ETHICS AND LAW IN MENTAL HEALTH ADMINISTRATION

ETHICS AND LAW
IN
MENTAL HEALTH
ADMINISTRATION

Walter E. Barton, M.D.
Professor of Psychiatry (Emeritus)
Dartmouth Medical School
Hanover, New Hampshire

and

Gail M. Barton, M.D., M.P.H.
Associate Professor of Psychiatry
University of Michigan Medical School
Ann Arbor, Michigan

Copyright © 1984 Walter E. Barton and Gail M. Barton

Library of Congress Cataloging in Publication Data

Barton, Walter E., 1906-
  Ethics and law in mental health administration.

  Bibliography: p.
  Includes indexes.
  1. Mental health laws—United States. 2. Psychiatric
ethics. I. Barton, Gail M. II. Title.
KF3828.B37   1984   344.73′044   84-4610
ISBN 0-8236-1765-3   347.30444

Manufactured in the United States of America

To Elsa, Duncan and Mariah

Contents

Preface

The administration of elements of the mental health system is enormously influenced by ethical and legal issues. We have written a text directed to clinician-executives, administrators, psychiatrists and mental health professionals who participate in the decision making process. Several books on law and on ethics and many articles on these subjects have appeared in the last few years. From this mass of material, we have attempted to select that which has application to administrative tasks and has value in practice. We have not attempted to explore in depth either moral philosophy or legal reasoning. We shared the issues and problems we have encountered and have drawn some general conclusions from our experience.

Because laws change and because every state has differing statutes, the administrator must become familiar with local laws and keep abreast of changes.

Knowledge alone seldom changes administrative behavior. It is the application in daily practice of what has been learned that effects change.

At the beginning of chapters we have used case examples. We suggest the development of illustrative cases from local problems. Out of the daily experience of problem solving, skills are acquired which will change administrative behavior.

Walter E. Barton
Hartland, Vermont
Gail M. Barton
Ann Arbor, Michigan

Foreword

This work by the Bartons describes a vast panorama of issues, problems, policies, laws, ethics and professional practice in mental health
administration. The range of issues the text encompasses is of far
broader relevance than conveyed by the title: *Ethics and Law in Mental
Health Administration*. Much of the book is relevant to *all* hospital
administration, as well as to general medical practice. Thus it will be
of interest to physicians at large, psychiatrists, psychologists, mental
health workers of all kinds, administrators, government policy makers,
bureaucrats, attorneys, educators, and students in related fields.

Many of the topics presented in the text have been pursued at length
in recent years in the various professional media, but rarely has one
the opportunity to see such an extensive review by a professional
twosome; commentary and analysis are included, along with a reasonable sampling of references and explanatory materials. As such,
it represents an ambitious endeavor. It succeeds in painting the kind
of broad picture one might capture in a photograph taken with a wide-
angle lens. Thus the panorama, the proverbial forest, is always clearly
in view. The book cannot go into the ultimate depths of every issue
it addresses, nor can it deal with all the minutiae without sacrificing
its pungency and its reality-oriented brevity. The reader must therefore
be cautioned that coverage in many areas may not be sufficient in
terms of amplification of all possible issues or all legal crosscurrents;
almost any of the chapters could justify a volume or even a set of
volumes. In particular, many areas of forensic psychiatry are addressed
in a relatively cursory fashion.

Another caution that the reader should keep in mind is that not only
is the law constantly changing, but also that the United States has fifty
plus jurisdictions with varying policies and rules. One is hard put to
state a general rule amid such diversity. Thus, some of the opinions
offered as representative of common practice may not accurately reflect

specific jurisdictions. The reader elicits a general principle, but must also know the specific rules or practices in a given locality. The reader cannot assume universality of principles where the law is at issue. Fortunately, the discussion of ethical matters involves issues that have been scrutinized by national professional groups, so here the guidelines expressed have more global applicability.

A third caution for the reader is the problem of interpreting legal cases. The authors are entitled to their opinion as to the meaning of a legal decision, at whatever judicial level it was tried. As we all know, however, higher courts disagree as to the meaning of lower court decisions, and attorneys, philosophers, and legal scholars have been known to argue about the specific meaning of a given legal decision. Many of the decisions cited have been rendered by trial courts whose influence is indeed minimal. On other occasions, a fifty-page judicial opinion may be summarized in a paragraph, or one element in a decision may be used to make a point while the rest of the decision is ignored. On occasion, I found myself disagreeing with the importance or meaning ascribed by the authors to a given case. I might be right and they wrong, or vice versa. Or we might be all right or, for that matter, all wrong. I make these remarks only to make clear to the reader that in some areas, particularly legal interpretation, there is often genuine disagreement and that overreliance on any one authority may not be justified—even in a book whose authors convey such a remarkable breadth of experience and knowledge.

A book like this is a guide to the professionally bewildered in a complex world. Where it does not answer questions, it clarifies issues. At the very least, it attempts to pinpoint in a succinct fashion major problems facing health professionals. Two most helpful aspects of the book are the lack of ambiguity and the frequency with which the authors state what they believe should be public policy or good professional practice.

In offering this opening commentary, I should like to stress what I consider the outstanding characteristic of this work. One can easily discuss ethics and law in the abstract and with cold reference to a specific issue. But one cannot read this book without an awareness of the aura of professionalism that permeates it. Though we may at times decry traditions of yore, we should never forget that the field of medicine has been enveloped by a nobility and a mystique, a mantle of human concern and decency that rises above individual practitioners and enwraps them in a cloak of the highest morality, desire for social betterment, and interpersonal concern. That essential humanism, the aim of alleviating suffering while respecting human freedom and human rights in a changing world, underlies much of the commentary and goes beyond the petty arguments of ethicists and sociolegal debaters. It amounts to human goodness, and that is a quality to be treasured.

One last matter. As is obvious, I was asked to write these introductory comments. I know one of the authors, Walter Barton—not well, but enough to know that exposure to a good man is an honor. Walter has spent a life in the service of his profession—as psychiatrist, administrator, author, and leader. He is no remote theorist telling the world what to do, and if he does not shy away from indicating what he thinks public policy should be, it is because he has been a soldier in the trenches as well as a general who has adapted to changing times and changing roles.

The Bartons have attempted a complex task. They cannot answer all the questions and resolve all the issues. No writers can. But they have succeeded in portraying the immensity of the challenge to health care professionalism with its ethical and legal entanglements. In the end, professionalism grows and lives within the soul of the individual. I think that this book will help toward that goal.

Irwin N. Perr, M.D., J.D.
Professor of Psychiatry and Community
Medicine (Legal Medicine), Rutgers Medical School
Lecturer in Law, Rutgers School of Law

Introduction

Ethics and law become intertwined as they seek to guide human conduct. "The law," Oliver Wendell Holmes Jr. once remarked, "is the witness and external deposit of our moral life. Its history is the history of the moral development of the race." In a society that has been torn away from its moral moorings, we scurry about seeking ways to regain control. New ethical codes are fashioned to guide professional behavior in areas where ethical dilemmas are posed by the swift advance of science. Impatient with the ruminations of scholarly philosophers, we seek a distillation of their wisdom to solve clinical and administrative ethical problems in everyday practice. Meanwhile the law, responding to a public outcry that individual rights be protected and practitioners be made responsible for their behavior, has spun so many strands that clinicians and administrators have become entangled, scarcely knowing which is the "right" course.

The resurgence of interest in ethics and the unprecedented outpouring of legislation and legal opinion have created a demand for instruction in these matters during the training of mental health professionals and administrators. In answering this demand, we have attempted to address current concerns as encountered in practice.

Our book begins with an exploration of moral rules, values, attitudes, and etiquette and of their impact on the behavior of clinician-executives. The topic of ethical guidelines and their application in human experimentation and other current ethical issues is next addressed, and is followed by a thirty-year study of ethical complaints received by a national organization. The legal issues selected for discussion in Part II are those which have proved most troublesome: informed consent, confidentiality, involuntary admission to hospital, patient rights, criminal responsibility, and liability.

Ethical and legal issues relating to persons with mental health problems are of concern to a number of different groups. Family physicians, psychiatrists, mental health professionals, administrators of hospitals and other facilities, behavioral scientists, lawyers, judges, police, and policy makers may all at one time or another become involved in mental health care issues.

The law articulates principles, sets boundaries, and clarifies what is best for individuals and the common good. Ethics seeks to guide professional conduct according to moral principles and values. The common good and the stability of a society is achieved when its leaders and its institutions pursue valued goals, and when public and private conduct conforms to the moral and ethical rules cherished by the community.

Laws and ethics change. Where once it was considered unquestionably immoral, unethical, and illegal to perform an abortion, today the procedure is viewed by large constituencies as ethical and legal, with only some constraints. Abortion has become a political issue in the 1980s.

In 1962 our *Administration in Psychiatry* focused on the ethical and legal problems encountered in hospital settings. Twenty years later, our *Mental Health Administration: Principles and Practice* (1983) reflected, in its focus on ambulatory care, a widespread shift in orientation. Where in the past, public policy had sanctioned admission of those society rejected and feared, today the emphasis is on appropriate treatment in the least restrictive setting and on preservation of autonomy and individual liberty. Then the legal issues of principal concern were commitment, competence, and responsibility; now they are liability, confidentiality, informed consent, patient rights, and judicial actions that directly impinge upon treatment.

The advance of science and technology now pose ethical issues that can be expressed in a series of questions: Have parents the right to demand that physicians shut off life support machines that keep "alive" a daughter vegetating in deep coma for several years? How is death to be determined in an age of such life-sustaining machines? Does a woman have the right to request an abortion if she does not wish to bear a child? If amniocentesis in the fifteenth week of pregnancy shows a genetic defect after three weeks of cell culture, can an abortion be performed in the second trimester, or would the operating surgeon be guilty of manslaughter? Is sterilization of the mentally ill and retarded ethical? Is fetal research ethical? Under what circumstances may a new drug that has shown promise in animals be tested in humans? Must patients on whom it is used suffer from conditions that may be alleviated or cured by the drug, or may it be used in a normal control? How can we be certain informed consent was given when the risks and unique responses of an individual are unknown? Should parents concur in consent on procedures involving their children? At what age may a child act independently in granting approval? May an adolescent secure treatment for a venereal disease without the parents being informed? Is it appropriate to treat adolescents with methods or medicines that coerce or modify behavior to secure conformity to authority? Is it proper to use psychiatric techniques to achieve socially desirable goals? Is it ethical to use a diagnosis less damaging than that actually determined on reports sent insurance companies? What guidelines are there to govern removal of a kidney from a dying person for purposes of organ transplant? May a physician have sexual relations with a patient? What constitutes a physician-patient relationship and how long does it last? Do professional organizations have an obligation to impose sanctions on grossly incompetent members? What are the criteria by which incompetence is determined? Is it ethical for a physician to inject a lethal drug in a state-ordered execution of a criminal? What shall determine what counts as acceptable moral and social behavior for physicians and administrators.

These ethical issues will not be answered by statements in codes. Individual morals and values, and those of society, insofar as both are incorporated into daily behavior, will provide solutions to ethical dilemmas.

From the many social forces shaping contemporary society several themes emerge that are relevant to current legal issues: distrust of institutions; the idea that environmental stress is more important than biological or psychological factors in producing mental illness; and an emphasis on individual freedom and participative management.

Distrust of institutions is widespread. Not only local government but the federal establishment, including the Presidency itself, have been targets of individual and group challenges to authority and traditions. The integrity of organizations and that of executives is questioned and accountability for stewardship demanded.

At one time society chained and imprisoned madmen; later, mental hospitals were created as sanctuaries under compassionate administrators who devoted their lives to humane patient care. But as these institutions grew in size and responded to various demands placed upon them by society, goals became confused and conflicting, causing the mental hospitals to lose their way. Neglected by the society they served and also by the medical profession, they came to be seen as coercive institutions corrupt in ideology and obsolete in practice. The place of these now despised institutions was soon to be filled by the community mental health center. This new approach, it was said, would prevent mental illness and abolish altogether the need for prolonged hospital care. Now environmental stress upon the individual was viewed as the dominant causative factor, and relevant interventions were devised. An idea that had been around for a long time, it was now being recycled as appropriate to modern society.

But when the legislative branch of government failed to set desired policy and allocate resources for these programs, and when the executive branch failed similarly, it became increasingly common for advocates of this approach to turn to the judicial system to gain their ends. A corps of a thousand lawyers, the "Mental Health Bar," was developed and trained to assist these advocates in reforming the mental health system through actions in case law.

Courts settle disputes and determine the constitutionality of laws passed by the legislature, but they do more. They also determine public policy. The clear enunciation of principles, the refinement of procedures, and the establishment of standards serve valued social ends. The courts do this well and in so doing serve the mental health field.

The problems that emerge are operational. A principle must be translated into action if systematic change is to result. Often resources are required to implement an action, and for this reason and others the legislative and executive branches must lend their support if the desired result is to be obtained. Much of the friction at the interface between law and mental health administration is the result of a lack of communication and coordination among governmental agencies. Sometimes, however, advocates of a position brought to the court may hold a view rejected by society as a whole. To effect the change desired, whether in a system, an institution, or a widely held practice or belief, a process of tempered persuasiveness is required. The bare juridical command that change occur ignores this process, so often change does not occur, or the command produces more problems than solutions. We will attempt to clarify some of these issues and problems so that the goal of system improvement and implementation of sound principles may be realised.

Walter E. Barton
Hartland, Vermont

Gail M. Barton
Ann Arbor, Michigan

Acknowledgments

We are grateful to those who have allowed us to quote opinions and findings from their remarks or published works. We have noted these in the text with an acknowledgment. Our special thanks to Phillip Margolis, Andrew Watson, and the late Bardwell Flower, who read our manuscript and made many helpful suggestions for its improvement.

Our wish was to enlist Mrs. Carol Davis as a full collaborator on the ethical section of this book. Demands on her time were so heavy, however, that she was unable to offer us more than her wise counsel on the thirty-year study of ethical complaints presented in chapter 5. It should be noted here that Mrs. Davis designed the system which made this analysis possible. We thank her for her help and for wanting to do more.

The Maurice Falk Foundation provided funds for typing and editing, for which we thank Philip Hallen and the Foundation.

Our special thanks goes to Nita Norman for her editing of early drafts of our work, and to our typists: Janet Lord, Sandra Green, Nancy Clark, Dorothy Kendall, Peggy Seaver, Janet Allen, and Roberta Kellogg.

W.E.B.
G.M.B.

Part I
Ethics in Mental Health
Administration

Chapter 1

Definitions and Concepts: Morals, Ethics, Values, Attitudes and Etiquette

> Moral virtues are the foundation of society in general, and of friendship in particular; but attentions, manners and graces adorn and strengthen them.
>
> —*Lord Chesterfield (1694–1773)*

Case example. A 35-year-old accountant, a bachelor, who lives alone in a rooming house, requests your help to overcome what he describes as his perversion. He says he is a homosexual and is lonely, unhappy, and isolated because of his fear of discovery. He believes his job is in jeopardy and hates his desire for male relationships. He has read about behavior therapy and wonders whether it might change his sexual orientation. He has dated women, rarely attends a social function with a woman but has never had an intimate relationship. He says while in college he had a male roommate who was his lover until the roommate married and "straightened himself out."

Will you agree to work toward the client's goal of sexual orientation change? Do you reject the client's goal as unrealistic and help him accept his difference and work toward reduction of self-disgust and

3

social anxiety? You live in a state where overt homosexual behavior is illegal. Will you encourage his illegal behavior?

In your decision, what values and attitudes of your own lead you to make the choice of one goal in therapy over the other? (Veatch, 1977)

Every day the administrator and clinician make decisions and take actions that are the consequence of their own observance of certain moral and ethical rules, values they cherish and express in their attitudes and behavior. What they decide may benefit themselves or express a duty to others. Moral and ethical rules govern our behavior and when violated they are followed by consequences that are perceived as evil by oneself and that may cause suffering for others.

Morality may also be a factor in the regulations governing professional practice. Licensure laws often require the applicant to be of good moral character. But what do these laws require and how is good moral character determined? Why are ethical codes necessary to lay down rules of professional conduct toward patients, toward the profession, and toward society? Why are values held by society expected to manifest themselves in the behavior of an administrator? Can one be immoral and succeed as an administrator? Is it possible for an administrator to possess the requisite knowledge and skill yet fail because his attitude was unacceptable to the group? Of what relevance to an administrator or clinician is etiquette in human relationships?

The answers to such questions may be more meaningful if we look first at human beings striving to relate to the world around them, and only then at morals, ethics, values, attitudes, and etiquette.

From the beginning of time, man has struggled to understand the meaning of life and of the world. The major religions all speak of a unifying principle in the universe to which everything relates. Each religion calls the experience of the unifying force by a different name (Offer and Sabshin, 1974). Man has sought self-awareness and relatedness to the unseen unifying force. Man soon learned that all of his desires could not be satisfied. Self-interest had to be set aside to gain harmony with nature and with his fellow men. In the Garden of Eden all desires were fulfilled by an omnipresent God. In a later day, when desires exceeded satisfactions, Buddha counseled curtailing desire.

Today one might be encouraged to adapt to existing resources. What then, are the basic needs among the many desires? According to the recent literature (Jahoda, 1958; Offer and Sabshin, 1974; Lerner, 1976) they are:

1. Developing one's abilities through growth, experimentation, learning, adapting to new environments, and self-actualization.

2. Achieving a sense of autonomy which is an awareness of self and a personal identity with an ability to decide what is best for one.

3. Having a sense of security in the structure and order of things, and in one's own boundaries in relationship with others.

4. Developing a sense of belonging to someone and to a group, feeling a concern for others, and having the ability to care for others.

5. Achieving integration of intrapsychic and extrapsychic forces into a unifying outlook on life.

6. Constructing a sense of mastery over self and environment by being able to love, work, play, and make choices, and to adapt, adjust and solve problems in daily living.

Hippocrates tried to construct a sense of perspective for the health care professionals of his day by stating that health was a state of universal harmony, and that the role of the physician was that of restoring equilibrium between the various components of the body and the whole of nature (R. T. Barton, 1965). While individuals may strive for a state of biological, psychological, and social harmony, when they seek help for illness it is because this balance is upset. It is expected that the clinician seek to restore that balance. Health is the objective in the prevention, cure, or management of disease. To whatever extent possible, the clinician seeks to help the individual avoid disease or injury, recover from it, or compensate for it (W. Barton, 1958).

Human striving toward gratification of basic needs, self-improvement, and a state of harmony within self, with others, and with nature involves choices—some good, some bad. The rightness or wrongness of conduct is the territory of morality. "Morality," Carl Jung once said, "is not a misconception invented by some vaunting Moses on Sinai but something inherent in the laws of life. . . . Nor can the optimum be reached by unbridled craving for individualistic supremacy, because the collective element in man is so powerful that his longing for fellowship would destroy all pleasure in naked egoism" (Warner, 1980). It may even be in one's self-interest to be moral.

Plato believed knowledge of the philosopher-king approached the attainment of the ideal of what is health for the soul. It was the philosopher, rather than the people themselves, who was to be entrusted with determining what was good and right for society. By contrast, Aristotle in his *Ethics* advanced the conception that the degree of virtue that each man must perfect within himself for his own happiness (gratified desires) was relative to each individual, his intellect, and his social position. The chief good, the principle of rationality, was always desirable and one's duty was to live a life of pure contemplation (Offer and Sabshin, 1974). With virtue, happiness, rationality, and contemplation as ancient concepts for right living let us examine present-day concepts of the common good and the professional duty to be actively moral.

MORALS

Moral philosophy is the study of what is right and wrong or virtuous and evil in human conduct and among groups of individuals. Morality is a system of rules for right conduct such as the Ten Commandments. Rules of morality are incorporated within each of us, reinforced by significant persons in our lives through praise for doing right and sanctions against wrongdoing.

Are there any moral absolutes, any principles of conduct that are universally held and constant over time? Moses' stone tablet had engraved upon it, "Thou Shalt Not Kill" (Exodus 20:2–17): It is moral to preserve life, it is immoral to take it away. Today a few would take the absolutist position, allowing no exceptions. These would be those who would refuse military duty on religious grounds because they might be required during the course of that duty to kill another person. Many others, meanwhile, would agree that a soldier may kill an enemy in combat. The majority of the general population grow uneasy when noncombatants are killed and no target of military consequence is involved in a strike. Most would concur that it is wrong to attack a hospital. Society is less certain whether a police officer may shoot a person escaping after a robbery, unless the officer's life is threatened. Laws today reflect the moral viewpoint that a householder or shopkeeper may not kill an intruder unless there is a visible weapon and a reasonable belief that one's life is endangered.

Perhaps closest to a moral absolute is the incest taboo, whereby sexual intercourse between siblings or between children and their mothers or fathers is forbidden. The taboo appears to be observed by most cultures, and such behavior is generally held to be wrong. Even so, sexual abuse of children by their parents does occur, in spite of social disapproval.

Today exceptions to many of the Ten Commandments are generally agreed upon. Swearing, in fact, seems more the rule than the exception. The Sabbath is no longer strictly observed as a holy day; instead shops and sporting events are widely attended on Sunday. Sexual behavior has become more varied and is less often sanctified by marriage. Coveting what our neighbors possess is commonplace. Even so, what we choose to do doesn't necessarily make it "right."

There is a moral position that holds that the right and good way is following God's rules for conduct; others believe every decision stating right or good is something to be discussed and reasoned, while others would ask what an ideal observer who is omniscient, disinterested, and consistent would do under the circumstances. Certainly we reject the rational egoism which holds that what brings happiness and pleasure is the ultimate good. What then is right and wrong? Perhaps the closest we can come is to favor Frankena's principles of beneficence and justice (1976) or Rawls's *Theory of Justice* (1971). There is a general utility in the moral positions "Do unto others what you would they would do unto you" and "Love thy neighbor as thyself." Gert (1976) set down properties essential before a reasoned judgment of rational action may be considered a *moral rule*:*

- It must apply universally without consideration of time, place, person, or group.
- It must specify the action to be taken or avoided.
- It must be obeyed without restriction on who shall obey. Also evident is the reality that the consequence of disobeying the rule would be disastrous.
- It must be understandable by all rational persons.
- It must be capable of being followed or of being broken.

* Quoted in summary fashion with the permission of the author. *The Moral Rules*, by Bernard Gert. Copyright 1966, 1967, 1970. Reprinted by permission of Harper and Row Publishers, Inc.

Since moral rules prohibit actions that have evil consequences, rational men generally advocate obedience to them, says Gert, and when they would justify an exception they must be willing to publicly advocate it. To act other than in accordance with moral rules brings evil upon oneself and will cause others to suffer evil consequences. Using his criteria, Gert derived five basic moral rules:

Don't kill
Don't cause pain
Don't disable
Don't deprive of freedom or opportunity
Don't deprive of pleasure

And then a secondary set of five moral rules:

Don't deceive
Keep your promises
Don't cheat
Obey the law
Do your duty

We prefer to state our interpretation of moral rules in the positive. Also, as our interest is interpreting the term used in licensure, "actively moral," we begin with the expectation that the clinician-executive will embrace a personal philosophy to explain his or her reason for being, demonstrate a compassionate interest in the welfare of fellow human beings, and place service to patients or clients above personal desire, convenience, or gain. We may, therefore, restate Gert's rules by saying that the actively moral clinician-executive:

Preserves life
Relieves suffering
Seeks to restore the wholeness of those that seek help
Is beneficent and just
Is honest and keeps promises
Obeys the law
Does his duty

George Santayana said the task of morals is to subdue nature as far as possible to the use of the soul (1962).

Moral Theories

The theory of *Natural Law* holds that there is a higher determinant than man of what is right and wrong for man and that natural laws delineate behavior which is morally appropriate for human beings (Beauchamp and Walters, 1978). Further, man must seek to understand the intentions of natural law. Aristotle, Aquinas, Kant, Teilhard, and Schweitzer contributed scholarly expositions in support of the natural law theory.

The *Utilitarian* theory states that an action is right if, and only if, it produces at least as great a *balance of value over disvalue* as any alternative action (Beauchamp and Walters, 1978).

Deontological theory is nonutilitarian; it holds an action is right if, and only if, the action is *required by a duty* which is at least as strong as any other duty under the circumstances. Rightness is determined by the features of an action.

The *pragmatic* theory holds that right and wrong are *products of human experience*. While belief in God or material law is the point of departure in this pragmatic theory, man is central as he seeks to subdue nature. Support is found for this view in Plato, The Talmud, and Maimonides. *Empiricists* such as John Locke, John Stuart Mill, and William James derive from the pragmatic principle the theory that our notions of right and wrong are the *products of human reasoning* and of what *society agrees is right* (R. Barton, 1965).

The timelessness of moral rules is reaffirmed in a free translation of Tao principles by C.S. Lewis, a medieval and Renaissance scholar at Cambridge. To each of the seven Tao principles, (quoted in Bird, 1973), we have added a clarifying quotation relevant to a health care professional's actions:

1. First of all do no harm.
   "Do the sick no harm; not even in thought."—The Ayur-Veda
2. Respect the sanctity of human life.
   "I will maintain the utmost respect for human life, from the time of conception." —Declaration of Geneva

3. Alleviate suffering.
   "To cure sometimes, to relieve often, to comfort always." —Lord
   Lister
4. Preserve confidentiality
   "Be true to him who puts his trust in you. Reveal not his secret
   and go not about as a talebearer." —Oath of the Hebrew Physician
5. Uphold the truth.
   "Devotion to the truth does not always require the physician to
   voice his fears or tell his patient all he knows. But, after he has
   decided the process of dying has actually begun, only in exceptional
   circumstances would a physician be justified in keeping to himself
   his opinion. In such cases his only question should be whether to
   tell the patient or the family and, when both should be told, which
   to tell first." —Alfred Worcester
6. Secure patient consent.
   "Among the experiments that may be tried on man, those that are
   harmless are permissible and those that do good are obligatory."
   —Claude Bernard
7. Support the right to die with dignity.
   "I hold it to be your duty to smooth as much as possible the pathway
   to the grave even if life is somewhat shortened." —S.B. Woodward

The blending of moral principles with ethical guides to clinical behavior
here becomes evident.

ETHICS

Ethics are rules of conduct recognized in respect to a particular class
of human action. Normative ethics, Gaylin says (Beauchamp and
Walters, 1978), are moral principles by which acts are judged to be
right or wrong, good or bad, obligatory, permissible, or forbidden.
Metaethics poses conceptual questions whose answers help us understand what we *mean* when we search for specific principles. For some,
ethics is the science of the human character in its ideal state. Others
use morals and ethics as if synonymous. We shall use the word ethics
in a more limited sense; rules for the conduct of a particular group
such as lawyers, clergy, physicians, and mental health professionals

or administrators. It is usual for the specified group to draw up its own code around the appropriate class of actions. For example, the International Code of Nursing Ethics sets guidelines for the conduct of all nurses. Among its provisions are directives to conserve life, alleviate suffering, promote health, provide the highest possible standard of care, maintain knowledge, upgrade skills, meet obligations, perform one's duties, and observe community moral standards in one's personal life.

To illustrate the relationship of morals, ethics, values, and attitudes, reference is made to Figure 1-1. The central area represents morals, schematized as the heart. From this moral foundation are derived val-

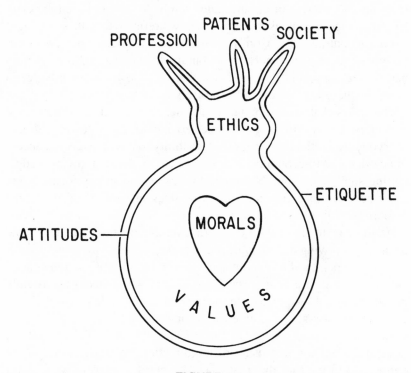

FIGURE 1-1

Schematic representation of morals at the core of one's values; attitudes and etiquette are expressed in contact with others. Ethics are rules which govern professional conduct toward patients, members of the profession, and society

ues. Ethics is shown as a constriction in the figure developed when applicable to a particular group. Morals and values are both involved in ethics. A professional group develops rules of conduct that are three-pronged, with specified responsibilities to patients or clients, to members of the profession (guild interests), and to society. Attitudes (beliefs systematized as determinants of behavior) are schematized in the figure as the covering visible to all on the outside, with etiquette the polish on the surface (good manners).

The amazing accomplishments of science have unsettled long-standing rules. Technological advances have made organ transplants possible; mechanical devices sustain life; there are miracle medicines and electrical controls of behavior; sperm banks exist now to assist the infertile and women offer surrogate wombs to bear children. Society has to change its values to keep up. Laws reflective of these changes are often contradictory. Conflict arises when two rights specify actions in opposition to each other, or even mutually exclusive. Society often has no reasoned solution and since there are no track records yet in many of these arenas, experience offers no help.

Questions that are cropping up for health care administrators and providers that arise from our unsettled era include the following: Should everyone, regardless of race, creed or ability to pay, have equal access to health care? In economic recession or fiscal crises involving budget cutting shall health care be limited to those who can pay for it, as are other services in a free market? How does one ration fairly limited resources to those unable to pay for care? Is allocation to be made randomly, or to those who come first until a quota is filled? Should a subsidy allowing access to health care be given only to those society feels have social utility, who make a valued contribution to the general welfare? We desire equal access for all, but when that is not fiscally possible, how do we distribute fairly what is available (renal dialysis, coronary bypass surgery, care for chronic mental illness)?

Interest in ethics, says Gaylin (Beauchamp and Walters, 1978), develops when we are unsure of the direction we are heading. When values are in conflict there is a need to clarify opposing views, for there may no single right answer. The goal of the clinician-administrator is to become ethically sensitive to the problems created by science and its technology and to be acutely aware of the individual's rights and those of society so they can be compared and contrasted and judgments made. In a later chapter we shall discuss the specific ethical actions pertinent to the mental health professions.

VALUES

A value has been defined as an enduring belief that a specific mode of conduct or state of existence is personally or socially preferable to an opposite mode of conduct or existence (Rokeach, 1973). A value is one of several kinds of beliefs; it is the kind on which a person acts by preference. Value expresses the worth or meaning or purpose of life. It is the basis for our striving and our commitment. For example, if I wish to attain security for myself and my family, enjoy reasonable prosperity, and gain the respect of colleagues and the esteem of the profession, I can be said to possess a series of values that will guide my actions. Quite a different set of values is evident if I say "The rat race is not for me. I don't wish to have either a family or material things to tie me down. I wish inner security and the freedom to do my own thing."

Since the tumultuous 1960s, traditional values have been under seige as new class and ethnic alignments developed and the values of respect for authority, sexual virtue, masculine domination, money, and power changed for many (but not for all).

Values are thought to be formed beginning in early childhood, from exposure to situations which lead to value judgments. We identify with role models among parents, family, friends, peers, teachers, and significant others. In school, at play, in worship, in work, in learning and loving others, our encounters make us choose among values. Just as we have done in acquiring morals, we test them, express them, and finally internalize them, as they become a part of our self (the superego). Values provide us the rationale for our attitudes and our actions. They guide our conduct and lead us to take one course of action among several, or to state a position on a social issue.

In a national survey of values, Rokeach (1973) presented an objective test in which 18 terminal values (e.g., a comfortable life, an exciting life, a sense of accomplishment, a world at peace, a world of beauty, self-esteem, true friendship, wisdom) and 18 instrumental values (e.g., ambition, broadmindedness, capability, cheerfulness, cleanliness, courage, lovingness, obedience, responsibility, self-control) were ranked in priority by participants. All the values on the list were socially desirable. Using the measure of central tendency and the nonparametric median test, Rokeach concluded that culture, society, and personality are major antecedents of values and that attitudes and behavior are their major consequences. We will not detail his findings here but will indicate only the overall priorities evident from the survey. When a choice was made among terminal values, a world at peace, family security, and freedom were chosen as top values, while an exciting life, pleasure, and social recognition were at the bottom of the list. Among instrumental values, honesty, ambition, and responsibility were chosen over obedience, imagination and intellect.

It is possible to express values as polarities to show how they reflect unresolved tensions in our society (Lerner, 1976):

work hard	work as much as necessary
make a living	make a life
develop an identity	build a family and
and follow a career	raise children
respect authority	be true to yourself
male dominance	equality of the sexes

Two principles of justice for institutions, stated by Rawls (1971), express the value of equality of opportunity: (1) Each person is to have an equal right to the most extensive basic liberty compatible with a similar liberty for others. (2) Social and economic inequalities are to be arranged so that they are both (a) of the greatest benefit to the least advantaged and (b) attached to offices and positions open to all under conditions of fair equality of opportunity.

The same basic rights should apply to everyone. The same opportunity to fill positions of authority should be open to all. Values may therefore express not only individual needs and priorities, but also the expectations of society and of its institutions. (The individual need for dependence may be expressed by the instrumental value of loyalty as demanded by an institution.) The advantage of thinking about a person as a system of values, rather than a cluster of units, is that it becomes possible to conceive of a person undergoing change as a result of changing values in the environment (Rokeach, 1973).

Some examples of the possible choices among values illustrate the relative priority given liberty, autonomy, and social responsibility:

- Those with contagious diseases should be confined for the protection of society.
- Those who cannot control their impulses and repeatedly aggravate others should be confined for the peace and comfort of society.
- Those who are unable to survive independently with grievous physical or mental illness should be given institutional care as an obligation of government.
- Only those who are dangerous to self and others and are mentally ill are to be confined involuntarily to a mental hospital.
- Society must learn to tolerate the mentally ill who are noisy, obscene, irresponsible, or a danger to property, for they may not be deprived of their freedom.

One may also develop hierarchies of values appropriate to directors of mental health facilities or, more generally, set down the qualities expected of professionals in leadership roles. One could also specify and rank the values determining the various degrees of responsibility the staff should carry. Does the manager believe the average worker dislikes work and needs a carrot on a stick to become motivated? Does the administrator believe that workers will exercise self-direction and assume responsibility for their actions if it is clear they are expected to do so? It may be felt unwise to incorporate one's own values into a decision which another should be making (Veatch, in Epanier, 1980).

ATTITUDES

An attitude is a position or bearing indicating an action, feeling, or mood. It is a behavior representing a state of readiness to act often accompanied by considerable affect. Whereas a value refers to a single belief of a very specific kind upon which one acts by preference, an attitude refers to the organization of several beliefs that are determinants of behavior.

A moral position might be that adultery is wrong because it is a sin against the law of God. Related values might express security within the family and loyalty to spouse and obedience to the marriage vows. The attitude of the administrator, based on the above, might then be characterized by maintaining social distance from staff members of the opposite sex and a prohibition against sexual affairs with any staff member. A different moral position is that fornication is an individual choice between consenting adults, or that it is sometimes right and sometimes wrong depending upon the depth of commitment between the two parties. The administrator with this moral stance and with associated values may attempt seduction or take an employee as a lover. Because society may disapprove, the consequences could be loss of job.

Administrators may have all the knowledge and skill to be competent in managing an institution and still fail because of values expressed in attitudes that are unacceptable to a societal group.

Attitudes expressed in actions toward employees that reflect the values of fairness, justice, equality of opportunity, demonstrated openness to criticism, tolerance for the opinions of others, sensitivity to needs, and willingness to share power and delegate authority are more likely to win the cooperation of workers that is essential to organizational efficiency.

To clarify values and attitudes in human service organizations and to improve individual functioning in task-oriented groups, Austin (1978) has developed a self-assessment test to reveal managerial philosophies. In the test one rates oneself on a 7-point scale as to agreement or disagreement with statements such as these:

- The greatest amount of reward for the least effort is the motto of most human service workers.
- If human service supervisors did not control and direct their subordinates, work toward the agency's goal would never get done.
- Under the right conditions the average worker will learn not only to accept but to seek responsibility.
- Most workers display a fairly high degree of imagination, ingenuity, and creativity.

Administrators would do well to identify their attitudes regarding such statements.

ETIQUETTE

Etiquette is the conformance of behavior to the conventional requirements of society. It concerns more than manners and the elementary rules governing acceptable standards for human interactions, for it includes the socially accepted ways of doing things. One can consult Emily Post's or Amy Vanderbilt's books on etiquette for correct behavior at engagements, weddings, funerals, entertaining, furnishing the home, or travel abroad. Etiquette is concerned with the rudeness, discourtesy, or bad manners that so frequently are major factors in the lodging of ethical complaints or lawsuits by patients or clients.

First impressions of the administrator contribute to the belief in his or her competence. Appropriate dress, cleanliness, and grooming, ease in introductions, thoughtfulness of the comfort of others, courtesy, and the ability to listen and to respect values and differing opinions are factors of importance in the initial impression. All of these relate to etiquette. Telephone courtesy, promptness in reply to inquiries by mail, remembering to inform referring physicians of a patient's progress, prompt investigation of complaints and correction of deficiencies, respect for the dignity of patients, and consideration for the feelings of others are all aspects of good etiquette that help build trust both in the administrator as a person and in the organization.

The conduct of some physicians and mental health professionals displeases the public and reflects on all. Shabby behavior, rudeness, and thoughtlessness are poor etiquette. Often these are simply affronts to the receivers of such ill treatment rather than clear violations of a professional code of ethics. An administrator's bad manners may nonetheless have an adverse effect on public opinion and on employees. Patients' refusal to return to see a clinician with poor etiquette may result in reduced fees and fewer word-of-mouth referrals.

SUMMARY

Morals, ethics, values, attitudes, and etiquette all are determinants of the administrator's behavior and affect both public and employee response. Morals are often viewed as universal rules to be obeyed for right conduct or evil consequences will follow. Ethics are principles formulated by a profession to guide a class of actions applicable to the behavior of members of the group. Values express the worth and meaning of strivings, commitments, and purposes in the lives of individuals. Attitudes are the positions, dispositions, or actions we express toward persons or things. They are a visible expression of morals, ethics, and values that have been internalized. Etiquette is the polish on the rough diamond, for it reveals the way things are done to meet the conventional requirements of social interchange with others. It is conducting one's business and expressing one's inner self and attitudes with good manners and thoughtful concern for others. This manifests itself for mental health professionals in their taking time to listen to patients or clients, and in respecting their values.

QUESTIONS

1. What evidence is required to support the requirement that an applicant be of good moral character?
2. What are six basic human needs?
3. Define morals, values, ethics, attitudes, and etiquette.
4. What is the *Natural Law* theory of what is right and wrong? The *Utilitarian* theory?
5. What are Professor Gert's ten moral rules?
6. What rules of conduct does the actively moral physician follow?
7. How does an individual acquire his or her morals and values?
8. Are values timeless and unchanging?
9. How do values and attitudes affect behavior? Give examples.
10. Of what relevance to the administrator are attitudes and etiquette?

REFERENCES

* Austin, M. J. (1978), *Management Simulations: For Mental Health and Human Services Administration*. New York: Haworth Press.

Barton, R. T. (1965), Sources of morals, *J. Amer. Med. Assn.*, 193:133–138.

Barton, W. E. (1958), Viewpoint of a clinician. In: *Current Concepts of Positive Mental Health*, ed. M. Jahoda. New York: Basic Books.

* Beauchamp, T. L., & Walters, L. eds. (1978), *Contemporary Issues in Bioethics*. Eucino, Calif.: Dickenson Publishing.

Bird, L. P. (1973), Tao principles of medical ethics. In: *Is it Moral to Modify Man?* ed. C. A. Frazier. Springfield, Ill.: Charles C Thomas.

* Block, S., & Chodoff, P., eds. (1981), *Psychiatric Ethics.* New York: Oxford University Press.

Bolen, J. S. (1979), *The Tao of Psychology: Synchronicity and the Self.* San Francisco: Harper and Row.

* Culver, C. M., & Gert, B., eds. (1982), *Philosophy in Medicine.* New York: Oxford University Press.

Epanier, R. (1980), Perspectives on parents' rights. *Forum,* 3:763–767.

* Frankena, W. K. (1976), *Perspectives on Morality,* ed. K. E. Goodpasture, South Bend, Ind.: University of Notre Dame Press.

* Gert, B. (1970), *The Moral Rules: A New Rational Foundation for Morality.* New York: Harper and Row.

* Hiller, M., ed. (1981), *Medical Ethics and the Law.* Cambridge, Mass.: Ballinger.

Jahoda, M. (1958), *Current Concepts of Positive Mental Health.* New York: Basic Books.

* Lerner, M. (1976), *Values in Education.* Bloomington, Ind.: Phi Delta Kappa Educational Foundation.

* Offer, D., & Sabshin, M. (1974), *Normality: Theoretical and Clinical Concepts of Mental Health.* New York: Basic Books.

* Pellagrino, E. D. (1979), *Humanism and the Physician.* Knoxville: University of Tennessee Press.

Rawls, J. (1971), *A Theory of Justice.* Cambridge, Mass.: Harvard University Press.

* Rokeach, M. (1973), *The Nature of Human Values.* New York: The Free Press.

Santayana, G. (1863-1952), The fact of morals. In: *The Practical Cogitator,* ed. C. P. Curtis & F. Greenslet. Boston: Houghton Mifflin, 1962.

* Vanderbilt, A. (1972), *Etiquette.* Garden City, N.Y.: Doubleday.

* Vaux, K. (1974), *Biomedical Ethics: Morality for the New Medicine.* New York: Harper and Row.

Veatch, R. M. (1977), *Case Studies in Medical Ethics.* Cambridge, Mass.: Harvard University Press.

Warner, R. (1980), *Morality in Medicine: An Introduction to Medical Ethics.* Sherman Oaks, Calif.: Alfred Publishing.

* Here and throughout this work, asterisks preceding entries indicate recommended reading.

Chapter 2

Human Experimentation

> For the chief malady of man is a restless curiousity about things he cannot understand; and it is not so bad for him to be in error as to be curious to no purpose.
>
> —*Pascal (1623–1662)*

Case Example. Suppose you were the superintendent of an institution for the mentally retarded and some research investigators presented to you a well-designed proposal for the following research. The experiment was to study infectious hepatitis in children between the ages of 5 and 8. Several times during the past few years a considerable number of cases had developed. Exposure, therefore, did occur with some degree of frequency. A mild form of hepatitis was to be induced into a selected population along with matched controls. Parents would be asked to give consent in each instance, on the basis that an exposure hazard already existed and "it was inevitable that some children would be infected anyway." What further steps would you take? Would you approve the experiment?

Mental health professionals and physicians apply scientific findings in their practice. This implies that the method of healing utilized will have been developed from controlled experimentation carefully documented and validated to demonstrate the efficacy of the procedure and any risk to the subject it might present. An ideal research investigation compares the experimental group with normal controls, often "double blind" in pharmacological trials so that subjects and observers cannot distinguish which individuals are receiving the active ingredient. An ethical obstacle would result if an investigator proposed to test an oral contraceptive in Catholic Chicano women, with one group to receive the active substance and the other a placebo.

An early investigation occurred in 1718, when Cotton Mather persuaded Zabdiel Boylston to inoculate healthy individuals with smallpox. The risk undertaken was enormous. For a very long time previously it had been known that pox scars meant lifelong protection from the epidemic disease. Even though discrete lesions did develop on inoculated individuals the mortality rate was found to be significantly lowered. In 1722, inmates of Newgate Prison who volunteered to be inoculated with smallpox did so as an alternative to hanging. When it became obvious that they had all survived the experiment, they were released as agreed. Experimentation on prisoners has been the practice for centuries. Even earlier examples were described by Beecher (1966), who tells of an ancient Persian king handing over condemned criminals for this purpose. The Ptolomies in Egypt and the Fallopines in Pisa also used the condemned for experimentation. More recently, Joseph Goldberger, his wife, and associates conquered pellagra by experimenting upon Mississippi prison inmates. Those confined were made fully aware of the details of the planned experiment. Although in a coercive environment, they willingly traded time, discomfort, and the risk of harm for earlier release than their sentences called for.

Before new drugs and procedures are readied for marketing, they must be tested for modes of action, side effects, and lethal effects. This testing is usually done first on mice, rats, dogs, or even primates. When some certainty of reasonable safety has been achieved, they then must be tried on humans. Once scientists of competence and integrity have reason to believe animal experimentation has demonstrated promise of benefit for human beings greater than the risks, they must then repeat the experimentation on human subjects. Only then can the drug or procedure be used routinely.

A frightful incident involving human experimentation in which risks and dangers far outweighed any benefit occurred in recent history when the Nazi scientists experimented on Jewish inmates in extermination camps. When the nature of their gruesome activities came to light, world opinion was outraged. The Nuremberg Code, which placed restrictions on human experimentation, was the official response.

In 1966, Beecher cited twenty-two research studies on humans in which he questioned the ethics of the experimenter. Later (1970) he reviewed one hundred studies involving human experimentation and found that even though they had been published in reputable scientific journals, there were twelve studies that he considered unethical.

Two recent incidents of human experimentation in the U.S. aroused the public and were debated in the medical press. One was a Tuskegee experiment initiated in order to determine the natural course of untreated syphilis. It was designed as a controlled study of treatments in use when the study was begun in 1932—even though it was recognized that the methods were not very effective. Most subjects were poor and black. Although they agreed to participate, they were not told whether or not they had syphilis. Even when penicillin came into use as an effective treatment agent, infected subjects were not administered it during the planned course of the experiment. The discovery of this omission led to public outcry (*Massachusetts Physician*, 1974). A federal court awarded damages to the four hundred original enrollees or their kin in the Tuskegee study. Each living participant received $37,500 in settlement; $15,000 was given to each control participant; $15,000 went to families of deceased subjects who had had syphilis; and $15,000 went to survivors of deceased controls (*JAMA*, 1975). The other incident was a Willowbrook, N.Y., study of infectious hepatitis in the mentally retarded, alluded to in the case example at the beginning of the chapter.

These incidents (as well as others such as the malformations thalidomide produced in developing fetuses; deaths from cardiac catheterization and liver biopsy; research with anesthetic agents; the use of homografts of skin, kidneys, heart, and corneas; and, the questioned use of psychosurgery) have led to the articulation of principles governing the use of humans as research subjects. They have also influenced the doctrine of informed consent and the promulgation of guidelines for experimentation involving children, the mentally retarded, the mentally ill, and criminals.

What, then, are the principles derived from this historical context to govern experimentation in humans? The following canons, guidelines, and rules have been formulated in such documents as the Helsinki Declaration and the Nuremberg Code (see Torrey, 1968).

Canons

1. Experimenters and their subjects are fellow human beings whose relationship is one of mutual trust and concern. They share a respect for the opinions of mankind.

2. Scientists must be free to use a new therapeutic modality if in their judgment it offers hope of saving life, establishing health, or alleviating suffering. The immediate benefit to the subject is the goal, and voluntary consent must be obtained.

3. Voluntary consent requires the legal capacity to give consent, as well as free power of choice without deceit, force, or duress, and with sufficient imparted knowledge to insure comprehension of the decision.

4. When the experiment is directed to the future benefit of society and the advancement of knowledge and not to the future benefit of the subject:

a. The experiment shall be undertaken only if it will yield results for the good of society unobtainable by any other means.

b. No experiment will be made where there is a prior reason to believe death or disabling injury will result.

c. The risk shall never exceed the importance of the problem.

Ethical Guidelines

1. The welfare of the individual must not be jeopardized.

2. The physician has an obligation to preserve subjects' rights and insure his or her safety.

3. Unnecessary physical and mental suffering will be avoided.

4. The experimenter should be able to recommend the procedure for his/her own loved ones—spouse and child.

5. Informed consent of the subject is essential.

6. The experimenter should not make himself the subject unless safeguards (such as screening by an institutional review committee for the protection of human subjects) are scrupulously maintained.

Disciplinary Rules

1. Precede human experimentation with animal experimentation.
2. Assess all risks carefully.
3. Determine if any possibility exists the personality will be altered by the procedure.
4. Approval by an institutional review committee for the protection of human research subjects is required. Each proposal must be scrutinized to ensure that all rules, guidelines, and regulations are followed and that a signed consent form demonstrates that the patient will be fully informed of risks as well as available options.
5. The experimenter must be qualified to undertake the experiment.
6. The subject shall have the right to terminate the experiment at any time.
7. The experimenter shall terminate the investigation at any point where it appears injury or death of the subject might occur.
8. Precautions shall be taken to prevent even the remote possibility of injury, disability, or death.

Expanded guidelines for human experimentation may be found in the Federal Health and Human Services Regulation (NIMH, 1981), in a handbook interpreting them (Levine, 1981), and in *Judicial Council, Opinions and Reports* (AMA, 1979) under Section 5.18. The AMA guidelines suggest disclosure of the fact that an investigational drug or procedure is to be used, and that a reasonable explanation be given of the nature of the procedure, followed by an offer to answer any questions before the experiment begins.

Minors and mentally incompetent persons may be used only if mentally competent adults would not be suitable subjects and only when written consent is given by a legally authorized representative of the subject. No persons may be used as subjects against their will. The guidelines state further that *"under no circumstances* is a doctor permitted to do anything that would weaken the physical or mental resistance of a human being except from strictly therapeutic or prophylactic indications imposed in the interest of the patient.'' When these guidelines are taken literally with respect to informed consent, "young children and the mentally incompetent" are categorically excluded from all investigations except those that may "directly benefit the subjects. Inglefinger (1973), though aware of these serious implications, suggests that the principle stated above is neither observed nor practical and that it should be modified by changing "under no circumstances" to "only when the risks are small and justifiable." He argues also that there are situations when insistence on the rule "it must directly benefit the child patient" will not hold. For instance, the courts have upheld the right of a child to donate a kidney to his twin and have indicated approval of the donation of skin for a graft to a burned cousin with the parents' consent.

Curran and Beecher (1969) state that for tissue and organ donation, donors should be 14 or older, intelligent and mature enough to give informed consent. Parental or guardian consent must also be obtained. Donation should be restricted to relatives or close friends.

If parents have the right to give informed consent for procedures on their minor children, they have also the right to deny consent. Permission withheld may result in certain death of the child, as in the case of a birth anomaly when corrective surgery is not performed. Ethical, moral, and legal questions then arise regarding the child's right to live, the obligation of the physician to preserve life, and society's right to intervene and overrule parental objection. The determination must be made, where appropriate, whether to appeal for court intervention under child neglect laws (Shaw, 1973). In a study of this question, Guff and Campbell (1973) analyzed 299 consecutive deaths in a special care nursery and found that 43 of them (14 percent) were due to treatment being withheld. Most of the 43 had multiple anomalies, and parents and physicians joined in a decision to withhold treatment when it was apparent that no meaningful life was possible and that treatment was relatively hopeless.

The AMA guidelines further suggest that when the patient is unable to make a rational decision, consent of the next of kin or legal guardian should be obtained. When a child under 14 is involved and is assumed to be below the age of understanding, the parents or guardian must consent.

Competence to consent to research requires that the subject have the requisite knowledge, the ability to reason, and the ability to make an appropriate choice. A person may be unconscious, out of contact with reality, or mentally retarded and thus unable to comprehend the facts presented. The ability to reason may be compromised in schizophrenia or in organic brain disorders. Action and judgment may be paralyzed in catatonia, delirium, and profound depression. When an individual is unable to act in an autonomous manner and lacks the capacity to make a rational decision, determination of competence follows tests similar to those for competency to stand trial.

Patients confined involuntarily in a mental hospital pose a special problem because it has been held that in such a coercive setting they may be unable to give valid consent. Admission, retention, and treatment of the mentally ill requires (1) informed consent of the patient; (2) court order; or (3) implied consent in an emergency where it is reasonable to assume that if a patient were competent he would give consent, e.g., where he is likely to inflict serious harm on self or others (Foster, 1978).

The administrator of a mental health program or institution will inevitably wish to do research. To do so requires careful observance of procedures designed to protect human subjects.* Each institution engaged in research with individuals is required to provide written assurance to the Secretary of Health and Human Services that it will comply with the regulations. To initiate the process the institution must file a statement of principles which protect the rights and welfare of subjects, provide the names and qualifications of the members of its Institutional Review Board (at least five members with a diversity of backgrounds, including one nonscientist such as a lawyer, ethicist, or clergyman), and spell out the procedures it will follow in the review process and in the continuing review of the investigation.

All research proposals on human subjects, except those classified

---

* Procedures are detailed in *Code of Federal Regulations* (45CFR46), Protection of Human Subjects, Revised January 1981. Regulations are authorized by the National Research Act PL 93–348, 1974. Every institution engaged in research on human subjects must obtain a copy of the regulations and follow the procedure regardless of the source of funding for the investigation. Material obtained from the Secretary of Health and Human Services will include detailed instructions and suggestions for application. Write: Director, Office for the Protection from Research Risks (OPRR), National Institute of Health, Bethesda, MD 20205.

for expedited review, must be reviewed at a meeting of the IRB with a majority of members present. The IRB may approve, disapprove, or modify the proposal. It will also insure there is documentation of subject's informed consent. It will follow projects with a continuing review appropriate to the degree of risk. The IRB will keep records of all proposals submitted, of its actions on them, and of its continuing review. Institution officials may further approve research investigations but may not approve any project not approved by the IRB. The IRB also has authority to terminate or suspend a project that harms subjects. When it takes this action it must notify institution officials and the Secretary of HHS.

Criteria for approval, all of which must be met, include the following:

1. By using procedures consistent with sound research design which do not necessarily expose subjects to risk.
2. Risks must be reasonable in relation to anticipated benefits.
3. Selection of subjects must be equitable.
4. Informed consent must be obtained.
5. Informed consent must be documented.
6. Provisions must be made for monitoring to insure subject safety.
7. Privacy of subjects and confidentiality of data must be protected.
8. Appropriate additional safeguards must be included to protect rights and welfare when the subject has an acute physical or mental illness, resides in an institution, or is economically or educationally disadvantaged.

Further duties are described in the regulations for research with fetuses, pregnant women, or *in vitro* fertilization.

Fortunately, this complicated process may be eliminated in the projects on the Expedited Review List (46FR8392–1981). All that is required is notification of IRB members and institution officials that the subject is not at risk and that the procedure falls under one or more of the following rubrics:

1. Collection of hair, nail clippings, or extracted teeth
2. Collection of excreta or external secretions

3. Data on subjects 18 years or older using noninvasive procedures routinely employed in clinical practice (weighing, testing for sensory acuity, sensors, EKG, EEG, thermography, etc. but not x-rays or microwaves)
4. Collection of blood (not exceeding 450 milliliters in an 8-week period or more often than twice per week)
5. Collection of dental plaque or calculus
6. Voice recording
7. Moderate exercise by healthy volunteers
8. Study of existing data, records, or specimens
9. Individual or group behavior where the investigator does not manipulate the subject's behavior and no stress is involved
10. Research on drugs or devices for which an investigational new drug or device exemption is not required

These regulations are workable and recognize the risk-benefit factors in research. Special care is exercised in conducting investigations on children, the mentally ill, and the mentally retarded to insure protection of their rights and welfare.

Administrators have the obligation to create a climate that encourages research. They must also use their influence to combat legal and regulatory barriers that may arise and impair the advancement of scientific inquiry into the correction and treatment of mental illness and emotional disorders. We have imported from abroad many innovative approaches to the care and treatment of mental illness. Creative and unusual new ideas that advance knowledge might well be snuffed out if the trend toward individualism and overemphasis upon rights blocks the greater good to society from the freedom to perform significant scientific studies. Scientific inquiry can be undertaken without sacrifice of either the welfare of subjects or their dignity and well-being.

OTHER ETHICAL ISSUES IN RESEARCH

Informed Consent

Participants in research, after reasonable explanation of the risks and benefits, must voluntarily consent to be a subject. Ethical issues arise when foreknowledge would doom the research to failure. Placebos may detect spontaneous remissions. Detailed explanations could bias results.

Controlled Trials

It is more ethical to employ random controlled clinical trials of a therapy than to rely upon clinical intuition. It is unethical to deny an effective therapy to patients who could benefit from it for purposes of an investigation comparing no treatment or placebo use. It is ethical to compare therapies only where knowledge is lacking that one method is better than another and both are believed effective.

Community Issues

The ethical problems of research in the community have been presented by Golann (1973). Researchers may learn of illegal acts in the course of investigation, and although they may promise confidentiality, they cannot guarantee legal protection to violators who are subjects of study. Minority groups frequently resist research that may potentially damage their self-image. Participant observations of homosexual acts in public restrooms may be taboo as a research investigation. Exploration of schoolchildren's knowledge about sex can mobilize massive community opposition to a research project.

Activities that offend public mores and demonstrate ethical irresponsibility of professionals will lose community support, Bell (1973) notes. For example, some recent procedures foster transient but often intense superficial relationships requiring no more than a commitment to personal gratification (Collahan, 1980). Mental health professionals caught up in such group movements may argue that nudity, public sex, and drug use, though illegal, are so only because laws are antiquated and do not reflect current social mores. Sensitivity to community attitudes is essential. The clinician had best steer clear of unconventional ways of relating and avoid association with those who shun scientific investigation of the efficacy of such methods. Encounters, sensitivity, and "far-out" groups are for "normal people" who seek self-fulfillment. The mental health profession has no obligation to police or supervise activities that bring pleasure or comfort. It is enough to make the public aware that ethical issues do arise out of group participation. Group leaders are often nonprofessionals and as such are not bound by an ethical code to prevent what is said or done in groups from being talked about in public.

Preservation of Privacy

Specific consent of the subject is required for recording on audiotape, videotape, or film, and the subject must have full knowledge of the use to be made of the record. Often the subject is unaware of the intensive explorations in depth that the record is part of, or of relationships revealed about significant others. Nor is the individual always aware of the meaning of what has been recorded. It is for these reasons that tight security is essential on all such material in order to protect the privacy of the subject. One disguises the data to prevent identification. Even with these precautions, the subject may read an article or book making use of this material and discover interpretations that are embarrassing or even damaging. There is no easy solution other than securing an enlightened informed consent. On the strictest interpretation of the informed consent principle, doubts could be raised as to the ethics of persons who pose as patients but who are actually observers engaged in data collection, of concealed observers behind a one-way glass, or of observers who feign symptoms to gain access to a hospital ward.

Publication and the Rights of Colleagues

Investigators discuss work in progress with colleagues. Project grants summarize ideas and methods. Manuscript drafts are submitted to readers for appraisal. It is wrong to steal ideas and race to publish them ahead of the scientist who is carefully checking the accuracy of his work. Even more immoral is the use of the work of a subordinate investigator, published as one's own research. The same applies to a team project, when the material of another is used without designating joint authorship. Investigators have the obligation to acknowledge contributors and to indicate data sources.

Patents and the Rights of Employers

A new and troubling consequence of the rapid advance of biotechnology has raised ethical issues and challenged traditional values. When a new technology is patentable, a scientist may delay publication of findings until industry gains an advantage in production. The scientist may become a consultant to industry and devote more time to this profitable venture than to basic research or give priority to investigations that are potentially profitable. It is possible for a scientist to become an instant millionaire from the proceeds of a patented technology. Is the profit to be shared with the department and the university or kept by the investigator? While the phenomenon of academia-industrial relations has occurred in the electronics field, industry has no basic research in life sciences and is therefore dependent upon university based research investigators.

SUMMARY

Freedom of scientific inquiry is essential to the improvement of health care. Clinical practice is based upon controlled human experimentation demonstrating one course of treatment more effective and at lower risk of hazard than another.

Questionable ethics in research have led to the restatement of ethical guidelines, rules, and regulations to be followed whenever humans are used as experimental subjects.

The canons specify that experimenter and subjects are fellow human beings whose relationship is one of mutual trust and concern who share respect for the opinions of mankind. The scientist must be free to use a new therapeutic modality which offers hope of saving life or relieving suffering. A voluntary informed consent must be obtained, with free power of choice. When the advancement of knowledge is directed to the future benefit of society, then the experiment is undertaken only if it will yield results obtainable in no other way. The risk must never exceed the importance of the problem.

The ethical guidelines require that the welfare of the individual not be jeopardized; that the subject's rights and safety be preserved; that unnecessary physical and mental suffering be avoided; and that the experimenter be willing that his own loved ones undertake the procedure.

The disciplinary rules require prior animal experimentation, assessment of all risks, approval by a human experimentation review committee, competence of the investigator to undertake the research, the subject's right to terminate the experiment at any time, termination if injury or death of a subject might occur, and precautions to avoid injury, disability or death.

The administrator has an obligation to approve the research protocol as significant and worth the expenditure of resources; to assure the competence of the investigator to carry out the project; to appoint an Institutional Review Committee; to create a climate supportive of research; and to work for education of the public and the removal of barriers to scientific inquiry in the field of mental illness and retardation.

QUESTIONS

1. Give an example of research on human subjects of questionable ethics.
2. How did the present concern over human experimentation arise?
3. What are the canons or principles which govern ethical considerations?
4. What are three ethical considerations?
5. What are the disciplinary rules to be observed?
6. What are the administrator's obligations with regard to research on human subjects?

REFERENCES

* AMA (1979), *Judicial Council Opinions and Reports*. rev. ed. Chicago: American Medical Association.

Beecher, H. K. (1966), Questionable ethics in experimentation. *N. Engl. J. Med.*, 274:1354–1360.

Beecher, H. K. (1970), *Research and the Individual: Human Studies*. Boston: Little, Brown.

Bell, J. E. (1973), Ethical issues in new group procedures. In: *Current Ethical Issues in Mental Health*. Rockville, Md.: National Institute of Mental Health.

* Bogomolny, R. (1976), *Human Experimentation*, Dallas, Tex.: Southern Methodist University Press.

Collahan, D. (1980), Shattuck lecture: Contemporary biomedical ethics, *N. Engl. J. Med.*, 302:1228–1233.

Curran, W. J., & Beecher, H. K. (1969), Experimentation in children. *J. Amer. Med. Assn.,* 210:77–83.

Foster, H. H. (1978). Ten rules that state principles of informed consent: Appendix A to chapter IV. In: *Law and the Mental Health Professions,* ed. W. E. Barton & C. J. Sanborn. New York: International Universities Press.

Golann, S. E. (1973), Ethical problems of research in the community. In: *Current Ethical Issues in Mental Health,* Rockville, Md.: National Institute of Mental Health.

Guff, R. S., & Campbell, A. G. M. (1973), Moral and ethical dilemmas in the special care nursery. *N. Engl. J. Med.,* 283:890–894.

Ingelfinger, F. J. (1973), Ethics of experiments in children. *N. Engl. J. Med.,* 288:791–792.

JAMA (1975), An unethical study to observe the long term effects of syphilis: Medical experimentation on the poor. *J. Amer. Med. Assn.,* 231:233–234.

* Levine, R. J. (1981), Ethics and regulations of clinical research. Baltimore: Urban and Schwartzberg.

Massachusetts Physician (1974), Unethical studies. *Mass. Physician* 33:19–20.

* NIMH (1981), *Code of Federal Reglations* (45CFR46) Revised 1981. Bethesda, Md.: National Institute of Mental Health.

* Rollin, B. E. (1981), *Animal Rights and Human Morality.* Buffalo, N.Y.: Prometheus Books.

Shaw, A. (1973), Dilemmas of informed consent in children. *N. Engl. J. Med.,* 283:885–889.

Torrey, E. F., ed. (1968), *Ethical Issues in Medicine.* Boston: Little, Brown.

Chapter 3

The Advance of Science: Bioethics

> The law is full of phraseology drawn from morals, and by the mere force of language continually invites us to pass from one domain to the other without perceiving it, as we are sure to do unless we have the boundary constantly before our minds.
> — *Oliver Wendell Holmes, Jr. (1841–1935)*

Case example. A frightened, 15-year-old adolescent, a sophomore in high school, comes to your office fearing that she is pregnant because she has missed two periods. Your examination and laboratory test confirm that she is pregnant and in the first trimester. The law in her state follows the 1973 U.S. Supreme Court decision (Roe v. Wade) in leaving the decision to have an abortion in the first three months to the woman and her doctor (Slovenko, 1973). The parents are aware of the daughter's concern, and her mother has in fact accompanied her. Do you recommend to the girl that she have the child? Raise it? Put it up for adoption? Will you recommend abortion? Do you advise counseling? May a minor consent to an abortion in your state? Is it ethical for a physician to perform an abortion? Does an unborn fetus have the right to life over the woman's right to her own moral choice?

34

Medicines With the Power to Maim and Kill

Powerful medications have been introduced that have produced deafness, caused deformities in the newborn, contributed to the formation of damaging thrombi, or upon continued use resulted in such symptoms as tardive dyskinesia. Others have induced fatal aplastic anemia or serious hypotension. Drugs must not only be proven effective in the treatment of a given condition, they must also be judged safe. To be effective some drugs, such as lithium, must be given in dosages that bring the blood level to a certain measurable concentration, and then be maintained within a relatively small range of variation. It sometimes seems that the more specific the action, the more likely it is that toxic side effects will follow deviation from the correct dosage. Of course, this is not a generalizable scientific fact but only a reflection that today's drugs are far different from those of the homeopathic-allopathic era. The potential for benefit from medications is greater than ever before, but so also is the potential for harm.

To protect the public, a new drug must undergo a prolonged period of gestation. Testing usually begins in animals and here its range of safety is explored. The investigation may proceed to trial with primates but eventually it must be tried in humans. Under stringent rules the new substance is tested in a research setting, after which attempts are made to replicate the findings elsewhere. Protocols are reviewed carefully by panels of experts before drugs are ready for release into commercial channels.

Some practitioners and drug manufacturers are impatient with the cautious and conservative approach of the Federal Drug Administration. This regulatory agency prescribes a slow and careful course to ensure the safety of each new product. Though its objectives are praiseworthy, these mandatory procedures cause such long delays that extensive trials of new drugs are often made outside of this country.

The introduction of new drugs poses ethical issues for investigators. They are expected to be honest, worthy of trust, and to document meticulously all the new drug's effects, both desired and undesired. They are expected not to make premature claims or rush into print. They are expected to avoid such conflicts of interest as being investors in the company that makes the substance or publishing their results in a journal over which they have editorial control.   The administrator has the obligation to insure that the institution endorses the use only of FDA-approved drugs, of course according to physicians the right to use their judgment in employing a listed drug in conditions other than those specified. When nonapproved drugs are proposed, procedure follows that outlined in chapter 2 for human experimentation.

MACHINES THAT SUSTAIN LIFE

Machines performing renal dialysis can sustain life in a person with damaged kidneys. Such a machine works by removing waste products from the circulating fluid. Artificial heart pumps propel the vital blood when cardiac valves and muscles fail. Artificial lung machines do the work of paralyzed chest muscles. Oxygen machines supply life-sustaining gas for breathing. Parenteral fluids drip into veins, supplying both nutrients and drugs to keep the organism alive. The ethical issues posed by these machines are expressed in such concepts as the right to die with dignity, termination of hopeless life, and the mode of selection of those given a chance to live when resources are limited.

Physicians have been trained to preserve life. They abhor involvement in decisions that would withdraw support. Dr. E. Stainbrook, rebelling at participation in such decisions, spoke for all physicians when he said, "I won't let society shove its problems off on me." Society has the responsibility to solve the central ethical issue of who has the right to live and who shall die now that machines are available to prolong life.

When a patient is judged hopelessly ill and the anticipated outcome is imminent death, serious medical, emotional, legal, and ethical issues arise concerning the justification for continued dependence upon life support efforts. Medical and nursing staff as well as the patient and his relatives face the dilemma whether maximal efforts to prolong life shall continue or whether such efforts should cease, allowing death to occur. To this end the establishment of a permanent Committee on Optimum Care was recommended following a study at the Massachusetts General Hospital (*NEJM*, 1976). The committee proposed a classification system with the following headings:

1. Maximal therapeutic effort without reservation
2. Maximal effort but with daily evaluation

3. Selective limitation of therapeutic measures, not to be admitted to the Intensive Care Unit; emphasis upon patient comfort
4. All therapy to be discontinued

The proposed system was then studied over two hundred admissions. As a result of the study, misunderstanding regarding prognosis was clarified with patient and family, communication was reopened between staff and patient, unified treatment objectives were decided upon by the staff, and responsibility for the patient was once again shared with the family.

Even with such a system, there is a growing concern that it may be inappropriate to apply technological capabilities to the fullest extent in all cases and without limitation (see Rabkin, Gillerman, and Rice, 1976). Heroic measures at resuscitation may be medically unsound. A patient with an irreversible and terminal illness may not wish to have heroic measures performed and should have a say in deciding what measures will be tried. Orders not to resuscitate should be issued only "upon the informed choice of a competent patient or with an incompetent patient by strict adherence" to established guidelines and "then only to the extent that all appropriate family members are in agreement with the views of the involved staff" (Rabkin et al., 1976). It is suggested that a committee assist the physician in arriving at the decision. In Michigan a patient who is not competent to decide may be assigned a guardian or advocate.

It is the administrator's responsibility to insure the development of appropriate standards and procedures for the employment of life-sustaining machines when recovery is not possible and death is inevitable without support.

Public concern over the inability to make decisions when hopelessly ill has led some to favor the "Living Will." This is a document prepared in advance that says in part: "If the situation arises in which there is no reasonable expectation of my recovery from physical or mental disability, I request that I be allowed to die and not be kept alive by artificial means or heroic measures." The legal status of such a document is uncertain. Several states have legislation pending that would recognize it (Bok, 1976).

In 1975 the news media focused national attention on a hopelessly ill patient, Karen Ann Quinlan. The parents asked physicians to shut off tubes and to disconnect the life-sustaining machines that had kept their daughter alive for more than a year in deep coma. Doctors refused to do so, whereupon the parents appealed to the court. Lacking convincing evidence of brain death, the judge denied their petition. Later the court returned responsibility for the decision to terminate life to the parents, subject to approval by a committee of physicians. The committee's vote was to confirm only the prognosis. It was not meant to decide the ethical issue of whether to treat or to withhold treatment (Veatch, 1980). Though the committee decided not to support life, the patient was able to survive without the life-sustaining equipment. She was subsequently moved to a nursing home, still unresponsive to her surroundings.

Two decisions rendered in cases heard by the Massachusetts courts, those of Saikewicz and Dinnerstein, further developed the process of interaction between law and medicine in ethical issues. Saikewicz, age 67, had, for over twenty years been a resident at the Belchertown State School for the mentally retarded. Communication with him was always difficult. His physicians diagnosed acute myeloblastic leukemia. In their judgment, the available treatment would extend life, with a 30–50 percent chance of temporary remission. Side effects would likely be severe, however, and would cause pain and discomfort that could not be interpreted to the patient. Without treatment he would die within a few months. The physicians decided not to intervene. The lay superintendent, for his part, felt that the need for treatment was urgent and asked the court to appoint a guardian. It took nearly four years until the Supreme Judicial Court issued its report. In the meantime a ruling was made that if an incompetent person refused therapy, a guardian might be appointed to act for the patient. The patient in this case died as had been predicted. The Court's decision, when it finally came, rejected the use of a committee in making treatment decisions. Further, it held, the family and physicians could not make the decision either. If an incompetent person is suffering from a condition that can be treated with some reasonable expectation of effecting a permanent cure or temporary remission which might lead to normal functioning, the Probate Court was mandated to decide if life-prolonging or life-saving treatment is to be withdrawn or withheld (MMS Newsletter, 1978).

In the Dinnerstein case, a woman in her sixties with advanced Alzheimer's disease, was immobile, bedridden, speechless, unable to swallow without choking, and certain soon to die. There was no known effective treatment. Her physician recommended that resuscitation not be undertaken if she developed heart or lung problems. The family agreed. The Massachusetts Appeals Court recognized the competence of physicians "to ease the passing of an irreversibly, terminally-ill patient in light of the patient's history and wishes of the family."

In another quite different situation, Brother Fox had made known his wish not to have his life prolonged by heroic measures if he should develop a terminal illness with no hope of recovery. The New York Court of Appeals voided the "substituted judgment" standard for determining the intent of incompetent patients with no hope of recovery and stated it was the obligation of the legislature, not the courts, to formulate guidelines for decisions. It added, "The decision to refuse treatment is the common-law right of every person of adult years and sound mind . . . to determine what shall be done with his own body." This right, it said, could be exercised for the incompetent patient only when the prognosis indicated a fatal illness existed with no chance of recovery, and clear and convincing evidence was present that the patient had provided instructions to terminate life-sustaining procedures (Pares, 1981).

The struggles of the courts to resolve the issues have not been successful. The Fox case leaves unanswered the question, What happens if the patient leaves no "clear and convincing" instructions before slipping into a vegetative state?

Perhaps the wise action, when an incompetent patient suffers from a terminal illness likely to result in death within a year, is to secure consultation to confirm the prognosis, and with the concurrence of the family order that no attempts at resuscitation be made in the event of cardiac or respiratory distress (*MMS Newsletter*, 1978).

EUTHANASIA

Blomquist (1974) has extensively debated the issue of euthanasia in Sweden. He states his belief that every human being has the right to his own death. Further, he argues, the physician ought to be free in certain situations to decline starting or stopping a treatment in order to maintain life; in certain instances a physician should in fact be allowed to directly hasten the patient's death.

In the U.S. it is a rare voice that is heard in support of helping a terminally ill patient end his suffering. Most fear the consequences of loosening moral restraints and argue that pain can be eased to allow a natural death. The debate and discussion of euthanasia must continue within this country, however, as there is still more ambivalence than agreement here. While the person in irreversible coma for several years might be seen as approaching the point where further measures to maintain life can be stopped, there is far less agreement that terminally ill individuals have the right to take their own lives. Suicidal feelings and self-destructive wishes, it is felt, will usually subside with active treatment. In this country it is usually considered the obligation of society and the psychiatrist to get the person into treatment. The terminal illness issue is dealt with separately.

Canons

• The medical profession is opposed to euthanasia, mercy killing, or any intentional termination of life. McFadden (1967) expresses the Roman Catholic viewpoint when he states that since "life is the creation of God, the direct killing of a private person is an absolute prohibition."

• When there is irrefutable evidence that biological death is imminent, the phyician may stop extraordinary measures to prolong life, if the patient and/or the immediate family request it.

Ethical Guidelines

• The physician has an obligation to preserve life.

• Any action that weakens patient resistance without therapeutic indication is unjustified. This applies both to experimental subjects and to the dying patient. When death is imminent, when the evidence is irrefutable that life cannot continue without life-sustaining machines, or when the remedy is either refused or not available, patient, family and physician may concur in withholding intervention.

Rules

In each case where a dilemma exists, there should be a method of review to determine whether maximum effort to prolong life is indicated or whether efforts should cease and death be allowed to occur. When irreversible and terminal illness is present, heroic measures to prolong life may be determined to be medically unsound. One way out of the dilemma is a Committee on Optimum Care which would share responsibility for the tough decision to withdraw life support systems. The use of consultants is another, followed by discussion with responsible family members.

The AMA House of Delegates stated in December 1973 that "mercy killing" is contrary to the policy of the medical profession and that "the cessation of employment of extraordinary means to prolong life of the body where there is irrefutable evidence that biological death is imminent is the decision of the patient and/or his immediate family." It added that the physician's advice should be available to both.

Rachels (1975) argues that the AMA position is unsound because active euthanasia may be more humane than the passive course, that decisions about life or death may be irrelevant grounds, and that the distinction between letting die and active termination has no moral importance. To buttress his position, Rachels cites the case of an adult with terminal cancer in terrible agony. By withholding treatment, suffering is prolonged. Although the doctor does nothing in this decision to "let the patient die," Rachels holds him as subject here to moral opprobrium as he would be had he administered a lethal injection that needlessly killed the patient. We do not agree with Rachels's position; rather we support that of the AMA.

Society must debate these differences in points of view and establish its legal rules of conduct which the physician is obligated to follow. Norman Frost (1976) dramatically demonstrated the ingredients of an ethical dilemma following the birth of a seemingly robust baby. Postnatal examination revealed Down's syndrome (mongolism) associated with intestinal atresia. When surgeons recommended an operation to open the intestinal passage and preserve life, the baby's parents refused permission. Two rights were in conflict: the child's right to live, which the physicians supported, and the parents' right to refuse treatment.

The alternative approaches to this dilemma are as follows: *legal decision,* which doesn't solve the moral issue, but does make a judgment in favor of one party; *the doctrine of relativism,* which holds that since there is no accepted principle, one does what seems right in the individual case; and *utilitarian doctrine,* which counsels us to act according to the probable consequences and to choose as the right course the one causing the greatest good for the greatest number. Using this last principle, one could assign points to the right-to-live position and, similarly, points to the parents' right to reject a congenitally damaged child. But this doesn't really help very much, for left is the question, Are fewer points to be given if the consequence will be a nonproductive individual?

Perhaps a better solution would be to employ the *decision-making model*. This approach seeks to gather all the facts, look at all the options and consequences, and then select an action for implementation. Data-gathering in the case cited goes beyond the physician-patient dyad. It shifts the conflict from privately held opinions to shared points of view. For example, the process of exploration may take into account the following factors:

• The parents don't want the child because of a belief that "mongoloids" live a miserable life in institutions and the only alternative is death.

• While the physician's duty is to preserve life and the operation will easily accomplish that purpose, the impairment of Down's syndrome will remain.

• An impartial advocate for the infant may clarify the unspoken arguments for survival, and nurses may describe their feelings at being commanded to give nothing by mouth and to await the patient's death.

• A sampling of other parents may reveal a shared opinion regarding birth defects.

In an open exchange with focus on process and not on what is right or wrong, a decision may emerge that is more acceptable to all; it may be for survival or for termination. In dealing with ethical issues there must be an awareness of the range of social values and the pluralism of moral views. It is helpful to define an ethical issue, to discuss it, and to realize there is no one correct answer to every question.

REPLACEMENT PARTS—TRANSPLANTS

Surgical skills make it possible to remove and replace a kidney, a liver, a lung, and even a heart. There are no reports, according to Ladimer (1971) of the National Transplant Information Center, of organ or tissue removal without express consent from relatives of deceased persons, "even though prior agreements to donate may have been recorded and would be sufficient by themselves under laws in practically all states."

It is possible to identify with Barnard's view (1973) that it is better to save a life through transplant of an organ removed post mortem than to leave it in the body of the deceased to putrefy. He would observe the law, use only a normal organ that is genetically close to the prospective recipient's body (this is determined by tissue matching), make certain of the absence of transmissible disease in the donor, use immune suppressants to combat rejection, and take appropriate measures to prevent infection. Heart transplants, discontinued for a time until resolution of immunological problems, have begun again in the 1980s.

The transplanting of an organ may be associated with psychiatric complications, as has been noted by Lunde (1973), consultant to the Stanford cardiac transplant team. Because of the centuries-old notion of the heart as the essence of life and the seat of emotion, the donor's family may feel that their loved one has "not completely died so long as his heart [is] beating in the chest of another." As a result, they may follow the life of the recipient with anxiety and may grieve when he dies. The recipient of the new heart may expect it will bring not only new life, but new loves and abilities.

Kidney transplants are another advance that may prolong life. After four years, "83% of kidneys from living, related donors are functioning well and 90–95% of patients are alive regardless of the source of the kidney" (*Medical News, 1979*).

Patients who receive kidneys from living donors do well, but about one half of all recipients of cadaver organs return sooner or later with symptoms of transplant rejection. Depression, anxiety, fear, and anger are expressed at this point. Even hemodialysis may not prevent death wishes or the determination to allow death to occur. While advances in technology may reduce the probability of rejection, the importance of a fresh organ to transplant is obvious. However, since there is not always available a living donor willing to give a kidney to save another's life, the organ may come from someone about to die from a cause other than renal failure. A redefinition of death and the criteria for its determination thus becomes essential with organ transfer as a reality.

The question "Will you authorize an organ to be transplanted to save a life?'' is asked of a family at a moment of high tragedy, when it has just learned that a loved one will die from an accident. Some would avoid this traumatic confrontation and use organs from bodies that will be unclaimed. Beecher (1968) notes that this course could lead to a market in organs involving coercion and an abhorrent abuse of the dignity of the poor. This was the subject of Robin Cook's popular recent novel, *Coma* (1977), subsequently made into a movie. Beecher says society can ill afford to discard the organs of the dying. All are agreed that the dying patient must be cared for by a medical team other than the one with responsibility for the recipient.

BRAIN DEATH

The concept of brain death emerged when it became possible to maintain patients in deep coma with the assistance of intravenous fluids and respirators, even when they lack reflexes and give no evidence of electrophysiological activity in the brain (Abram et al., 1981). The use of organs for transplant, obtained from persons whose brains are destroyed but whose respiration and circulation are artificially maintained, has made it urgently necessary to change the way death is determined.

Death—the cessation of life—was traditionally judged to have occurred when the blood ceased to circulate. The absence of breathing and of heart action were primary determinants of death. However, in respirator-maintained patients, new criteria are necessary to establish permanent loss of brain function. The "Harvard criteria" formulated in 1968 are quite reliable (Abram et al., 1981). They are:

1. Unreceptivity and unresponsitivity to externally applied stimuli and inner need
2. Absence of spontaneous muscular movements or spontaneous respiration
3. No elicitable reflexes

Social policy is slowly moving toward a statutory definition of brain death. By 1981 twenty-six states had enacted legislation incorporating the cessation of all brain functions as a criterion for declaring death (Alabama, Alaska, Arkansas, California, Colorado, Connecticut, Florida, Hawaii, Idaho, Illinois, Iowa, Kansas, Louisiana, Maryland, Michigan, Montana, Nevada, New Mexico, North Carolina, Oklahoma, Oregon, Tennessee, Texas, Virginia, West Virginia, and Wyoming). In addition, the President's Commission for the Study of Ethical Problems in Medicine has urged Congress to adopt a statute providing a clear and socially accepted basis for determination of death (Abram et al., 1981). Support for legislation is advanced by Caprow and Kass (1972) and Veith, Fein, Tender, Veatch, Kleiman, and Kalkines (1977a,b).

Veith et al. bluntly state that there is no adequately documented instance in which recovery occurred when the criteria for brain death were fulfilled. Present determination of death is based upon the following criteria (Abram et al., 1981) whereby an individual presenting the clinical picture described in either Section A (cardiopulmonary) or section B (neurological) is considered dead.

A. Irreversible cessation of circulatory and respiratory functions.
1. Clinical examination: absence of responsiveness, heartbeat, and respiration (may require EKG).
2. Irreversibility recognized by persistent cessation of functions during an appropriate period of observation and/or trial of therapy.
B. Irreversible cessation of all functions of the entire brain, including the brain stem.
1. Cerebral functions absent, deep coma, unreceptivity and unresponsivity (may require EEG or bloodflow study).
2. Brain stem functions are absent. Tests should show no pupillary-light, corneal, occulocephalic, occulovestibular, or oropharyngial reflexes, and adequate testing for the exclusion of apnea must be done: (O_2 or O_2 + CO_2 for ten minutes).
3. Irreversibility is recognized when evaluation discloses findings (1) and (2) above and when following findings are present:
a. cause of coma is established and is sufficient to account for findings.
b. possibility of recovery is excluded (reversible conditions include sedation, overdose of drug, hypothermia, neuromuscular blockade, and shock).
c. cessation of all brain functions persists for an appropriate

period of observation and/or trial of therapy (complete cessation of circulation in the *normothermic adult* brain for more than ten minutes is incompatible with survival of brain tissue).

Further elaboration of the concept of brain death and its medicolegal aspects may be found in Black (1978) and Coe and Curran (1980).

The ethical and moral position of Jewish, Catholic, and Protestant scholars supports the concept of brain death. To be human and alive requires some ability to think, perceive, and respond as well as to integrate experience and body function. It is morally wrong to regard as alive a person who has *irreversibly* lost these capacities. It is morally wrong to maintain circulation and respiration in such an individual.

PSYCHOSURGERY

A surgical procedure, prefrontal lobotomy, reported in 1936 by Egaz Moniz of Portugal, won for him the 1949 Nobel Prize for Medicine. A swirling controversy ever since has mixed legitimate doubts regarding the procedure's scientific validity with fear that it may be employed as an instrument of social control of those who use violence as a political strategy or for the subjugation of minorities confined in institutions. Ethical issues have been raised regarding its risk benefit ratio, the experimental use of psychosurgery in humans, and the different claims and responsibilities of physician and society in an area where the acknowledged expert is the medical doctor seeking to restore the patient to function. Some see the principal issue to be the brain as the organ of the mind and the locus of self and identity; any intervention, they argue, carries with it the hazard of damage to self.

In the early 1970s, when we were visiting an APA District Branch in Jackson, Mississippi, we discussed psychiatrist participation in reviewing cases of psychosurgery in children. Dr. Peter Breggin visited APA headquarters to express his concern at the resurgence of the procedure and to enlist APA support in opposing it. This led to the formation of a Task Force to prepare an APA position. A year or so later we visited U.C.L.A. at a time when an organized protest halted a research project intended to validate the use of psychosurgery. The

APA Task Force defined psychosurgery as "surgical intervention to sever fibers connecting one part of the brain with another or to remove, destroy or stimulate brain tissue with the intent of modifying or altering disturbances of behavior, thought, or mood for which *no* organic pathological cause can be demonstrated by established tests and techniques" (APA, 1977). There is little resemblance between yesterday's prefrontal lobotomy and today's technology in doing psychosurgery. The advance of scientific knowledge of brain anatomy and function as well as of this type of procedure and the technique involved has made the difference. It is now known that the limbic system mediates human emotions and behavior, and it is the current focus of surgical attention in psychosurgery. Present technology is sufficiently refined that it can be brought to bear on specific parts of that system.

A national survey (APA, 1977) has determined that about five hundred psychosurgery operations were performed annually in 1971, 1972, and 1973. Earlier, a drastic decline in the number of such procedures had ensued upon introduction of ECT and drug therapy; a smaller decline accompanied attempts at regulation. The therapeutic uses of these procedures are to relieve pain, as in inoperable cancer, and to treat symptoms of epilepsy when objective evidence of organic central nervous system disease is lacking but where these symptoms are associated with episodic or continuing aggressive behavior or other behavioral disturbance. It is primarily the experimental uses of psychosurgery that engender controversy. Psychosurgery has never become accepted therapy with positive indications and specific and predictable results. Rather it has been employed when all other treatments have failed and in an attempt to restore some function to one otherwise doomed to chronic distress and permanent incapacity.

The consequences of lobotomies performed in the 1940s included loss of initiative, dependency, seizures, and no improvement; others with long-standing illnesses did improve and returned to full function. Psychosurgical procedures as presently performed may have fewer serious potential side effects than those attending the prolonged use of antipsychotic drugs. Surgery has not helped much in eliminating thought disorders, delusions, or hallucinations, but it has had a beneficial effect on the affective components that accompany them (APA, 1977).

The lack of convincing evidence that modern psychosurgery produces no permanent personality change and the fact that the procedure once performed is irreversible and results in what is seen as permanent "brain damage" has persuaded the courts to impose controls and the states to develop restrictive and regulatory laws. Several states and Congress have had bills introduced that would limit the use of psychosurgery. Oregon enacted a law in 1973 that created a review board to approve or disapprove a petition by a physician or hospital intending to perform either psychosurgery or intracranial brain stimulation. California enacted a similar statute. Regarding such legislation, the APA Task Force observed "that removing clinical decisions from physicians and placing them in the hands of government officials generates the very possibility which the proponents of legislative control fear—the utilization of medical technology for political purposes" (APA, 1977).

Congress, after prolonged hearings, passed PL 93–348, which established a National Commission for the Protection of Human Subjects of Biomedical and Behavioral Research. The report of this commission, made in 1977 after five years of study, rebuts the position that all forms of psychosurgery are unsafe and ineffective. It endorsed research and validation but called also for stringent safeguards when the procedure is recommended for prisoners and involuntarily committed mental patients, as well as those on voluntary status in institutions, children, and persons with guardians.

With this very lengthy preamble, let us return briefly to the ethical issues emerging from the psychosurgical controversy. They include the precept "do no harm" vs. the idea that some harm is acceptable when the benefit outweighs the risk; the legitimacy of experimental research on humans; the right of a patient or his proxy to request and to receive treatment when involuntarily confined in a hospital or prison; and the question of when a procedure may move from the experimental category to that of accepted treatment.

It is difficult to squeeze psychosurgery into the presentational framework of ethics, but let us try.

Canons

Psychosurgery may be used in the small number of psychiatric disorders which are characterized by severe distress and functional incapacity and which fail to respond to any other presently available treatment. As a treatment of last resort, it should be performed only in a facility that meets established standards including a qualified team of experts (neurosurgeon, skilled nurses, psychiatrist, and clinical psychologist.)

Ethical Guidelines

Explicit protocols should be required, with assessment before and after operation and follow-up studies on outcome. A national registry for collation and evaluation should be established with a view to determining the scientific validity of the procedures in use and in a variety of conditions.

Rules

The procedure should not be used on children and young adults, or in prisoners if the indications are related to criminal behavior. (In all rules there are exceptions that constitute unusual indications. When such is the case, a conservator, proxy, advocate, or legal counsel shall represent the patient.)

A human experiment review committee shall be established and investigate each case proposed for psychosurgery as a treatment of last resort. Evidence must be presented to the review committee that trial during twenty-four months had demonstrated the failure of all alternative appropriate therapy.

The National Commission recommended the creation of a National Psychosurgical Board which would in each case determine that (1) the procedures to be undertaken have a demonstrated benefit for symptoms or disorders present in the patient, and (2) informed consent has been obtained and has been affirmed as in order by the relevant institution's review committee.

In the case of prisoners and persons involuntarily admitted, and in instances where the institutional review committee has determined a person incompetent to give informed consent, a court at which the patient is represented must give approval for the procedure, provided it meets the National Psychosurgical Board's criteria.

ELECTROCONVULSIVE THERAPY

"The electrical induction of a series of generalized seizures (ECT) remains an effective means of treating severe endogenous depression and, under certain circumstances, schizophrenic disorders" (Weiner, 1979). Max Fink (1978) states that ECT is as effective as pharmacotherapy in acute schizophrenic disorders. It is frequently the treatment of choice in agitated depression when there is a high risk of suicide, as often the lag before drug therapy can become effective is quite perilous for such patients.

All treatment alternatives to ECT are associated with such risks as neurological and cardiovascular complications. Attention has focused upon memory loss as an argument against ECT use. An anterograde and retrograde amnesia may occur for a few weeks after a course of ECT. An unresolved issue is the occasional persistent loss of memory. Weiner (1979) presents a discussion of the research on the subject. For a further review of the subject, the American Psychiatric Association's Task Force report (APA, 1978) is valuble, as are two recent books (Fink, 1979; Shagrass, Autry, Cole et al., 1980).

While use of ECT declined following the introduction of psychoactive drugs in the 1960s, it has lately been making a comeback, not only as a useful therapeutic alternative to pharmacotherapy when the patient fails to respond or develops undesirable side effects, but as an accepted treatment modality in its own right and sometimes the treatment of choice. There have of course been abuses of ECT, including its application in inappropriate cases, its too frequent prescription, and its extension over too many treatment sessions. Opponents of the procedure would eliminate it because of these abuses, citing irreversible brain damage and memory loss in those subjected to it. Legislative remedy was therefore sought to at least control these abuses.

The same California statute that limits the use of psychosurgery also deals with electroconvulsive therapy. The so-called "Vasconsellos Bill" allows ECT to be used when a competent patient has given informed consent, when a relative, guardian, or conservator concurs, when documentation shows that all other treatments have failed and critical need of therapy is demonstrated, and when a review board agrees that all conditions have been met. A petition to the California Supreme Court (in which the APA and the California Psychiatric Association were amici curiae) resulted in an order that the case be assigned to the Court of Appeals in San Diego. That body declared the statute unconstitutional on April 23, 1976 (*Psychiatric News,* 1976). The California Court of Appeals responded in its ruling to all points by petitioners:

• Denial of equal protection under the Fourteenth Amendment: argument rejected as without merit. The Court held that "regulation of intrusive and possibly hazardous forms of medical treatment is a proper exercise of the state's police power." The objective of the challenged law is to ensure that certain medical procedures are not performed on unwilling patients.

• Prescribed disclosure conflicts with legal precedent on standards for informed consent.

• The requirement that the procedure was critically needed for the patient's welfare was impermissibly vague.

• Once the competency of a voluntary patient has been confirmed and the truly voluntary nature of his consent is determined, the state has little excuse to invoke the substitute decisionmaking process. The court agreed there was no justification for infringing on the right to privacy in selecting and consenting to the treatment.

• It was proper to require a substantive review for involuntary or incompetent patients because of the need for a substitute decision-maker.

We believe that the ruling which requires a review of a physician's judgment to use an accepted mode of therapy poses a formidable barrier to treatment which often is urgently needed. Peer review of indications, appropriate use, and number of treatments should be sufficient to safeguard the patient if care is taken in obtaining informed consent. If the patient lacks competence or understanding, a relative or guardian may join in the decision process. A retrospective medical audit by peers is a reasonable way to deal with improper use rather than denial or restriction of application of an accepted form of treatment.

In Berkeley, California (November 1982) voters banned ECT in that city. Court action was introduced to declare the local ban invalid for it is in conflict with a state law which permits it. State law has precedence. The controversy between ECT as an accepted form of treatment and ECT as morally wrong (a position held by only a few) continued into the 1980's.

BEHAVIOR MODIFICATION

Parents have always used rewards, admonition, persuasion, and punishment to shape the behavior of their children. Societies have long rewarded those who modify their behavior to accept its goals and have punished those who violated its laws. Most treatment in psychiatry is intended to effect a change in a patient's behavior.

In 1949, Orwell's *1984* raised the specter of a controlled society. By that time Pavlov's pioneering work in conditioning had been replicated and expanded in a variety of ways. Insulin, electroconvulsive therapy, and lobotomy were used in modifying undesirable behavior. One of us observed early experiments in Boston in which the simple reward of a cigarette or a piece of candy provided sufficient incentive for psychotic patients to temporarily abandon handicapping mannerisms. From such simple beginnings emerged operant conditioning and the token economy, a procedure which assists in shaping behavior into desired patterns through rewards or by giving tokens that can be exchanged for privileges and comforts.

Circus animals perform at the will of their masters when the principles of behavior modification are employed. First in animals and then in humans, Delgado implanted an electric device that was able to stop rage reactions and substitute placid or pleasurable sensations. Skinner (1971) and his pigeons led to the formulation of theory and projected change in human behavior from the application of similar techniques.

The power to change man's behavior in religious conversion was described by Sargant (1957), in the control of thought by the Chinese in Korea by Lifton (1957), and as a treatment technique by Wolpe (1969), Yates (1970), and Sargant (1957). Behavior therapy is the systematic application of conditioning and learning theory to the treatment of mental disorders. The demonstration of the effectiveness of behavior control in a variety of settings, along with technological advances, has led society to look more closely at the procedures in use, the circumstances under which they are applied, and the social consequences as it gropes toward social policy to monitor practices.

Extremists challenge all use of drugs, ECT, and behavior therapy and publicly accuse psychiatry of being a "conspiracy" to control the behavior of citizens who deviate from social norms. There is even on record an action by a court to restrain a doctor from administering phenothiazine. Halleck (1974a,b) classifies the use of behavior modification under three headings:

1. Situations in which the patient consents to treatment or requests it. The meaning of the symptoms to be modified is clarified and informed consent is secured.

2. Situations in which the patient consents to treatment but may be under duress, as in those involuntarily committed to a mental hospital or in jail or prison. There must be no retaliation of any kind to the individual's responses or any promise of release if he or she consents. In this setting clear explanations of the consequences of treatment, the choice of alternatives, and informed consent are essentials. Before treatment is undertaken, it should be approved by a human rights committee.

3. Situations in which the patient does not verbally consent to the treatment. The patient may be incompetent and incapable of participating in the process of informed consent. The application should be reserved for individuals who are dangerous to self and to others, and then only when there is reason to believe the treatment will be of benefit: (The restriction upon appropriate therapy unless the patient is dangerous bothers us. When a mental disorder is present, we believe that a treatment should be employed with obtained consent when there is evidence that it is an appropriate remedy.)

The techniques used in the behavioral therapies (see Agras, 1972) include *desensitization* (training in relaxation), including the construction of anxiety hierarchies (determining all the stimulus situations that provoke anxiety and grouping these into themes such as being criticized or being in high places, in crowds, or in confined spaces). The procedure of desensitization employs relaxing, imagining the least anxiety-provoking situation, and repeating it until counter-conditioned. Other techniques are *shaping by positive reinforcement* (as in token economy, rewarding the desired behavior); *aversive therapies* (use of a nausea-inducing drug followed by presentation of alcohol to a problem drinker); and *flooding* (exposing the subject to the feared situation, as in anxiety-based behavior, and demonstrating a nonfearful approach and shaping behavior until the situation can be tolerated).

The ethical concerns involved in behavior therapies and in psychosurgery and electroconvulsive therapy involve informed consent, use in those involuntarily confined in mental hospitals, jails, or prisons, and the potential for abuse in social control by conforming behavior to some norm arbitrarily set by an elite. The ethical issues may be clarified by stating them as polarities:

• *Enslavement vs. adaptation.* The first challenges the right to alter a person in such a manner that he does someone else's bidding. The latter accepts the desirability of relieving incapacitating symptoms of distress, making possible behavior that approaches a norm for society.

• *Coercion vs. compliance.* Patients involuntarily confined to a mental hospital may be told that the treatment is essential to gain release; the prisoner knows release is dependent upon cooperation with authorities. On the other hand, pressures from family to consent, the awareness that one's job may depend on behavior change, and the therapist's advice that one will be helped by the preferred treatment are acknowledged aspects of the everyday world as desirable forces in the patient's or client's interet.

• *Regressive dehumanization vs. enlightened self-interest.* The use of electric shocks, electric prods, and chemicals that produce nausea are demeaning and subhuman. These same interventions may be viewed as transient inconveniences in a process that extinguishes behavior the individual knows is harmful to self.

• *Political control vs. social stability.* Some see the behavior therapies a a gigantic conspiracy to control citizens, forcing them to abandon their protests against a sick society. Others approve change in behavior of sick persons and of dangerous criminals so that they may resume their places in the community.

We believe, and judicial rulings emphasize, that aversive techniques used in behavior therapy are neither legally nor ethically acceptable when they are used solely for oppressive purposes or without the consent of the patient or client and/or his guardian (Bogomolny, 1976).

POPULATION CONTROL

Is it right to encourage contraception and sterilization as a means for controlling population? May abortion be made readily accessible to all classes to interrupt unwanted pregnancies? May the government offer incentives (as in China) to encourage couples to have fewer children and thus prevent a population explosion?

Nearly everyone agrees that the number of people on earth has reached crisis proportions. Most would agree that zero growth is a desirable goal. The concern is with the loss of freedom that follows the imposition of involuntary birth control. Debate over the morality of the issues, Shinn (1973) says, will not stop the geometric progression of population growth. He points out that the human species took millions of years on this planet to reach the first billion mark. Now population increases at an awesome rate. According to Pinson (1973), 250 million people lived in our world when Christ was born. By the year 1600 the population had doubled, and it was to double again in 250 years to reach one billion in 1850. The two billion mark was reached in 1930 and the three billion level in 1972. Pinson predicts it will double yet again, reaching six billion, in thirty-seven years. The fastest growth is in Latin America, with Asia next. The U.S. population is predicted to reach 400 million by the year 2000. Recent U.S. figures indicate a marked slowing in population growth, but zero growth can be achieved in fifty years only if immigration, legal and illegal, can be stopped, a very unlikely possibility.

Rodents when overcrowded behave strangely; so do humans. Crowding in concentration camps produced overactivity of the captives' adrenal glands and death from stress syndrome even when prisoners were fed and housed adequately. Social relations collapse above certain levels of crowding, says Williams (1973), and people with low flash points for violence explode with assaultiveness induced by overcrowding. In some cases, mannerisms which are the product of a state of hyperirritability become intolerable to others.

The ecological impact of overcrowding is enormous (Odum, 1963; Ward and Dubos, 1963; Commoner, 1971). We have witnessed the spread of cities into what once was farmland or forest. Trees and plants give way to houses and pavement. The more people, the more energy they consume and the more cars they drive. To park them near places where they work, shop, or visit requires more pavement. Their extravagant use of energy fills the air with wastes, and automobiles and other machines spew poisonous gases into the air. Oxygen-producing plants and trees have been sacrificed, and with them much of the earth's capacity to regenerate itself. The smog over cities is but a warning that the mantle of air may soon not sustain life. An overheated atmosphere may result, which has its own dire consequences.

Industrial waste, chemical fertilizers, and raw sewage have contaminated the waters until rivers and lakes are dead or dying. When land is used for the expanding population to live upon, cultivatable land is reduced, thus endangering the food chain. Starvation and famine are with us, and unless population growth is halted will cause the death of millions. We value a world of beauty and abhor the pollution of the environment. However, to deplore the erosion of the quality of life will not suffice. It is not enough to aid a country to raise more food, improve sanitation, and prolong life if population increases even faster and makes things worse than before. The agricultural countries cannot raise enough food for an additional billion persons.

Control of population growth and limitation of family size is therefore imperative. Japan has achieved the lowest birthrate of any country. India, sixteen years ago, started a similar campaign to reduce births. It began with a growth rate expressed as 1.3; at the end of the period it was 2.5 and 150 million more people attested the failure of the campaign. Latin American countries, largely Roman Catholic in religion, have, as was mentioned, the highest growth rate. They also still have land to expand upon, and so more time to debate traditional ideologies and to discover remedies. India has no tomorrow, nor does China. The People's Republic of China has launched a massive attempt to change attitudes, control births, and reduce family size. It has made contraceptives available and provided disincentives to early marriage and to having more than two or three children. The program appears to be working in the cities, but not so well in the rural area.

In the U.S. the principle of contraception is accepted, although not everyone accepts the pill or intrauterine devices. Sterilization is legal in all states except Utah, where medical necessity must be proven. Formerly in the U.S., about 100,000 men and women chose sterilization annually. In 1971 the number was 700,000. Vasectomy for male sterilization is the preferred technique because of its safety.

The reported national abortion rate in 1979 was 30.2 per thousand women of reproductive age. Women who obtained abortions were mainly young, white, unmarried, and childless. These were their first abortions. One third were teenagers, one third 25 or older, and 69 percent were white; 75 percent of abortions were obtained by white women. There were 1.5 million women who had abortions in 1979. This was a 9 percent increase over 1978. About 29 percent wished abortions but could not obtain them. No facilities were available in nonmetropolitan areas and there were no state or Federal funds—Medicaid—to finance them; more nonwhites than whites required financial assistance (Henshaw, Forrest, Sullivan, and Tietze, 1981).

Childbearing among unmarried American women reached its highest point ever in 1980 (665,747 or 18.4 percent of all births), according to the report of the National Center for Health Statistics (December 1982). The increase in births among the unwed was almost entirely in white women and represented a 21 percent increase over 1979. The smallest increase was in the age group 15-17. Stigma of pregnancy in the unwed and to abortion prior to 1973 forced those who did not want a child to seek an illegal abortion.

Prior to 1973 the stigma attached to pregnancy in the unwed and to the abortion procedure itself forced pregnant single women to bear children or to seek illegal abortions.

Fourteen states (Arkansas, California, Colorado, Delaware, Florida, Georgia, Kansas, Maryland, Mississippi, New Mexico, North Carolina, Oregon, South Carolina, and Virginia) followed the American Law Institute's proposal that abortion be allowed only when birth would endanger the physical or mental health of the mother, when pregnancy was the result of rape or incest, or when the child was likely to be born with a defect.

Texas and thirty-one other states allowed abortion only when the life of the mother was endangered. The U.S. Supreme Court, in a 7–2 decision, struck down restrictive state laws and in so doing ruled also on the reform laws of the fourteen states.* The ruling (Roe v. Wade) upheld the right of a woman to obtain an abortion until the stage of viability—i.e., during the first trimester—the decision to be that of the woman and her physician without interference of the state. States may regulate the abortion procedure in ways reasonably related to maternal health during the final six months of pregnancy, and during the last ten weeks (when the fetus is capable of surviving) may prohibit abortion

---

* The ALI acceptable grounds for abortion were unsatisfactory to most women and to many physicians, for perhaps no more than 10 to 15 percent of women requested abortions because of rape or for medical or genetic reasons. The vast majority were needed for economic or social reasons (the women could not afford to raise another child, were unmarried, etc.). The ALI rules also established an approval mechanism that caused delay due to red tape and thereby increased emotional trauma.

except where an operation may be necessary to preserve the life and health of the mother.

In 1981 a Constitutional amendment was under consideration in Congress, as well a Senate Bill 158 (the so-called human life bill), that would reverse the Supreme Court decision. The Senate proposal, on which testimony has been heard, holds that present-day scientific evidence indicates a significant likelihood that actual human life exists from conception. It would thus use Fourteenth Amendment protection of all human beings to prohibit destruction of a fetus without due process of law.

A single living cell, multiplying and dividing, does contain genetic material which has the potential for human life. But there is no consensus in the scientific community on when the organism becomes a human being. The concept "actual human life" is a moral and religious one, not medical or scientific.* The debate over public policy in abortion was a hot issue as the decade of the eighties began. Legislative attempts to erode access to family planning and to abortion will have a devastating effect upon health and mental health in our view.

Alaska, Hawaii, Washington, and New York legalized nontherapeutic abortion. Slovenko (1973) discussed the problem of nonresidents coming to those states and noted that abortion is "simply a backstop in a system of birth control."

Acceptance of a terribly damaged infant requires a vital decision. We believe it ethical to withhold support when serious birth defects are present to threaten life, if the parents after discussion determine this is the course they wish the physician to take. It is essential also to discuss fully with parents the results of prenatal diagnostic tests which reveal severe fetal disease. When fetal therapy is possible, it must be fully explained, including the risks to both fetus and mother. If the choice is made to abort, one must follow state and Federal laws.

Today there are many techniques available for prenatal diagnosis: sonography, amniography, fetoscopy, and amniocentesis. There are also treatable defects in the fetus. Some treatments are indirect, with medications given to the mother; others are direct, with transfusion into the fetal peritoneal cavity or into the amniotic fluid. Serious mal-

---

* In the hearings before the Senate Judiciary Committee all but one of eight qualified medical experts agreed that life began at conception. The leap from a living cell to endowment of the conceptus with constitutional rights is a quantum one. "Don't ask medicine to justify the course (anti-abortion); ask your priest, minister or rabbi" (Meyer, 1981).

formations incompatible with normal life may be detected early and may lead to a decision to terminate the pregnancy (see Harrison, Golbus, and Filly, 1981). Some of the ethical issues here are (1) conflict of interests "between the perceived interests of the fetus with a correctable defect and the stated interests of the parents"; (2) the conflict between the fetus's right to life and parental choice; (3) the conditions essential to research while long-term results are compiled; and (4) the social and economic priorities assigned the study of risks and benefits of fetal therapy. (Fletcher, 1981).

The view is held by some that abortion must be considered wrong unless we are prepared to accept also the termination of the life of newborn infants with malformations incompatible with life. (Ramsey, 1970). Others hold that, once born, a separate life from that of the mother exists, making the fetus "a person"; that state creates an ethical difference.

GENETIC COUNSELING AND ENGINEERING

Through thousands of years of his existence, man has evolved in ways that enable him to adapt to changes in his environment. Now that the technology exists, it is appropriate to discuss the question, Should man deliberately influence evolution?

Genetic information resides in the DNA of all body cells. A small number of genes may determine behavioral potentials (*JAMA, 1972*). It is possible to influence the mechanism of cell differentiation, replace defective genes, and introduce new ones. The fascinating potential of genetic engineering can be glimpsed from the recently achieved growth of a fertilized ovum in a test tube. The conceptus has been successfully implanted into the uterus of a woman otherwise unable to conceive and has produced a child. Cloning, successful in frogs, if applied to humans (discounting environmental influences) could theoretically produce identical copies of the selected donor. If the trait of cooperation with others is judged to be more essential to future individuals, theoretically they could be produced with that socially valued trait. Similarly, intelligence, artistic ability, or any personality trait could be copied.

The power to transform living organisms exists today with a potential similar to that of nuclear fission to transform matter. It is now possible with recombinant DNA technology to remove DNA from an organism, to divide the substance enzymatically, and to rearrange it and then implant the genes into a new host (Goldstein, 1977). While research is currently conducted using a virus or plasmid and vector animal, plant, or bacterial cells, the possibilities are endless. The short-circuiting of centuries of evolution, the unpredictability of the effects of transplants, and the potential of life once created to be self-perpetuating and uncontrollable have stirred an ethical controversy. The potential for harm vs. the potential for good is the central issue here. Alarmists would halt all research as too dangerous, while others hold there are no generally applicable principles that would justify halting these investigations. A reasoned approach calls for constraints, rigid guidelines, risk assessment panels, safeguards for containment, and cautious study in a few selected centers where all researchers are trained to follow containment procedures.

At present, the appearance of an affected offspring calls attention to a couple at risk for the transmission of a genetic defect. If parents at risk were detected before reproduction, they could choose to take the risk or not. Medical genetics seeks to detect the individual whose own health or whose offspring's health is threatened (Littlefield, 1972). Cytogenetic studies of fetal cells detect fetal abnormalities resulting from abnormal chromosomes (as in mongolism). Biochemical analysis detects abnormal or absent enzymes (as in galactosemia, phenylketonuria or Tay-Sachs' disease). Now a new technique, nucleic acid hybridization, extends the possibility of detecting abnormal genes (Teplitz, 1980).

Families faced with the prospect of serious genetic disorders may take genetic information into account in making responsible decisions about having or not having children (Lappe, Gustafson, and Roblin, 1972). The Institute of Social Ethics and Life Decisions (Torrey, 1968) has provided valuable guidelines for genetic counseling that include attainable goals, community participation in program objectives and design, equal access to information, accurate test procedures, no constraints on child-bearing or compulsion to take the counselor's advice, informed consent, access by clients to test information, well-trained counselors, and protection of the right of privacy.

Artificial insemination may be an alternative to not having children when there is hereditary disease in the husband (Torrey, 1968). It also may be employed as an alternative to adoption when there is absolute male sterility. Sperm banks provide storage for easy access when needed. The Roman Catholic view contends that the procedure violates natural law and is therefore immoral. As yet there is scant recognition of the procedure in law. A Canadian judge ruled it adultery, but a U.S. court held it was not and ruled a child produced by it legitimate.

The above discussions bring into focus sharply differing viewpoints that Gustafson (Lappe, Gustafson, and Roblin, 1972) expressed in four propositions:

1. A scientist has a moral right to do anything he has the technical capacity to do as he seeks truth in research.

2. A scientist has no right to intervene in natural processes in such a way that he might alter what men believe to be of value as the most distinctly human characteristics.

3. A scientist has no right to intervene in the natural processes of human life because life is sacred.

4. A scientist has the right to intervene in the course of human development in such a way that the uses of his knowledge foster growth of those distinguishing qualities of life that humans value most highly and remove those qualities that are deleterious to what is valued.

We find some problems with all of the above, but reject the first and third and agree in principle with the second and fourth. Potential benefits are balanced against risks in the formulation of public policy. Prohibition of research is unsound, but constraint and caution are imperative.

PL 94–278, the Health and Research and Health Services Amendments of 1976, has ushered in a new era of detection and prevention of genetic disorders (Schmidt and Curran, 1976). The act provides for basic and applied research, training, testing, counseling, information, and education of both professionals and the public in genetic diseases such as sickle cell and Cooley's anemias, Tay Sachs' disease, cystic fibrosis, dysautonomia, hemophilia, retinitis pigmentosa, Huntington's chorea, and muscular dystrophy. Participation in programs must be voluntary. The community resentment that followed mandatory mass screening procedures led to provisions in the act for voluntary enrollment, informed consent, strict confidentiality of test results and of records, and community involvement in developing testing and counseling centers.

SUMMARY

Among the advances in science that have led to a revival in bioethics are the development of powerful new drugs which can change mood and behavior, machines that sustain life indefinitely, organ transplants, the concept of brain death, new techniqes in psychosurgery and electroconvulsive therapy, behavior modification, abortion, and the emerging science of genetic engineering. Ethical issues have produced guidelines to assist investigators in observing moral and social obligations when in pursuit of truth:

- Be alert to socially sensitive issues.
- Observe the Nuremberg Code; safeguard the health of subjects; any act or advice that may weaken physical or mental resistance is to be used only in the subject's interest.
- Assess all inherent risks.
- Be alert to any possibility of personality damage.
- The importance of the objective must be in proportion to the risk.
- The investigation must be conducted by persons scientifically qualified who are aware of all potential risks.
- The subject must give free and voluntary consent. The mental, physical, and legal state of the subject must permit exercise of free choice.
- Respect the right of the subject to safeguard personal integrity.
- The subject must be free to withdraw from the study at any time.
- All studies performed on human subjects must be sent for clearance to a Human Experimentation Review Board.

Federal agencies have formulated regulations on such activities as human experimentation, DNA research, and the use of psychosurgery.

The law has attempted to clarify the conditions under which treatment may be withheld from terminally ill patients or treatment be given to prolong life; has moved to allow women the choice of having an abortion in the first trimester of pregnancy and to permit states to specify allowable interventions in the second and third trimesters; to define in statute brain death and to control the use of psychosurgery and ECT as well as intrusive drug therapy.

The ethical issues upon which a consensus seems to have been reached during the 1970s are: the government's right to regulate research on human subjects, the criteria for brain death, and the imposition of conditions on heroic efforts keeping patients alive when their condition is irreversibly terminal. There is as yet no consensus on euthanasia, the allowable limits of genetic engineering, or abortion.

QUESTIONS

1. Why is there an ethical concern over the use of drugs, ECT, and behavior modification which are accepted, effective treatment modalities?
2. What is a Living Will?
3. What is the significance of the Quinlan case? of Saikewicz and Dinnerstein?
4. What are four criteria essential in the determination of brain death?
5. What rules are to be followed in the use of psychosurgery?
6. How should abuses in the use of ECT be controlled?
7. What was the 1973 decision of the U.S. Supreme Court regarding abortion?

REFERENCES

* Abram, M. B. et al. (1981), *Defining Death: A Report on the Medical, Legal and Ethical Issues*. Washington, D.C.: U.S. Government Printing Office.
* Agras, W. S. (1972), *Behavior Modification: Principles and Clinical Applications*. Boston: Little, Brown.
  APA (1977), Task Force Report on "Psychosurgery." Washington, D.C.: American Psychiatric Association.
* APA (1978), Task Force Report #14: Electroconvulsive Therapy, APA Washington, D.C.: American Psychiatric Association.
  Barnard, C. (1973), Heart transplants. In: *Is It Moral to Modify Man?*, ed. C. A. Frazier. Springfield, Ill.: Charles C Thomas.
  Beecher, H. K. (1968), Ethical problems created by the hopelessly unconscious patient. *N. Engl. J. Med.*, 278:1425–1430.
  Black, P. McL. (1978), Brain death: Parts I and II. *N. Engl. J. Med.*, 299:388–344, 393–400.
  Blomquist, C. (1974), The ethics of medicine and its position in Sweden. *Viewpoint*, Feb. New York: Swedish Consulate General.
  Bogomolny, R., ed. (1976), *Human Experimentation*. Dallas: Southern Methodist University Press.

Bok, S. (1976), Personal directions for care at the end of life. *N. Engl. J. Med.,* 295:367–369.

* Caprow, A. M., & Kass, L. R. (1972), A statutory definition of the standards for determining human death: An appraisal and a proposal. *University of Pennsylvania Law Review,* 121:87–118, No. 5

Coe, J. I., & Curran, W. J. (1980), Definition and time of death. In: *Modern Legal Medicine, Psychiatry and Forensic Science,* ed. W. J. Curran, A. L. McGarry, & C. S. Petty. Philadelphia: F. A. Davis.

Commoner, B. (1971), *The Closing Circle.* New York: Knopf.

Cook, R. (1977), *Coma.* Boston: Little, Brown.

* Fink, M. (1978), Is ECT a useful therapy in schizophrenia? In: *Controversy in Psychiatry,* ed. J. P. Brady, & H. K. H. Brodie. Philadelphia: W. B. Saunders.

Fink, M. (1979), *Convulsive Therapy: Theory and Practice.* New York: Raven Press.

* Fletcher, J. C. (1981), The fetus as patient: Ethical issues. *J. Amer. Med. Assn.,* 246:772–773.

Frost, N. (1976), Seminar. Mendon, Vt., April 23.

* Goldstein, R. (1977), Public policy and recombinant DNA. *N. Engl. J. Med.,* 206:1226–1228.

Halleck, S. L. (1974a), Legal and ethical aspects of behavioral control. *Amer. J. Psychiat.,* 131:381–385.

Halleck, S. L. (1974b), Reply to letter to the editor from Yoell and Cole. *Amer. J. Psychiat.,* 131:928.

Harrison, M. R., Golbus, M. S., & Filly, R. A. (1981), Management of the fetus with a correctable congenital defect. *J. Amer. Med. Assn.,* 246:774–777.

Henshaw, S., Forrest, J. D., Sullivan, E., & Tietze, C. (1981), Abortion in the United States, 1978-1979, *Family Planning Perspective,* 13:6–17.

JAMA (1972), Genetic engineering in man: Ethical considerations. *J. Amer. Med. Assn.,* 220:721.

Ladimer, I. (1971), Ethics and the law. *Mass. Physician,* 30:42–48.

Lappe, M., Gustafson, J. M., & Roblin, R. (1972), Ethical and social issues in screening for genetic disease. *N. Engl. J. Med.,* 286:1129–1132.

Lifton, R. J. (1957), Psychiatric aspects of Chinese Communist thought reform. *Symposium,* 43:234–252. New York: Group for the Advancement of Psychiatry.

Littlefield, J. W. (1972), Genetic screening. *N. Engl. J. Med.,* 286:1155–1156.

Lunde, D., ed. C. A. Frazier. (1973), Heart Transplants. In: *Ethical Issues in Biology and Medicine,* ed. P. Williams. Cambridge, Mass.: Schenkman.

McFadden, C. J. (1967), *Medical Ethics.* 6th ed. Philadelphia: F. A. Davis.

Medical News (1979), New approaches to prolonging survival of transplanted organs. *Medical News, AMA,* 242:2265–2273.

Meyer, H. S. (1981), Science and the "human life bill." *J. Amer. Med. Assn.,* 246:837–839.

MMS Newsletter (1978), Clarification of the Saikewicz decision. *Newletter, Mass. Med. Society,* 18:1–4, July/Aug.

NEJM (1976), Optimum care for hopeless ill patients. *N. Engl. J. Med.,* 295:362–364.

Odum, E. P. (1963), *Ecology.* New York: Holt Rheinhart & Winston.

Orwell, G. (1949), *1984.* New York: Harcourt Brace.

Pares, J. J. (1981), The New York Court of Appeals on the rights of the incompetent dying patient. *N. Engl. J. Med.*, 304:1424–1425.

Pinson, W. M. (1973), Population. In: *Is it Moral to Modify Man?*, ed. C. A. Frazier. Springfield, Ill.: Charles C Thomas.

Psychiatric News (1976), ECT law declared unconstitutional. *Psychiatric News*, 11:1–4.

Rabkin, M. T., Gillerman, G., & Rice, N. R. (1976), Orders not to resuscitate. *N. Engl. J. Med.*, 295:364–366.

Rachels, J. (1975), Active and passive euthanasia, *N. Engl. J. Med.*, 292:78–80.

Ramsey, P. (1970), Reference points in deciding about abortion. In: *The Morality of Abortion*, ed. J. T. Noonan. Cambridge, Mass.: Harvard University Press.

Sargant, W. (1957), *Battle for the Mind*. New York: Doubleday.

Schmidt, R. M., & Curran, J. J. (1976), A national genetic disease program: Some issues of implementation. *N. Engl. J. Med.*, 295:819–820.

Shagass, C., Autry, J., Cole, J. et al., eds. (1980), *ECT: Efficacy and Impact*. New York: Grune & Stratton.

Shinn, R. (1973), Population. In: *Issues in Biology and Medicine*, ed. P. Williams. Cambridge, Mass.: Schenkman.

Skinner, B. F. (1971), *Beyond Freedom and Dignity*. New York: Knopf.

* Slovenko, R. (1973), *Psychiatry and Law*. Boston: Little, Brown.

Teplitz, R. L. (1980), Genetics. *J. Amer. Med. Assn.*, 243:2186–2188.

Torrey, E. F., ed. (1968), *Ethical Issues in Medicine*. Boston: Little, Brown.

Veatch, R. M. (1980), Courts, committees and caring. *AMA News Impact*, 1–2, May 23.

* Veith, F. J., Fein, J. M., Tender, M. D., Veatch, R. M., Kleiman, M. A., & Kalkines, F. (1977a), Brain death: I. A status report of medical and ethical considerations. *J. Amer. Med. Assn.*, 238:1651–1655.

Veith, F. J., Fein, J. M., Tender, M. D., Veatch, R. M., Kleiman, M. A., & Kalkines, F. (1977b), Brain death: II. A status report of legal considerations. *J. Amer. Med. Assn.*, 238:1744–1748.

Ward, B., & Dubos, R. (1963), *Only One Earth*, New York: Norton.

Weiner, R. D. (1979), The psychiatric use of electrically induced seizures. *Amer. J. Psychiat.*, 136:1507–1517.

Williams, P. (1973), *Ethical Issues in Biology and Medicine*. Cambridge, Mass.: Schenkman.

Wolpe, J. (1969), *The Practice of Behavior Therapy*. New York: Pergamon Press.

Yates, A. J. (1970), *Behavior Therapy*. New York: Wiley.

Chapter 4

Ethical Codes

> Inspire in me a love for my art and for thy creatures let no thirst for profit or seeking for renown or admiration take away from my calling . . . keep within me strength of body and of soul, ever ready, with cheerfulness to help and succor rich and poor, good and bad, enemy as well as friend. In the sufferer let me see only the human being.
> —*The Prayer of Maimonides (1135–1204)*

The principles of ethical behavior for all physicians and mental health professionals may be summed up in this modification of the Canadian Medical Association's Code of Ethics:

Consider first the well-being of the patient.
Honor your profession and its traditions.
Recognize your limitations and seek consultation.
Preserve the confidentiality of your relationship
    with patients and protect their right to privacy.
Teach and be taught. Improve your knowledge and skills.
Be responsible in setting a value on your services.
Participate in activities to improve the health of
    the community.

66

The priest-physician, in the dawn of human life on earth, embodied in one person the roots of theology and medicine. In 2500 B.C. rules for ethical conduct were chiseled upon 21 eight-foot stone columns to record Hammurabi's code (Davidson, 1973). The Ten Commandments, inscribed upon stone tablets, were presented by Moses to the Israelites about 1500 B.C. as principles for moral conduct.

A description of the situation in the age of Pericles (490–429 B.C.) reminds us that our day is not really so very different from earlier times: "Among educated men everything was in dispute, political sanctions, literary values, moral standards, religious conventions, even the possibility of reaching the truth about anything" (W. C. Greene, quoted in Lippmann, 1929).

Hippocrates wrote guides for physicians' behavior about 400 B.C., which, elaborated through the centuries by his followers, are still widely quoted and still recited as a pledge by fledgling physicians in some medical schools (Davidson, 1973). The basic guidelines to professional conduct expressed in the Oath of Hippocrates over two thousand years ago are still valid. The precepts for the physician are applicable to all in the health services: be moral, improve one's knowledge, use one's best judgment in the patient's interest, do no harm, give equal treatment to all who seek help, and protect "as holy secrets" what is learned from patients as well as other things that ought not be made public. Hippocrates admonished the physician, when making a home visit, not to commit acts of injustice or mischief and to abstain from sexual relations with patients—men, women, or slaves.

An ancient medical student oath in the Charaka Samita manuscript of India (1 A.D.) pledges the student to live the life of an ascetic with personal sacrifice and commitment to duty. There was to be no drunkenness, crime, or adultery. Patient needs were to be above personal interests and professional secrecy maintained (Konold and Veatch, 1972).

The Chinese in the sixth century A.D. set down an ethical code in Sun Ssu-maio's *The Thousand Golden Remedies* and in the seventeenth century it was expressed in *Five Commandments and Ten Requirements* by Chen Shih Kung in a treatise on surgery (Konold and Veatch, 1972). Physicians were enjoined to treat all equally and the poor without charge, to protect secrecy, to be humble, and not to insult one's colleagues.

Moses Maimonides, a Jewish physician (1135–1204 A.D.), in an elegant and moving prayer, asked for wisdom to soothe the suffering and heal the sick letting no thirst for profit or seeking of admiration interfere. The physician was to aid rich and poor, good and bad, enemy as well as friend. Guidance was requested to improve knowledge and skills in the service of mankind.

It was Thomas Percival's "Medical Ethics: On a Code of Institutes and Precepts Adapted to the Professional Conduct of Physicians and Surgeons" (1803) which influenced the development of a code of medical ethics in the United States (Braceland, 1969). Percival stressed the etiquette of inter- and intraprofessional relationships. He advised physicians to treat their patients with fidelity and compassion, to eschew fraudulently advertised remedies, to embrace temperance, to comfort the dying, and to subordinate desire for wealth to patient welfare.

Benjamin Rush, the father of American psychiatry, was a stern moralist who opposed smoking, drinking, gambling, and desecration of the Sabbath. If Rush were alive today, not only individual morals but those of society would be his target.

One hundred and forty years ago an editorial, "Professional Etiquette" (*NEJM, 1844*), stated the following:

1. *Dissatisfaction* with his own treatment should lead to a request for consultation. It should also be provided when the patient or friends wish it. When a fatal outcome is likely to occur, he should disclose it so the family may avail themselves of consultation should they wish.
2. *To the consultant* he should state his findings, treatment, and its effects. He should follow strictly the consultant's directions until dissatisfied with the effects when he should advise and confer on the proper course to be pursued.
3. *When called* to visit another physician's patient he should notify the physician of his intended call, see the patient together, but in an emergency, grant aid in silence, doing nothing to detract from his neighbor's character.
4. He should not seek business through the pretense to superior skill but in all things pertaining to his profession should conduct himself in a manner best calculated to promote the welfare of his patient, the peace of society and the honor of his profession, irrespective of the opinion of those whose knowledge is necessarily limited and views oftener incorrect than otherwise.

The German doctors who performed experiments on living prisoners in Auschwitz followed the precepts of science in seeking truth and attempting to solve problems of disease and injury. Science is not value free. The Nazis flouted social norms that must always be an integral part of science. Ignored were the ethical constraints upon experimental practice and the relationship to men and to nature which is an essential part of the process of understanding men and nature (Gorovitz and MacIntyre, 1975). The shocking revelations of Nazi atrocities on prisoners, justified as legitimate scientific inquiry, led to new codes of ethical conduct in the area of human experimentation. These codes included the Nuremberg Code and the Helsinki Declaration (Torrey, 1968), those adopted by the American Medical Association in 1948, and the Declaration of Geneva, adopted by the World Medical Association in September 1948. This latter includes an oath to be taken when a physician is admitted into the medical profession:

- I solemnly pledge myself to consecrate my life to the service of humanity.
- I will give to my teachers the respect and gratitude which is their due.
- I will practice my profession with conscience and dignity.
- The health of my patient will be my first consideration.
- I will respect secrets which are confided in me.
- I will maintain, by all means in my power, the honor and the noble traditions of the medical profession.
- My colleagues will be my brothers.
- I will not permit consideration of religion, nationality, race, party politics or social standing to intervene between my duty and my patient.
- I will maintain the utmost respect for human life from the time of conception; even under threat, I will not use my medical knowledge contrary to the laws of humanity.
- I make these promises solemnly, fairly and upon my honor. [AMA, 1979]

In the post–World War II period, Thomas J. Held developed a credo and code of ethics for psychiatrists. It was presented in a manual of seventy-six pages to the governing council of the American Psychiatric Association in May 1949. It was not adopted, perhaps for two reasons: the wish to remain identified with all of medicine, and its great detail.

Menninger's *Whatever Became of Sin?* (1973) is enjoyable reading. Once there were seven deadly sins: envy, anger, pride, sloth, avarice, gluttony, and lust. All are actions hurtful to self or others. Menninger argues that we have redefined sin into other categories: crime, symptoms, collective irresponsibility.

Some mental health professionals participated in the protests of the turbulent sixties. They joined in the opposition to such social injustices as U.S. participation in the war in Viet Nam. Expression of opinion is acceptable behavior in a democratic society. What was not ethical, and was a rather widespread practice then, was the certification of nonexistent physical or mental disorders to enable individuals to escape the draft.

In 1957 the AMA approved an ethical code consisting of a preamble and ten short sections. It was expressed in 525 words and for twenty years endured unchanged. The ethical conduct of medical specialists and all physicians in the United States is guided by the American Medical Association's Principles of Medical Ethics. In addition, each of the mental health professions has developed its own code, and these will be briefly noted later. It should be noted that in 1981 a revised physicians' code, was made official. Instead of ten sections, it had but seven. The retrospective analysis of complaints that follows in chapter 5 could not have been made using the new version. We therefore present, in its entirety, the preamble and ten sections of the physicians' code, followed by annotations applicable to psychiatry.

Preamble

These principles are intended to aid physicians individually and collectively in maintaining a high level of ethical conduct. They are not laws but standards by which a physician may determine the propriety of his conduct in his relationship with patients, with colleagues, with members of allied professions, and with the public.

THE PRINCIPLES OF MEDICAL ETHICS*

Section 1

The principle objective of the medical profession is to render service to humanity with full respect for the dignity of man. Physicians should merit the confidence of patients entrusted to their care, rendering to each a full measure of service and devotion.

The patient may place his/her trust in his/her psychiatrist knowing that the psychiatrist's ethics and professional responsibilities preclude him/her from gratifying his/her own needs by exploiting the patient. This becomes particularly important because of the essentially private, highly personal, and sometimes intensely emotional nature of the relationship established with the psychiatrist.

The requirement that the physician "conduct himself with propriety in his profession and in all the actions of his life" is especially important in the case of the psychiatrist because the patient tends to model his/her behavior after that of his/her therapist by identification. Further, the necessary intensity of the therapeutic relationship may tend to activate sexual and other needs and fantasies on the part of both patient and therapist, while weakening the objectivity necessary for control. Sexual activity with a patient is unethical.

The psychiatrist should diligently guard against exploiting information furnished by the patient and should not use the unique position of power afforded him/her by the psychotherapeutic situation to influence the patient in any way not directly relevant to the treatment goals.

Physicians generally agree that the doctor-patient relationship is such a vital factor in effective treatment of the patient that preservation of optimal conditions for development of a sound working relationship between a doctor and his/her patient should take precedence over all other considerations. Professional courtesy may lead to poor psychiatric care for physicians and their families because of embarrassment over the lack of a complete give-and-take contract.

* Permission has been granted to reproduce the American Psychiatric Association's *The Principles of Medical Ethics: With Annotations Especially Applicable to Psychiatry* (with changes approved by the Board of Trustees in 1974) by the Medical Director and the *American Journal of Psychiatry,* 130:1057–1064 (Official Actions). Copyright © 1973, The American Psychiatric Association. The 1978 Edition, with later amendments, was also used. It is not copyrighted.

Section 2

Physicians should strive continually to improve medical knowledge and skill, and should make available to their patients and colleagues the benefits of their professional attainments.

Psychiatrists are responsible for their own continuing education and should be mindful of the fact that theirs must be a lifetime of learning.

Section 3

A physician should practice a method of healing founded on a scientific basis and he should not voluntarily associate professionally with anyone who violates this principle.

Section 4

The medical profession should safeguard the public and itself against physicians deficient in moral character or professional competence. Physicians should observe all laws, uphold the dignity and honor of the profession and accept its self-imposed disciplines. They should expose, without hesitation, illegal or unethical conduct of fellow members of the profession.

It would seem self-evident that a psychiatrist who is a lawbreaker might be ethically unsuited to practice his/her profession. When such illegal activities bear directly upon his/her practice, this would obviously be the case. However, in other instances, illegal activities such as those concerning the right to protest social injustices might not bear on either the image of the psychiatrist or the ability of the specific psychiatrist to treat his/her patient ethically and well. While no committee or board could offer prior assurance that any illegal activity would not be considered unethical, it is conceivable that an individual could violate a law without being guilty of professionally unethical behavior. Physicians lose no right of citizenship on entry into the profession of medicine.

A psychiatrist who regularly practices outside his/her area of professional competence should be considered unethical. Determination of professional competence should be made by peer review boards or other appropriate bodies.

Special consideration should be given to those psychiatrists who, because of mental illness, jeopardize the welfare of their patients and their own reputations and practices. It is ethical, even encouraged, for another psychiatrist to intercede in such situations.

Where not specifically prohibited by local laws governing medical practice, the practice of acupuncture by a psychiatrist is not unethical per se. The psychiatrist should have professional competence in the use of acupuncture; or if he/she is supervising the use of acupuncture by nonmedical individuals, he/she should provide proper medical supervision.

When a member has been found to have behaved unethically by the American Psychiatric Association or one of its constituent branches, there should not be automatic reporting to the local authorities responsible for medical licensure, but the decision to report should be on the merits of the case.

Section 5

A physician may choose whom he will serve. In an emergency, however, he should render service to the best of his ability. Having undertaken the care of a patient, he may not neglect him; and unless he has been discharged he may discontinue his services only after giving adequate notice. He should not solicit patients.

A psychiatrist should not be a party to any type of policy that excludes, segregates, or demeans the dignity of any patient because of ethnic origin, race, sex, creed, age or socioeconomic status.

What constitutes unethical advertising in an attempt to solicit patients varies in different parts of the country. Local guidance should be sought from the county or state medical society. Questions that should be asked include: To whom are materials distributed, what is distributed, and when and in what form is it distributed?

Section 6

A physician should not dispose of his services under terms or conditions which tend to interfere with or impair the free and complete exercise of his medical judgment and skill or tend to cause a deterioration of the quality of medical care.

Contract practice as applied to medicine means the practice of medicine under an agreement between a physician or a group of physicians, as principals or agents, and a corporation, organization, political subdivision, or individual whereby partial or full medical services are provided for a group or class of individuals on the basis of a fee schedule, for a salary, or for a fixed rate per capita.

Contract practice per se is not unethical. Contract practice is unethical if it permits features or conditions that are declared unethical in these Principles of Medical Ethics or if the contract or any of its provisions causes deterioration of the quality of the medical services rendered.

The ethical question is not the contract itself but whether or not the physician is free of unnecessary nonmedical interference. The ultimate issue is his/her freedom to offer good quality medical care.

In relationships between psychiatrists and practicing licensed psychologists, the physician should not delegate to the psychologist or, in fact, to any nonmedical person, any matter requiring the exercise of professional medical judgment.

When the psychiatrist assumes a collaborative or supervisory role with another mental health worker, he/she must expend sufficient time to assure that proper care is given. It is contrary to the interests of the patients and to patient care if he/she allows himself/herself to be used as a figurehead.

In the practice of his/her specialty, the psychiatrist consults, associates, collaborates, or integrates his/her work with that of many professionals, including psychologists, psychometricians, social workers, alcoholism counselors, marriage counselors, public health nurses, etc. Furthermore, the nature of modern psychiatric practice extends his/her contacts to such people as teachers, juvenile and adult probation officers, attorneys, welfare workers, agency volunteers, and neighborhood aides. In referring patients for treatment, counseling, or rehabilitation to any of these practitioners, the psychiatrist should ensure that the allied professional or paraprofessional with whom he/she is dealing is a recognized member of his/her discipline and is competent to carry out the therapeutic task required. The psychiatrist should have the same attitude toward members of the medical profession to whom he/she refers patients. Whenever he/she has reason to doubt the training, skill or ethical qualifications of the allied profesional, the psychiatrist should not refer cases to him/her.

Also, he/she should neither lend the endorsement of the psychiatric specialty nor refer patients to persons, groups or treatment programs with which he/she is not familiar, especially if their work is based only on dogma and authority and not on scientific validation and replication.

In accord with the requirements of law and accepted medical practice, it is ethical for a physician to submit his/her work to peer review and to the ultimate authority of the medical staff executive body and the hospital administration and its governing body.

In the case of dispute the ethical psychiatrist has the following steps available:

- Seek appeal from the medical staff decision to a joint conference committee including members of the medical staff executive committee of the governing board. At this appeal, the ethical psychiatrist could request that outside opinion be consulted.
- Appeal to the governing body itself.
- Appeal to state agencies regulating licensure of hospitals if, in the patient's state, they concern themselves with matters of professional competency and quality of care.
- Attempt to educate colleagues through development of research projects and data and presentations at professional meetings and in professional journals.
- Seek redress in local courts, perhaps through an injunction against the governing body.
- Public education as carried out by the ethical psychiatrist would not use appeals based solely upon emotion, but would be presented in a professional way and without any potential exploitation of patients through testimonials.

When involved in funded research the ethical psychiatrist will advise human subjects of the funding source, retain his or her freedom to reveal data and results, and follow all appropriate and current guidelines relative to human subject protection.

Section 7

In the practice of medicine a physician should limit the source of his professional income to medical services actually rendered by him, or under his supervision, to his patients. His fee should be commensurate with the service rendered and the patient's ability to pay. He should neither pay nor receive a commission for referral of patients. Drugs, remedies or appliances may be dispensed or supplied by the physician provided it is in the best interests of the patient.

The psychiatrist may also receive income from administration, teaching, research, education, and consultation.

Charging for a missed appointment or for one not canceled twenty-four hours in advance need not, in itself, be considered unethical if a patient is fully advised that the physician will make such a charge. The practice, however, should be resorted to infrequently and always with the utmost consideration of the patient and his circumstances.

Psychiatric services, like all medical services, are dispensed in the context of a contractual arrangement between the patient and the treating physician. The provisions of the contractual arrangement, which are binding on the physician as well as on the patient, should be explicitly established.

It is ethical for the psychiatrist to make a charge for a missed appointment when this falls within the terms of the specific contractual agreement with the patient.

An arrangement in which a psychiatrist provides supervision or administration to other physicians or nonmedical persons for a percentage of their fees or gross income is not acceptable; this would constitute fee-splitting. In a team of practitioners, or a multidisciplinary team, it is ethical for the psychiatrist to receive income for administration, research, education or consultation. This should be based upon a mutually agreed upon and set fee or salary, open to renegotiation when a change in the time demand occurs.

Section 8

A physician should seek consultation upon request; in doubtful or difficult cases; or whenever it appears that the quality of the medical service may be enhanced thereby.

The psychiatrist should agree to the request of a patient for consultation or to such a request from the family of an incompetent or minor patient. The psychiatrist may suggest possible consultants, but the patient or family should be given free choice of the consultant. If the psychiatrist disapproves of the professional qualifications of the consultant or if there is a difference of opinion that the primary therapist cannot resolve, he/she may, after suitable notice, withdraw from the case. If this disagreement occurs within an institution or agency framework, the differences should be resolved by the mediation or arbitration of higher professional authority within the institution or agency.

Section 9

A physician may not reveal the confidences entrusted to him in the course of medical attendance, or the deficiencies he may observe in the character of patients, unless he is required to do so by law or unless it becomes necessary in order to protect the welfare of the individual or of the community.

Psychiatric records, including even the identification of a person as a patient, must be protected with extreme care. Confidentiality is essential to psychiatric treatment. This is based in part on the special nature of psychiatric therapy as well as on the traditional ethical relationship between physician and patient. Growing concern regarding the civil rights of patients and the possible adverse affects of computerization, duplication equipment, and data banks makes the dissemination of confidential information an increasing hazard. Because of the sensitive and private nature of the information with which the psychiatrist deals, he/she must be circumspect in the information that he/she chooses to disclose to others about a patient. The welfare of the patient must be a continuing consideration.

A psychiatrist may release confidential information only with the authorization of the patient or under proper legal compulsion. The continuing duty of the psychiatrist to protect the patient includes fully apprising him/her of the connotations of waiving the privilege of privacy. This may become an issue when the patient is being investigated by a government agency, is applying for a position, or is involved in legal action. The same principles apply to the release of information concerning treatment to medical departments of government agencies, business organizations, labor unions, and insurance companies. Information gained in confidence about patients seen in student health services should not be released without the student's explicit permission.

Clinical and other materials used in teaching and writing must be adequately disguised in order to preserve the anonymity of the individuals involved.

The ethical responsibility of maintaining confidentiality holds equally for the consultations in which the patient may not have been present and in which the consultee was not a physician. In such instances, the physician consultant should alert the consultee to his/her duty of confidentiality.

Ethically the psychiatrist may disclose only that information which is immediately relevant to a given situation. He/she should avoid offering speculation as fact. Sensitive information or fantasy material is usually unnecessary.

Psychiatrists are often asked to examine individuals for security purposes, to determine suitability for various jobs, and to determine legal competence. The psychiatrist must fully describe the nature and purpose and lack of confidentiality of the examination to the examinee at the beginning of the examination.

When a psychiatric examination is performed at the request or order of a court, an attorney, or a litigant, the examinee shall be fully informed as to whom the psychiatrist represents, the purpose of the examination, the lack of doctor-patient relationship, the absence of confidentiality and what will be done with the information gathered.

Ethical considerations in medical practice preclude the psychiatric evaluation of any adult charged with criminal acts prior to access to legal counsel. The only exception is the rendering of care to the person for the sole purpose of medical treatment.

Psychiatrists at times may find it necessary, in order to protect the patient or the community from imminent danger, to reveal confidential information disclosed by the patient.

Careful judgment must be exercised by the psychiatrist in order to include, when appropriate, the parents or guardian in the treatment of a minor. At the same time the psychiatrist must assure the minor proper confidentiality. When the psychiatrist is ordered by the court to reveal the confidence entrusted to him/her by patients he/she may comply or he/she may ethically hold the right to dissent within the framework of the law. When the psychiatrist is in doubt, the right of the patient to confidentiality and by extension, to unimpaired treatment, should be given priority. The psychiatrist should reserve the right to raise the question of adequate need for disclosure. In the event that the necessity for legal disclosure is demonstrated by the court, the psychiatrist may request the right to disclosure of only that information which is relevant to the legal question at hand.

With regard for the person's dignity and privacy and with truly informed consent, it is ethical to present a patient to a scientific gathering if the confidentiality of the presentation is understood and accepted by the audience. It is ethical to present a patient or former patient to a public gathering or to the news media only if that patient is fully informed of enduring loss of confidentiality, is competent and consents in writing without coercion.

Section 10

The honored ideals of the medical profession imply that the responsibilities of the physician extend not only to the individual, but also to society where these responsibilities deserve his interest and participation in activities which have the purpose of improving both the health and well-being of the individual and the community.

Psychiatrists should foster the cooperation of those legitimately concerned with the medical, psychological, social and legal aspects of mental health and illness. Psychiatrists are encouraged to serve society by advising and consulting with the executive, legislative and judiciary branches of the government. A psychiatrist should clarify whether he/she speaks as an individual or as a representative of an organization. Furthermore, psychiatrists should avoid cloaking their public statements with the authority of the profession (e.g., "Psychiatrists know that . . .").

Psychiatrists may interpret and share with the public their expertise in the various psychosocial issues that may affect mental health and illness. Psychiatrists should always be mindful of their separate roles as dedicated citizens and as experts in psychological medicine.

On occasion psychiatrists are asked for an opinion about an individual who is in the light of public attention or who has disclosed information about himself through public media. It is unethical for a psychiatrist to offer a professional opinion unless he/she has conducted an examination and has been granted proper authorization for such a statement.

The psychiatrist may only permit his/her certification to be used for the involuntary treatment of any person following his/her personal examination of that person. To do so he/she must find that the person, because of mental illness, cannot form a judgment as to what is in his/her own best interest, and that without which treatment substantial impairment is likely to occur to the person or to others.

In July 1980 the AMA House of Delegates adopted a new ethical code. It was the first revision since 1957. The intent was to modernize the language, eliminate reference to gender, conform to present legal requirements, and be responsive to social reality. The change goes beyond questions of wording. The new code is silent on fees, contracts, and conflict of interest. Association with cults or with nonscientific healers has become a matter of choice.

The AMA *Judicial Council Opinions and Reports,* 1981 edition, added several contemporary guides: (1) The physician has a duty to do all that can be done for the patient "without total responsibility for equitable disbursement of society's limited health resources." As in a triage system, when resources are scarce, allocation will be as fair and as humanistic as possible with priority given to those likely to benefit from treatment. (2) The quality of life is to be considered in determining what is best for a deformed newborn or severely deteriorated person. (3) Terminally ill incompetent patients require a determination of the possibility of extending life and comfort, the attitude of the family, the accuracy of the diagnosis before any decision to discontinue life support systems. (4) Advertising in any medium is approved so long as the communication is not false, misleading, or designed to deceive the public. One may not use patient testimonials in advertisements (*JAMA,* 1981).

THE PRINCIPLES OF MEDICAL ETHICS
(1981 REVISION)

Preamble: The medical profession has long subscribed to a body of ethical statements developed primarily for the benefit of the patient. As a member of this profession, a physician must recognize responsibility not only to patients, but also to society, to other health professionals, and to self. The following principles adopted by the American Medical Association are not laws, but standards of conduct which define the essentials of honorable behavior for the physician.

I. A physician shall be dedicated to providing competent medical service with compassion and respect for human dignity.

II. A physician shall deal honestly with patients and colleagues, and strive to expose those physicians deficient in character or competence, or who engage in fraud or deception.

III. A physician shall respect the law and also recognize a responsibility to seek changes in those requirements which are contrary to the best interest of the patient.

IV. A physician shall respect the rights of patients, of colleagues, and of other health professionals, and shall safeguard patient confidences within the restraints of the law.

V. A physician shall continue to study, apply and advance scientific knowledge, make relevant information available to patients, colleagues, and the public, obtain consultation, and use the talents of other health professionals when indicated.

VI. A physician shall, in the provision of appropriate patient care, except in emergencies, be free to choose whom to serve, with whom to associate, and the environment in which to provide medical services.

VII. A physician shall recognize a responsibility to participate in activities contributing to an improved community (APA, 1981).

The American Psychiatric Association (APA, 1979) has developed a series of questions and answers called "Opinions of the Ethics Committee" in the manner of the interpretations of ethical principles that appear in the AMA *Judicial Council Opinions and Reports* (AMA, 1981).

The Canadian Medical Association's code amplifies its principles under three headings:

1. Responsibilities to the patient: practice the art and science of

medicine to the best of ability, improve the standard of care, respect the patient, observe his/her rights, except in emergency the freedom to choose whom one will serve, once accepted continue to serve until no longer required or arrangements made for another to accept responsibility, observe personal morality, adhere to rules for human experimentation in clinical research, care for the dying with compassion and allow death to occur with dignity.

2. Reponsibilities to the profession: personal conduct above reproach, contracts to be controlled by the physician, communicate research through recognized scientific channels, identify own opinions as distinct from those generally held, build practice on merit, avoid personal profit motive in drugs, appliances or procedure from any facility in which he/she has a financial interest.

3. Responsibilities to society: improve standards of care, share responsibility for matters relating to public health, health education, and legislation affecting health or well-being of the community.

The National Association of Social Workers used a very modern approach in the development of its revised ethical code. It identified about three dozen codes of physicians and organizations and put the principles into a computer after analysis for their relevance to social workers. They discarded duplicates and retained those best expressing the desired conduct under six categories:

1. The social worker's conduct: high standard of personal conduct, integrity, become and remain proficient in professional practice, a primary service obligation to clients, scholarship and research.

2. Ethical responsibility to clients: primary responsibility to clients, foster self-determination, respect right of privacy, set fair reasonable fees for services.

3. Responsibility to colleagues: treat with respect, courtesy, fairness and good faith, relate to clients of colleagues with consideration.

4. Responsibility to employers: adhere to commitments.

5. Responsibility to the profession: advance values, ethics, knowledge and mission, make services available to the general public, develop knowledge.

6. Responsibility to society: promote the general welfare of society (*NASW News*, 1980; Levy, 1976).

The Ethical Standards of Psychologists (1979) has a Preamble and nine Principles. Psychologists respect the dignity and worth of the individual and preserve human rights. They are committed to increase their knowledge of human behavior and to promote human welfare. The nine principles cover:

1. Responsibility: value integrity and maintain the highest standards.
2. Competence: recognize boundaries of competence, update knowledge.
3. Moral and Legal Standards: be aware of impact of public behavior.
4. Public Statements: aid consumer in making informed judgments.
5. Confidentiality: safeguard client information.
6. Welfare of the Consumer: protect welfare and fully inform consumer.
7. Professional Relationships: act with regard to needs and competencies of colleagues and other professions.
8. Utilization of Assessment Techniques: persons examined have the right to know results and interpretations made.
9. Pursuit of Research Activities: respect dignity and welfare of subjects.

The Code of Ethics (1976) of the American College of Hospital Administrators requires accountability to the college as members and observance of the American Hospital Association's "Guidelines on Ethical Conduct and Relationships for Health Care Institutions." Principles for health services administrators and facilities will be discussed in a later chapter.

SUMMARY

The ancient code of ethical conduct and codes revised in the last decade underscore basic principles to be observed by physicians and mental health professionals. The primary objective is to serve patients or clients to the best of one's ability, with competence and responsibility, with protection of the confidential relationship. Current ethical practice, to insure against invasion of privacy, is to inform patients or clients that failure to pay fees may result in the release of their names and other relevant information to a collection agency. This is very different from release of names to an insurance company for the patient is aware of this necessity for reimbursement and has signed a waiver permitting access.

An unexpected finding of a survey of current practice of clinical psychologists showed 61 percent used a collection agency and less than half had told their clients verbally or obtained written consent on this limit of confidentiality (Hastings Report, 1982).

There is a responsibility to improve one's knowledge and skill and to base one's practice on scientific methods.

Except in emergencies one may choose patients or clients. There is an obligation to safeguard the public from the incompetent and immoral practitioner. One practices in situations where one has the freedom to exercise professional judgment. An obligation exists to seek consultation when the case at hand exceeds the recognized limits of one's competence. All have a responsibility to society to improve the health of the community.

QUESTIONS

1. What is the primary ethical obligation of physicians and of mental health professionals?
2. What are some of the obligations to patients or clients? to the profession? to society?
3. When must one seek consultation?
4. What are the ethical issues on fees for services rendered?
5. Is there an ethical requirement for continuing education? If so, why?

REFERENCES

* AAAS (1981), *Professional and Ethical Activities of Scientific and Engineering Societies*. Washington, D.C.: American Association for the Advancement of Sciences.
   AMA (1979), *Judicial Council Opinions and Reports*. rev. ed. Chicago: American Medical Association.
* AMA (1981), *Judicial Council Opinions and Reports*. Chicago: American Medical Association.
* APA (1979), *Opinions of the Ethics Committee on the Principles of Medical Ethics*. Washington, D.C.: American Psychiatric Asociation.
* APA (1981), *The Principles of Medical Ethics* (Revised). Washington, D.C.: American Psychiatric Association.
   Braceland, F. J. (1969), Historical perspectives on the ethical practices of psychiatry. *Amer. J. Psychiat.*, 126:230–237.

* Code of Ethics (1976), Chicago: American College of Hospital Administrators.

Davidson, H. (1973), The vanishing oath. *Medical Insight,* 5:28–29.

Dunning the client: The ethics of debt collectors by therapists. (1982) *Hastings Center Report,* 12.

* Ethical Standards of Psychologists (1979). Washington, D.C.: American Psychological Association.

Gorovitz, S., & MacIntyre, J. (1975), Toward a theory of medical fallibility distinguishing culpability from necessary errors. *Hastings Center Report 5,* pp. 13–23.

JAMA (1981), AMA insights. *J. Amer. Med. Assn.,* 245:819.

Konold, D. E., & Veatch, R. M. (1972), Codes of medical ethics; History of the codes of medical ethics. In: *Encyclopedia of Bioethics,* ed. Center for Bioethics, Georgetown University. New York: The Free Press.

* Levy, C. (1976), *Social Work Ethics.* New York: Human Science Press.

Lippmann, W. (1929), *A Preface to Morals.* New York: Macmillan.

Menninger, K. (1973), *Whatever Became of Sin?* New York: Hawthorne Books.

NASW News (1980), *National Association of Social Work (NASW) News,* 25:19.

NEJM (1844), Professional etiquette. *N. Engl. J. Med. (Boston Medical and Surgical Journal),* 21:440–441.

Torrey, E. F., ed. (1968), *Ethical Issues in Medicine.* Boston: Little, Brown.

Chapter 5

A Study of Ethical Complaints: 1950–1980

Consider first the well-being of the patient.
—*Canadian Medical Association Code of Ethics*

Case example. A complainant alleged, in writing, that her psychiatrist had sexual intercourse with her on several occasions while she was a patient in psychotherapy. The District Branch held a hearing at which both complainant and defendant were present. The defendant admitted the statement made in the complaint was true, defending his action as therapeutic. During questioning it was further revealed that on several occasions a social worker served as the psychotherapist, but the bill which had been rendered specified a charge for services by the psychiatrist. The District Branch found the complaint confirmed, directed that the member be expelled, and notified the Secretary of the American Psychiatric Association. The Board of Trustees, in executive session, reviewed the evidence and affirmed the action of the District Branch. The report did not note any complaint directed against the social worker.

This case illustrates a violation of Section I of *The Principles of Medical Ethics with Annotations Especially Applicable to Psychiatry* (APA,

86

1978). These ethical principles, which are intended to guide the behavior of psychiatrists, apply to the medical profession generally and so should serve as guides to other mental health practitioners as well. As we have seen in chapter 4, in 1981 a new *Principles of Medical Ethics*, with but seven sections and with content differing from the earlier version, was adopted. As its more general language and relative paucity of detail make retrospective analysis of complaints an even more formidable task, and as the earlier code was in use during the period of our study, we have naturally chosen the latter as the basis for the analysis that follows. Using American Psychiatric Association information, we reviewed all complaints alleging violation of ethics received by the APA during a thirty-year period: 1950–1980. The purpose was to learn the nature of the complaints and to relate them to sections of the earlier principles. The complaints were divided into decades—1950s, 1960s, 1970s—in order to detect trends. The hypothesis was explored that more ethical complaints would follow as a result of the revised procedures established in 1973. In that year, all District Branches of the American Psychiatric Association and academic training centers were given copies of the ethical principles and explicit instructions for the reporting of complaints.

Mental health professionals have ethical responsibilities to patients, to peers, and to society, as do psychiatrists. While the thirty-year analysis involved only complaints lodged against psychiatrists, the findings will be of concern to each of the mental health professions and to clinician-administrators as examples of the kind of abuses which occur and which reach the stage of reporting and judgments.

METHOD

As each complaint was received by the APA, it was recorded on a file card without the name of the accused. A decision was made as to the section of the ethical code violated and immediately classified by section. Frequently the complaint alleged violations of more than one section of the code. When this occurred, a decision was made as to which was the primary complaint. This decision was often assisted by the action taken. Fortunately one person made the coding decision during most of the period studied.

The progress of the investigation was posted step by step on the cards to the conclusion of the case. The nature of the complaint often made possible a further classification according to the various subsections of the code. The actions taken showed whether the complaint was confirmed (guilty), not substantiated (not guilty) or no action taken (none). The latter category included: withdrawal at the request of the complainant, unavailability of the parties at the hearing, insufficient evidence for a finding to be rendered, and failure by the District Branch to report. Also included under the "no action taken" category are cases still open because of ongoing lengthy court trials and appeals, or because the investigation is still under way. More recent complaints, as expected, were unresolved at the cut-off point for the study.

FINDINGS BY SECTION

Table 5–1 classifies 273 complaints of alleged violation of ethics by sections of the ethical code and subdivides these into the decade in which they were lodged. The total number of complaints received in the 1950s was 35, as compared to 45 in the 1960s. By the 1970s the

TABLE 5–1
A Study of Complaints by Decades and by Sections of the Medical Ethical Code

	1950–1960	1960–1970	1970–1980	Total
Section 1	2	11	72	85
Section 2	0	0	0	0
Section 3	1	3	5	9
Section 4	17	14	55	86
Section 5	3	6	24	33
Section 6	1	1	1	3
Section 7	4	4	11	19
Section 8	0	0	2	2
Section 9	6	4	18	28
Section 10	1	2	5	8
TOTAL	35	45	193	273

total number of complaints, 193, was six times greater than in the previous decade.*

The hypothesis proved true that more complaints would be received after procedures on how to report ethical violations were made very explicit and were publicized. There were, of course, other factors operating, including an increased concern in society and in the professions about ethical issues. Greater awareness undoubtedly stimulated the filing of complaints, as did the belief that action would be taken.

Section 1: Improper Conduct or Treatment; Sexual Intercourse or Misconduct

A total of 85 complaints alleging violation of this section of the ethical code were received in the thirty years 1950–1980. Two were received in the 1950s, 11 in the 1960s, and 72 in the 1970s.

Although complaints alleging unethical behavior might have been subdivided into many categories, we chose to group them under three headings (see Table 5–2): *Improper conduct* (38 complaints); *sexual intercourse or misconduct* (35 complaints); *improper treatment* (12 complaints).

Complaints alleging *improper conduct* were affirmed in 13 instances and unsubstantiated in 13. Twelve complaints were either still open or no action had been taken to resolve the case. Examples to illustrate the outcome of such cases follow:

1. A patient in long-term therapy complained that the therapist was rude and discourteous in person and abusive on the telephone. The complaint was confirmed by the District Branch, which officially admonished the therapist.

2. A patient complained that the therapist did not supply information about fees and refused to accept insurance payments. The District

* Two additional instances of alleged ethical violations in the 1970s were reported since the conclusion of our study. Both are still open, pending a court decision. Both cases were being tried in 1981. One of the additional cases, filed under Section 4, was for alleged falsification of records to cover up a fatal drug overdose, an improperly prescribed drug, and a narcotics violation. The other case, filed under Section 7 (also under 8 and 9), alleged a charge for an examination of a child which was not done, refusal to consult with two psychologists who had examined the child, and violation of confidentiality with discussion of irrelevant family matters with attorneys. Adding these two cases to the study, the total number of complaints is 275, with 195 complaints in the 1970s.

TABLE 5-2

A Study of Ethical Complaints

Complaints that reached the national Ethics Committee of the American Psychiatric Association in 30 years (1950–1980) classified under the section of the AMA Ethical Code applicable.

	I	II	III	IV	V	VI	VII	VIII	IX	X	Guilty	Not Guilty	None* or open**
					SECTION								
Improper conduct	38										13	13	12
Sexual relations or misconduct	35										11	5	19
Improper treatment	12										0	4	8
Failure to improve skills		0									0	0	0
Use of unscientific methods			9								0	3	6
Failure to safeguard public				17							3	4	10
Immoral or illegal behavior				39							13	15	11
Incompetence				13							3	7	3
Failure to uphold dignity of the profession				19							1	8	10
Failure in duty to patient					15						1	8	6
Solicitation of patients, improper advertising					18						7	7	4
Poor judgment, inadequate skill						3					1	0	2
Billing for services not rendered							3				0	1	2
Excessive fees							16				3	6	7
Failure to secure consultation								2			1	1	0
Violation of confidentiality									28		5	15	8
Failure to improve health or safeguard the community										8	1	5	2
										273	63	102	108

TOTAL ——273

* none: includes no record of action taken, insufficient evidence for a finding, not an ethical matter, or case withdrawn by request of complainant.
** open: under investigation, in trial or appeal process

Branch did not confirm the complaint at the hearing. The patient was upset at the use of a collection agency to obtain payment of fees. The District Branch found the defendant not guilty and closed the case.

3. A patient complained that the therapist missed scheduled appointments, fell asleep or read during treatment hours. This case is classified as "no action" and is still under investigation.

A total of 35 complaints alleged *sexual intercourse or sexual misconduct* during the period of the study; 7 in the first two decades and 28 in the 1970s. Examples include the following:

1. A patient alleged that the therapist was her lover, legal advisor, and business manager. At the hearing the charge that the therapist had sex with the patient in a therapy session was confirmed. The therapist was expelled from the District Branch.

2. A patient alleged sexual misconduct by her therapist. An investigation was carried out by the Board of Medical Licensure, who did not substantiate the charge. The case was closed.

3. A patient alleged sexual intercourse during her therapy. She also filed a civil action in court. In the study the action taken is listed as "none," which in this case means open pending court action. Once the court has ruled on the matter, District Branch will decide what action, if any, it will take.

Improper treatment was alleged in 12 instances; 4 in the first twenty years of the study and 8 in the 1970s. Outcomes are illustrated by the following:

1. A patient alleged that the therapist gave improper treatment. Upon investigation the charge was not substantiated.

2. A patient alleged that incarceration in hospital was illegal. Further, the patient complained that electroconvulsive therapy was given without consent. Investigation by the District Branch could not substantiate any ethical violation but stated that the therapist's records were "inadequate."

3. A patient alleged physical abuse by being beaten and kept in a cellar room. Further, the patient was charged $5000 for a month of care. A newspaper account of the case stated that the Department of Public Welfare was complaining that the therapist was operating an

unlicensed psychiatric facility. The District Branch declined to investigate the charges they received because the therapist practiced in two states and it was unclear which state had jurisdiction. As a consequence the American Psychiatric Association appointed two Fellows as investigators. Though the action taken is listed as "none," the complaint is still under investigation.

Section 2: Failure to Improve Medical Knowledge and Skills

There were no complaints during the thirty-year study period alleging failure to improve medical knowledge and skills. This does not mean all psychiatrists kept abreast of advances in their field; it indicates only that no written complaints were received. Recently some states have made evidence of continuing medical education a condition for licensure, and many professional bodies make it compulsory for continued membership. Theoretically, an ethical complaint could follow noncompliance of the continuing medical education requirements of the state. Except for nurses, the other mental health professions have yet to require continuing education.

Section 3: Failure to Practice Based Upon Scientific Principles

According to this section, an ethical physician should practice a method of healing based on scientific principles and should shun association with anyone who violates that principle. In thirty years there were 9 allegations of the use of unscientific methods, but no complaint was confirmed upon investigation. Examples follow:

1. One complainant alleged that the therapist used "operant conditioning" in the hospital. Investigation found operant conditioning to be an accepted scientific therapy and not an ethical violation. The case was closed.

2. Another complainant alleged that the therapist considered her mental disorder an allergy and prescribed high doses of vitamins. Upon investigation, the complainant was unwilling to appear or to supply detailed information, and no action was taken.

3. A complainant alleged that she was put into a closet with a heat lamp on as therapy for her mental disorder. No action could be taken

because the therapist was not a member of the professional association being asked to investigate. The District Branch did, however, forward the complaint to the state's licensure board. Follow-up as to their findings and action was not noted.

Section 4: Failure to Safeguard the Public

This section was identified more than any other section of the ethical code as being the primary complaint. There were 86 complaints related to this section made during the period under study: 17 in the 1950s, 14 in the 1960s, and 55 in the 1970s. Complaints were grouped under four subheadings: *failure to safeguard the public, immoral or illegal behavior, incompetence,* and *failure to uphold the dignity of the profession.*

Failure to safeguard the public was alleged in 17 instances with 3 found guilty, 4 not guilty, and 10 with no action taken or with investigation still in progress. Examples follow:

1. The complainant alleged that the psychiatrist was training unqualified persons to be lay analysts for clinical practice. Investigation confirmed the truth of the complaint. The therapist was admonished for the action and the psychiatrist subsequently resigned from the APA.

2. A cover-up of a grievance and falsification of records was alleged in a complaint. As the complainant at the hearing was unable to provide evidence, the defendant was found not guilty and the case was closed.

3. The complainant alleged that essential evidence was withheld by the defendant when on the witness stand. Civil action was also taken, but when the complainant died the case was closed.

Immoral or illegal behavior accounted for 37 complaints. Thirteen were confirmed, 15 were unsubstantiated, and in 9 there was no action taken or the case remained open for further investigation. Examples follow:

1. A patient's complaint to the District Branch alleged Medicare and Medicaid fraud as well as bribery. The matter was also in court, where the defendant pled guilty to ten counts of fraud. The defendant was subsequently convicted and sentenced. The complaint was confirmed by the District Branch.

2. A complaint stated that the therapist had sexual relations with the wife of a patient. An investigation was conducted by the medical society. It was found that no patient-therapist relationship had in fact been established, so the case was closed.

3. Another patient's complaint alleged fraud and billing for services not rendered. No action to confirm or deny was taken because the District Branch held it had no ability to investigate fraud.

Incompetence was alleged in 13 instances with guilt established in 3. Seven complaints were unsubstantiated and 3 were followed by no action or are still open for investigation. Examples follow:

1. The complaint alleged unprofessional conduct and the practice of "bad" medicine. Investigation showed the defendant advocated ECT for patients who did not meet the hospital's criteria for appropriate use of ECT. When the psychiatrist was refused access to the hospital beds he wrote letters to his patients decrying the decision. Charges were affirmed and the defendant reprimanded by the District Branch.

2. A complaint alleged improper diagnosis and treatment. Investigation did not substantiate the charge. Though there was no ethical violation, evidence did show that the therapist had been rude to the patient.

Section 5: Failure of Duty to Patients; Solicitation

In the three decades there were 33 complaints alleging violations of ethics under Section 5. Three instances occurred in the 1950s, 6 in the 1960s, and 24 in the 1970s. The complaints were grouped under the headings *failure in duty to patients,* and *solicitation of patients or improper advertising.*

Failure in duty to patients was the basis for 15 complaints. One resulted in a finding of guilty, 8 not guilty, and in 4 no action was taken or the investigation is still ongoing. Examples follow:

1. One complaint alleged abandonment of the patient and failure to share information with the therapist who assumed subsequent responsibility for treatment. The complainant and the therapist negotiated a settlement.

2. The patient's complaint alleged abandonment as well as a charge

for a missed appointment even though due notice had been given (Section 7). At the hearing, evidence was presented that the therapist had properly informed the patient's family of his intention to leave the case and that billing was proper. The charge stood unsubstantiated.

3. Another complaint alleged that a therapist terminated the patient without adequate notice and violated confidentiality (Section 9). District Branch investigation revealed that the complainant's attorney had negotiated a settlement. Upon District Branch review, the therapist was asked to respond fully on the ethical issues. Since this is not yet completed the case remains open.

Solicitation of patients or improper advertising generated 18 complaints. Seven were confirmed, 7 unsubstantiated, and in 4 no action was taken or the case is still open. Examples follow:

1. The complaint alleged that the therapist solicited patients for encounter groups by mail. At the hearing guilt was established and the therapist admonished. The complainant had enclosed an advertisement by the therapist which outlined a weight loss plan with a refund guarantee if unsuccessful. The manufacturer of the product in the advertisement had been sued for mail fraud. At the District Branch hearing it was ruled the therapist had exceeded the Federal Trade Commission ruling on the right to advertise. The therapist resigned from the APA.

2. A complaint alleged solicitation of patients for hypnosis. The hearing found the defendant had mailed a notice to physicians to offer a training course to his peers. The charge was unsubstantiated.

3. Publication of a book on self-diagnosis and treatment was the basis for a complaint. No finding by the District Branch was made in response to the complaint and no action was taken.

Section 6: Poor Judgment or Inadequate Skills

There were 3 complaints under section 6 in the thirty years under study, one in each decade. *Poor judgment or inadequate skills* was confirmed in one instance and no action was taken in two. Examples follow:

1. One complaint alleged that a psychiatrist aided the "illegal" practice of psychotherapy because the supervision given was a

"sham." The claim was substantiated and the therapist was admonished.

2. A complainant alleged that a group of therapists planned to review each other's work and list the name of the group in the telephone directory and on stationery. Upon investigation it was found that the intent was to generate referrals. When the group agreed to abandon the plan, no action was taken.

Section 7: Billing for Services Not Rendered; Excessive Fees

There were 19 complaints alleging violation of Section 7 in the study period. Four complaints were received in the 1950s, 4 in the 1960s, and 11 in the 1970s. Alleged ethical improprieties were grouped under the headings *billing for services not rendered* and *excessive fees*.

Billing for services not rendered: 3 were confirmed, 1 was unsubstantiated, and in 2 instances no action was taken. Examples follow:

1. A complainant alleged a charge was made for a missed appointment and bills failed to indicate that no service was given. Investigation made by the state medical society found no ethical violation. The psychiatrist was subsequently dropped from their membership rolls for nonpayment of dues.

2. A complainant alleged misdiagnosis and no professional courtesy granted a fellow physician, with consequent overcharge. Although an eight-year lapse was noted between the time of the incident and the complaint, and evidence substantiated the diagnosis, the case was continued as "open" for the report on the overcharge and the courtesy issue.

Charges of *excessive fees* generated 16 complaints over thirty years. In 3 instances the defendant was found guilty, in 6 not guilty, and in 7 the action was listed as none. Examples follow:

1. A complaint alleged excessive fees and that the insurance company had named a lower fee as proper. At a hearing the charge was confirmed, the therapist admonished, and reduced fees negotiated.

2. Another complaint alleged that an excessive hourly fee had been charged. At the hearing the charge was unsubstantiated because the fee had been discussed beforehand with the patient. It was suggested

to the therapist that charges be discussed during the first therapeutic session.

3. A complaint alleged excessive fees and enclosed a clipping from the *AMA News* indicating that the psychiatrist was expelled from the state medical society. The defendant appealed his expulsion. No action was reported as to outcome of the appeal or whether the District Branch took action.

Section 8: Failure to Secure Consultation

There were but 2 complaints received of violations of Section 8. Both were received in 1970. One was substantiated and one was not. Examples follow:

1. This complaint alleged that the physician did not agree to a requested consultation. The defendant was found guilty and admonished. When he was informed of his right of appeal, he declined to exercise it.

2. The other complaint alleged failure to secure consultation. At the hearing it was revealed that the issue had been fully discussed with the patient. The charge was unsubstantiated and the case closed.

Section 9: Violation of Confidentiality

Twenty-eight complaints alleging violation of Section 9 were received during the study period: 6 in the 1950s, 4 in the 1960s, and 18 in the 1970s. Allegations of violation of confidentiality were confirmed in 5 instances, unconfirmed in 15, and in 8 no action was taken. Examples follow:

1. A complaint alleged breech of confidentiality in a report made to a probation officer. The hearing confirmed the violation and the defendant was instructed on the legal and ethical issues of the situation. Review by the national organization stated that a reprimand should have been given.

2. A complainant alleged that a report was sent to an insurance company without authorization and that a consultant's report was withheld. At the hearing it was found that the charge was unsubstantiated. The consultant's report was not released but was read in his office by

an appropriate reviewer. It was held that the report made to the insurance company was not unethical.

3. A complaint alleged that a videotape made of the patient was shown in violation of his privacy. At the hearing it was learned that precautions had been taken to protect privacy. No action was taken when the defendant agreed to withdraw the tape.

Section 10: Failure to Improve Health or Safeguard the Community

In the thirty years, 8 complaints were received alleging violations of Section 10. One complaint was received in the 1950s, 2 in the 1960s and 5 in the 1970s. The charge was substantiated in 1 instance and unconfirmed in 5. In 2 cases no action was taken. Examples follow:

1. A complaint alleged that a book was written about a prominent person which brought discredit upon the profession. At the hearing it was revealed that the book went beyond prudent recording of psychohistory and the complaint was confirmed. The defendant was reprimanded and he chose not to exercise his right of appeal.

2. A complaint alleged that the psychiatrist sent a telegram to an attorney about the patient's mental disorder and that this was done without examination. At the hearing it was found that a two-hour mental examination had in fact been made. The patient's attorney had requested a report and this had been given via a letter. The telegram was requested by the same attorney for use in court. The charge was not substantiated and the case was closed.

3. A complaint alleged that after an office visit the therapist revealed that the patient suffered a job-related neurosis, a revelation which exposed him to loss of job. A civil action was filed in court and was unresolved with the case still open. In the meantime the defendant moved to another state.

Discussion

If one looks at Table 5–1 it can be seen there were 35 complaints of ethical violations in the 1950s. In 1950, when the American Psychiatric Association had 5,856 members there were 6 complaints generated for each 1000 members. In 1960 there were 11,037 members and 45 complaints or about 4 per 1000 members. In 1970 there were 18,407 members and 193 complaints or 10 per 1000 members. In 1980 there were 25,345 members, 4.5 times the number of psychiatrists in 1950. They generated 5.5 times as many complaints.

There is no doubt that in the earlier period there was an underreporting of ethical violation allegations. Further, complaints received locally by District Branches may not have been sent to the American Psychiatric Association's office for review and recording in every instance. There are also a significant number of "no actions taken" by the District Branches to either confirm or deny the allegations and a demonstrated failure to follow a case through to closure in many instances.

To be sure, District Branches lacked resources for running an investigation. Often medical society or licensing board records were confidential and not available to a local ethics committee. Hearings could be held, however, and did allow both parties to be heard. Legal counsel was not provided nor were there firm rules of procedure. The subsequent reporting to licensing boards, the judicial system, or hos-, pital boards seems never to have been considered. Nor was publicity ever given to reprimands.

Responsibility Toward Patients

Three sections of the code—Sections 1, 5, and 9—address therapists' responsibilities toward patients. When allegations of unethical behavior under these sections are combined they total 146 complaints and comprise 53 percent of all complaints received.

Mental health professionals do have the obligation to thoroughly investigate and evaluate the patient's disorder and to institute appropriate treatment. To keep abreast of new developments in diagnosis and treatment, mental health professionals must continually update their knowledge and skill. They should seek to improve their standard of patient care and to render services of the highest quality.

Other responsibilities, under Section 1, 5, and 9 include the obligation for continuity of care, securing informed consent, observing patients' rights, keeping adequate records, discussing fees for services, and observing personal morality. These are serious responsibilities, and patient rights advocates, third-party payers, and hospital accreditation procedures force some professionals to be more rigorous in their compliance than they might otherwise be.

The unique relationship of the psychotherapist to the patient demands the development of complete trust and a special awareness implemented in practice that preserves secrets shared in confidence.

The patient's system of values should be respected. The therapist-patient relationship is meant to assist patients in establishing new and more effective behavior patterns to deal with stress and conflict and in improving their skills in interpersonal relationships. The therapist should not exclude, segregate, or demean any patient by reason of ethnic origin, sex, religion, age, or economic status. He or she should strive to gain for patients their enjoyment of the wholeness of spirit that has come to be known as "quality of life."

Special ethical dilemmas will arise to confront the mental health professional that each must resolve for himself. One such dilemma might derive from the patient's right of access to his records. The "right to know" the uses to which these records may be put does not entail the "need to know" their specific content. Another dilemma has to do with confidentiality which is not absolute. In an emergency, confidentiality can be an impediment to proper care. A job may depend upon the answer to a seemingly harmless query about a patient. Payment by an insurer of the expense of treatment requires substantiation that the patient was seen and that treatment conformed to a benefit covered under the patient's policy. The patient should be made aware that information to the insurance company is routinely sent, without any special procedure for release of information.

Mental health professionals are faced with difficult decisions related to Sections 1, 5, and 9, dilemmas which can be illustrated by the following questions:

- What will you do when the patient confesses to a murder and forbids you to tell the police?
- What will you do when the patient who is mentally ill threatens to kill someone and you believe he may?
- What action will you take when the patient confesses to embezzling money and is continuing to do so?

• What action will you take when the heroin-addicted patient reveals the illegal source of his continuing supply of drugs?

The dilemma posed by the first question expresses the conflict between two obligations, the duty to safeguard society and the duty to preserve the patient's secrets shared in confidence. The competing duties will be weighed in each instance and may have differing outcomes depending upon the risk that the patient will repeat the crime, the goal of therapy, and the likelihood of achieving it.

The second question requires an action to involuntarily detain the patient as dangerous to others and in California (see the Tarasoff case) an obligation to warn the potential victim.

The third and fourth questions are central problems in therapy. There will be a time in the process when the patient must cease the activity and work toward restructuring his or her life and must face the consequences or the treatment will be a failure. Encouragement toward disclosure will be continuous.

Some believe that confidentiality should be preserved under any circumstance. Others hold that there are situations where the rights of society outweigh the right of an individual to privacy.

Recently the conflict between the therapeutic role and the institutional role has come into focus. The therapist may be obligated by the conditions of his employment to serve the institution rather than primarily serve as therapist to the patient. When the court assigns the task of examining a patient for competency to stand trial or of determination of responsibility for an act, the patient has the right to know that what he says may be used against him and that this situation is not the usual therapeutic one. Far more serious and less obvious role conflicts can occur in which the political views of a society direct what the psychiatrist shall do, subordinating patient welfare to the collective will of the system. The ethical duty of the physician is to the patient and the obligation is to do no harm.

Zitrin and Klein (1976) called attention to the demand by consumers and by the government for greater accountability from psychiatry, noting that the traditional system of self-policing has been challenged. They reviewed the experience of a large (1,535-member) District Branch Committee on Ethics over an eight-year period. Forty-four complaints were received in the four years 1970–1974, double the number for the previous four years. The authors expressed dissatisfaction with the limited resources available for investigation, as well as with the potential for bias when misconduct is judged by one's colleagues. They suggested that public confidence will grow only when indications are given that professions enforce their ethical standards.

We believe the mental health professions should develop state committees on ethics able to make impartial decisions. It must be recognized that it is difficult to get evidence. An ethics committee does not have the responsibility to employ trained investigators and to take over the function of either the courts or a police department. It is the complainant's responsibility to produce sufficient information to demonstrate cause for a hearing. The vexing problem of confidentiality prevents digging up evidence that could damage the defendant by making known the reasons for the inquiry. Sometimes sources of information may be unavailable without the defendant's permission.

There are reasons for the powerlessness of associations. Inaction can sometimes result from the complainant's wish to avoid involvement. It can come also by the complainant's refusal to supply essential information, because of the very real barrier of confidentiality, the reluctance of one colleague to bring charges against another, unfamiliarity with the system for taking an action, or the belief that nothing would be done anyway, which has been all too true in the past.

Perhaps the first steps toward the development of a better system for handling ethical complaints are to ensure knowledge of ethical codes, provide guidelines, and publicize where and how to file a complaint and what actions can be taken.

The question of liability of ethics committee members merits some comment. Membership in a professional organization is a valued privilege. It may not be taken away unless there is a specific charge, a hearing, an opportunity to confront accusers, and careful adherence to procedures made clear in by-laws. The principal legal problem arises when it is shown that there was a failure to follow procedure. It could also be claimed that the decision made was unfair or incorrect and that it damaged the physician's reputation or impaired earning capacity. If a member is expelled for soliciting patients and advertising, a claim for damages might be made under antitrust laws. All states except

Alaska, South Carolina, and Vermont have a qualified immunity statute that applies to peer review committees which exempts members if they act in good faith and without malice. This protection has relevance to ethics committees which review the conduct of peers. Florida and Rhode Island laws specify there shall be no liability for actions taken in a medical society's disciplinary procedures. The best protection against liability claims is a clearly defined, written procedure that is carefully followed, conducted in good faith, without malice, and in the interest of safeguarding the public.

Responsibilities Toward the Profession

Sections 6,7, and 8 of the Ethical Code generated only 24 complaints (about 9 percent) in thirty years, with 19 percent of these in Section 7, where most were allegations of excessive charge. The sections include such obligations as contracts which allow freedom to exercise judgment in the patient's interest, collaborative relationships with other professions, consultation, submission of work to peer review, limitation of charges to services actually rendered, responsibility to set a proper value on services (avoidance of excessive fees), prohibition of fee splitting, informing the patient when one's own opinions diverge from that of the profession, and building a reputation on ability.

The AMA *Judicial Council Opinions and Reports* (AMA, 1979) offers rules and guidelines on contract practice, work for corporations, payment under different arrangements, billing procedures, use of collection agencies, relation to commercial enterprises, and use of consultants. These suggestions may be quite helpful for practitioners who wish to make certain they are staying on the ethical side of practice issues.

Responsibilities Toward Society

The sections of the code concerned with responsibilities to society are 2, 3, 4, and 10. Alleged violations of these four sections numbered 103 in thirty years, about 38 percent of the total number of complaints received. Most were under Section 4. The obligations included in these sections are: to improve knowledge and skills, to practice healing founded on a scientific basis, to safeguard the public (personal morals, competence, observation of laws, upholding the dignity and honor of the profession), to improve standards of practice both individual and institutional, to advocate health education and health legislation affecting the health or well-being of the community.

The AMA *Judicial Council Opinions and Reports* add to this additional guidelines by citing responsibility, clinical investigations, organ transplants, relationships with others in the healing services, and details on announcements of practice, use of advertising, and relationships with the press and electronic media.

Sexual Activity with Patients

Nadelson, Grunebaum, and Macht (1976) surveyed the members of an APA District Branch as to their knowledge of ethical violations on the part of their colleagues, including sexual activity with patients. With only a 30 percent return of questionnaires from a small random subsample of 100 members, 12 instances of sexual activity of therapists with patients were reported. Of these 9 were held justified and 3 probably so.

Stone 1976 examined the gap between Dr. William Masters' opinion that "any therapist who exploits the power and position of his or her professional status to have sexual intercourse with a patient should be charged with rape" and existing sanctions in law. Rape charges in such cases are rarely brought to court and even more rarely do they succeed. He cited two cases. One was a psychiatrist who gave his patient ECT and/or injections of a hypnotic drug and then had intercourse. The doctor was convicted and sent to prison. The other was a psychiatrist who had intercourse with a 16-year-old adolescent referred because of promiscuity. He was convicted of statutory rape.

When a competent patient is told in advance, before the transference relationship is developed, that sexual intercourse is to be the treatment and the patient consents, there is no rape and neither is there coercion or fraud. Michigan has a statute which could make sexual intercourse in the course of therapy considered rape because it uses language which relates exploitation of examination or treatment to unethical behavior. Ohio's statute uses the words "knowingly coerces the other person to submit by any means that would prevent resistance by a person of ordinary resolution.''

Under civil law, a therapist who engages in sexual activity with a patient as part of treatment may be held liable for malpractice. One court states, ''there is a public policy to protect a patient from the deliberate and malicious abuse of power and breach of trust by a psychiatrist when that patient entrusts to him, her body and mind'' (Stone, 1976).

The greatest deterrent to sexual intercourse with a patient perhaps will be the fact that a California jury awarded $4,500,000 to a woman who testified she had suffered psychological damage after seduction by her therapist during therapy sessions. The *AMA News* (July 24, 1981) cited the findings of the malpractice suit and reported that the therapist had attempted unsuccessfully to settle out of court for $100,000.

The ethics and the legality of employing a sexual surrogate in sex therapy is a hot issue. It is recognized that dual sex therapy is essential in the customary mode of male and female therapists treating the marital couple. The problem surfaces when the single person comes for therapy. The supplying of a partner creates the ethical problems. It is strongly opposed on moral grounds. As to sexual activity by the therapist, we agree with Gaylin (quoted in Stone, 1976) that ''there are absolutely no circumstances which permit a psychiatrist to engage in sex with his patient.''

Kardener, Fuller, and Mensh (1973) surveyed 460 physicians as to erotic attitude and practice with their patients. Eighty percent of psychiatrists and 83 percent of obstetricians and gynecologists believe erotic overtures are improper and do not engage in them. None of the psychiatrists in the author's survey, and only 1 percent of the obstetricians had intercourse with patients. Two percent of surgeons and 1 percent of general practitioners did. As West (1969) has bluntly stated, ''the overwhelming majority of psychiatrists would agree that it is unethical to seduce patients and foolish if not outrageous to call it treatment.''

A related issue surfaced recently under what appeared at first glance to be a tangential question, ''What is the definition of the physician-patient relationship and how long does it last?'' If a physician gives a prescription for a tranquilizer to his secretary for emotional upset, is there a physician-patient relationship? If a week later the physician begins a sexual relationship with the secretary, is she still his patient? What if the affair begins a year later? Does the physician-patient relationship continue indefinitely, or does it have an end point only when either party announces it is terminated? A variation on this theme occurred when a resident presented a patient at Grand Rounds. The resident began a sexual relationship with the patient following her discharge from the hospital. Does the doctor-patient relationship end when the patient leaves the hospital?

In the first instance, the physician's signature on the prescription established a physician-patient relationship that exists until withdrawn with notice to the patient long enough in advance for her to secure another physician. In the second instance, if the patient presented at Grand Rounds was the resident's case, the fact of release from the hospital does not automatically end the relationship.

It is to be noted that under Section 4 there were five complaints that the physician was mentally ill. The AMA's former Council on Mental Health noted that occasionally the functioning of a physician was impaired by psychiatric disorders, alcoholism, or drug dependence. Because of the potential hazard to patients, the Council outlined a procedure to be followed and the AMA prepared a model bill (available on request) for management of disabled physicians. Two states, Texas and Florida, pioneered legislation. Utah, New Mexico, Nebraska, and Kansas enacted legislation in 1976, and by 1981 all but six states had identifiable mechanisms to formulate programs to identify, treat, and rehabilitate disabled physicians. When the physician can't be persuaded to seek treatment and is on a hospital staff, the matter should come before a hospital committee. If that is not feasible, the state or county medical society should act. If necessary, the matter should go to the medical licensing board to restrict, suspend, or revoke the physician's license to practice (*JAMA, 1973*).

Many complaints received do not reach the status of an accepted violation of ethics and thus are dropped without investigation under the established procedure. To illustrate the range of complaints: the divorced wife of a therapist complained that her former husband had stopped his child support payments (she was referred to the judicial system); a psychiatrist accused another of plagiarizing his work (he was encouraged to seek justice, if he wished, under copyright laws); an anonymous caller charged a physician with selling methadone (the caller was encouraged to put the complaint in writing so the accused could face accuser at hearing).

Policing of its members is an important function of a medical specialty organization. Often, however, professionals are reluctant to initiate complaints against a fellow without hard evidence or even with it, for being a "stool pigeon" is anathema to most Americans. Hospitals, medical organizations, and state licensing boards are the agencies primarily responsible for the enforcement of discipline and for guarding the public against unethical conduct and incompetence. Derbyshire (1974) concluded that serious deficiencies exist in enforcement performance. Hospital administration can be held responsible for the competence of staff members, according to court decisions. While some hospitals evaluate performance, few require certificates of ability to return to work after serious mental or emotional illness. Many permit the incompetent to resign and apply for hospital privileges elsewhere, uing their voluntary resignation as proof of professional competence.

AMA statistics compiled in 1980 showed the number of disciplinary actions it took against its members increased from 685 in 1977 to 1,476 in 1978. The number of physician licenses revoked also increased threefold.

Two model bills were endorsed by the House of Delegates at the 1976 AMA Annual Convention. One required physicians and medical peer review committees to report "gross or repeated medical malpractice or professional incompetence" to state licensing boards. The other granted those boards the authority to take disciplinary action. Both bills provided immunity for those making the report and included a mechanism for appeal by the accused. As a result, forty one states enacted amendments to their medical licensing acts. Eleven state boards can only suspend or revoke a physician's license, but 38 have authorized additional disciplinary actions that include public reprimand or probation and supervision of practice as a condition for license. Fourteen states require continuing education as a condition for renewal of license and 27 include medical malpractice or professional negligence as a basis for disciplinary action (*AMA Newsletter*, 1976).

For any ethical system to work efficiently in maintaining the integrity of the profession and safeguarding the public, it must be generally known how to file a complaint, what process it will go through, and what the possible outcomes are. There must also be a trust in the integrity and fairness of the organization, its ethical committee, and the individuals on it.

The defendant, in an alleged violation of ethics, should receive notice of the charge, reasonable notice of the date of hearing, and the right of confrontation and cross-examination of the complainant. If the defendant is dissatisfied with the outcome, there should exist the right to an appeal, to be heard before an impartial body, usually the profession's national committee on ethics.

In the past, the educational process failed to prepare mental health professionals for ethical responsibility. Most schools were content to include a lecture on ethics in the curriculum (*JAMA*, 1976). Today things are very different, as schools rush to remedy this defect. A recent survey (Veatch and Sollito, 1976) of 112 medical schools brought replies from 107, of which 97 had some teaching of ethics. Six had required courses, 56 offered seminars and conferences on ethics, 26 discussed ethical issues in other courses, and 47 offered ethics as an elective. Some schools have even established a separate department of ethics.

State Boards of Medical Examiners seldom get involved in minor ethical violations, very few licenses are revoked, and reprimands are uncommon. However, 41 states have in the past few years initiated actions that may be expected to accelerate activity in this area.

The following example illustrates that licensure boards may be held responsible for discipline. The case, cited in *AMA News* (1976), is that of a physician with a severe drinking problem who after treatment relapsed and lost his hospital privileges. He continued to see patients, although all were aware of his impaired judgment. When he diagnosed a patient as being pregnant and it was ultimately discovered by another physician to be an ovarian cancer too advanced for operation, a malpractice suit was filed. The physician fled the state and could not be found. The suit was then filed against the Board of Examiners, on grounds they had knowledge of the problem, did nothing, and so shared liability. The aftermath was an action by the Medical Society to enlarge the Board from four (one M.D.) to eleven (six M.D.s) with one of their tasks being to codify misconduct as a basis for loss of licenses.

SUMMARY

A study of 273 complaints received by the American Psychiatric Association over thirty years, all alleging violations of ethics, was analyzed by decades, by the sections of the ethical code in use over the entire period, and by the nature of the complaint and its outcome: guilty as charged, not guilty, or no action taken (or still open for investigation).

During the 1950s, about 6 members in 1000 were charged with unethical behavior. During the 1960s, complaints were received on about 4 members per 1000. In the 1970s, 10 members in 1000 were alleged to have behaved unethically. As expected, there was a marked increase in the number of complaints filed after an explicit procedure was publicized in 1973. Interest in ethical matters in the professions and in society generally also heightened during the seventies. Both factors led to more complaints being made.

The most common allegations of ethical violations were improper conduct (38), immoral or illegal behavior (37), sexual relations with patients (35), and violation of confidentiality (28). As to outcome, 63 complaints were confirmed, 102 unsubstantiated, and in 108 no action was taken or the case was still open for investigation.

The responsibilities of all mental health professionals toward patients, toward colleagues, and toward society are similar to those of psychiatrists, on whom the study of complaints was made. There is a need for the mental health professions to study the nature of complaints received regarding alleged unethical behavior by their members. Trust in the ability of a profession's ability to discipline its members is built upon the demonstrated will to take appropriate action when evidence proves unethical conduct. Confidentiality in the patient-therapist relationship is to be preserved. Even though society appears to tolerate sexual relationships between consenting adults, the therapeutic situation allows no sexual exploitation of vulnerable patients. Fraudulent behavior that cheats and steals from government mental health programs, as well as fee gouging, must be punished. Society has chosen to honor and reward those in the health professions, who relieve pain and restore the ill to productive lives. The morals and the values of mental health professionals and psychiatrists are reflected in their behaviors. Though ethical guidelines are observed by almost all mental health professionals, the few who are unethical must be identified and sanctions applied if the trust of society is to be maintained.

QUESTIONS

1. How significant is the increase in complaints alleging violation of ethics?
2. What are the most common alleged ethical violations?
3. What is the procedure to be followed when an ethical complaint is received?
4. Are the ethical issues analyzed in the thirty-year study applicable to mental health professionals generally? How do they differ for each profession?
5. Is it ethical to have a sexual relationship with a former patient a few weeks after termination of treatment?
6. Is it ethical for a physician to supervise a clinic of Chinese acupuncturists or to refer patients to a licensed chiropractor?
7. Is it ethical for a practitioner to insert his name in the yellow pages as a psychoanalyst if he has never had any form of analytic training?
8. Is it ethical to see a patient in private practice that one began treating in a public institution?
9. If it is generally considered ethical for psychiatrists to teach principles of counseling to clergymen, is it ethical also to give them advice in the management of specific cases?
10. Is it ethical to charge for missed appointments?

REFERENCES

AMA (1979), *Judicial Council Opinions and Reports*. Rev. ed. Chicago: American Medical Association.
* AMA (1981), *Judicial Council Opinions and Reports*. Chicago: American Medical Association.
AMA Newsletter (1981). MD liable for releasing patients. *AMA Newsletter* 24:7, July 24.

AMA News (1976), Medical board inaction stirs debate, *AMA News,* May 3.

AMA Newletter (1976), Two new AMA model bills on medical discipline. *AMA Newsletter* 8:4, Aug. 2.

* APA (1978), *The Principles of Medical Ethics: With Annotations Especially Applicable to Psychiatry.* Washington, D.C.: American Psychiatric Association.

Derbyshire, R. C. (1974), Medical ethics and discipline. *J. Amer. Med. Assn.,* 228:57–62.

JAMA (1973), The sick physician: Impairment for psychiatric disorder including alcoholism and drug dependence. *J. Amer. Med. Assn.,* 223:684–687.

JAMA (1976), Medical ethics, education and the physician's image. *J. Amer. Med. Assn.,* 235:1043–1046.

Kardener, S. H., Fuller, M., & Mensh, I. N. (1973), A survey of physician's attitudes and practices regarding erotic and nonerotic contact with patients. *Amer. J. Psychiat.,* 130:1077–1081.

Nadelson, C., Grunebaum, H., & Macht, L. B. (1976), Therapist-patient sex: survey findings speak. *Psychiatric News,* 11:28–29, Oct. 1.

Stone, A. A. (1976), The legal implications of sexual activity between psychiatrist and patient, *Amer. J. Psychiat.,* 133:1138–1141.

Veatch, R. M., & Sollito, S. (1976), Medical ethics teaching: Report of a national medical school survey. *J. Amer. Med. Assn.,* 235:1030–1033.

West, J. L. (1969), Ethical psychiatry and biosocial humanism. *Amer. J. Psychiat.,* 126:226–229.

Zitrin, A., & Klein, H. (1976), Can psychiatry police itself effectively? The experience of one district branch. *Amer. J. Psychiat.,* 133:653–656.

Chapter 6

Ethics and Law of Institutions

> The law is the witness and external deposit of
> our moral life. Its history is the history of the
> moral development of the race.
> —*Oliver Wendell Holmes, Jr. (1841–1935)*

The statements which follow suggest the range of ethical issues, often with legal overtones, which fall into the domain of institutional ethics.

- A patient was discharged without medical approval for release when unable to pay for care.
- An award was made to a contractor who had paid for a luxury vacation trip for the administrator.
- The incompetence of a drug-abusing clinician was covered up.
- Sexual harassment of employees was ignored after a formal complaint was made.
- A hospital's governing board made a unilateral change in the by-laws that required clearance by the Medical Executive Committee.
- A copy of a patient's medical record was released without that patient's authorization.
- Medication was given to a disturbed voluntary patient over her objection.
- An inebriated person was turned away from the admitting room after an accident and died a few hours later of internal bleeding.

• An employee was fired for unsatisfactory performance by her superior, who bypassed the procedure which called for written notice of poor work and a discussion of deficiencies with the employee.

Let us assume acceptance of the statement expressing a social value: there shall be equal access to treatment based upon patient or client need. Three problems in the ethical arena of organizations will illustrate some of the kinds of issues to be resolved: cost of a procedure, social policy favoring minorities, and legal barriers.

First of all, there is cost. Technological advances have sometimes involved the purchase of expensive equipment, yet its use will increase cost. With an established need, will the patient unable to pay for the procedure have equal access?

Second, social policy may dictate that minorities are to be favored in order to correct past social injustices. When funds will not pay for access to treatment for all who need it, will admission of a minority group member take precedence over the admission of a child or elderly person with an equal need? A choice might well have to be made between the (in principle) equal rights of children and those of the elderly, both of whom are designated as underserved groups.

Finally, legal barriers may arise, including barriers that stand in the way of sound medical judgment. For example, while the treatment of choice in a particular case may clearly be electroconvulsive therapy, its use may be restricted by law to a defined emergency situation or to the status of treatment of last resort after other therapies have failed to produce improvement.

As far as the administrators of a mental health organization are concerned, they have an obligation to be ethical in the conduct of personal and business affairs (Code of Ethics, 1975). "Leadership is a process of morality to the degree that leaders engage with followers on the basis of shared motives, values and goals" (Burns, 1978). "A successful leader draws out, promotes and defends attitudes and values that are shared by the group, class or nation he leads" (Maccoby, 1976).

The concern for morality, ethics and values which forms the reciprocal relationship between administrators and staff is illustrated by the following statements:

- Human dignity shall be preserved with respect for all persons regardless of race, ethnic group, sex, or religious preference.
- An individual has responsibility for his/her own bodily integrity (unless adjudicated legally incompetent or in an emergency) with the freedom to determine his/her treatment or permitted intervention among alternatives.
- Truthfulness is to be followed at all times except when it may cause harm (see *JAMA*, 1982).
- Delegation down-the-line to staff is the preferred mode.
- Participation in decision making is expected.
- Professionals will follow the ethical code of their discipline.

Another set of ethical guidelines for administrators is to be found in the "Guidelines on Ethical Conduct and Relationships for Health Care Institutions"* of the American Hospital Association (AHA, 1974):

1. Good health is of utmost importance to the nation, to the community, and to every individual. Health care institutions should be interested in the overall health status of people in addition to providing direct patient care services.

2. The public has accorded high priority to the availability of services to the sick and injured, but there are limits to the individual and collective resources available for this purpose. Recognizing this, health care institutions should:

a. Support the most effective use of economic and other resources to ensure access to comprehensive services of high quality.

b. Deliver services efficiently.

3. The community's health objectives are advanced when all health care providers and social welfare, educational and other agencies work together in planning and offering improved services. Health care institutions should promote and support cooperation among each other, all providers, and community agencies in efforts to increase the results they could achieve separately.

4. Patient care services are inherently personal in nature. Health care

---

* Reprinted with permission of the American Hospital Association and the American College of Hospital Administrators from Appendix II of the Code of Ethics. Copyright © 1974 American Hospital Association.

institutions should maintain organizational relationships, policies, and systems that produce an environment that is conducive of humane and individualized care for those being served.

5. Individual religious and social beliefs and customs are important to each person. Health care institutions should, wherever possible be consistent with ethical commitments of the institutions, ensure respect and consideration for the dignity and individuality of patients, employees, physicians and others.

6. Health care institutions should establish and maintain internal policies, practices, standards of performance, and systematic methods of evaluation that emphasize high quality, safety, and effectivenes of care.

7. Health care institutions, being dependent upon community confidence and support, should accept an ethical sense of public accountability; reflect fairness, honesty, and impartiality in all activities and relationships; manage their resources prudently; and ensure that reports to the public are factual and clear in interpreting institutional goals, status, and accomplishments.

8. Health care institutions should relate to their communities and to each other constructively and in ways that merit and preserve public confidence in them, both individually and collectively.

The primary purpose of a facility or program for the mentally ill or retarded is quality care and treatment for patients or clients. There is an obligation to create a safe and wholesome environment in support of that purpose. The organization should merit the respect and confidence of the patients or clients it serves.

Klerman (1980), classified the ethical dilemmas of Federal-level administrators into four categories:

1. *Remaining virtuous:* resisting the temptation to accept bribes, allocating discretionary funds equitably. The more discretionary authority one has the more potentially corruptible one is.

2. *Coping with conflicting values:* allocating resources on the basis of equal social values or to minorities on the basis of correcting of past injustices.

3. *Generation of new ethical principles:* public funds to be expended only for those treatments demonstrated to be safe and efficacious.

4. *Conflicting loyalties:* approving budget cuts favored by the administration that will be deleterious to patient care.

''The administrator must understand and integrate the disparate values of clinicians, consumers, third party payers, politicians, etc. if the facility is to be morally relevant and fiscally viable'' (Schulberg and

McClelland, 1981). To this end the following grouping of ethical guidelines for the mental health administrator will illustrate the range of issues (AMA, 1981):

Personal

Integrity: merit trust, accept no favors, gifts or bribes that might influence decisions.

Open communications: hear complaints and be fair and just in their correction.

Mutual respect: develop harmonious relationships, avoid racism, sexism, and discriminatory practices.

Fulfillment of obligations: perform faithfully prescribed duties.

Priority of patient/client welfare: observe the need of the patient or client, because the contracted service has precedence over one's own financial interests.

Organization

Conflict of interest: awareness that personal interests may be in conflict with those of the organization, or patient/client relationship in conflict with organizational interests. There is an obligation to inform the patient or client of the circumstances and take appropriate action to resolve the conflict. It is unethical to prolong the stay of a patient for financial benefit to the organization.

Fees: bill only for services actually performed, no separate and distinct fee for securing admission to the facility.

Use of inside information: no use of inside information in the transaction of business of the organization for personal gain.

Ownership disclosure: it is not unethical for a physician or mental health professional to own or to have an interest in a mental health facility or service for profit, but if one does then there is an obligation to disclose the fact of ownership or interest to the patient or client.

Reporting of criminal activities: it is ethical to report to appropriate governmental agencies *evidence* of alleged criminal conduct of any physician or mental health professional.

Compulsory assessments: it is unethical to collect assessments (for building funds, etc.) under penalty of any kind.

PUBLICITY AND ADVERTISING

Is it ethical to present the patient or a family group to a public audience via the media and to detail the problem and its solution? Should the mental health professional appear on TV or radio when the sponsor is a drug manufacturer and the audience may assume endorsement? May one pose in the nude for a magazine or endorse cigarettes in an advertisement without damage to the image of the profession? Is it ethical to promote a treatment that has no scientific evidence to validate its usefulness?

A five-year battle waged by the American Medical Association with the Federal Trade Commission ended up in the U.S. Supreme Court (1982). The result was a 4–4 deadlock which upheld the FTC action. The FTC held that law and medicine were subject to the same regulations as private enterprises and the ethical ban on "solicitation" was in restraint of trade. The AMA held that medicine, as a learned profession with an obligation to society, was properly protecting the public in expressing its right to self-regulation. The courts found for the FTC and barred the AMA from prohibiting truthful advertising or solicitation of patients. The action also forbade the AMA from interfering in the amount or form of compensation that could be offered in a contract for physicians' services. It does, however, allow peer review of fee practices. The AMA's *Judicial Council Opinions and Reports* (AMA, 1981) said, "a physician may advertise in any medium as long as the communication is not false or misleading or designed to deceive the public." The new ethical code of the AMA omits any reference to publicity or advertising. Legislation presently before Congress would exempt all state-licensed professions from FTC jurisdiction.

As all know, advertising often extols a product and makes comparisons, claiming it is better. While lower price may be used to entice the purchaser, often it is not included. Hawking one's special talents and boasting of prowess is reprehensible to most mental health professionals and psychiatrists. Only a few have departed from the values of their peers to utilize display advertisements in attracting patients.

In this period of transition here are some things you may not do (Klerman, 1980):

- Violate the patient/client right to privacy.
- Use false, deceptive, or misleading information in advertisements or directory listings.
- Use testimonials or statements in advertising which create an unjustified expectation of favorable results or self-laudatory statements that imply the possession of skills superior to those of others.
- Engage in practice for gain that interferes with professional judgment and skill or causes a deterioration in the quality of practice.
- Pay commissions or rebates for referral of patients/clients.

ORGANIZATIONS

Mental health organizations often insert advertisements in newspapers and journals to encourage referrals and admissions. We have yet to see one that states that its fees are lower or that the quality of care is better than that provided by competitors. Health Maintenance Organizations (HMO's) often use a "hard sell" to attract purchasers of their service, but they refrain from qualitative judgments of their physicians and mental health professionals.

Admission to a program or service, or membership in a professional society, may not be denied because of race, color, religion, creed, ethnic affiliation, national origin, or sex.

An ethical problem may arise when there is a legal duty to report communicable diseases, such as venereal disease, or gunshot wounds. Reports may be required within a specified time, usually within twenty-four hours, to state health or police authorities. In such cases, the patient should be informed of this duty. The report of a gunshot wound may arouse media interest. The only information that may be given without the consent of the patient (or the parent or legal guardian) is verification that the patient is in treatment or was treated and released, and a general statement of the patient's condition (good, fair, or poor).

In brief, an organization may not offer commissions for referrals; use false or misleading information in advertisements; or violate the patient or client's right of privacy.

LAW AND THE MENTAL HEALTH FACILITY

Much of what follows under the sections on law is pertinent here. We cite here only principles that apply generally and provide examples to illustrate the administrator's responsibilities. Because state laws vary and because the issues are complex, we urge the administrator to consult such helpful references as: (Health Law Center, 1978), *Law of Hospital, Physician and Patient* (Hayt, Hayt, and Groeschel, 1972), and *Nursing and the Law* (Springer, 1970).

Facility Obligations

Some general principles are offered as guides to ethical behavior:

1. The facility must be in compliance with all Federal, state, and local laws and regulations, including licensure, fire inspection, and other safety requirements. Upon inspection, when deficiencies are noted, it must act promptly to take all reasonable steps to correct them.

2. The facility should move with all possible dispatch to conform to the principles and standards set forth in the accreditation manual for mental health facilities (Joint Commission, 1981).

3. The facility owes the duty to its patients or clients to provide the standard of care and skill in treatment exercised by facilities of the same general type in similar communities.

4. The facility owes the duty to its patients to furnish reasonably adequate equipment in good working order for use in diagnosis and treatment. This equipment must be suitable for the purposes intended. It must have no obvious or known uncorrected defects.

5. The premises of the facility must be kept in a reasonably safe condition for their expected use.

6. The facility should have enough staff properly trained and supervised to carry out the necessary diagnostic and therapeutic procedures owed as a duty to its patients.

7. The facility should assume individuals will retain their civil rights when they become patients.

A facility may be held liable for the wrongful acts of its employees (not physicians, however, because they may be held independently liable) under the legal concept of *respondeat superior,* which obtains when a master-servant relationship is shown to exist between hospital or facility and a class of its employees. Interns, residents, nurses, aides, and technicians usually are the classes of employees so designated. Care and supervision to avoid the allegation of negligence is essential. The facility is also responsible for the proper sterilization of supplies and equipment or must use presterilized disposables, and for maintaining vigilance through established procedures to prevent the spread of infection, including screening to identify employees in certain posts who might be carriers of infectious diseases.

RESPONSIBILITY OF ADMINISTRATOR AND GOVERNING BODY

As the top level of the management system of a hospital or psychiatric facility, the governing body and the administrator are accountable for entrusted resources and efficient management. We have said it is their responsibility to maintain the standard of care provided by similar facilities in like communities. As the management system and the clinical system interrelate, this is a joint enterprise.

The boundaries of authority are roughly defined by the acts of incorporation of the facility, or in statute and regulations governing institutions. If the corporation transgresses these boundaries, it may be challenged for operating an "unrelated business activity." The operation of canteens, gift shops, newsstands, and parking lots may be profitable to the hospital, but such activities are at least on the borderline of related activity, as they serve the relatives and visitors of patients. A hospital so fortunate as to have an operating oil well on its grounds would clearly be conducting an unrelated business activity and could be compelled to dispose of this taxable business.

Some years ago Butler Hospital, a private mental hospital in Providence, Rhode Island, rented or sold space in unused buildings to medically related organizations. In the years that followed, other hospitals have developed medical office buildings on their grounds, as well as a varied complex of enterprises such as intermediate care facilities, nursing homes, and boarding houses. Tax exemption usually requires exclusive use of hospital property for the purposes stated in the original incorporation presentation. Nevertheless, at least one court has recognized that related activities which contribute to the hospital's primary purpose are acceptable and held it could construct a professional office building on its land (Health Law Center, 1978).

The governing board of a hospital or community mental health center recruits and appoints the administrator, who is its employed agent. The qualifications, authority, and duties of the administrator should be specified in the bylaws of the facility.

The board, usually with the concurrence of the medical or staff executive committee, adopts bylaws and procedures which include criteria for selection of professional staff. The medical or clinical executive committee should recommend for appointment and reappointment those qualified by training and performance. It may also after careful study and appraisal recommend that a professional staff member not be reappointed or that his services be terminated. (Such an action must follow the procedures of due process—notice, right to be represented by counsel, confrontation of evidence that serves as the basis for the action, and appeal.)

Extent of professional privileges may also be defined. There is clear recognition in law of the need for evaluation of staff performance for the protection of the public. Rulings have tended to protect administrators and boards from charges of libel and slander if their actions were supported, for cause, and without malice.

A member of the governing board shares in full responsibility for any action which that body takes, and which he did not actively oppose, as recorded in the transactions of the governing body.

The governing body also has a duty to protect the property from damage, whether by vandalism or other destructive loss. This extends also to loss from the negligent acts of those it employs.

The governing body has a duty to employ enough persons to cover emergency and standby situations as well as to maintain day-to-day standards of care.

The administrator is usually responsible only to the governing body, or to the appointing authority, for in some states in public mental hospital systems, boards recommend the selection of an administrator and the Department of Mental Health appoints. In some public systems, there are no boards of control.

The administrator usually has a voice in policy determination (in proprietary or private mental hospitals he/she may also be the owner of the institution).

The administrator must be competent and qualified at the level of statutory requirements. It is expected that he/she will carry out management tasks in such a manner as to minimize both injury through fault or negligence of staff and invasion of patients' rights. He/she will also insure supervision and accountability for staff performance.

Medical Staff Appointments

The standards for accreditation (Joint Commission, 1979, 1980, 1981) specify that the governing body shall delegate to the medical staff authority to evaluate the professional competence of medical staff members and applicants for staff privileges. The medical staff is responsible to the governing board for the achievement and maintenance of high standards of medical practice.

The medical or clinical staff through its bylaws establishes a procedure for evaluating applications and for granting staff privileges. For example, minimal standards for medical staff appointment to a psychiatric facility include:

1. A degree of doctor of medicine from a medical school acceptable to the Coordinating Council on Medical Education.

2. Graduates of a medical school outside the U.S. or Canada must pass the Visa Qualifying Examination (VQE) or parts I and II of the National Board Examination and be competent in oral and written English (PL 94–484, January 10, 1977).

3. Evidence of satisfactory completion of an internship and/or residency in an approved training program listed in the Directory of Residency Training Programs (AMA, 1979–1980).

4. A valid license to practice medicine in the state. This license in some jurisdictions requires regular renewal, evidence of continuing education, and registration of license in town or county.

5. Evidence of competency in the specialty of designation as demonstrated by a certificate of an American Board such as Psychiatry and Neurology, issued after successfully passing a qualifying examination. As this is written, many psychiatrists are not so certified and acceptance is judged by evidence of satisfactory completion of three years in an approved residency program with additional clinical experience and satisfactory references. General membership in the American Psychi-

atric Association is granted after evaluation by peers upon evidence required above.

6. Evidence of good character and ethical practice.

7. Sometimes membership in local and state medical societies is a requirement, as may be citizenship or evidence of interest and action to become one. Sex, race, creed, color, or national origin may not be the basis for denial of medical staff membership.

8. Evidence of competence, a specified length of experience, and special training may be required for staff privileges in certain areas such as child psychiatry or forensic psychiatry, and for such posts as director of residency training and a supervisor of long-term psychotherapy.

Other Staff Appointments

Licensure, certification, or registration may be required for staff appointments in a psychiatric facility for other mental health professionals. While one may practice as a nurse without a license, one may not be designated an R.N. without having been registered after an examination. Similarly a psychologist may not call himself a clinical psychologist or practice as one without qualifying by certification or license in most jurisdictions.

No purpose is served by repeating required details of medical or clinical staff organization and responsibility, or of the standards for the services that must be available to patients both in direct treatment and in support. They are covered in full in the accreditation manuals for psychiatric facilities, which every top-level administrator must study (Joint Commission, 1979, 1980, 1981).

No one element in the triad of authority represented by the triangle in Figure 6–1 can unilaterally make policy for the hospital or facility. To effect change all three elements must be in agreement. All three are united in a single purpose—to provide the best possible patient service. Yet the governing body of a voluntary hospital may be legally responsible for the duty of providing a service which it has no organizational means to render (Guest, 1972).

The governing body in a general hospital appoints the administrator and upon recommendation makes appointments to the medical staff.

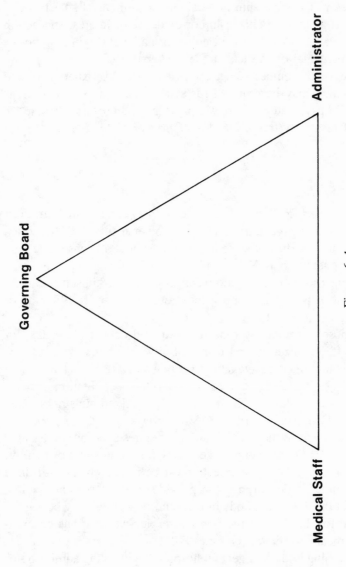

Figure 6–1
The Triad of Authority: Common in hospital administration

The physicians, however, are not paid by the facility (exception: salaried department heads who are physicians). Their contractual arrangements are with the patient served, whose advocates they are. The administrator cannot exercise line control over the physician; there is no legal authority that permits one to tell doctors how to practice. The resources the physician needs in equipment, special facilities, and personnel are under the control of the administrator. Cooperation of members of the triad is therefore essential to its operation. Negotiation and persuasion are tools in the process of securing agreement. The medical staff executive committee is the medical staff unit that relates to administrator and governing body. To involve physicians in the management process, appointment to the governing body has been urged as essential. Linkage is also facilitated when members of each element meet with the other. However, many physicians would shun an active role in governance. They prefer to retain their status as patient advocate.

Mental hospitals with salaried staff may have the same triad of responsibility or a very different one. For example, they may have no legal requirement for a governing body; if the administrator is a psychiatrist, he or she heads a hierarchy of colleagues.

Community mental health centers and other mental health agencies frequently have an organizational structure in which mental health professionals are in charge of its major subsystems. The psychiatrist may have a defined role which limits his function to the diagnosis and treatment of physical and mental illnesses and a consultation-liaison function. We have elsewhere discussed organizational structure, community mental health centers, and the roles of the psychiatrist (Barton and Barton, 1983).

RECENT LAWS AND COURT ACTIONS OF SPECIAL CONCERN TO
PSYCHIATRIC FACILITIES

Control of Drugs and Alcohol

The Federal Drug Abuse Prevention and Control Act of 1970 consolidated into one omnibus law scattered legislation controlling various drugs. The Act has five schedules based on relative potential for abuse, safety, and likelihood of developing dependence. Schedule I lists those regarded as most dangerous; the higher the number of the schedule the less dangerous and less severe the penalty for any violation. Illegal sale or distribution may call for penalties that range up to fifteen years for a violation in the control of a schedule I drug and up to one year for violation in handling a schedule II drug. The judge is allowed discretion to impose a fine, or to allow probation instead of a prison term.

Mental health facilities must register and must file a physical inventory of drugs on these schedules every two years. While not required, a perpetual inventory is suggested for schedule I drugs. A registered dispensing unit must keep its separate inventory.

Controlled substances must be dispensed only on a physician's order (or doctor's order sheet for any patient).

Controlled drugs must be protected against theft or diversion. This requires responsible monitoring and procedures for accountability. Narcotics are protected in a safe in the pharmacy and in a locked box in locked containers. Similarly, other controlled drugs are kept in locked cabinets. Daily the inventory is checked against orders on all schedule I drugs. Drugs are administered by trained personnel under a physician's supervision. Procedure should call for an automatic stop order and review at regular intervals in any prolonged use. Self-administration of drugs by patients is permitted when specifically ordered by the patient's physician. Quantities issued should be limited to a safe minimum. Similar controls are needed on tax-free alcohol locked storage, with all withdrawals recorded and reports at stated intervals of stock on hand.

While describing safeguards, it would be well to note here the responsibility in every mental health facility to safeguard poisonous substances that could be used for suicidal purposes or may be carelessly left about for a mental patient to ingest. Containers for all poisonous substances must bear a distinctive label that describes the contents and indicates their poisonous nature. Only that amount of poisonous substance needed for a specific purpose is issued for immediate use. No secondary storage should be permitted in ward or other patient areas. All poisons must be stored in a locked compartment, not a place used for storage of drugs or foodstuffs.

Refusal of Treatment

In New Jersey (Rennie v. Klein), and in Massachusetts (Rogers v. Okin), the right to refuse treatment has been upheld by the courts. A class action suit at the Boston State Hospital was entered to stop the use of medication and seclusion when patients refused them and there was no emergency. The defendants argued that patients, who were held under civil commitment, were not competent to decide whether the treatment was necessary or not. They maintained that a constitutional right to refuse treatment did not exist.

On October 29, 1979, the U.S. District Court, Judge Tauro, presiding, "held that voluntary and involuntary committed patients in state mental institutions are presumed competent to make decisions with respect to their medical treatment and unless adjudicated incompetent have a constitutional right to refuse forced antipsychotic medication and seclusion in nonemergency situations (*MMS Newsletter,* 1981). The court held there is an obligation to make treatment available but not to impose it. During the four years the court was deliberating, Boston State Hospital physicians applied for incompetency rulings when patients refused medication.

The decision of the District Court was substantially modified on November 25, 1980 by the First Circuit Court of Appeals. The court stated medical treatment decisions are to be made by a qualified physician while the court's role is limited to the design of procedures to insure protection of the patients' interests. It asked the District Court "to fashion a procedural mechanism whereby medical judgment can be made in a manner consistent with due process." The court attempted to balance patient rights and needs in a mental hospital. Awaited is the District Court's standards for insuring that patients' interests are protected and that antipsychotic medication and seclusion are not forcibly administered without a finding by a qualified physician that those interests are outweighed in a particular situation and that less restrictive alternatives are unavailable. It will still be necessary to review the treatment history and adhere to court-developed standards when making a decision a patient would make for himself if competent.

Every patient should be encouraged to consent to treatment and should be informed of the risks and benefits of what is recommended. It is well to make the patient as full a partner in the responsibilities for compliance with a therapy as his capabilities will allow. The psychiatric facility has the obligation to have a written policy for the use of medications and seclusion, which should take into account the hazards of prescribing them without the patient's consent.

Withholding Treatment

In chapter 3 we noted the ruling of the Supreme Judicial Court of Massachusetts, in Supt. of Belchertown State School v. Saikewicz, that the decision to either continue or to withhold artificial life support systems in a dying patient was to be made by the court. The court stated that physicians, families and patients, and hospital committees are not to make life-and-death decisions. However, in the Dinnerstein case (also discussed in chapter 3), the Massachusetts Appeals Court said further judicial approval need be sought only where the treatment in question has "some reasonable expectation of effecting a permanent or temporary relief from the illness being treated."

While there is doubt that the court rulings in Massachusetts or in California have general applicability nationally, they are representative of the erosion of medical decision making and the weakening of the doctor-patient relationship. Instead we see the substitution of a one-sided advocacy of freedom by civil liberty lawyers with no advocate to represent the patient's need for appropriate treatment (Stone, 1979b).

The institution can issue "Do Not Resuscitate" orders when the patient is dying to allow death from natural cases. Court approval is to be sought when the treatment in question has some reasonable expectation of effecting a permanent or temporary cure or relief from the illness being treated. One cannot withhold treatment if there is any likelihood the patient can return to normal functioning and an integrated existence; in such instances the court is to be asked before treatment is withheld.

Limiting Treatment

Seclusion and restraint, intrusive treatments, overmedication, electroconvulsive therapy, behavior modification, and psychosurgery have all been the subject of court-ordered limitation in use. The intent is to safeguard patients from excessive or coercive use of certain treatments. The advocates pressing for limited use or abolition may be opposed to ECT or to pharmacotherapy.

Electroconvulsive therapy (ECT) is a standard medical treatment in general use throughout the country. There exist fairly specific indications for its use. Despite this, a 1974 California law forbade its use until all other appropriate treatment modalities have been exhausted; the law also required approval by a three-person review board (*Psychiatric News*, 1975). Fortunately for sound medical practice, the law was found unconstitutional.

A survey made in Massachusetts (Grosser, Pearsall, Fisher, and Geomonte, 1975) turned up excessive use of ECT in several private hospitals: ECT given to children as young as 9, and as many as 200 to 300 treatments given a single patient in a year. Efforts at control by statute were headed off to forestall the precedent of legislating the conditions of medical practice. A task force developed guidelines that restricted the use of ECT in children under 16, requiring in such cases the concurrence of two child psychiatrists, and that limited treatment in all patients to 35 treatments in a 12 month period. Monitoring insured compliance without the rigid and unwarranted delay of cumbersome legal procedures.

Legal reformers have proposed a change in informed consent (Stone, 1979a). This change would force doctors to give the patient enough knowledge to make him an equal bargaining partner. The principle is flawed, however, because evidence demonstrates that the majority of patients do not comprehend or retain the information; some are too anxious or dependent, others lack the capacity to make appropriate choices in their own interest.

Permit us a digression to explain our belief that the legislative and judicial route is not always the best way to correct a fault. The consequences of regulation subtract valuable time from patient service and remove the flexibility that individualized patient care demands. One of us in the 1930s and again in the 1950s studied European educational approaches and paid factory employment for mental patients. A major effort was made to translate the best of the European experience into practice in the United States. That endeavor succeeded in the VA system and in many progressive mental hospitals. Contracts were secured for work in shops by patients who were paid for their labor; patient-employees were hired for special tasks designed to prepare them for living outside the hospital. From their earnings, they paid for room and board at minimal rates, and they learned to manage their affairs. At the same time effort was accelerated to provide alternatives to hospitalization. The hospital stays of all patients were reviewed to move out all who could go into their own living quarters or into substitute families or group living. From this pressure for minimal use of hospitalization (reserving it for those who would benefit from it and with the consequent emphasis on short hospital stays, the pattern for the new hospital psychiatry began to emerge.

The courts have held (Wyatt v. Stickney) that no patient shall be required to perform labor which involves the operation and maintenance of the hospital. In Souder v. Brennan it was ruled the Fair Labor Standards Act applied to mental patients and that therefore fair payment should be made for their work. The institution must secure a certificate from the labor department for a work center, it must keep time and wage records, and must make deductions for income taxes and social security.

As a consequence of the concept that patients who work must be paid for their services, progressive institutions requested funds for an administrative unit to operate a patient worker payroll section. In a period of budget cutting no additional funding for the purpose was allowed. As a result, patients did not work and most were idle.

The chronically ill need a total program that includes something meaningful to do. Most who work in hospitals need intensive supervision and could not be employed in the competitive labor market. If they could, they likely would be out working. What was needed was not a legislative approach but one of professional education and leadership to bring antiquated mental hospital practices up to date. If any legislative battle should have been waged, it should have been a militant advocacy for ability and responsibility to appropriately treat each patient and to press upon society its obligation to supply the resources to make that goal possible.

MEDICAL RECORDS

In New York in 1975, the court ruled (Glotkin v. Miller) that regulations which apply uniformly to all may be used to deny the patient access to medical records that are property of the hospital. The right of patient access to his medical records was a topic of lively debate in 1980. We would not deny the patient this right; we in fact advocate patient right of access and would favor each individual's maintaining his own lifelong record which would be brought to the physician and to the hospital facility. We would also establish various needs to know, with patient concurrence on the uses for which information from his record is sought. We would advocate that tertiary records such as peer review and PSRO profiles on the work performance of individual physicians be protected by law and made undiscoverable.

DISCLOSURE OF INFORMATION ABOUT PATIENTS

Mental health facilities are asked every day to answer inquiries regarding patients. Relatives and friends ask for information; social agencies, other institutions, third-party payers, physicians, and attorneys also seek data. Sometimes the press wants information in instances where some spectacular incident has occurred or when the admission of a celebrity is suspected.

The basic principles to be followed are contained in these statements:

- Patient and therapist share in determining what shall be released, to whom, and for what purpose.
- The patient has a right to privacy.
- The need to know must be established.
- The patient's best interest is protected as far as possible.
- The patient (so long as he is not found incompetent by a court) has control over personal information, and his consent is required for release even to relatives or friends.

Mental health professionals, physicians, and institutions responsible for care of the patient and the patient's attorney may have as much data as is consistent with discharge of their responsibilities. This may be a copy of the complete record.

Insurance companies require data on which to judge the disorder within the provisions of their contract. This usually means they need to know the nature of the illness, its severity, onset, probable duration, and prescribed treatment, as well as detail of charges and the projected frequency of future visits for treatment. Copies of the record are not usually released. We do not condone the practice of insurance companies whereby their customers are made to sign a blanket waiver allowing unlimited access to the psychiatric record. Rather, we feel it appropriate that insurance carriers may be given the dates of visits, their length, the procedures carried out, prognosis, and diagnosis. Better yet, the insurance companies should ask for specific information which patients can obtain through a written request which they may then sign. The therapist's interest should not be to withhold information from the insurance company which they would need to justify payment of a claim, but rather to protect the patient's right to privacy. The insurance company should not be privy to the details of the patient's problems and their working through.

The press, investigating an incident that has attracted public attention, often involving the police, may be given a reasonable response to satisfy public interest. We suggest this response be in very general terms. Where these incidents involve suicide attempts, no statement should be made regarding motive or means, and no indication of progress given. Similarly, in cases of injury we advise no statement be given on how it was received or on probable outcome. We may describe the injury itself—fracture, head injury with unconsciousness, penetrating wound of abdomen—and may list condition as satisfactory or serious.

When in cases involving celebrities the press calls, we suggest telling the reporter his call will be returned. This serves two purposes. It verifies the legitimacy of the person on the other end of the phone, for one can call the "city desk" and ask for the reporter by name. Time also becomes available to discuss with the patient what he or she wishes to reveal. Sometimes it is sufficient simply to indicate the patient's presence for rest and relaxation or for examination.

Requests from outside agencies and facilities may be required in writing. The need to know and the patient's willingness to release information may then be established.

Videotaping, filming, or photographing patients requires an informed consent covering purpose, intended use, and the audience that will view the pictures. Signed statements of permission to photograph are essential. The wholesome trend toward full-face photographs of recognizable individuals is encouraged, for it admits the person to membership into a human society without concealment and without shame. It goes without saying that photographs are permitted only in the patient's interest and with full knowledge of the use to be made of the picture.

ABORTION

The startling conviction of Dr. Kenneth C. Edelin in Massachusetts in 1975 and his sentencing to one year of probation on a charge of manslaughter for an abortion performed at the request of a patient during the second trimester of pregnancy focused attention again on the uncertain legal status of abortions (*Medical World News,* 1975). The U.S. Supreme Court, in a test of the constitutionality of the Texas and Georgia abortion laws, found both laws unconstitutional and indicated what states could lawfully do. (The American Psychiatric Association filed a brief in support of the position the court was to take.) States cannot restrict abortion during the first trimester of pregnancy. The physician and the woman may make the decision for or against an abortion. States may legislate abortion in ways reasonably related to the health of the woman in the second trimester (fourth to sixth month) and may, if they choose, prohibit all abortion in the third trimester. The 1973 Supreme Court decision made invalid nearly all state abortion laws. Hospitals, psychiatrists, and mental health professionals who may be called upon to provide opinion as to the consequences of continued pregnancy on the health of a woman, will wish to be aware of the following:

1. Hospital personnel and physicians are not required to participate in the performance of abortions.

2. Government hospitals may be required to allow legal abortions under valid state laws.

3. Regulations should be developed that restrict abortions in conformance to state laws and that establish procedures for determining the effect on maternal health of continuation in the second trimester.

4. Some modification of law and regulation is essential to permit genetic screening that may lead to advice to abort early in the second

trimester. Amniocentesis is usually not reliable until at least the fifteenth week of pregnancy. Allowance must also be made for three weeks in which to develop cell cultures. This brings the time for decision on findings very close to deadline, particulary if estimates are faulty or if repeat cultures are necessary (*Medical World News,* 1975).

After 1977, Congress and state legislatures debated the wisdom of legislation to pay for abortion out of public funds (Berger, 1978). (About 270,000 of one million legal abortions in 1976 were paid for under Title XIX (Medicaid) or Title XX (Social Service.) In 1980 Congress denied payment of abortion from Medicaid funds and this was upheld by the U.S. Supreme Court.

STERILIZATION

The desire to limit family size or to have no children has increased the demand in males for vasectomy and in females for salpingectomy. Castration, removal of testes or ovaries, is not considered here since that procedure is related to removal of a diseased organ and not to statutes concerned with fertility control, which is the subject of this section. Psychiatrists and hospital administrators are involved in eugenic sterilization and in therapeutic sterilization.

Eugenic sterilization has one of two purposes: to prevent the transmission of hereditary defects or to prevent procreation by persons unable to care for the offspring (Springer, 1970; Health Law Center, 1978). Some states authorize sterilization in the mentally ill or mentally retarded and sometimes for sex offenders and habitual criminals. Where state statutes authorize eugenic sterilization, great care must be taken to carry out due process procedures such as: specific authority granted to facility administrator to carry out sterilization; notice to the person to be sterilized and, if incompetent or unable to understand a notice, to the responsible relative, guardian, or legal counsel; and hearing before a board to determine that sterilization is indicated. At the hearing the patient and his relatives, guardian, or counsel must be present. A period of up to thirty days should elapse between hearing and actual sterilization (longer if necessary) to allow ample opportunity for appeal of the decision.

Because therapeutic sterilization is justifiable upon evidence that a woman's life or health will be endangered if she is allowed to become pregnant, the psychiatrist is frequently a partner in the decision making, giving evidence of medical necessity and the possibility of mental illness in the event of pregnancy. All states recognize the necessity for medical and surgical treatment to preserve life and health, and no need exists for a specific statute on therapeutic abortion.

There are no laws which prohibit single persons of legal age from obtaining voluntary sterilization. Married persons should discuss the decision with the spouse. Only three states (Georgia, Virginia, New Mexico) require the spouse's consent. While the physician or hospital would not be liable for performing a sterilization at the request of a competent adult without the consent of the spouse, most physicians wisely require it, for a legal action between husband and wife could be entered. Courts have frequently struck down spousal consent requirements. Sometimes the spouse has deserted, or is irresponsible, vindictive, or incompetent.

The added safeguard of allowing thirty days to elapse after consent is obtained seemed wise, in order to permit deliberation on events that might revive the wish for another child: divorce with custody of the children to the spouse; death of spouse or children; remarriage and the desire to have a child to share with the new spouse.

AUTOPSY AND DONATION OF PARTS OF BODY

The performance of an autopsy is accepted as a standard of good hospital and medical practice. It advances medical knowledge of disease and should improve the precision of diagnosis and prescription of appropriate treatment. It may also provide evidence that death resulted from a crime, that an occupational disease existed that could be the basis for compensation, or that death occurred from a disorder compensable under an insurance policy. It can provide peace of mind for troubled relatives who desire certainty as to the cause of death.

Before the important issue of securing permission for autopsy can be addressed, it is necessary to explore who has the right to claim the body for burial. The uniformly recognized rule in this country is that "the person entitled to possession of a body for the purpose of burial has certain legally protected rights" (Health Law Center, 1978). Liability may occur if those rights are not observed. Some state statutes specify an order of priority based on closeness of kinship: spouse, child, parent, uncles and aunts, etc. Other states have laws that do not indicate priority but indicate that autopsy permission may be obtained from the person who claims the body for burial. Rarely, several will claim the right and it will fall to the hospital to determine which of these has the duty and priority of custody. The nearest of kin may be the criterion most useful.

The permision to make a postmortem examination may then be obtained in writing or set into writing after telephone conversation with the authorized person, who has been informed that a witness will confirm the conversation.

About half of the autopsy consent statutes allow authorization of an autopsy upon one's own body. A witnessed consent form should be obtained. While an increasing number of individuals accept the enlightened view of donating their corneas to an eye bank or donating other organs, many still regard solicitation of such permits before death as a gruesome business.

In states without an autopsy consent law and where no statute exists specifically permitting donation of parts or all of the body, we would recommend that the spouse confirm the consent of the patient (or where appropriate the nearest of kin), if that individual has a right to claim the body for burial. It is equally important to note that the person who gives consent to an autopsy may specify that it be limited, for example, to the abdomen, the head, or the thorax. An autopsy done under such a consent must not exceed the specified limitation. It will also be important to specify if organs may be removed, for there are court rulings of liability for failiure to return all organs to the body after examination. Separate consent for removal of organs from the body is required.

When a body is unclaimed for burial, a reasonable attempt must be made to reach responsible relatives. This is best done when the patient is admitted by a vigorous attempt to locate relatives and friends. Efforts to trace relatives after death should be made; if unsuccessful after twenty-four hours, an advertisement should be placed in local newspapers requesting relatives or friends of the individual to call immediately a phone number given in the ad. Most states have statutes that authorize the administrator of the facility to turn over unclaimed bodies to medical schools for educational and scientific purposes. The administrator then calls the designated person at the school for transportation and removal. If it is known the deceased was a veteran, the nearest Veterans Administration Center or benefit office may be called to assist in the disposition.

LABOR LAWS

The Labor Management Relations Act defines certain unfair labor practices and provides for hearings on complaints. The intent was to encourage employers to acknowledge the right of employees to organize and to bargain for their rights. The administrator must not interfere with the right of employees to organize or to bargain collectively.

The Equal Opportunity Employment Act prohibits discrimination on the basis of sex, race, color, religion, or national origin. Help wanted ads may not specify male or female, unless reasonable evidence can be shown that being of one or the other sex is an essential requirement of the job. The Girl Friday may become the Boy Friday, but the R.N. to be hired by a male physician examining disrobed women needs to be a female, and the want ad may reflect this.

An employee is engaged to render a service under the direction and control of the employer—the hospital or clinic (Hayt, Hayt, and Groeschel, 1972). This service is performed for wages, a salary, or a fee, and this constitutes a contract for hire. The employer retains the right to control the details of work in the area of designated skill. The employee agrees by acceptance of the job to (1) render loyal, efficient service for the full working period; (2) be ready for emergencies; (3) safeguard the welfare of patients; (4) follow instructions; (5) promote goodwill toward the hospital among patients and public; and (6) give reasonable notice of intent to leave.

The broadening of the 1938 Fair Labor Standards Act by Public Law 89–601 in 1967 included hospital employees but exempted professionals, executives, and administrators from the forty-hour provision. Its principal provisions are: forty-hour work week; a minimum wage; paid overtime for work in excess of eight hours; equal pay for equal work. Child labor laws set minimum age for employment. Equal opportunity legislation forbids discrimination by sex, race, color, creed, age, or national origin.

The Wagner-Walsh-Healy and Taft-Hartley Acts apply to hospitals and give employees the right to organize, establish provisions for election of a representative, and forbid the employer to interfere in ways to be described later. Amendments made in 1974 extended the application of the Act beyond hospitals to include other health service delivery facilities.

The administrator may not attempt to control the union or support one of two competing unions. Impartiality should be the rule, leaving the choice to the employees and offering equal opportunity to unions wishing to be certified as the collective bargaining agent. Sometimes a separate bargaining unit represents physicians, another the nurses, another maintenance employees, etc. There has also been a trend toward limiting the court's power to issue an injunction to interfere in labor disputes and to define the circumstances when an injunction may be granted to halt activities when they imperil patient care or when unlawful acts or property damage have occurred. About a third of the states have "right to work" laws which forbid closed shop contracts. Laws may also require the provision of a safe place to work. There are also laws in many states that restrict the employment of minors below a specified age. These may require presentation of a certificate to be able to work and may specify that minors not be put on the night tour of duty (Health Law Center, 1978).

SUMMARY

The ethical standards of an institution often exceed but must never be less than those required by law. The administrator has an obligation to be ethical in the conduct of personal and business affairs. The primary purpose of a facility or program for the mentally ill or retarded is the provision of quality care and treatment for patients or clients. The organization should merit the confidence of the public it serves.

The American Hospital Association's "Guidelines on Ethical Conduct for Health Care Institutions" require: available direct services of high quality and an interest in the health status of the people in the community it serves; the effective use of resources at its disposal; cooperation with other health agencies engaged in a common purpose; individualized care with respect for human dignity and for individual religious and social beliefs; creation and maintenance of high standards of performance and a safe, wholesome environment that fosters improvement; accountability to the public it serves; the practice of medicine with integrity; and the meriting of public trust.

The administrator accepts no gifts or favors which may influence decisions; is careful to avoid conflicts of interest; is open to complaints and is fair and just in their correction; maintains harmonious relationships; fulfills prescribed duties; and does not prolong the stay of patients for financial gain.

Laws and regulations of the local, state, and Federal governments require compliance. When a deficiency is identified it must be promptly corrected or resources must be requested to do so. Accreditation standards should be met. The staff should be competent to carry out assigned tasks, for the organization may be held liable for the wrongful acts of its employees under the concept of *respondeat superior*.

The responsibility of the administrator and of the governing body were noted. Professional staff credentials should be reviewed to insure they meet educational and experiential standards for the position to be filled.

As examples of laws pertinent to institutional management we cited the Federal Drug Abuse Control Act and the Fair Labor Standards Act. Court decisions on the right to refuse treatment or to withhold treatment, and the payment of patients who perform useful work were cited as examples.

The disclosure of information about patients is an ever-present issue involving many employees in an organization.

All of what follows in Part II on law is pertinent to this chapter. We have noted as examples in this chapter the relevance of ethical issues on abortion and sterilization.

QUESTIONS

1. What are four organizational obligations cited in the American Hospital Association's "Guidelines on Ethical Conduct for Health Care Institutions"?

2. Is it ethical for a mental health professional to own or have a financial interest in a hospital or facility?

3. Is it ethical for an administrator to accept financial support for the organization's continuing education program from a drug company?

4. Is it ethical to extend the period of care or treatment of individuals to increase the institution's income?

5. What are six principles in hospital or facility law?

6. How does the legal concept *respondeat superior* apply?

7. Describe the administrative triad and some of the stress points in facility governance.

8. What are minimal standards for medical staff appointments?

9. Under what circumstances may a patient perform work in a facility?

10. What are the guidelines for release of information on a facility patient?

11. What is the importance to facility management of the Wagner-Walsh-Healy and Taft-Hartley Acts and the 1974 amendments?

REFERENCES

* AHA (1974), "Guidelines on Ethical Conduct and Relationships for Health Care Institutions." Chicago: American Hospital Association.

AMA (1979–1980), *Directory of Residency Training Programs*. Chicago: American Medical Association.

* AMA (1981), *Judicial Council Opinions and Reports*. Chicago: American Medical Association.

Barton, W. E., & Barton, G. M. (1983), *Mental Health Administration: Principles and Practice*. New York: Human Sciences Press.

Berger, L. R. (1978), Abortions in America: The effect of restrictive funding. *N. Engl. J. Med.*, 298:1474–1477.

Burns, J. M. (1978), *Leadership*. New York: Harper Colophon.

* Code of Ethics (1975). Chicago: American College of Hospital Administrators.

Grosser, G. H., Pearsall, D. T., Fisher, C. L., & Geomonte, G. (1975), Regulation of ECT in Massachusetts: A follow-up. *Mass. J. Ment. Health*, 5:12–25.

Guest, R. H. (1972), The role of the doctor in institutional management. In: *Organization Research in Health Institutions*, ed. B. Georgopoulos. Ann Arbor: Institute for Social Research, University of Michigan.

* Hayt, E., Hayt, L. R., & Groeschel, A. H. (1972), *Law of Hospital, Physician and Patient*. 3rd. ed. Berwyn, Ill: Physicians Record Co.

* Health Law Center (1978), *Problems in Hospital Law*. 3rd ed. Rockville, Md.: Aspen Systems Corp.

Hospital Law Manual (1980), 3 volumes. Germantown, Md.: Aspen Systems Corp.

JAMA (1982), Telling the truth. *J. Amer. Med. Assn.*, 247:651–654.

* Joint Commision (1979), *Principles for Accreditation of Community Mental Health Service Programs.* Chicago: Joint Commission on Accreditation of Hospitals.

* Joint Commission (1980), *Accreditation Manual for Hospitals.* Chicago: Joint Commission on Accreditation of Hospitals.

* Joint Commission (1981), *Consolidated Standards for Child, Adolescent, Adult Psychiatric Alcoholism and Drug Abuse Programs.* Chicago: Joint Commission on Accreditation of Hospitals.

Klerman, G. (1980), Ethical administrative dilemmas at the Federal level. Paper presented at the NIMH Conference on Ethical Issues in Mental Health Policy and Administration, Bethesda, Md.

Maccoby, M. (1976), *The Leader: A New Face for American Management.* New York: Simon & Schuster.

Medical World News (1975), 16:6–7, March 10.

MMS Newsletter (1981), Rogers v. Okin: First Circuit modifies patients' right to refuse forced medication and seclusion. *Newsletter, Mass. Medical Society,* 21:7, January.

Psychiatric News (1975), 10:1, Feb. 5.

* Saklein, S., & Baron, J. (1978), *The Affirmative Action Handbook.* New York: Executive Enterprises Publication.

Schulberg, H. C., & McClelland, M. (1981), Ethical dilemmas. *Administration in Mental Health,* 9:20–32.

* Southwick, A. R. (1978), *The Law of Hospital and Health Care Administration.* Ann Arbor, Mich.: Health Administration Press.

Springer, E. W., ed. (1970), *Nursing and the Law.* Pittsburgh: Health Law Center, Aspen Systems Corp.

Stone, A. A. (1979a), Informed consent: Special problems for psychiatry. *Hosp. Community Psychiat.,* 30:321–327.

Stone, A. A. (1979b), The Myth of Advocacy, *Hosp. Community Psychiat.,* 30:819–822.

Part II
Law in Mental Health Administration

Chapter 7

Informed Consent

Concern for man himself and his fate must always form the chief interest of all technical endeavors.

—*Albert Einstein*

Case example. A woman, aged 73, was admitted to the hospital with depressed mood and a wish to die. The onset followed the death of her husband six months previously. She had been quite dependent upon him because of her blindness due to diabetic retinitis. Her grieving was followed by feelings of helplessness and then dread of being placed in a nursing home, as there were no relatives to turn to. Her depression deepened, she neglected her grooming, was sleepless, ate poorly and finally ingested pills from the medicine chest at home, hoping they would kill her. After being found by her neighbor, she was admitted to the local general hospital.

The psychiatrist asked the ward nurse to secure the patient's consent to taking tricyclic medication. The nurse described the drug treatment to the woman and the expected results. She read the consent form to the blind woman and helped the patient sign it. Was this an informed consent? May the physician delegate responsibility for explanation in the manner described?

145

The concept of informed consent has two very different roots. One is old, deep, and firmly fixed; the other new, shallow, and on unstable ground. *Voluntary consent* has been acknowledged for a very long time as a principle and prerequisite for a given treatment or procedure. Less certain is an informed agreement based on the principle of sharing with the patient information as to what will be done, why it is necessary, with what expected outcome, the risks and benefits, the alternative courses of action and their consequences with the intent to involve the individual as an equal partner in the decision making process. Obviously, the knowledge of the physician, the limited comprehension of the patient, the variability of response, and a host of other factors make this ideal difficult to achieve. The concept of partnership in decision making is sound. Trust in the competence of the physician usually leads the patient to accept the doctor's judgment that what is proposed is in the patient's best interest.

While written consent is not necessary it is good practice. Even when a verbal contract is made, it is best to document the agreement in the patient's clinical record.

Treatment of the patient without consent exposes the clinician to a potential charge of battery and, if the patient suffers harm, to a malpractice suit. Those who suffer an untoward event may seek compensation in the belief that if they had been told all the consequences, they would not have consented.

The distrust of authority and rebellion of the 1960s moved us toward a more open society. The courts articulated the goal of the consent process to be patient participation in treatment decisions with a fuller understanding of the relevant factors in making the decision whether to accept a specific treatment or procedure.

WHAT TO TELL?

In Cobb v. Grant (California, 1972) it was ruled that the physician was obligated to inform the patient of *all* benefits and risks which a "reasonable man" would need to know in order to make a "rational decision" with respect to submitting to the treatment. The "reasonable man" decision and the "rational decision" in the above ruling pose problems. The chronic psychotic patient may not be such a person or be capable of rational choice. The court is correct, however, in stating the principle that the patient's participation in the decision making process requires enough information about risks and benefits to make a choice between a proposed treatment, alternative courses of action, and no treatment.

In Small v. Gifford Memorial Hospital (1975), the Vermont Supreme Court held "it is the duty of the physician, in terms of Informed Consent, to give a patient whose situation otherwise permits it, *all* information material to the decision to undergo the proposed treatment." The charge to give "all information" is not based upon what the physician feels is reasonable or what conforms to what other doctors do, but is to be determined by what a reasonable patient would feel is significant. Because the ruling created a vague standard of care to be applied on a case by case basis, the Vermont Medical Society urged clarifying legislation. The statute as passed established the standard as what physicians in a similar type of practice and under similar circumstances would do, and what a reasonable practitioner would have disclosed to help the patient make a knowledgeable decision.

In Canterbury v. Spence (1972) the decision for a neurosurgeon was reversed upon appeal because the patient was not informed of a 1 percent risk of paralysis following a laminectomy. The court thereby included the requirement that information be given concerning infrequent complications. The court added that "dependence upon the physician for information affect his well-being in terms of contemplated treatment is well-nigh abject. . . . He cannot possibly make a reasoned decision without being told what the physician intends to do and why, what the alternatives are and what the probability of success and the risks may be" (Rennie, 1980).

Most patients can take bad news without becoming upset. However, some are made so anxious that they become unable to objectively weigh the risks and benefits. The physician always faces the reality that the information given will be judged from hindsight as to whether it was sufficient and understood, and also the prospect that what was said may be later repudiated because of psychiatric illness present at the time.

In Kaimowitz v. Michigan Department of Mental Health, psychosurgery was prohibited because a prisoner was incapable of giving a legally valid informed consent. The prisoner, Doe, was confined under an indeterminate sentence, charged with murder and rape. He had given informed consent and a Human Rights Review Committee found his consent met required criteria. The subject was chosen for the procedure in a research study of uncontrollable violence to be treated by ablation of part of the amygdala. If an individual, involuntarily confined, cannot give a legally valid, informed consent to experimental psychosurgery, then the rule has wide application both to this surgical procedure and to any other treatment modality. As Ralph Slovenko (1978) has written, "Contemporary law, having marched up the hill, formulating a rule on informed consent, then marches down, with exceptions, and the doctor is left not knowing where he stands."

Prisoners, children, and mental patients pose a special problem when held involuntarily. If the patient is free to leave the facility, the concern expressed here is of no consequence. It is relevant if there exists any direct or even subtle connection between the granted consent and its bearing on release from the institution now or later. Most mental patients are competent to make a free choice. Some may not be. The spouse or the nearest of kin may share in the decision. In the case of a minor, a parent's consent as well as the minor's is wise. When there is a legal guardian that person's consent is necessary. It is hindsight that gives the court and jury a different perspective from the here and now of the clinical setting. Long after the fact, a judgment is made that the consent given was or was not an informed one (Mills, 1974).

Consent is asumed in a life-threatening emergency when the patient is either physically or mentally unable to comprehend or respond to questions. Parents may give permission for the treatment of minors and guardians for those adjudicated incompetent. Consent may be either verbal or implicit in the patient's action, as when the sleeve is rolled up to receive an injection (MMS, 1974). Jurisdictions that have ruled on consent acknowledge the patient's right to know and the physician's duty to inform. The doctor may not rely upon others to give the information but must convey it in person. The same is true when one is a consultant carrying out a procedure already explained by a referring physician. Consent once given may also be withdrawn.

SOME ADDITIONAL PROBLEMS

Variability of Response

Scientific error arises not only from the limitations of the present state of the art or from the negligence or ineptitude of the clinician, but also from the inability to predict what a particular treatment or procedure will do to a unique individual under a variety of circumstances beyond physician control. The best possible judgment of the physician may prove erroneous. Individual reactions are variable and unpredictable.

> What patients and the public have to learn is to recognize, accept, and respond reasonably to the necessary fallibility of the individual physician. The physician-patient relationship has to be redefined as one in which necessarily mistakes will be made, sometimes culpably, sometimes because of the state of development of the particular medical sciences at issue, and sometimes inevitably because of the inherent limitations of the predictive powers of an enterprise that is concerned essentially with the flourishing of particulars of individuals. [Gorovitz and MacIntyre, 1975]

Unavoidable Accidents and Unreasonable Expectations

In a procedure monitoring sleep in an NIMH sleep laboratory considered to be of very low, even negligible risk, a 23-year-old female was found dead in the morning, presumably of cardiac arrest. Investigation revealed a four-year history of heart difficulty she had concealed from the investigators (Elliot, 1980).

Even with care taken to explain risks and expected benefits, unavoidable accidents may occur. Examples include the following: a patient given disulfiram as aversive therapy for alcoholism tested his tolerance for liquor and in the violent vomiting that followed suffered a detached retina; a patient with delirium tremens under medical therapy was given a paraldehyde enema which resulted in acute severe proctitis.

Until recently, people were exposed to the threat of dread diseases such as polio, meningitis, infectious diseases, septicemia, tuberculosis, and others. Many persons now reach adulthood, notes Osmond (1980), without ever having suffered a life-threatening illness. In the day of miracle drugs, advanced technology, and TV doctors who overcome every obstacle, one expects scientific medicine to produce in every case a quick and certain cure. In an earlier day there was an awesome respect for illness, and the physician was honored not as an omnipotent being but as a dedicated partner in the struggle for survival.

Limitation of Comprehension

Pain, discomfort, inability to concentrate, memory impairment, profound depression, delirium, dementia, preoccupation with hallucinations or delusions, and cognitive impairment are symptoms encountered in mental disorders. All interfere with the comprehension of consent forms and the oral explanations intended to assist the patient in making an informed agreement. Other factors which limit comprehension, in addition to mental status (related to inadequate recall) are education and the care with which patients read the consent form. In a study of 200 patients by Cassileth, Zupkis, Sutton-Smith, and March (1980), a test of the recall of the consent form and oral explanation was given. Sixty percent understood the purpose and nature of the procedure and 55 percent could correctly list one major complication or risk. Only 40 percent read the form carefully. Most believed the purpose of the informed consent was to protect the physician.

Most consent forms are written in legal language and fail to pass readability tests. Grunder (1980) analyzed five representative forms with two standardized readability tests to ensure the average patient could understand them. Four of the five were written at the level of a scientific journal and one at the level of an academic magazine. To be understood by the average person, they need to be written in simple language at the high school student's level.

In addition, Katz, Capron, and Glass (1972) have described some inherent barriers to informed consent. The achievement of an expression of "free will" is often hindered by unconscious motivation or subtle external pressures; rational decision making can be compromised by transference, countertransference, or psychological regression; and comprehension can be precluded by failures of communication and understanding.

The way information is presented to patients also influences their choice between alternative therapies. McNeil, Pauker, Sox, and Tversky (1982) presented a group of 238 ambulatory patients, 491 graduate students, and 424 physicians a theoretical situation of lung cancer and the choice of surgery or radiation as a proposed treatment. The information on which the choice was to be made was supplied in several ways. With some subjects the two therapies were not named but simply designated A and B. In addition, survival rates and life expectancy data were presented to separate groups in different ways: positively, as probability of living; and negatively, as probability of dying. Surgery was preferred over radiation when the two therapies were named and when the information was framed in terms of probability of living rather than chances of dying. It is evident that the quality of the patient's decision making can be improved by the way information is presented and the nature of the data. What is evident from the studies cited is that truly informed consent is an ideal seldom achieved.

Twenty-six states have specific statues on informed consent. Several states (Delaware, Idaho, Nebraska, New Hampshire, North Dakota, and Tennessee) specify the need to supply "only such information as disclosed by physicians similarly situated and with similar training and experience." A modified standard adopted in Florida, Kentucky, Maine, and North Carolina requires disclosure "in accordance with an accepted standard of practice and presented so that a reasonable person would have understanding." Two states (New York and Vermont) add the requirement that information be disclosed regarding risks and alternative modes of treatment. Several states (Pennsylvania, Washington, Texas, Ohio, Alaska, Oregon, Utah, Iowa, Hawaii, and Louisiana) add that the disclosure must cover the nature and purpose of the procedure and "reasonably known risks" (Miller, 1980).

Although state statutes on informed consent usually refer to physicians, they apply with equal force to mental health professionals and administrators who are responsible for the diagnosis and treatment of patients or clients.

Does a Child or Adolescent Have the Right to Consent?

A rule in common law holds that if a physician treats an unemancipated minor, even without negligence and even if the treatment leads to a satisfactory result, the parents can bring a legal action for assault and battery. (An emancipated minor is one not subject to parental control. Usually the minor does not live at home, is self-supporting, is a runaway, in the military service, or married.) The rule holds today in all nonemergency situations involving very young children, but does not apply in most situations involving adolescents (Holder, 1980).

Most states have enacted statutes for the treatment of minors between the ages of 14 and 18. Ten states (Delaware, Louisiana, Maine, Maryland, Massachusetts, Minnesota, Montana, Nevada, Utah, and Vermont) have laws requiring parents be informed when clinicians treat minors. The other forty have statutes that do not specifically require this. All states permit physicians to *treat* minors for venereal disease without parental consent. However, parents must be *informed* about venereal disease care in fifteen states (Alabama, Alaska, Arizona, Connecticut, Idaho, Indiana, New Mexico, North Dakota, Ohio, Pennsylvania, Rhode Island, South Carolina, Washington, Wisconsin, and Wyoming). Two more states have a variation of the duty to inform: South Dakota requires parents be informed when the clinician is not working in a public agency, and Vermont law makes it necessary to inform parents only when venereal disease is found. Statutes change so it is well to keep abreast of the law.

It is important to note that about forty states have laws which permit the treatment of minors without parental consent under specified conditions. The child must be mature enough to understand both the nature of the predicament and the consequences of treatment. The recognition of the child's right of privacy encourages treatment, for example, of venereal disease. If the right to consent is acknowledged, so also must be the right to refuse.

WHAT IS REQUIRED

Canons

The right to physical integrity and self-determination is expressed as the right of a person to determine what will be done with his or her body. There shall be informed participation between the physician and any patient who has the legal capacity to give consent and who is free to exercise choice.

Ethical Guidelines

The patient's right to know is recognized as well as the physician's duty to inform as to the risks and benefits or probable consequences of no treatment. The development of an understanding decision shall be based upon a reasonable explanation of the facts essential to a free choice among alternatives.

Rules

Participation in the decision making process requires a fair explanation of the nature of the treatment or procedure, its purposes, the methods to be employed, what discomforts or inconveniences the patient may experience, the more frequent complications, risks, and hazards, and the likelihood of their occurrence. Alternative courses of action may also be described, along with their probable consequences (ACOG, 1974). Emphasis is upon "informed participation" with mutual discussion of all material information (including alternative treatment options and possible outcomes) necessary to arrive at a decision.

"Legal capacity" becomes important in those who are mentally ill or retarded and in children. The phrase "freedom to exercise choice" alerts one to the special circumstances of the individual who is confined against his will in a mental hospital or prison. The "material information" includes the nature of the procedure, its purpose, methods to be employed, possible discomforts or inconveniences, the risks or hazards, and the likelihood of their occurrence. Relevant alternative procedures may be described, along with their anticipated outcomes and the consequences of choosing one treatment over another.

SUGGESTIONS FOR ACTION

Persons shall be admitted to a medical facility when there is informed consent by the patient, in an emergency where consent is implied, or upon a court order.

The patient's informed consent shall be obtained for procedures and treatment. The consent form should be readable and understandable by the average person. (It has been proposed that package inserts on prescribed drugs be given patients, yet in their present form they are nearly incomprehensible to the average individual.)

An oral explanation in simple language should be given by the therapist. Printed sheets, if comprehensible, may serve to cover the usual complications and risks.

An interesting approach to these problems is a two-part informed consent form suggested by Miller and Willner (1974). The first part resembles the usual consent form. It states the purpose for which consent is requested, the procedure and method, the possible discomfort, inconvenience, risks, and hazards, the alternative courses of action open, and, in the case of experimental procedures, any benefits that may ensue as well as the right to withdraw consent at any time. The second part of the form is a list of questions designed to determine how well the information has been understood. The number of questions used varies with the complexity of the procedure. Six areas are covered: benefits, any departure from ordinary medical practice, risks, inconvenience and discomfort, purpose, and rights the patient may exercise. For example, the question on risk asks, "Are there any dangers to you from the procedure to which you have consented? If so, what are they?" The patient's answers to such questions may then be used as a basis for further discussion to ensure communication and understanding.

SUMMARY

It has been traditional for physicians to secure voluntary consent of the patient for treatment and procedures. Added recently is a new requirement that there be an informed agreement which would make the patient an equal partner in the decision making process.

In Cobb v. Grant, the court held that the physician is obligated to inform the patient of *all* the benefits and risks which a reasonable man would need to know in order to make a rational decision with respect to submitting to treatment. The problem of how much to tell was not resolved in Small v. Gifford, where the ruling stated it was necessary to give all the information material to the decision making process. In Canterbury v. Spencer a decision called for information of a 1 percent risk. Kaimowitz v. Michigan concerned the risk of a procedure where all safeguards and review had been carefully followed. The court held a prisoner incapable of giving a legally valid, informed consent. The decision raised the question, Can any individual involuntarily confined give an informed consent?

Some of the problems highlighted were the high degree of variability of response (even aspirin, a relatively safe drug, can harm a few, and common vaccines can produce rare adverse reactions); unavoidable accidents; unreasonable expectations of cure; limitation of comprehension; unconscious motivation; and competence of children, adolescents and emancipated minors. If a right to consent exists, there is also a right to refuse treatment.

The right to physical integrity and self-determination implies the right of a person to determine what will be done with his or her body. There shall be informed participation between the physician and any patient who has the legal capacity to give consent and the freedom to exercise choice. The right of the patient to know is recognized as well as the physician's duty to inform.

What is required is a fair explanation of the nature of the treatment or procedure, its purpose, the methods to be employed, the discomforts or inconveniences one may expect, the risks and benefits, and the likelihood of their occurrence. Alternative courses of action and their consequences may also be described.

QUESTIONS

1. What is the intent of the concept of informed consent?
2. What did the court rule in Cobb v. Grant? in Canterbury v. Spencer? in Kaimowitz v. Michigan?
3. What information must one give to a severely depressed person for whom tricyclic antidepressants are proposed?
4. Can a physician accept the consent of a 15-year-old adolescent? Under what conditions is the consent valid?
5. Define informed consent.
6. What procedures should be established to ensure there is informed consent?

REFERENCES

ACOG (1974), Informed consent statement of the American College of Obstetrics and Gynecology.

* Barton, W. E., & Sanborn, C. J., (1978), *Law and the Mental Health Professions,* chaps. 3 & 4. New York: International Universities Press.

Cassileth, B. R., Zupkis, R. V., Sutton-Smith, K., & March, V. (1980), Informed consent: Why are its goals imperfectly realized? *N. Engl. J. Med.,* 302:890–900.

Elliott, J. (1980), Trouble at NIMH. *AMA News,* May 2, p. 2.

Gorovitz, S., & MacIntyre, J. (1975), Toward a theory of medical fallibility distinguishing culpability from necessary errors. In: *Hastings Center Report 5,* pp. 13–23.

Grunder, T. M. (1980), On the readability of surgical consent forms. *N. Engl. J. Med.,* 302:900–902.

Holder, A. R. (1980), Informed consent and the adolescent patient. *Malpractice Digest,* Jan./Feb., pp. 1–2.

* Katz, J. (1981), Disclosure and consent in psychiatric practice: Mission impossible? In: *Law and Ethics in the Practice of Psychiatry,* ed. C. K. Hofling. New York: Brunner/Mazel.

Katz, J., Capron, A. M., & Glass, E. S. (1972), *Experimentation with Human Beings,* pp. 521–724. New York: Russell Sage Foundation.

McNeil, B. J., Pauker, S. G., Sox, H. C., & Tversky, A. (1982), On the evaluation of preference for alternative therapies. *N. Engl. J. Med.,* 306:1259–1262.

Miller, L. J. (1980), Informed consent. *J. Amer. Med. Assn.,* 244:2556–2558.

Miller, R., & Willner, H. S. (1974). The two part consent form: A suggestion for promoting free and informed consent. *N. Engl. J. Med.,* 290:964–966.

Mills, D. H. (1974), Whither informed consent? *J. Amer. Med. Assn.,* 229:305–310.

MMS (1975), *Professional Liability Guide.* Boston: Massachusetts Medical Society.

Osmond, H. (1980), God and the doctor. *N. Engl. J. Med.,* 302:555–558.

Rennie, D. (1980), Informed consent by "well-nigh abject" adults. *N. Engl. J. Med.,* 302:917–918.

* Rosoff, A. J. (1980), *Informed Consent: A Guide For Health Care Providers.* Gaithersberg, Md.: Aspen Systems.

* Slovenko, R. (1973), *Psychiatry and Law.* Boston: Little, Brown.

Slovenko, R. (1978), Psychotherapy and informed consent: A search in judicial regulation. In: *Law and the Mental Health Professions,* ed. W. E. Barton & C. G. Sanborn. New York: International Universities Press.

Chapter 8

Confidentiality

> Whatsoever, in the course of practice, I see or
> hear (or even outside of my practice in social
> intercourse) that ought never to be published
> abroad, I will not divulge but will consider such
> things to be holy secrets.
> —*Oath of Hippocrates (5th Century* B.C.*)*

Case example. The pastor of a local church identifies your patient as
a member of his parish. He states he is presently seeing the mother
in counseling sessions once a week. He asks for details as to the nature
of the illness, attitude toward both parents, the role of parents in the
patient's illness, your treatment, and the expected outcome. Do you
supply the answers? What steps do you take to assist the clergyman?

There is confusion in the field about the definition of confidentiality.
Some use confidentiality and privilege as if they were synonyms.
Confidentiality is the ethical understanding that the clinician will keep
a patient's secrets and not disclose what is said to anyone else. *Privilege*
is the right of the patient to privacy. A patient may bar the clinician
from testifying about the treatment or may wish to waive this privilege
and request that the mental condition which led to treatment be revealed. The "all-or-none" tradition of the courts creates the problem.

157

Waiver of privilege makes all the records available, not just the evidence desired. The patient, not knowing what is in the record, may desire to present some facts and leave others out. The reasonableness of this view has led to the adoption of the concept of "relevance of material to the issue at hand."

"The legal duty of confidentiality or secrecy is the obligation not to release information about a client or patient without his or her permission except when divulgence is required by law" (Slovenko, 1973). The law holds that in certain exceptional instances the ethical tradition of the clinician and the right of privacy of the patient may be abrogated for the greater good of society. English common law early recognized that justice could not be done unless there was absolute privilege between client and lawyer. The struggle for a similar privileged relationship with the clergy, the physician, the psychotherapist, the spouse, and the news reporter has not ended. The search continues for a reasonable balance between confidentiality and the legitimate needs of a complex society for information.

PERSPECTIVES: PAST AND PRESENT

In 1606 Father Henry Garnet, a Jesuit priest, was hanged in England because he refused to divulge what was told him in the confessional. His conviction was on criminal grounds of complicity in a plot to assassinate James I (Slawson, 1969).

The first physician-patient privilege rule was made in England in 1776, when a surgeon was compelled to reveal personal information about his patient that was not relevant to his services. In a bigamy case involving the Duchess of Kingston, her surgeon was asked to tell the court whether the Duchess had admitted to an earlier marriage.

In 1828 New York state enacted the first medical privilege law in the U.S. It fostered frank revelation by patients in a situation of complete trust in the physician. In the 1952 case of Binder v. Ruvell, a husband accused another man of stealing his wife's affection. The wife had instituted divorce proceedings. The husband's attorney subpoenaed hospital records and sought an order to compel Roy Grinker, Sr., M.D., to testify concerning information obtained during the wife's psychotherapy. Dr. Grinker refused to testify. At the time, no Illinois law protecting confidentiality existed. The court's decision recognized the importance of confidential relationships as different in psychiatry from that in general medicine and ruled that communications between the wife and her psychiatrist was privileged, as were the records.

For forty years now, third parties have eroded the confidential doctor-patient relationship. With the development of health insurance has come the demand for information for the administration of contracts. If the insurance company is to reimburse for medical expenses, it needs to know that a psychiatric disorder is present, when it began, the nature and frequency of treatment, and the fees charged. However, a blanket waiver signed by the patient upon application for insurance frequently accompanies a demand for a copy of the medical record.

The family has always been a third party requesting information. It was the psychiatrist or mental health professional who determined what information should be disclosed in the patient's interest. Schools also request information, for the purpose of modifying programs to the child's benefit. Employers seek to learn about the emotional health of workers when this becomes relevant to performance in a job. And of course company insurance plans require the same basic data other carriers do.

To meet these demands and for other purposes, records expanded as more and more data was collected. For the past twenty years computers have been used to store records and supply information. The insurance industry established the Medical Information Bureau as a center for hundreds of carriers. The Multi-State Information System accumulated psychiatric data for the states it served. Millions of health records found their way into Social Security computers for those receiving service under Medicare and Medicaid. People began to be aware that there were computer networks not only for health care for groups such as migrant workers, but also for information regarding crimes and credit. We leave computerized tracks when we fly, rent a car, or get a hotel room. Gradually the public developed an awareness that others not concerned with health care had access to confidential data. Data collected for one purpose was used for another through linkages and leakages between computer systems.

The psychiatric profession was shocked out of its indifference to these developments by two related incidents. The first was a break-in by snoopers and character assassins into the office of Dr. Lewis Fielding, a psychiatrist who had been treating Daniel Ellsberg. Ellsberg, who had access to secret documents, had outraged government officials when he released material to the press. The other incident occurred at the Senate Watergate hearings, when John Ehrlichman, testifying before the television cameras, seemed unaware that any wrong had been done in this breach of a psychiatrist's files. Further, he suggested that anyone in a white coat could walk onto a hospital ward and read any case record he had a mind to. The smouldering issue of confidentiality burst into flame, and the various medical specialities scrambled to bring it under control.

Confidentiality, as it is traditionally understood, no longer exists according to Siegler (1982). He says, that in a hospital, some 25 to 100 professional and administrative personnel may have a legitimate need to use the patient's clinical record. Access to information in it may be needed by attending physicians, consultants, house officers, nurses, pharmacists, students, unit secretaries, financial officers, record reviewers and various others. In circumstances such as these it is almost impossible to insure confidentiality (Siegler, 1982).

The quote, at the beginning of this chapter clearly states the ethical principle: the physician has a duty to preserve the patient's privacy. Trust in the psychiatrist's promise of confidentiality assures the patient it is safe to reveal personal matters. In so doing, anything that might be potentially embarrassing, or capable of harm will not be divulged under the physician's ethic to consider such information as "holy secrets".

Because in the real world of institutional practice, others than the patient's personal therapist must have access to the clinical record, procedures must be developed to establish the "need to know". Patients should be informed as to the limits of confidentiality. A balance is required between the confidentiality that is a prerequisite to effective psychiatric treatment and the legitimate needs in society for information. The patient can readily understand that his insurance company must have certain information about his illness to pay the bill for care.

However, the improper release of a private communication between patient and therapist that causes harm may be the basis for a claim for malpractice. So deep is the conviction that the secrets entrusted to a therapist be protected, that some psychiatrists go to jail rather than reveal them; others fight costly court battles or lead efforts to mobilize public opinion in support of new state laws and Federal rules of evidence.

THE PROBLEMS

1. You receive a phone call asking, "Is John Doe able to return to work as a truck driver?" (meaning "Can he obey traffic rules; is he on any medication that might make him drowsy?"). Do you answer "John who?" or do you supply the information?

2. You receive a letter asking, "Is there any contraindication for the admission of Jane Doe to college?" What answer will you give?

3. You receive a phone call requesting detailed medical information from a person who identifies himself as a physician. Will you answer the questions? (Factual Services Inc., with fifteen branch offices in major cities, used this technique to obtain medical information without authorization, a grand jury in Denver was told.)

4. You receive a letter from an insurance company; in it is a copy of your patient's signed release of information waiver. They wish a complete copy of the patient's record. Do you send it?

5. You have just examined a 14-year-old girl and found her pregnant. She asks you not to tell her parents. Will you respect her wishes?

6. A state trooper comes to your office, displays his badge, and asks to examine the record of one of your patients. He says he is investigating a homicide. How can you offer assistance without violating the confidential relationship?

7. You are the superintendent of a state mental hospital. The governor, your superior in the state employee hierarchy, asks you to report to his office and bring with you for his examination the records of all patients who "escaped" last month. Will you bring the records?

8. A news reporter has learned you are treating a famous person and asks for details. What do you tell the reporter?

9. You have been asked by the court to make an examination to determine an individual's competency to stand trial. In court you are asked by the prosecuting attorney to state your diagnosis and the supporting evidence for it. Do you limit your reply only to your findings on competency or do you comply?

10. In your mental health facility could a person not on staff but who was wearing a white coat and name tag request a patient's record and obtain it?

THE ISSUES

Patient-Physician Relations

For over two thousand years the ethical tradition preserved patient confidences. Institutions and individuals safeguarded personal information, releasing it only to those with direct responsibility for treatment of the individual or to those authorized by the patient. In today's more open society, we recognize the right of an individual to know that a record has been made. Under the Federal Freedom of Information Act a citizen has the right to know what is in the record. Even so, patient access to clinical records is still debated. Accumulating evidence supports this practice of disclosure. If it is done tactfully and carefully, we are in favor of it. There is increasing interest in giving patients the right to determine the use that will be made of the information in records. Some facilities have patients sign a release each time information is requested to be released. The forms state what type of information will be divulged and to whom. It is a one-time release. We strive for the ideal of total confidentiality but recognize that the patient's interest and those of society have created some exceptions. In practice we are required by law to report gunshot wounds, child abuse, and contagious diseases.

Psychotherapist Confidentiality

As we mentioned earlier, in 1952 Dr. Roy Grinker, Sr., risked a contempt citation when he refused to testify or allow the records of his patient to be examined in a divorce case. The judge, upon hearing the basis for the refusal, ruled confidentiality a *sine qua non* of diagnosis and treatment of mental and emotional disorders.

Two cases (Lifschutz v. California, Supreme Court, April 15, 1970 and Caesar v. Mountanos, U.S. District Court of Appeals, 9th Circuit) have attracted the attention of psychiatrists. Under "a properly limited interpretation'' of the California privilege law, ''psychotherapists can be compelled to disclose information about a former patient . . . where the patient himself has made his mental condition an issue'' (*Citation,* 1970). A former patient of Dr. Lifschutz sued an individual who allegedly assaulted him. The patient asked for damages for physical injury and emotional suffering. It should be noted that Dr. Lifschutz had treated the plaintiff for six months, a good ten years before the suit. When Dr. Lifschutz responded to the subpoena, he refused to disclose any information at all, including even a statement that the individual had in fact been in treatment. Because the patient had introduced his mental condition into the suit, a real donnybrook ensued, with writs and appeals that brought the case to the State Supreme Court. Lifschutz was held in contempt and jailed for three days. The action underscored his belief in absolute privacy for the psychotherapist-patient relationship. It also affirmed the state's obligation to seek the truth, for ''a patient should not be permitted to claim emotional suffering and at the same time foreclose inquiry into the relevant aspects of his mental health.'' More important, the decision held that ''when confidentiality is at issue the psychotherapist may request the court to limit the scope of inquiry'' and specified that the request could be made at any time in the trial.

Dr. Caesar (Caesar v. Mountanos, California) also was sentenced to jail for contempt. Caesar challenged the constitutionality of the following section of the California Evidence Code: ''There is no privilege under this article as to communication, relevant to an issue concerning the mental or emotional condition of the patient if such an issue concerning the mental or emotional condition of the patient has been tendered by . . . the patient by filing a lawsuit.'' Caesar reasoned that revealing confidences might be harmful to the patient and there was no valid consent to testify. He felt his answers might not be relevant to the lawsuit and would be an unnecessary and unwarranted breach of confidentiality. Therefore he refused to answer questions on a required deposition, claiming privilege under the Bill of Rights and the Fourteenth Amendment. The courts overruled him and ordered Dr. Caesar to testify. He refused, maintaining the essential requirement of absolute confidentiality in the psychotherapist-patient relationship. This case focused the debate. Privilege is usually seen as the right only of the patient. The Illinois statute provides also for that of the psychotherapist.

Another arena of struggle was the battle to include Rule 504 in the Federal Code of Evidence. Rule 504 would establish the confidential relationship and communications between psychotherapist and patient on the same basis as the privileged relationship between attorney and client. In 1966 Chief Justice Earl Warren appointed an advisory committee to recommend uniform rules for evidence in all Federal courts. In 1969 a subcommittee of the group recommended abolition of all physician-patient privilege. When a joint AMA–American Bar Association committee recommended this be accepted, the AMA House of Delegates refused to go along with it but was unsuccessful in having it quashed.

In 1970 the American Psychiatric Association entered the arena and advanced the argument that there was a constitutional basis for safeguarding communications between psychotherapist and patient. They noted that the practice of psychotherapy could not proceed without a guarantee of confidentiality. Rule 504 was introduced into Congress with the support of the Federal Advisory Judicial Committee. For a time, the AMA opposed it, seeking instead to revive its earlier recommendation that privilege be extended to all physicians. Later the AMA supported the position of psychiatry. Congress, though it deleted Rule 504 from the code, did so because of pressure to include, in addition to psychotherapists, clergy, spouses, physicians, and newsmen. Seeing no partial compromises, Congress indicated that the states would need to develop their own protective laws.

Section 333 of the 1970 Alcohol and Drug Abuse Act authorized the Secretary of HEW to award an absolute privilege to withold names of subjects. Later this was modified (Section 408 Drug Abuse Office and Treatment Act 1972) with respect to records of drug abusers, by imposing a duty to maintain the confidentiality of drug abuse patient records as distinguished from authorizing the Secretary to confer the privilege of doing so.

Patient Clinical Records

Primary health care records are those kept during an active episode of treatment. Those who are directly concerned in the patient's care must have access to it and enter appropriate data. All others (administrators, students, faculty, etc.) must secure permission to examine the record from both patient and therapist. We are among those who believe that patients also should have the right of access to their records, though in a supervised setting. Studies have shown that while some patients become anxious when they read their charts, the experience often serves to open communication; most patients benefit from subsequent interpretation and explanation of findings (Stevens, Stagg, and Mackay, 1977; Stein, Furedy, Simonton, and Neuffer, 1979).

At some point in time, the clinical record of the episode is closed and then it becomes the responsibility of the medical records librarian or of data handlers who generate secondary records. These are reports to insurance companies, courts, human service agencies, accreditation surveyors, researchers, and peer review committees. In each instance the need to know must be established and access limited by due process guarantees either legislated or regulated. The patient's right of privacy continues with exceptions for legitimate cause only.

Tertiary records are generated in the process of quality control. Peer review of physician performance and medical record audits are procedures designed to improve patient care. The findings must be undiscoverable, in order to allow freedom to criticize and to change behavior without the threat of public disclosure and malpractice action. Unless there is absolute confidentiality, the process will be destroyed. We favor legislation to make findings inadmissible evidence in a lawsit. A Federal district judge decided that PSROs which are agencies of the Federal government (many are) must comply with requests to make records available to the public. The case was pending before the U.S. Court of Appeals in 1980 while legislation was introduced in Congress to protect tertiary records from disclosure.

In treatment the patient makes willing disclosure of many personal problems, with the expectation that there will be no use of the information beyond that setting. The blanket waiver one often signs on purchase of an insurance policy, which gives the company access to all manner of personal information, is not in our view an informed consent, except to the release of data pertinent to the specifics of the policy contract. There is a legitimate need by the insurer to know onset, diagnosis, treatment, and prognosis, in order to determine whether treatment is covered by the contract. A complete copy of a patient's psychiatric record, however, is not essential to that purpose and may contain information of which the patient has no recollection and which could be damaging and violate his right of privacy.

Research Records

Published case records should have all identifiers removed. When photographs, videotapes, or identifiable data are used, the patient's informed consent (covering the proposed use, its purpose, and the intended audience) must be obtained.

LEGAL DECISIONS

Tarasoff v. Regents Univ. of Cal. 1974

A devastating blow to the confidentiality of the psychotherapist-patient relationship was struck by the California Supreme Court in a 5–2 decision, which ruled that psychiatrists and psychotherapists in that state have a legal duty to warn intended victims of patients they see in their practice who they conclude are dangerous (Grossman, 1978). The court decreed such warnings were not a breach of confidentiality. The majority opinion by Justice Tobriner said: "The protective privilege ends where public peril begins. In this risk-infested society we can hardly tolerate the further exposure to danger that would result from a concealed knowledge of the therapist that the patient is lethal." The ruling followed the murder of a student at the University of California by a graduate student who was receiving outpatient psychiatric therapy. The graduate student was alleged to have told his therapist he intended to kill the student. The therapist did warn the campus police, who detained the man briefly but released him. In the dissenting opinion, Justice Clark stated that without a substantial guarantee of confidentiality, those needing treatment will be deterred from seeking it and patients will be reluctant to make disclosures necessary for treatment.

The American Psychiatric Association, joined by other organizations, petitioned for a rehearing, noting that a warning to a potential victim is no protection, and that a patient who drops out of therapy is more dangerous. Hostility and threats toward others are a constant accompaniment of the therapeutic process. Violent and destructive impulses and homicidal fantasies are common. In the therapeutic process, feelings are ventilated and attempts are made to deal with them. Dr. Maurice Grossman, Chairman of APA Task Force on Confidentiality, remarked that "even in those patients where the control is tenuous and the violent impulse is severe, the patient is helped to control the impulse in the therapeutic process." In part, it is the patient's trust in his therapist that helps the patient control his behavior. Fortunately, psychiatric patients do not kill as frequently as people not in therapy do—which says something about the value of working through problems and feelings (*Psychiatric News*, 1975).

An extension of the Tarasoff decision, which applied only in California, was made by a District Court in Nebraska (Lipari v. Sears, Roebuck Co., July 17, 1980). It stated that psychotherapists have a duty to warn potential victims of a dangerous patient. In this case, a former committed patient in the psychiatric care of a VA facility bought a gun one month before he terminated treatment. A month after termination he shot into a crowd at a nightclub and killed a patron. According to an *AMA News* story (March 20, 1981), the court found the VA negligent in failing to detain the patient, the psychotherapist at fault for failure to take reasonable precautions to prevent danger to others, and the store that sold the gun as sharing in the negligent acts. The VA held it could not warn unknown persons, but the court countered that warning was expected to all persons forseeably endangered.

The decision of the Nebraska court raised questions difficult to answer. How does one warn all potential victims? How does a gun shop determine the customer's potential for being dangerous to others?

In Janet Gotkin v. Alan Miller (U.S. Court of Appeals, 2nd Circuit), attorneys from the Mental Health Law Project and the American Civil Liberties Union asked if courts erred in holding that despite the common law right of a patient to access to her records, the hospitals could deny that right based on policy that applied to all former patients. The final ruling denied access. The U.S. Supreme Court decision in Zurcher v. Stanford Daily (1978) upheld the validity of a search warrant allowing local enforcement officials to search the newspaper' files for evidence in an investigation. A consequence of the decision was to make the personal files of physicians, lawyers, legislators, and other citizens vulnerable to similar search procedures.

In 1980 Congress passed a law barring search warrants by Federal law enforcement officials to obtain newspaper and communication media files. Guidelines issued by the Justice Department restrict the use of search warrants to obtain records of physicians, attorneys and clergymen "except when there is substantial jeopardy that the information might be destroyed or rendered useless." Some protection of patient or client records is likely, for permission to use a search warrant requires approval of a high-ranking Justice Department official except in emergencies (*AMA News,* 1981). The intent of the law and the guidelines is the protection of innocent parties who share a privileged relationship from improper search and seizure.

A recent landmark Federal District Court Decision (Hawaii Psychiatric Society v. Arisyoshi, 1979) struck down as unconstitutional a state Medicaid fraud law because it violated the patient's right to privacy and the physician's right to be free from unreasonable search and seizure. The court held that "confidentiality of a psychiatrist-patient communication is essential to preserve the individual's freedom of choice in deciding whether to seek psychiatric care, to encourage the patient to volunteer sensitive personal information in the course of treatment, and to enable a psychiatrist to conduct such treatment in the best manner."

Laws and judicial decisions using the words "psychiatrist" or "physician" may be expected to apply as well to the clinical psychologist and psychotherapist.

THE NEED FOR ACTION BY STATES

Senator Sam Ervin, long a champion of individual rights, had this to say in encouraging actions by states:

> A good case can be made for the proposition that the state ought to aid the psychiatrist to keep inviolate his obligation of confidentiality to his patient when demand is made upon him by subpoena to make confidential information concerning his patient available for use as evidence in a civil or criminal case.

No one can gainsay that a surprisingly large proportion of people are subject to mental illness in some form at some time in their lives, and that the state has a profound interest both economically and governmentally in preserving for psychiatry the right to employ its most potent therapeutic techniques—the confidence and cooperation of its patients—to cure or alleviate the mental illness of as many of them as possible.

If the state will establish an effective policy to this end, psychiatry will cure or alleviate the mental illness of many of its citizens, and thus enable them to observe the norms of society, and lead satisfactory lives outside the institutions which the states must maintain for those for whom custodial care is essential.

To establish a policy of this character, the state must make a law providing that confidential communications between psychiatrist and patient constitute privileged communications, and are to be kept secret in judicial proceedings for the benefit of the patient, even in the face of a subpoena demanding their disclosure for evidential purposes. [Ervin, 1974]*

The struggle of those who would protect the confidentiality of the psychiatrist-patient relationship and build new legal safeguards often seems remote to psychiatrists and mental health professionals as they go about their daily practice. But it has relevance to daily requests for information that is supplied if need to know is felt to be established. One can take Dr. Caesar's position and decline to give any information at all, declining even to affirm that the person is in treatment. One can avoid having case records stolen, as happened to Dr. Fielding, by keeping no written records. However, neither position is tenable in daily practice. Unless the insurance company knows who you are treating and for what, no payment will be made. If no records are kept, scientific practice may suffer and colleagues may be unable to pick up treatment where someone leaves off. Malpractice suits are much more likely to be successful when no records or very brief ones are kept.

Yet laws can be changed or new laws enacted. Rules and standards can be promulgated. Insurance forms can be redesigned to change a patient's blanket waiver of all rights to a selective waiver for a specific purpose valid for a limited time. Clinicans can be ever vigilant that only for a highly valued social purpose will there be an override of the basic right of privacy.

* Permission granted by Sen. Ervin to use this quote from an address delivered at the 1974 Conference on Confidentiality of Health Records, Nov. 6–9, 1974, Key Biscayne, Florida.

In 1960, a model statute for privilege, accompanied by an appropriate rationale, was proposed by the Group for the Advancement of Psychiatry (GAP, 1959–1962). It read: "The confidential relations and communications between psychiatrist and patient shall be placed on the same basis as regards privilege provided by law between attorney and client."

The Connecticut Psychiatric Society, a District Branch of the American Psychiatric Association, found the proposed statute oversimplified, arguing that some very real problems arise that require exceptions. The Connecticut statute (1961) "provided for the patient's privilege of relevant confidential communications with three exceptions: when the psychiatrist determined a need for hospitalization and the patient was unwilling to go voluntarily; when the judge informed a defendant of nonprivilege under the special circumstance of an examination made by a court-appointed psychiatrist; and when the patient introduced his or her mental condition as an element of his or her claim or defense in civil litigation.

Another very similar law was enacted in Illinois in 1971. It added a significant amendment (Beigler, 1972) and read in part:

> In civil and criminal cases, in proceedings preliminary thereto, and in legislative and administrative proceedings, a patient or his authorized representative have the privilege to refuse to disclose and to prevent a witness from disclosing communications relating to diagnosis or treatment of the patient's mental condition between patient and psychiatrist, or between members of the patient's family and the psychiatrist or between any of the foregoing and such persons under the supervision of a psychiatrist in the accomplishment of the objective of diagnosis or treatment.

As in Connecticut, there was no privelege for communications relevant to effecting hospitalization, court-ordered psychiatric examination, or instances where the patient introduced his mental condition as a claim or defense (Slawson, 1969; Citation, 1970; Grossman, 1978). The amendment, however, assures privilege for both patient and psychotherapist in divorce cases and in child custody cases resulting from a divorce action unless either the psychotherapist or the patient testifies as to communications between them.

The Connecticut statute served as a model for new statutes in Illinois, Florida, Kentucky, and California. To these five may be added two additional states, Georgia and Massachusetts, that also have psycho-therapist-patient privilege laws. The exception in the Connecticut law (when the patient introduces his mental condition) has proven to be a hazard to the patient's right of privacy and a threat to the confidential relationship between doctor and patient.

Some thirty-six states and the District of Columbia have physician-patient privilege statutes. Where there are no privilege laws, privilege does not exist, for it must be established by statute.

STEPS TO PRESERVE CONFIDENTIALITY

A National Commission on Confidentiality of and Access to Health Care Records was established in 1975 (Barton, 1975). One of its objectives was to propose legislation and regulations and to study and analyze those being formulated or already introduced. The passage of protective laws in states where they do not exist was recommended.

Because existing statutes provide an exception, permitting intro-duction of evidence regarding mental condition when the patient is the litigant and waives confidentiality, sensitive information may be re-vealed that can damage parties. Three suggestions are offered:

1. Relevance of evidence should be decided by the judge in his chambers in the presence of attorneys for both parties.

2. In divorce proceedings based on grounds of mental cruelty, the patient-litigant exception should be disallowed.

3. "Pain and suffering" should not be considered a mental condition.

Those responsible for the active treatment of the patient have access to the primary record, as stated above; all others must secure permission for such access from both the patient and the therapist in charge of the patient's treatment. The purpose of PL 93–579, The Privacy Act of 1974, was an attempt to safeguard individual privacy by regulating data collected, its use and dissemination. It became effective at the end of September 1975. The act prohibits and provides penalties for disclosure of private information. Under another act, the Federal Free-dom of Information Act, the individual has the right to know whether or not a Federal agency keeps a file on him, can obtain copies of any such file, and can learn the names of any persons requesting to see his file and for what purpose. One may also challenge and correct personal information and demand change as well as notification of all who used the file before the correction was made.

As is usual, good legislative intent is accompanied by problems in implementation. Federal agencies must keep a record of all disclosures and details as to when and for what purpose the information was released. If the patient demands access to his record and it seems likely that disclosure would be harmful, then the individual will be requested to designate in writing a medical representative to whom copies of the records will be sent. Underscored is the importance to physicians that prepared reports be objective when submitted to the Social Security Agency.

There is an assumption in privilege law that there is always a congruence between the needs of an individual and those of his agent, and that the patient will act in his own best interest in the decision to waive privilege (Dubey, 1974). While this is usually true, it may not always be in psychotherapy. A patient involved in ligitation may disingenuously display dramatic symptoms in treatment sessions in order to present the therapist sound evidence of his disability, and this may be directly contrary to the patient's therapeutic interest.

Destruction of Records

- Records may be destroyed after seven years. The statutes of limitations vary in states from three to seven years.
- Records of children should be kept for seven years after they reach the legal age of majority.
- Workmen's Compensation records and those of industrial accidents must be kept indefinitely.
- Mental health facilities should retain clinical records indefinately, either in the original or on microfilm.
- When records are destroyed, they must be shredded or burned and not dumped into cans for waste disposal.

THE ADMINISTRATOR'S OBLIGATION

Educational Activities

All who handle sensitive confidential information should be instructed in the concepts of confidentiality and privilege. Preservation of the patient's privacy depends on the integrity of the individuals to whom one's secrets are entrusted. The generation of secondary records follows an established need to know and observes carefully specified procedures. All information handlers must be familiar with the guidelines and procedures.

System for Protection of Records

The nurses' station in a hospital, with its chart rack out of reach of passersby, is manned by personnel who know that records may be released only to members of the active treatment team. Charts are not left about, but are replaced in the rack immediately after use.

The doctor or therapist may take patients' records to his office but may not leave them lying unattended in an empty office. All records of active cases must be returned to the file at the end of the working day. Anyone who has been called to treat an emergency involving another therapist's patient quickly understands—in the event the chart can't be found—the reason for this rule.

Health care records of individuals in a mental health facility that have been stored in a medical records room are under the control of personnel fully informed of procedures. This will prevent access by unauthorized persons. At the close of the working day, all patient records are returned to the files and the files and the room are locked. Data bank personnel are also instructed in procedures to assure access only to authorized persons. Entrance to confidential information files is allowed to those with coded numbers or cards. Some facilities further protect confidential data rooms with security alarms, photoelectric beams, or TV monitors. Preservation of confidentiality, however, will in the last analysis be assumed not by technical devices to prevent unauthorized access to computers or data repositories, but by the affirmative action of human custodians who zealously guard confidential information.

Lobby for Legislation

We would hope that administrators would actively press for legislation in their states similar to the statutes on confidentiality in Connecticut and Illinois. Also needed is legislation to prevent disclosure of internal medical record audits and therapist performance reviews ensuring quality in patient care.

SUMMARY

Physicians have for two thousand years followed the ethical tradition of keeping patient disclosures confidential. During the past forty years, third parties have intruded into the doctor-patient relationship. The growth of data banks for many different purposes permits linkages never intended and leakages of information. Concern over confidentiality is of recent origin.

"The legal duty of confidentiality or secrecy is the obligation not to release information about a client or patient without his or her permission except when divulgence is required by law" (Slovenko, 1973). It is the rare exception that poses a social good greater than the moral and ethical tradition of psychiatrists and the patient's right of privacy. Psychiatrists urge that the psychotherapist be granted the same privilege as now exists between attorney and client. The Connecticut and Illinois statutes on confidentiality are enlightened laws that approach this desired goal. These acts, however, allow no privilege to communications relevant to involuntary hospitalization, court-ordered psychiatric examinations, or situations where the patient has introduced his mental condition as a claim or defense. It is the last exception that still poses a problem: suggested remedies would limit disclosure to evidence relevant to the issue at hand, prohibit the exception in divorce proceedings alleging mental cruelty, and determine that "pain and suffering do not constitute a mental condition."

Because certain information is necessary for an insurance company to determine its contractual obligation for payment, patient waiver of privilege is required. Once again, information relevant to settlement of claims is required, not copies of the entire record. The need to know and the right to privacy must be kept in balance. All who handle confidential information must at all times act in a responsible manner to protect the patient's right to privacy.

The adminitrator has an obligation to educate staff in the concepts of confidentiality and privilege, to establish procedures to safeguard information, and to press for protective legislation.

QUESTIONS

1. Why has confidentiality become a current concern?
2. What is confidentiality and what is privilege?
3. Who has the right to see the primary clinical record? Does the patient have the right to see his record?
4. Why did psychiatrists react so strongly to the Tarasoff decision in California?
5. What information is proper to release to an insurance company? to an employer? to a school?
6. What steps should be taken to protect the confidential relationships of psychotherapists?

References

AMA News (1981), M.D.'s offices protected from search. AMA News, 24:2, Jan. 16.

AMA News (1981), Psychiatrist required to protect victims. AMA News, 24:16, Mar. 20.

* APA (1975), Confidentiality and Third Parties: Task Force Report. Washington, D.C.: American Psychiatric Association.

Barton, W. E. (1975), Should a national commission for the preservation of confidentiality be formed? Psychiatric Opinion, 12:15–17.

* Barton, W. E., & Sanborn, C. J. (1978), Law and the Mental Health Professions, chaps. 7 & 8. New York: International Universities Press.

Beigler, J. S. (1972), The 1971 amendment of the Illinois Statute on confidentiality: A new development in privilege law. Amer. J. Psychiat., 129:311–315.

Citation (1970), Confidential relationship with patient. The Citation, 22:49–50, Dec.

* Dubey, J. (1974), Confidentiality as a requirement of the therapist: Technical necessities for absolute privilege in psychotherapy. Amer. J. Psychiat., 131:1093–1096.

Ervin, Sam J., Jr. (1974), The Right of the Psychiatric Patient to the Confidentiality of His Revelations. Address to Conference on Confidentiality of Health Records, Key Biscayne, Fla., Nov. 7.

GAP (1959–1962), Confidentiality and Privileged Communications in the Practice of Psychiatry. GAP Report 45, Vol. 4. New York: Group for the Advancement of Psychiatry.

Grossman, M. (1978), Confidentiality: The right to privacy versus the right to know. In: Law and the Mental Health Professions, ed. W. E. Barton & C. J. Sanborn. New York: International Universities Press.

* Health Records and Confidentiality: An Annotated Bibliography (n.d.), Washington, D.C.: National Commission on Confidentiality of Health Records.

* Plaut, E. A. (1974), A perspective on confidentiality. Amer. J. Psychiat., 131:1021–1024.

Psychiatric News (1975), Therapists ordered to report dangerous patients. *Psychiatric News,* 10 (3) Feb. 5.

Siegler, M. (1982), Confidentiality in medicine: A decrepit concept. *N. Engl. J. Med.* 307:1518–1521.

Slawson, P. T. (1969), Patient-litigant exception: A hazard to psychotherapy. *Arch. Gen. Psychiat.,* 21:347–352.

* Slovenko, R. (1973), *Psychiatry and Law.* Boston: Little, Brown.

* Spingarn, N. D. (1976), *Confidentiality.* Washington, D.C.: American Psychiatric Association.

Stein, E. J., Furedy, R. L., Simonton, M. J., & Neuffer, C. H. (1979), Patient access to medical records on a psychiatric inpatient unit. *Amer. J. Psychiat.,* 136:327–329.

Stevens, D. P., Stagg, R., & Mackay, I. R. (1977), What happens when hospitalized patients see their records. *Annals Internat. Med.,* 86:474–477.

Chapter 9

Admission to Hospital

> In the first place, the law should put no hindrance in the way to prompt use of those instrumentalities which are regarded as most effectual in promoting the comfort and restoration of the patient. Secondly, it should spare all unnecessary exposure of private trouble, and all unnecessary conflict with popular prejudices. Thirdly, it should protect individuals from wrongful imprisonment. It would be objection enough to any legal provision that it failed to secure these objects in the completest possible manner.
>
> —*Isaac Ray, 1869*

Case example. A 43-year-old man, severely schizophrenic since the age of 19, had received many years of treatment in and out of the finest private mental hospitals in this country. During a ten-year period, the family spent more than $200,000 on hospitalization and psychoanalytic, electroconvulsive and drug therapies. The patient remained grossly delusional. He hallucinated, looked withdrawn and often exhibited silly and inappropriate behavior. While hospitalized in a public institution, he was released on a trial visit but refused to return after a specified time as agreed. He was ultimately discharged when efforts to return him failed.

At home his condition worsened. He refused his medication, he threatened and attacked his elderly, enfeebled parents who then lived in terror of him. The parents eventually engaged a lawyer, and after tremendous effort on all their parts, admission to a general hospital was arranged two months later. A petition for involuntary admission was prepared. This commitment was disallowed because admission to the general hospital had been voluntary. After his discharge, an amended petition was filed and a hearing set for the next month. The finding of "likely to injure himself or others" led to a recommendation for outpatient treatment in a community mental health center. Pursuant to local statute the case was referred to the Superior Court for hearing a month later. After a second hearing, the next week, an order for involuntary admission was issued. Additional court hearings on how reimbursement would be handled dragged on for six more months when the case was declared closed. [adapted from Lebensohn, 1978]

This case shows that it can take over four months to overcome obstacles to commitment in a case clearly requiring hospital treatment and seven months more to closure, at considerable expense to public and relatives, anguish to the parents, and lost treatment time for the patient. Community confusion and uncertainty exist about how one can admit to hospital a mentally ill individual who has not attempted suicide or murder. A decade of legislation and court action has significantly changed the ground rules.

To insure minimal deprivation of freedom, the least restrictive environment is sought through preadmission screening. This determines the appropriateness of the proposed admission to the mental hospital and decides whether an available alternative to hospitalization would be more appropriate. When a therapist has been treating a person for months and his or her judgment as to the need for hospitalization is questioned by others less familiar with the situation, there is often expressed resentment.

Self-determination on the part of the patient, as well as professional opinion regarding treatment in a hospital setting, seem thwarted by a system of justice whose procedures are formulated to protect the sane. The debate between law and the mental health profession about who decides hospitalization—patient, physicians or courts—was intense as the 1980s began. Society is becoming frustrated and may be unwilling to await the outcome of reasoned debates. Practice sometimes finds a way around barriers.

We shall look at various types of admission: (informal; voluntary; emergency; involuntary; court-ordered observation), review the criteria for hospitalization, point out ways that have been used to get around barriers, and discuss some of the unsolved problems.

CRITERIA FOR HOSPITALIZATION

There are medical, substantive and procedural criteria for admitting a mentally ill person to hospital:

- Severe mental illness uncontrolled by ambulatory care
- Suicidal—dangerousness to self
- Violent—dangerousnous to others
- Withdrawal, confusion, and severe memory impairment with an inability for survival independent of others' help
- Bizarre, antisocial, or inappropriate behavior that creates a nuisance in the community
- Acute alcohol or drug intoxication
- Unmanageable behavior in another hospital unit or institution with request for assistance from the staff
- Transportation to outpatient care unavailable or difficult
- Initial stabilization of therapy imperative (as in lithium carbonate therapy, (the leveling off of blood levels to therapeutic range)
- When alternative arrangements are not immediately available and must be developed
- Intensive diagnostic and evaluative studies indicated (G. Barton, 1974)

In these rare instances in which protection of the patient, the family, or society is required but the patient is unwilling to accept treatment, the hospital may initiate the legal steps to involuntary detention in an appropriate facility after notification of nearest of kin.

Society is left with the problem of the few patients who are a genuine social nuisance as a consequence of mental illness but who are not considered dangerous. In some states with restrictive laws, they may not be admitted if they cannot be persuaded to request admission. The confused elderly patient may repeatedly wander into the city traffic stream; the mentally ill recluse may live in a cluttered apartment and be severely malnourished; the paranoid individual may daily haunt public offices seeking redress for imaginary bodily invasion by electrical rays; the disordered individual may damage property; and the severely ill employee may deposit each morning a wrapped prackage of feces on the boss's desk. Ordinary citizens are offended by these mad acts and are not in sympathy with laws which withhold treatment for persons so obviously in need of help. They would vocalize their insistence that treatment is a right, as is protection for themselves. Civil libertarians on the other hand view personal liberty as supreme; it should not be sacrificed simply because the person is a proper subject for care, or would benefit from treatment, or is in need of observation and therapy. The view of the mental health professional that the patient's need for treatment is paramount clashes with the legal view to protect individual liberty first.

This latter view is natural in a democratic society that views loss of liberty as a most serious event. "Railroading" (malicious confinement of a person by a relative to remove and discredit the offensive one) has been much feared; consequently, procedural safeguards have been developed so that a person thought to be in need of confinement has the right to examination by impartial experts. On the other hand, society has not divested itself of the myth that the insane have a proclivity for violence; the news media, TV, and films wallow in the "mad killer" theme. This mad killer theme elicits public support for the many advocates of legal reform who would make dangerousness the sole basis for deprivation of liberty and would negate the need to hospitalize those who damage property and endanger the health and welfare of their families or who simply cannot care for themselves. Litigants have joined in developing procedural safeguards similar to those of the judicial criminal system.

The rationale for legal intervention in the decision to hospitalize rests on two major principles. The *first* is the protection of society from individuals who are dangerous to themselves or others. However, the definition of dangerousness may be so broad and imprecise as to encompass a variety of behaviors. It may, for example, be so broad and imprecise as to encompass a variety of behaviors where the potential for harm to others is great, such as speeding in an automobile or driving while intoxicated. It is not the intent of legal standards to allow such a loose interpretation of dangerousness.

The *second* principle is the right of the state to protect its sick and helpless citizens from potential harm (*parens patriae*). This is interpreted to mean the protection of individuals who are incapable of survival in the community without the help of others or who have such impaired judgment that hospital care is essential to prevent physical harm to themselves.

There has been a statutory trend during the past decade toward limiting the doctrine of *parens patriae* and toward more precise standards of dangerousness. For example, the Massachusetts 1971 revision of its civil commitment statute defines "likelihood of serious harm" as:

1. a substantial risk of physical harm to the person himself, as manifested by evidence of threats of, or attempts at, suicide or serious bodily harm;
2. a substantial risk of physical harm to other persons as manifested by evidence of homicidal or other violent behavior or evidence that others are placed in reasonable fear of violent behavior and serious physical harm to them; or
3. a very substantial risk of physical impairment or injury to the person himself as manifested by evidence that such person's judgment is so affected that he is unable to protect himself in the community and that reasonable provision for his protection is not available in the community. [Mass. General Laws, Ch. 23, Sect. 1; see McGarry, Schwitzgebel, Lippsett, and Lelos, 1978]

To protect the individual who may lose his or her liberty if involuntarily admitted to a hospital, the law has evolved both substantive criteria and procedural safeguards. [Roth, 1980]

Substantive Criteria

- Serious mental illness which poses an immediate danger to self or others
- Inability to provide the basic necessities of life such as food,

clothing, and shelter, and inability, due to the illness, to make rational decision as to the need

Additional criteria in statutes not specifically requiring a determination of dangerousness are:

* Treatability of the disorder
* Impaired judgment with inability to understand the need for care and treatment
* Essential need for care and treatment in a hospital

In 1974, only four states explicitly cited dangerousness to self or others as a requirement. By 1978, twenty state laws used this criterion. Statutes using the concept of "likely to cause serious injury or harm" to self or others increased from 10 to 28 in the same four-year span.

Procedural Safeguards

The purpose of commitment procedures is not fact finding as the basis of determining criminal guilt but determination of the necessity for loss of liberty for treatment. Safeguards include:

* Notice of hearing to the individual
* The right to be represented at hearing by counsel
* A statement of findings justifying involuntary detention
* The right to a hearing within a few days in emergency admissions and to a second hearing before involuntary indefinite admission
* Mandated periodic review of the need for continuing care

The statement of findings necessary to justify involuntary detention is viewed by the law according to three standards of proof:

1. Beyond a reasonable doubt—the standard used in criminal cases. It implies a 90 percent certainty. Five states use this standard.
2. Clear and convincing proof—implies a 75 percent certainty. Twelve states use this standard.
3. Preponderance of evidence—Implies a 51 percent certainty. Texas and Mississippi are the only states using this standard.

California's Civil Commitment Law, the Lanterman-Petris-Short Act (1969) was a landmark on the way to criminalization of the mental health system for it marked almost total abandonment of the concept "need for care and treatment" in favor of the concept of "dangerousness" (McDonald 1980). The Act provided legal safeguards against improper commitment, established the right to a hearing, representation by counsel, examination by impartial experts and procedural guidelines similar to those noted above.

There is accumulating evidence that the pursuit of limitation of admission to hospital of only the dangerous has diverted a member of mentally ill individuals to the criminal justice system, increased recidivism, and many in need of care failed to receive it.

Competence to Make a Decision

A patient's judgment may be so impaired that he is unable to understand the need for care and treatment; in such cases the state may protect the patient from potential harm. The act of commitment for a serious mental disorder does not in itself determine the individual's competence to make decisions regarding admission or to refuse treatment. All states have laws concerned with competency which traditionally are oriented toward inability to manage property. A separate hearing is necessary to determine competence and many variables are considered in this determination. This is such a complex topic that a separate chapter has been devoted to it (see chapter 12). Here we shall say only that a person is legally competent to make a decision regarding admission to hospital unless the contrary has been established; usually a determination that an individual is incompetent requires a separate hearing.

Patient Participation

Admission to hospital may be initiated by the patient, or at least involve his active participation. Often, however, the patient's mental illness interferes with initiative or decision making capability. The individual may make no objection when hospitalization is suggested or may acquiesce to others' urging. While relatively few are reluctant to seek help, there are some who resist hospitalization. In these cases judicial action or medical certification may be initiated to impose confinement. Usually the duration of hospitalization is time-limited to permit review, to assess an individual's willingness to remain without compulsion, or to determine the propriety of further detention (Rock, 1968). As a consequence of the varying degrees of cooperation or resistance, different admission categories—informal, voluntary, emergency, involuntary—have been developed.

INFORMAL ADMISSIONS

An informal admission is the intake into a hospital or facility of one who requests service without any form of legal process. It should be possible for any patient with a mental disorder to seek treatment and to obtain it, if the admitting officer concurs, without recourse to the legal system. Admission should be possible to general hospitals or to public or private mental hospitals on such a nonstatutory basis.

There is a wealth of experience to show that even those with severe mental disorders may seek to enter, be treated, and leave without court intervention. Required only is sufficient comprehension of their need for treatment and an understanding that their permission for use of a therapeutic modality is essential.

In *Administration in Psychiatry* (Barton, 1962) we told of the impact the late Dr. Duncan MacMillan had upon us when we visited the Mapperly Hospital in Nottingham, England, some twenty years ago. All patients were voluntarily admitted and a significant number were admitted informally. Each new arrival was asked to sign an agreement to leave the hospital in thirty days. The dramatic shift in emphasis led us to adopt that approach at the Boston State Hospital in 1959. The practice was adopted slowly: in 1975, out of every 11,000 admissions to the Massachusetts mental hospital system, only four hundred were informal admissions. In 1971 some eight states had statutes authorizing this form of intake (Brakel and Rock, 1971), but we doubt if statutory authority is even required for its use. Interpretation of the statute in your state may be required to learn if informal admission is excluded as an alternative route to care; it probably is not. It should also be mentioned that many private mental hospitals, perhaps the majority, accept patients informally.

It should be evident that when a patient in this category asks to leave he or she may do so. No advance notice is required. The comparison can be made with any patient on the medical or surgical wards of a general hospital. Decisions about intake, care and treatment, and departure are discussed with the patient, and recommendations are made, perhaps even urged by the physician, but the patient retains the right to disagree or to reject this advice.

When patients previously familiar with involuntary procedures are admitted for the first time informally, they may test the sincerity of the therapist by exploring the limits of their rights. They may demand release, resist efforts to change their mind, and leave, fully expecting that someone, perhaps the police, will stop them and return them to the ward. Frequently, when this does not occur, they return and ask to be taken in, relieved that they can be admitted and astonished that the choice was truly theirs to make.

VOLUNTARY ADMISSION

There is another form of admission, defined by statute, which we refer to as voluntary admission to distinguish it from informal admission. In Michigan it is called "formal voluntary." Critics who advocate abolition of mental hospitals as well as all commitments hold that the threat of commitment and coercion to remain represents a covert practice in involuntary detention. It is true that statutory voluntary admission in all states but two usually requires a written notice of intention to leave. Usually a period up to five days is required after filing an intention to leave, so that a hospital may initiate involuntary admission procedures in the meantime. It is this required notice and the intent to make it possible under the law to detain a patient involuntarily that makes this a very different procedure from the informal admission. Frequently private hospitals allow patients to leave against advice without notice or signing a release. Voluntary mental hospitalization is a fraud, writes Szasz (1972), as "regardless of the method of admission to a mental hospital, the patient in such an institution does not, as a rule, have an unqualified right to leave." The recommended routine practice of admitting patients under informal admissions described above renders the Szasz charge invalid, yet for formal voluntary admissions he has a point.

Massachusetts data for 1975 show involuntary admission was employed in 33.3 percent of 11,096 total admissions. A change from voluntary status to involuntary was exceedingly rare. McGarry and Greenblatt (1978) made a study of 3,669 admissions to three mental hospitals and found only 42 petitions for involuntary admission, of which only 21 were actually granted by the court.

What about the patient who insists on leaving and creates that rare situation where it is the therapist's opinion that he will kill himself or murder someone? If efforts to persuade the patient to remain on an informal status fail, then there is an ethical and social obligation on the part of the therapist to notify the family and to initiate procedures for involuntary admission (McGarry and Greenblatt, 1972).

Several states have interesting variations in the voluntary admission process. In Virginia all patients in state mental hospitals not charged with a crime were reclassified as voluntary on November 1, 1974, unless another commitment procedure was undertaken with a hearing as provided for in a revised mental health law (Shaffer, 1974). A major revision of the New York mental health laws in 1964 provided for informal admission, voluntary commitment, and a nonstatutory admission on the certification of two physicians. In recognition of the need to insure individual freedom, judicial safeguards were set up that required notification of patients of their right to a hearing, with the requirement that it be held within sixty days, with notice given also to the patient's attorney and an independent review body, the Mental Health Information Service. The law recognized the positive indications for hospitalization of the mentally ill and the need for immediate treatment as overriding considerations. In two years of application, involving committed patients for the most part, all but 10 percent were admitted through the voluntary and nonstatutory route.

In 1971 Massachusetts also revised its general laws pertaining to mental health. The statute required that every patient brought to the hospital on an involuntary emergency status be informed of an absolute right to elect to become a "conditional voluntary patient," a label intended to remind all that a three-day notice for release is all that is required. Sixty-six percent of all 11,000 admissions in Massachusetts mental hospitals in 1975 were conditional voluntaries, either self-initiated or elected at admission. Massachusetts was the first state to adopt voluntary admission (1881) and over many years its use has grown to become the major route to admission.

Statutes now permit voluntary admission in most states. One may be admitted, if the institution concurs, on one's own signature. The need for notice in advance of departure, when medical opinion holds the individual unready for release, is prescribed in law. The statute may specify the right to hold a patient for three days or even several weeks after notice is given, to permit initiation of the legal process to involuntarily detain the individual if that is deemed necessary. Often in practice the actively suicidal patient or the one who is potentially dangerous is asked to sign a formal voluntary commitment and thus is ineligible for informal admission.

Opposition to voluntary admission was described many years ago in *Administration in Psychiatry* (Barton, 1962, p. 253). Experience has shown that an open admission policy does not increase the number seeking service, and the demand for immediate release after the decision to seek help is infrequent. It is true that patients admitted voluntarily can't be transferred to other facilities serving their home district unless they agree to move. This can present the admitting facility fewer alternatives in financing the patient's care if the person resides in another county. As a result, patients are often directed to their home district for admission in the first place.

One of the concerns about the formal voluntary admission is the aspect of deprivation of liberty. Some states have revised their laws limiting involuntary admission and tightening indications for its use. The potential shift from voluntary status during the period after advance notice of intent to leave has been given is openly stated on the formal voluntary admission form which the patient signs in Michigan.

The concept that all hospitalization is "bad" is in our view false. We disagree with the position taken against the free use of the mental hospital by persons in need of therapy. We believe that it helps both patient attitudes and staff attitudes to have patients seek help on their own initiative and that voluntary admissions are therefore desirable. On that premise a way must be found to achieve a greater latitude in the use of voluntary admission.

The formal voluntary admission serves an important function beyond that offered by the informal admission and release procedures. Formal voluntary admission carries with it the patient's agreement to remain under therapy and to give advance notice of any intention to leave. He or she may not be the best judge of the need for further treatment and may not be able to control hostile impulses. The legal safeguards in the voluntary admission statutes do permit steps to be taken to protect both patient and the public. We do, however, doubt the wisdom of forcibly detaining a patient who gives written notice that he or she wishes to leave *except* in those rare instances where the patient *is* potentially dangerous to himself or others. Even though voluntary admission is still the preferred route to mental hospital admission as indicated by growth in its use, we insist informal admission should be the preferred category for most patients.

EMERGENCY ADMISSION

Emergency admission is quite frequently the route taken by patients. In Massachusetts, where the law allows a ten-day emergency detention, each individual must be offered the option of becoming a conditional voluntary patient. In a study (McGarry et al., 1978) which sampled 688 emergency admissions to mental hospitals, 36 percent were referred from general hospitals, police brought 21 percent, and family or friends 18 percent. Over a third had evinced symptoms of schizophrenia, and just under a third suffered affective disorders. Sixteen percent showed signs of organic brain syndrome. Even so, 41 percent of all admissions were discharged within two weeks.

Arizona's mental health law states that a written application for an emergency admission may be made to a licensed health care facility by any person with knowledge of the facts. The application must be on a prescribed form and if the admitting officer determines there is reasonable cause to believe that the patient is a danger to self or others or is gravely disabled (unable to provide for his or her survival by reason of degenerative brain disease or other chronic long-standing disorder), the patient may be admitted. On the same day, or the succeeding court day, a petition must be filed for a court-ordered evaluation.

Maine and New Hampshire follow a procedure which is more commonplace. Certification by a physician is required stating that the
individual is mentally ill and as a result is likely to injure himself or
others if not immediately detained. The procedure may be initiated by
a health or police officer or any other person who completes the form.
Admission must be within three days of signing. The applicant may
make private arrangements for transportation or may request it of the
sheriff or police. Within three days of an emergency admission, the
patient must be released, or someone must initiate the procedure for
involuntary commitment. Most states now have a legal method permitting immediate, direct admission to a mental hospital when the
patient is dangerous or violent or requires emergency psychiatric care.
A few do not (Peske, 1975).

There are two issues associated with emergency procedures that
deserve exposition here. The first is the elimination of the "command
to receive" a patient that once characterized the court-ordered commitment. It was the source of frustration to admitting officers who
could find no evidence of mental illness to warrant detention. When
this occurred, the custom was to speed up the evaluation of the case
by quick discharge. This often annoyed the court. Newly enacted laws
sometimes give the hospital's admitting physician the right to refuse
admission. Yet, as some local physicians feel their opinions should
not be challenged when they send a patient to be hospitalized, the
issue remains a very sensitive one.

The second issue is the controversial concept of dangerousness.
Does it imply that one is *likely* to cause serious injury or harm to self
and others? Is one dangerous only when one overtly *threatens* another?
The 1976 Pennsylvania Mental Health Act excludes threats to harm
as an act sufficient to establish dangerousness. The statute requires a
recent proven *act* or *attempt* (Roth, 1980). In practice, because of the
lack of precise definition, a rather wide range of behavior may be
labeled dangerous in order to gain a patient admission to hospital.

Most of the research on the prediction of violence has been done
on institutionalized mental patients and prisoners with a history of
violence. Reluctance to release them was based upon a fear of further
violence. Follow-up studies made after release have revealed that the
vast majority do not repeat the violent behavior expected of them.

Monahan (1978) suggested there was a need to study the later history of mentally ill persons admitted under short-term emergency statutes who were predicted to be dangerous if they remained in the community.

It should be quite clear to every psychiatrist that the reluctance to pass legislation permitting emergency admission in some states is due to the concern over loss of liberty. Since 1964 the New York Mental Hygiene Law has required persons believed to be mentally ill to appear before a magistrate. Emergency psychiatric admission may be ordered if the disorder is apparent. Zusman and Shaffer (1973) studied the warrants issued under this law and noted that mentally ill persons were detained in jail, sometimes overnight, then transported by police to the hospital in handcuffs, with no attempt made to negotiate or help them make up their own minds. It seems to us that the jailing of individuals and the "criminalization" of the mentally ill in the name of liberty is as wrong as the abuse of involuntary hospitalization. We still favor informal admission. If that is not possible, the next best alternative is the Massachusetts procedure of voluntary admission with the absolute requirement that every patient (who may be brought in at any time of day or night) be allowed to elect conditional voluntary status.

Some recent judicial decisions concerning commitment are of interest here. Lessard v. Schmidt in Federal District Court of Wisconsin (1972) ruled that the state's commitment laws were defective: that they failed to give notice of charges justifying detention, failed to require notice of right of jury trial, and failed to provide full hearing in forty-eight hours without proof of mental illness and dangerousness. The Supreme Court vacated the lower court's order on technical grounds without deciding on the merits of the case. In Bell v. Wayne County General Hospital, the Federal District Court struck down Michigan's temporary commitment procedure because it did not require a preliminary hearing to determine probable cause and violated due process and the right to privacy in permitting unwilling patients to be subjected to physically intrusive treatment such as ECT and chemotherapy. The impact of this decision could be far-reaching if applied generally. Several other cases have challenged commitment laws as violations of due process and would institute, therefore, notice to patients, representation by counsel, and hearings with right to cross-examine and application of the criminal standard of proof beyond reasonable doubt (Kopolow et al., 1975).

INVOLUNTARY ADMISSION

All states have statutes that provide for involuntary admission to a hospital for mental disorders. Usually the family and sometimes others complete an application that must be sworn. A majority of states also require examination by two physicians and their certification that hospitalization is needed for a mental disorder, the existence of which they have verified. The intent of the laws for involuntary admission is to provide prompt examination of the individual with suspected mental illness, to protect the public from harm, and to protect the patient from his own irrational acts. According to Brakel and Rock (1971),

> Legislation in forty-two jurisdictions authorizes some form of judicial procedure [for involuntary admission]. In sixteen, notice to the person who is alleged to be mentally ill is not mandatory. A number of states do not require the presence of the alleged mentally ill person at the hearing. Twenty-four states authorize the discretionary appointment of counsel in all cases in which the alleged mentally ill person is unrepresented.

In 1974 Arizona revised its laws to require that before an individual can be committed as dangerous there must be evidence that in the recent past an attempt to inflict harm has been made or actual harm done, or that the individual is a danger to self or is grievously ill. After working with the law for three years, the Arizona Psychiatric Society declared it impossible to hospitalize anyone involuntarily unless the person had broken a law.

Most mental health professionals and psychiatrists are opposed to legal admission procedures that resemble traditional criminal court trials. Even the term "commitment" has been avoided in this discussion, for it connotes an order employed in criminal proceedings. We have followed the Group for Advancement of Psychiatry (GAP, 1966) in their attempt to avoid words which convey an inappropriate attitude. The trauma to the patient of hearing symptoms recounted for the purpose of producing evidence of his or her "guilt," in the instance of a jury trial to determine "insanity," is intolerable. Clinicians are often further distressed by the archaic language used in such proceedings:

"insane," "lunatic," "weak-minded." These terms do harm by increasing the stigma of mental illness.

Massachusetts currently retains only 2 percent of those admitted under involuntary emergency status beyond the initial six-month period. The local district court within whose jurisdiction the facility is situated has the responsibility for involuntary hospitalization and under the 1971 statute must act to extend detention beyond six months.

In California the law provides an initial seventy-two hours of emergency detention for evaluation and treatment, with a hearing required within that time. A Sacramento study of 226 patients revealed that all but 42 (19 percent) were either discharged or had accepted voluntary status within five days (the seventy-two hours applies only to days court is in session, so weekends and holidays can stretch the period of detention to four or five days; (see GAP, 1966). All of the 42 patients who remained were placed on a fourteen-day extension. The law allowed this with the appointment of legal counsel and a member of the court staff to personally discuss the extension with the patient. Within the fourteen-day period, 22 additional patients accepted voluntary status. Only those who are dangerous to self or others or who are gravely disabled may be involuntarily detained any longer.

The procedure in Vermont has six steps:

1. An interested party, a licensed physician, the head of a hospital, a selectman, a town service officer, or the state commissioner of mental health may make application by filling out a form. The application must identify the applicant and his or her relation to or interest in the patient and then state what facts lead the applicant to believe the proposed patient needs to be hospitalized against his or her will. The completed application serves as an order to determine the subject's mental condition.

2. An examination will then be made by a physician licensed in Vermont. The Physician's Certificate must set forth in detail all statements and events heard or observed by the physician or reliably reported on which an opinion is based. Available alternative forms of care must be considered instead of hospitalization. The physician then signs the medical certificate stating that in his or her opinion the individual is *mentally ill* (specifying particular disorder where possible) and *in need of hospitalization*.

3. The completed Physician's Certificate, together with the application form, is then sent to the district court serving the area in which the patient resides, or if the patient is not a resident of Vermont, to any district court.

4. The district court appoints counsel and notifies the patient and his attorney, legal guardian, spouse, parents, or children that an application has been filed. If the judge has any reason to believe that such notice would likely be injurious to the patient, the notice may be omitted, with the consent of the patient's attorney.

5. After giving such notice, the district court schedules a hearing for the purpose of receiving testimony. *The patient need not be present.* The applicant and the physician who has completed the certificate may be summoned to appear.

6. If upon completion of the hearing, in consideration of the record, the district court finds that the patient is mentally ill and because of illness presents a substantial risk of injury to self or others or lacks sufficient capacity to make a responsible decision concerning his or her mental condition, the judge orders hospitalization.

The potential value of a hearing is illustrated by a New York study. Since 1965 a dramatic increase in the discharge rate occurred at Bellevue Hospital as a consequence of lawyers' involvement in decision-making. Patients admitted could be discharged, kept for short-term therapy, or transferred to a state hospital on either voluntary or involuntary status. When patients requested a court hearing the chance of being discharged was increased by nearly 50 percent (Kumasaka, Stokes, and Gupta, 1972).

WHAT EFFECT HAS SUBSTANTIVE AND PROCEDURAL CHANGE HAD
UPON PRACTICE?

Thirty-four states have enacted new civil commitment laws between 1973 and 1978. The trend has been toward more explicit criteria and the use of the standard of "clear and convincing evidence." Schwitzgebel (McGarry et al., 1978) surveyed all 50 states and found that all statutes included a requirement that mental illness or disability be present. Twenty-eight states used the criteria "likelihood of harm to self and others," while 20 directed that there be evidence of "danger to self or others." The choice of one criteria over the other seemed to be a matter of preference. Twenty-three states defined a "need of treatment" and 31 used the criterion "gravely disabled." The category "other criteria" included most frequently the requirement that the "least restrictive alternative" to hospitalization be considered, that the individual be a resident of the state, that he be likely to improve, or that he has committed acts constituting a felony. One state (South Carolina) uses the criterion "lacks sufficient insight or capacity to make reponsible decisions with respect to his treatment." One consequence of the trend toward more explicit criteria has been to curtail the discretion allowed the psychiatrist and mental health professional in involuntary admissions to hospitals.

In a study of the courtroom behavior of judges, lawyers, and psychiatrists, Lelos (McGarry et al., 1978) observed a sample of 688 patients from three state hospitals in Massachusetts. Evidence was presented that met the requirements of the statute for both mental illness and harm in only slightly more than half the cases. The intent of the law was not upheld. There was no increase in the factual reporting of pathology and no change in the frequency of appropriate involuntary admissions in cohorts of patients processed before and after a law was enacted with specific criteria. Patients were poorly represented by counsel; the lawyers typically failed to bring forth the crucial issues of the presence or absence of mental illness and the likelihood of harm. If the best interest of the patient is to be served, better representation by the lawyer is needed or, as Lelos suggests, examination and testimony by an independent psychiatrist should be offered.

The Florida Supreme Court upheld a civil commitment statute permitting hospitalization of a person found to be mentally ill and "in need of care or treatment and [who] lacks sufficient capacity to make a responsible application on his own behalf." The court interpreted the "in need of care or treatment" standard to mean that a judge must find that a person's "mental illness manifests itself in neglect or refusal to care for himself, that such neglect or refusal poses a real and present threat of substantial harm to his well being, and that he is incompetent to determine for himself whether treatment for his mental illness would be desirable" (*Psychiatric News*, 1977).

The best and most comprehensive statement on criteria for involuntary admissions was issued by the American Psychiatric Association in 1983. "The Guidelines For Legislation on the Psychiatric Hospitalization of Adults" is highly recommended to states planning revisions of the entire civil commitment law or portions of it (APA, 1983). The guidelines cover emergency evaluations, voluntary and involuntary admissions as well as patient rights and other topics related to hospitalization.

The "Guidelines" state a person may be involuntarily committed for a period up to thirty days (and recommitted for 60 days, followed by a 180 day recommittment) after a hearing (notification, presence may be waived, representation by counsel, finding within 1 day) provided the court finds clear and convincing evidence, that:

1. the person is suffering from a severe mental disorder, and
2. there is a reasonable prospect that this disorder is treatable at or through the facility to which he is to be committed, and such commitment would be consistent with the least restrictive alternative principle; and
3. the person either refuses or is unable to consent to voluntary admission for treatment; and
4. the person lacks capacity to make an informed decision concerning treatment; and
5. as the result of the severe mental disorder the person is (1) likely to cause harm to himself or to suffer substantial mental or physical deterioration, or (2) likely to cause harm to others (APA, 1983).

The statute in Utah enacted in 1978 closely follows the above with required criteria of mental illness, inability to engage in rational decision making, no other appropriate less restrictive environment treatment exists and because of mental illness an immediate danger of physical injury to others and self exists, which may include the inability to provide the basic necesities of life (food, clothing, shelter) if allowed to remain at liberty (Lebeque and Clark, 1981).

Pennsylvania, after a study (1982) of the functioning of its 1976 act providing full procedural protection, recommended both substantive and procedural changes. Recommended were expansion of the commitment standard to include "serious property damage or seriously endanger the health and welfare of their families'' and to broaden the concept of harm to self to include ''serious inability to exercise customary judgment and discretion in the conduct of personal affairs and social relations which will cause major harm or lead to serious distress.'' The procedural change recommended would make the hearing informal, perhaps at meetings of the treatment team with a patient advocate assigned to assist the patient present his/her case (Applebaum, 1982).

The U.S. Supreme Court has addressed the issue of admissions. In 1979 in two decisions on admissions the court seemed to reverse the trend from criminal standards toward a free and independent evaluation rather than a formal fact-finding adversarial process. The court expressed concern about the consequences of denying care to those who desperately need it. In Addington v. Texas, the Supreme Court chose neither the criminal standard ''beyond a reasonable doubt'' nor the traditional standard of simple preponderance of evidence. Instead it selected a midground ''clear and convincing evidence'' standard of proof for involuntary hospitalization (Spensley, Barter, Werme, and Langsley, 1974; Curran, 1979; Williamson, 1979). In a consolidation of two opinions (Parham v. J. L. and J. R. and Bartley v. Kremens, the Supreme Court answered two questions: Do children have a constitutional right to challenge their parents' decision to ''voluntarily'' commit them to institutions for the mentally ill or mentally retarded? And if they do, what must be done to protect their interests? The decision provided a definitive answer to a dispute that had lasted four years. It all began with a ruling by a three-judge Federal panel in Pennsylvania (Bartley v. Kremens, 1975) declaring unconstitutional a 1966 statute allowing parents to commit children. The second case, from Georgia (Parham v. J. L. and J. R., 1977), was similar, in that a lower court had ruled that voluntary commitment of children by parents or guardians violated due process rights. Finally, in 1979, the Supreme Court ruled that while some parents may at times act against the best interests of their children, this is hardly reason to discard the human experience that parents generally do act in the child's best interest. Rather than recommend either a medical decision as sufficient or an adversary hearing, it stated that children up to age 14 could have up to six weeks' hospitalization before requiring an adversary hearing.

However, children who are wards of the state shall have a hearing. The court further indicated that due process did not require a formal hearing unless the state wished it; a full and independent evaluation by a staff physician would be acceptable (*HCP*, 1979; McDonald, 1979; *Mental Disability Law Reporter*, 1979).

SPECIAL SITUATIONS

What about admission to general hospital wards? The admission to the wards of a general hospital of patients with all forms of mental disorders, serious mental illness in particular, is increasing. Usually the action to admit has required no legal action. Admission is at the request of the patient with concurrence of the physician. However, the pressure to accept involuntary admission as well is also greater than it was formerly. Acceptance of the involuntary patient to the general hospital should be contingent on the ability to limit entrance to those who can benefit from available resources and the range of services offered (Leeman and Berger, 1980).

What about the patient leaving before the staff believes the person healthy enough to go? When the patient comes of his or her own volition he or she may be neither coerced to enter nor forcibly detained from leaving. The hospital may, however, require a signed release indicating that the act of leaving was against medical advice, clarifying for the record that it was the patient's decision to leave.

Involuntary care requires the availability of an organized psychiatric unit, with specially trained staff, a range of programs and services, and both open and locked wards. Some patients may for a time require a locked ward while acutely psychotic, suicidal, violent, or intoxicated. This change of the general hospital from a treatment center for only those who come voluntarily to one that admits those with a defined legal status and troublesome overt behavior may occasion a deterioration in the quality of services unless there are additional resources and program changes. The development of the psychiatric intensive care unit similar to cardiac care units may facilitate the conceptualization, funding, and generation of sufficient general hospital services to accommodate psychiatric inpatients.

OTHER FORMS OF ADMISSION

Most states also have special laws that cover the admission to mental hospitals of epileptics, the mentally retarded, drug addicts, and sexual deviates. Only thirteen states, for example, have provisions for the voluntary admission of persons suffering from chronic alcoholism. Massachusetts provides that the alcoholic patient accepted for inpatient care must agree to remain under treatment for thirty days.

Persons who develop a mental illness before sentence or after confinement in prison are hospitalized according to a range of practices varying widely from state to state.

Massachusetts requires under its Briggs Law that any person charged with a capital crime be examined by two psychiatrists designated by the state's Department of Mental Health. Anyone indicted for a crime, or who pleads guilty, who is suspected of having a mental illness or of being mentally retarded is either examined at the place of detention or is sent to a public mental hospital for a period not to exceed twenty days. Male criminal offenders may be detained at the Bridgewater State Hospital, a security institution run by the Department of Corrections, while women offenders are sent to state hospitals when found mentally ill.

California law, as of October 1975, requires that a prisoner's attorney be notified if the prisoner is to be transferred to a mental health facility. Further, each judicially committed individual must be examined to determine if security measures are essential in their confinement. Confidentiality is breached to allow mental health records to be obtained by the jail, the judge, or the probation officer. The time spent under mental health treatment in a facility other than the prison is credited to the prisoner's sentence. As a general rule, all mentally ill sex offenders who do not require a secure treatment setting are treated as near their homes as possible.

It would appear that the legal correctional concept of human behavior holds that control is achieved by reward and punishment. The usual tests seem to be: Is the behavior nonbizarre or commonplace? Is there an understandable motivation? If behavior is bizarre and motivation obscure, then it is a proper concern of the medical profession. When individuals fail to respond to reward and punishment, it is assumed they must be sick. This rationalizes the use of the medical system as a repository for correctional failures.

PROBLEMS, ISSUES AND CURRENT CONCERNS

Dangerousness

If one accepts that "the only legitimate justification for civil commitment of any kind should be a proven likelihood of dangerous acts" then serious problems remain (Stone, 1975):

1. Present research is inadequate to assess the likelihood of dangerous behavior.

2. If society must wait for an attempt at suicide or murder to prove the likelihood of danger, then many seriouly ill mental patients will go untreated until a tragedy or near tragedy occurs.

3. The serious mental illness reflected in damage to property, family disruption, and societal disarray will go untreated.

4. The diagnostic categories that describe mental illness and the treatment required have no relationship to dangerousness.

5. The precarious balance between the individual's freedom and the protection of the family from exhaustion and terror and the public from mad acts must be the focus of continued debate.

Least Retrictive Alternative

The legal theory of the *least restrictive alternative to hospitalization* holds that if community facilities exist, patients who need limited services should be given access to them rather than be forced to enter or remain in a mental hospital. The Mental Health Law Project sought to force the District of Columbia to provide community alternatives to admission to St. Elizabeths Hospital. (Dixon v. Weinberger USDC, CA74–285, Dec. 1975; see Stone, 1977).

Since the 1960s, American medical opinion, social policy, and legal theory have changed the preferred locus of treatment of the mentally ill from the mental hospital to nursing homes in the welfare system for institutional care. In this conceptual shift the large state hospital is seen as undesirable, and often as an agent that might well worsen a patient's condition. Although it was anticipated that the community mental health center would accept responsibility for all the mentally ill in its catchment area, including those with chronic mental illnesses, it did not do so. Instead it was expected that the community would exercise leadership in stimulating the private sector to develop alternatives to hospitalization and to provide group homes for those with mental illness when their own homes were unsuitable.

Budson (1979) has identified ten kinds of housing that serve as alternatives to hospitalization: halfway houses, long-term group residences, cooperative apartments, lodges, work camps, family (or foster) care homes, crisis centers, skilled nursing homes, board and care homes, and hotels.* Safety for residents living in alternative settings (including smoke detection devices and easy escape routes from sleeping areas) is as important as quality care. Further, "it is unwarranted to assume," notes Bachrach (1980), "that the quality of restrictiveness: (a) resides outside of the patient in the environment (certain places may be good or bad for a chronic patient), (b) is primarily a function of a class of residential facilities (factors affect restrictiveness such as the type of facility, its location, etc. staffing, programs, expectations, goals, etc.), (c) is a relationship between restrictiveness and residence that can be expressed on a continuum (all of one type of facility are similar)."

With these factors in mind, questions reveal the problems that remain: How does one monitor decentralized services? How does one determine that one setting is the least restrictive among options? Are the services relevant to the individual's needs?

It is usually most desirable to treat an individual as an ambulatory patient while he or she continues to live at home. However, a change in living arrangements may be a desirable option when the home presents the patient with untherapeutic stresses which cannot be altered. Sometimes the mental hospital is the least restrictive place to reside, for it can be a place where individual dignity is retained, where self-determination is encouraged, and where a great variety of treatment modalities exist to speed remission of symptoms.

Screening, Preadmission

A determination of the appropriateness of hospitalization for individuals is part of the screening process. It also attempts to find an

* A lodge is a cooperative communal society in which a group of individuals organizes itself into a self-sustaining business. A work camp accepts individuals into a totally supervised rural setting with farming chores.

alternative service if hospitalization is inappropriate. In Vermont and in most areas served by Federally funded community mental health centers, all patients admitted to the state hospital must be screened prior to acceptance. This rule applies whether admission is voluntary or involuntary. The purpose is to determine that inpatient service is required and that no other alternative is available.

Screening agents are designated by the state mental health department and are required to know state law, admission criteria, and treatment capabilities of state hospitals; the current availability of community resources; and the funding system for payment of suppliers of treatment. Agents must be available seven days a week, twenty-four hours a day.

Problems that serve as obstacles to admission include the interposition of a third party, often unfamiliar with the previous medical history, who may upset the fragile self-determination that leads a person to seek therapy to prevent a relapse; resentment by the treating physician, who has had the patient under care perhaps for years, and who has full knowledge of family stress, toward a review of his or her judgment by one often less qualified; the unavailability of suitable community resources, which reduces the procedure to a meaningless ritual.

In 1979 NIMH reported a decline in the number of inpatients residing in state and county mental hospitals (from 308,983 in 1971 to 170,619 in 1976). Factors other than legislative changes and court decisions were in part responsible for this change, including improved medical therapy, administrative policy, screening, and a greater use of outpatient services and general hospital inpatient beds where actual increases in utilization occurred. In California, according to Roth (1980), voluntary admissions dropped 84 percent. Long-term involuntary admissions increased and more patients were admitted who had arrest records. Though reports indicated no change in actual practice, with perfunctory hearings still the rule, there were nonetheless increased costs for hearings in terms of both money and time spent away from direct service to patients. In addition, judges seem more likely to view behavior as dangerous than are psychiatrists, and legal decision makers do not scrupulously follow new laws.

SUMMARY

Three major trends are reducing the number of patients who require involuntary hospitalization.

1. The growth of ambulatory care and informal admission to general hospitals has reduced drastically (by more than 50 percent) the statutory need for confinement in a mental hospital.

2. The admission of most patients to mental hospitals is under informal or voluntary admission procedures or by emergency certification. During the emergency period the patient is often discharged or, if further treatment is indicated, he elects to stay as a voluntary patient.

3. New statutes limit involuntary admissions by more sharply defining likelihood to cause harm.

Patients who are most likely to be admitted to mental hospitals from the ambulatory care system are those with a history of previous hospitalization, those with a diagnosis of schizophrenia, and single men with few family resources for support (Roth, 1979). The patient who cannot make reasoned decisions in his best interest, and who needs hospital treatment because he may harm himself, is protected by *parens patriae* provisions in many statutes. The government, in depriving the dangerous patient of his liberty, has also acted to protect the rights of those who might otherwise be harmed. In so doing, the need for treatment to ameliorate symptoms or to effect a cure is acknowledged. The law has set standards for its involvement in involuntary hospitalization. They are:

1. A substantial risk of physical harm to the person himself, manifested by evidence of attempts at suicide or serious bodily harm, or of threats likely to be acted upon.

2. A substantial risk of physical harm to other persons, manifested by evidence of violent behavior, or attempted homicide or evidence that others are placed in reasonable fear of violent behavior or serious bodily harm.

3. A very substantial risk of physical impairment or injury to the person himself, manifested by evidence that the person's judgment is so affected and that he is so gravely disabled that he is unable to protect himself or that reasonable provision for his protection is not available.

Once the action to deprive a person of liberty is initiated, most statutes now provide for notice and a hearing and the right to be represented by counsel. Court decisions indicate the need to modify statutes to provide a hearing within seven days. Occasionally recourse to a jury trial, if requested, is also provided. Evaluation of the need for hospitalization and review after admission at stated intervals (to insure proof exists for continued care) is provided for in some new mental health laws.

Every administrator has the obligation to become informed as to the specific statutes governing admission in the state in which his or her facility is located.

On occasion a mental patient is released by a psychiatrist who judges him capable of withstanding the normal stresses of daily life outside an institution, and contrary to expectation the patient assaults another or manifests behavior that causes difficulty. In such cases, the normal rules of negligence apply. The courts generally allow for a policy of release for mental patients whenever possible and construe operative statutes to allow immunity (Williamson, 1979). This conclusion was reached in a case where a child died as the result of an assault by a mental patient. The court allowed no recovery of damage and indicated the statutory purpose was to protect state-employed psychiatrists who acted in good faith and after careful assessment arrived at the opinion that the mental condition of the patient warranted his release. The second conclusion was reached in a New York case where a patient on an open ward of a mental hospital left the grounds and attacked a person in a park. The court denied recovery of damages because no evidence showed the decision to allow the patient reasonable freedom was a medically unsound judgment. To rule otherwise would force every psychiatrist to overprescribe incarceration.

Mental health professionals may be guided by the rulings applied to psychiatrists. The interests of the patient or client are primary in all determinations of the need for admission or the readiness to leave an inpatient service.

QUESTIONS

1. What are the medical, substantive, and procedural criteria for the admission of the mentally ill to the hospital?
2. What are the differences between informal and voluntary admissions?

3. How has the admission procedure employed in Massachusetts changed practice? Does counsel for the patient insure evidence is clear and convincing?
4. What is the trend in newer state laws for involuntary admission?
5. Discuss the pros and cons of dangerousness as the primary criterion for involuntary mental hospitalization.
6. How does one determine the "least restrictive alternative" to hospitalization?
7. What has been the impact of the laws requiring a recent overt dangerous act for involuntary admission?
8. What are some of the elements which should be considered in developing a more ideal involuntary admission statute?

REFERENCES

Applebaum, P. S. (1982), Civil commitment in the pendulum changing direction. *Hosp. Community Psychiat.*, 33:703–704.

Bachrach, L. L. (1980), Is the least restrictive environment always the best? Sociological and semantic implications. *Hosp. Community Psychiat.*, 31:97–103.

Barton, G. (1974), Criteria for admission to a psychiatric hospital. In: *A Practical Handbook of Psychiatry*, ed. J. Novello. Springfield, Ill.: Charles C Thomas.

Barton, W. E. (1962), *Administration in Psychiatry*. Springfield, Ill.: Charles C Thomas.

Brakel, S. J., & Rock, R. S. (1971), *The Mentally Disabled and the Law*. Rev. ed. Chicago: University of Chicago Press.

Budson, R. D. (1979), Sheltered housing for the mentally ill. *McLean Hospital J.*, (1980) 4:140–157.

Curran, W. (1979), Law-medicine notes: The Supreme Court and madness. *N. Engl. J. Med.*, 301:317.

GAP (1966), *Laws Governing Hospitalization of the Mentally Ill*. New York: Group for the Advancement of Psychiatry.

HCP (1979), Parents, children and due process: The case of Kremens v. Bartley. *Hosp. Community Psychiat.*, 27:705–706.

Kopolow, L. E., et al. (1975), *Litigation and Mental Health Services*. NIMH DHEW Publication (ADM) 26-76. Rockville, Md.: National Institute of Mental Health.

Kumasaka, Y., Stokes, J., & Gupta, R. K. (1972), Criteria for involuntary hospitalization. *Arch. Gen. Psychiat.*, 26:399–404.

* Lebegue, B., & Clark, L. D. (1981), Incompetence to refuse treatment: A necessary condition for civil commitment. *Amer. J. Psychiat.*, 138:1075–1077.

* Lebensohn, Z. M. (1978), Defensive psychiatry: On how to treat the mentally ill without being a lawyer. In: *Law and the Mental Health Professions*, ed. W. E. Barton & C. J. Sanborn. New York: International Universities Press.

Leeman, C. P., & Berger, H. S. (1980), The Massachusetts Psychiatric Society's position paper on involuntary psychiatric admissions to general hospitals. *Hosp. Community Psychiat.*, 31:318–326.

McDonald, M. (1979), Supreme Court upholds parents' right to commit. *Psychiatric News*, 14:1–14, July 20.

McGarry, A. L., & Greenblatt, M. (1972), Conditional voluntary mental hospital admissions. *N. Engl. J. Med.*, 287:279–280.

* McGarry, A. L., Schwitzgebel, R. K., Lipsitt, P. D., & Lelos, D. (1978), *Civil Commitment and Social Policy*. Rockville, Md.: National Institute of Mental Health.

Mental Disability Law Reporter (1979), Decisions: Historic Supreme Court decision on the voluntary admission of minors. July-August, pp. 231–234.

Monahan, J. (1978), Prediction research and the emergency commitment of dangerous mentally ill persons. *Amer. J. Psychiat.*, 135:198–201.

Peske, M. A. (1975), Is dangerousness an issue for physicians in emergency commitment? *Amer. J. Psychiat.*, 132:825–828; 829–831.

Psychiatric News (1977), Court upholds Florida law on commitment. *Psychiatric News*, 12:15, Aug. 19.

Rock, R. S. (1968), *Hospitalization and Discharge of the Mentally Ill*. Chicago: University of Chicago Press.

* Roth, L. H. (1980), Mental health commitment: The state of the debate. *Hosp. Community Psychiat.*, 31:385–396.

Shaffer, B. (1974), New law gives Virginia mental patients a bill of rights. *The Washington Post*, A–7, Aug. 10.

Spensley, J., Barter, J. T., Werme, P. H., & Langsley, D. G. (1974), Involuntary hospitalization: What for? How long?, *Amer. J. Psychiat.*, 131:219–222.

* Stone, A. A. (1975), *Mental Health and Law: A System in Transition*. DHEW Publication (ADM) 75–176. Washington, D.C.: U.S. Government Printing Office.

Stone, A. A. (1977), Recent mental health litigation: A critical perspective. *Amer. J. Psychiat.*, 134:273–279.

Szasz, T. S. (1972), Voluntary mental hospitalization: An unacknowledged practice of medical fraud. *N. Engl. J. Med.*, 287:277–278.

Williamson, P. W. (1979), New developments in civil commitment of the mentally ill: Impact for patient, family and psychiatrist. *J. Amer. Med. Assn.*, 242:2307–2309.

Zusman, J., & Shaffer, S. (1973), Emergency psychiatric hospitalization via court order: A critique. *Amer. J. Psychiat.*, 130:132–136.

Chapter 10

Patient Rights

The spirit of liberty is more than jealousy for
your own rights. It is a decent respect for the
rights and opinions of others. We are free, not
because we have freedom but because we serve
freedom. The love of liberty cannot be separated
from loving your neighbor or yourself.
—*Christian A. Herter*

Case example. A 40-year-old woman, from a family of social standing
and high achievement, had a 20-year history of hospitalization in a
Massachusetts mental hospital. The diagnosis was paranoid schizophrenia, and all the usual forms of treatment had been tried without
success. Her parents had died and she had no siblings. Without going
into the dynamics of her distressing behavior, we will focus upon her
belief that those about her were attempting "to steal her birthright."
She claimed to sense their interest by sensations in her genitalia. When
these occurred, she would without warning strike the person beside
her. The force of these blows at times broke or bloodied noses, or
toppled the unsuspecting victim. On occasion other patients would
retaliate with their own violent blows.

Massachusetts law permits the use of restraint and seclusion in
emergencies, and a 1979 court decision defines an emergency as a

206

situation where there is "a substantial likelihood of physical harm to the patient, other patients or to staff members of the institution."

The hospital staff, wishing to prevent injury to everyone concerned, decided it would be best to apply a leather strap around her waist with cuffs to restrain her arms. She would enjoy progressively longer periods out of these restraints if she refrained from striking others. Failing that, she would be secluded for thirty days, with brief periods out each day. These would be lengthened each day if she struck no one.

The reasons for restraint and seclusion and the procedure to be followed were to be carefully explained to the patient. She objected, insisting she could control her behavior and that it would not recur if only others would stop trying to steal her birthright.

Would you respect her right to refuse? May the procedure as outlined be instituted? If not, what action would you take to protect the patient and others? You have tried medications, ECT, psychotherapy, and behavior therapy several times over without success.

HISTORICAL PERSPECTIVE

The rights of individuals to freedom and protection from intrusions by the state into their private affairs are the subject of Amendments One through Ten of the Constitution of the United States, commonly known as the Bill of Rights, and also of the Fourteenth Amendment. In somewhat the same spirit, psychiatric reform was begun in the late eighteenth century by Pinel in France, by Tuke in England, and by others with some recognition that the rights of patients were being disregarded. Corrective steps were embodied in moral treatment of the insane in the early nineteenth century. Dorothea Dix, and later (around 1910) Clifford Beers, aroused awareness of the suffering of the mentally ill in jails, almshouses, and asylums. New institutions were founded and old ones improved as a consequence of the crusade led by these two individuals.

Moral treatment, however, became ineffective as institutions grew large. It was replaced by custodial care: food, lodging, occupation, and symptomatic relief for the undifferentiated mass of individuals. Dehumanizing routines crushed the human spirit.

The 1930s brought insulin, metrazol, prefrontal lobotomy, and electroconvulsive therapy, which restored the conviction that mental disease was curable. It was ECT that truly started a therapeutic revolution, as its application brought quick relief to depressed and overactive patients.

World War II depleted hospital personnel and diverted essential resources. This led to shocking exposés of the miserable conditions of patients in mental institutions. The American Psychiatric Association reacted by establishing a Mental Hospital Institute, the journal *Mental Hospitals,* and a Central Inspection Board to improve the conditions in facilities caring for the mentally ill. Teams visited Europe to study their methods of service delivery and returned with the determination to change the system in the United States (Casey and Rackow, 1960; Barton, Farrell, Lenehan, and McLaughlin, 1961; Furman, 1965). Emphasis was on the dignity and responsibility of patients, informal admissions, open hospitals, paid work programs, family care, and ambulatory care. Hospitals improved, entire systems of delivery were changed as in Saskatchewan (Smith and McKerracher, 1963), and for the first time patient census began to decline while admissions continued high.

In the 1950s the discovery of effective new drugs to treat depression and excitement and to relieve hallucinations and delusions produced dramatic changes in the course of mental disorders. It was now possible to treat most patients on an ambulatory basis or in a brief time in a general hospital.

The 1960s focused national attention upon discriminatory practices against blacks, a concern which quickly spread to encompass discriminatory practice directed at other groups in society. The movement had overtones of a revolt against all institutional authority. In this climate one of us, in *Administration in Psychiatry* (Barton, 1962), called attention to patient rights. To Morton Birnbaum goes the credit for articulating the mentally ill patient's right to treatment. *Wyatt v. Stickney* (1972) was a landmark decision on the civil rights of patients. The rise of the mental health bar in the 1970s to press for patient rights aroused public awareness and led to legislation and judicial rulings which had a profound impact upon the attitudes and values associated with the rights of the mentally ill.

Another step in defining the rights of patients was the Developmentally Disabled Assistance and Bill of Rights Act of 1975. It required states to develop protection and advocacy systems for persons with developmental disabilities as a condition of continued Federal funding. In 1978 the President's Commission on Mental Health recommended a similar advocacy system for mentally disabled individuals. The Commission also asked all Federal agencies to enforce existing laws and regulations which prohibit discrimination against those with mental illness. States were asked to review mental health laws and to revise them if necessary to insure both procedural and statutory rights.

PROCEDURAL AND STATUTORY RIGHTS

The rights of patients may be subdivided into two major categories, procedural and substantive. Procedural safeguards encourage screening of potential commitment cases, a hearing preceded by adequate notice to concerned parties, the right of the patient to be present, representation by counsel, use of the "clear and convincing evidence" standard, and a specified period of confinement with review of progress (President's Commission, 1978). This emphasis restricted the use of involuntary commitment and diminished the states' protective role toward those unable to make decisions essential to their own interest.

Substantive rights were defined in a series of court decisions. For example, the Eighth Amendment "right to freedom from cruel and unusual punishment" was applied in the Willowbrook case in New York State to upgrade facilities for the care of the retarded. The "right to treatment" was given recognition in Wyatt v. Stickney, as was the "right to the least restrictive alternative to hospitalization" in Dixon v. Weinberger (Stone, 1975; Barton and Sanborn, 1978).

Many states have recodified their mental health laws in the past few years. Some, including Massachusetts, have incorporated a bill of rights for mental patients. The Massachusetts statutes apply to all facilities and specify that the rights statement is to be posted and given to every patient upon admission. Rights covered include: access to the names of all personnel responsible for his or her care, prompt response to all reasonable requests, a copy of any rule or regulation which applies to conduct as a patient or resident, and inspection of medical records and of any financial statement sent to a third party.

There are limitations in the legislative and judicial approach to protecting patient rights. Judicial rulings articulate principles and set standards by which practice will be judged. But the legislature determines the distribution of resources available to meet citizen needs in a climate of intense competition for scarce funds, and the executive branch conducts operations. The latter has the authority and responsibility to prepare policy statements and regulations to assure that patient rights will be protected, but has often failed to formulate, implement, or enforce them, as has been demonstrated in several successful court cases. This was brought out clearly in Morales v. Turman, where the judge stated that since the agency involved did not exercise it's authority to set regulations and standards, the court would therefore do so.

This historical perspective leads us to the present and to a statement: *The responsibility for the enforcement of patient rights rests with the state's mental health authority and with the administrator of every mental health facility. A state's Department of Mental Health is given the responsibility for developing rules and regulations essential to achieving its assigned mission. It is the facility administrator who puts policy into operation and then assures that patient rights are preserved.*

PATIENT RIGHTS

Principle II of the Standards for Psychiatric Facilities drawn up by the Joint Commission on Accreditation of Hospitals states, "The psychiatric facility shall acknowledge the dignity and protect the rights of all its patients" (Joint Commission, 1981). Let us examine these rights.

The Right to Health

"The enjoyment of the highest attainable standard of health is one of the fundamental rights of every human being without distinction of race, religion, political belief, economic or social condition," according to the preamble of the World Health Organization's constitution.

The U.S. Congress declared in the Comprehensive Health Planning Act of 1966 (Public Law 89–49) that "the fulfillment of our national purpose depends on promoting and assuring the highest level of health attainable for every person in an environment which contributes positively to healthful and family living'' (Curran, 1971).

If the right to health is conceptualized as society's obligation to assure every citizen the highest attainable level of health, then that goal is unattainable. Government cannot guarantee health. It can provide only the resources for exercising the right of access to health care. The actual maintenance of health is an individual's own responsibility. Health is not something legislated into existence or granted a person by a benevolent society. It may not be a gift even at birth; it may be destroyed by accident, intention, or through ignorance. If attained, it must be preserved through an individual's own efforts.

We are aware that health is affected by personal lifestyles. We are aware also that those who eat and exercise moderately and regularly, don't smoke cigarettes, use alcohol in moderation or not at all, and sleep seven or eight hours each night have observed the imperatives of good health. Some choose to smoke, overeat, and drink excessively; refuse immunizations, overexpose their skin to the sun, and take no exercise; or ride motorcycles, race automobiles, hang-glide, or play football. Those who choose to do so are at greater risk of ill health or injury. "Does justice require," asks Veatch (1980), "that the public bear the health costs of truly voluntary health risks that some choose to take?"

The Right of Equal Access to Treatment

A person with an injury or acute illness should have the right of immediate access to appropriate treatment. Those with less urgent needs may be prescreened to insure that intake into the health care system is indicated.

We remember the case of an individual with acute delirium tremens who was shuttled between hospitals and refused admission because "they didn't admit alcoholic patients"; the person died in the ambulance. We recall a professional colleague struck down by a truck which resulted in terrible injuries. His admission to hospital was delayed for hours while geographical jurisdiction was argued. One hears of patients whose admissions were delayed while ability to pay was established. Psychiatrists have been alleged to turn away desperately depressed and suicidal patients because they believed individuals have the right to kill themselves.

Over a hundred years ago Isaac Ray (1869) said that any law to regulate hospitalization of the mentally ill:

> should put no hindrance in the way to prompt use of those instrumentalities which are regarded as most effectual in promoting the comfort and restoration of the patient. Secondly, it should spare all unnecessary exposure of private trouble, and all unnecesary conflict with popular prejudices. Thirdly, it should protect individuals from wrongful imprisonment. It would be objection enough to any legal provision that it failed to secure these objects in the completest possible manner.

In many places it is standard practice for the mentally ill to be held in jail while awaiting transportation or completion of legal arrangements for admission to a mental hospital. We abhor the practice. Transport should neither be left to the sheriff's department nor police as if the mentally ill were criminals. Emergency Medical Technican Paramedics and their ambulances may offer a more humane and suitable alternative. Do we need a Dorothea Dix to undo the snarls in our age that serve as barriers against access to treatment? There should be no room in our social philosophy to delay admission because of race, color, creed, sex, ability to pay, jurisdiction, or legal machinery.

The Right to Treatment

The President's Commission on Mental Health recommended that "each state review its mental health laws and revise them, if necessary, to ensure they provide for a right to treatment and to habilitation." A number of states had already done so. The Florida statute declares "that it shall not deny treatment for mental illness to any person." The Wisconsin law states all patients "have a right to a humane psychological and physical environment within the hospital facilities" (President's Commission, 1978).

In a 1979 decision by U.S. District Court Judge Lenore J. Conte (Rone v. Fineman, Ohio), it was held that no constitutional right to treatment exists by itself. The constitutional right of freedom is the issue; it is not whether treatment is overly restrictive but whether the treatment method is overly restrictive of liberty. As long as treatment within the hospital does not restrict one's liberty by comparison with other feasible settings in which therapy might be given, it is acceptable. Treatment doesn't have to be given in an alternate setting (McDonald, 1979).

In Wyatt v. Stickney the court did society and the profession a service in restating the principles of good patient management in a safe environment, to ensure that individual treatment needs were met. It went further than the right to the "highest standard of medical care . . . possible in light of the facilities and personnel available" (Slovenko, 1973, chapter 14). "Adequate treatment" as set forth in Judge Frank M. Johnson's landmark decision included a comprehensive physical and mental examination made within forty-eight hours after admission, and an individualized treatment plan for each patient developed by "qualified mental health professionals" (including a psychiatrist) no later than five days after admission. Required in the plan was a statement of the specific nature of the problem; the specific needs of the patient; the least restrictive treatment conditions to achieve the purposes of commitment; a description of short- and long-range goals and a timetable for their achievement; a description of staff responsibilities and their relation to achieving goals; criteria for release and discharge; and a posthospitalization plan to be reviewed at least every ninety days by the mental health professional assigned responsibility for follow-up.

Eight years after Judge Johnson made his decision, he placed the Alabama hospitals in receivership because of failure to comply with these standards (*Psychiatric News*, 1979). The order required a remedial plan to achieve compliance and cited several critical areas for correction: lack of habilitation planning, inadequate staff, failure to provide privacy, lax medication policies, overrestrictive environment, and lack of proper medical and dental care.

Sufficient time has elapsed to assess the overall impact of Wyatt v. Stickney on the Alabama system, (Burrier, 1969; Tancredi and Clark, 1972; Leaf, 1977; Byrne, 1981).

• The standards were workable.
• Patient care improved.

- Where limited funds had been used to perpetuate an obsolete institutional system, attention to priorities should have created a balanced system.
- An inordinate amount of the time of professionals was diverted from patient service to reports to the court and to legal reviews.
- Recruitment of staff of quality was hampered by the damage to the system's reputation.
- The courts are not an operating agency or an acceptable alternative to the executive branch of government.

THE RIGHT OF THE RETARDED TO TREATMENT

On June 18, 1982, the U.S. Supreme Court established for the first time the constitutional rights of the mentally retarded. The ruling, in Youngberg v. Romeo, may be expected also to affect those under involuntary admission for mental illness. The court indicated that patients should have at least the constitutional protection afforded prisoners, such as the right to safe conditions and the right to be free of unnecessary physical restraints. The court based itself on the due process clause of the Fourteenth Amendment, granting protection from cruel and unusual punishment. The decision emphasized that ''the court must show deference to the judgments exercised by a qualified professional'' and advised minimal interference by the judiciary with internal operations unless there is a substantial departure from accepted professional judgment, practices, or standards.

The court said institutions have an obligation, enforceable in courts, to provide limited guarantees that a minimum level of training and development would be given patients. It noted problems with the ''right to treatment'' because the Constitution guarantees no substantive services to anyone. The ruling showed flexibility in allowing for professional judgment and budgetary limitations. The ruling did affirm the right to training and development to enhance the ability of patients to function safely.

THE RIGHT TO REFUSE TREATMENT

Individuals have the right to participate in decisions that affect them. The concept of informed consent assumes that patients, given a reasonable explanation of the treatment proposed, its expected benefits, the risks and side effects, the alternative therapeutic options and their consequences, and the probable course of the disorder without treatment, will make a decision in their own best interest. This holds for both voluntary and involuntary patients or clients. The psychiatrist and the mental health professional have no more power than anyone else to override the patient's wishes. Most accept the right of a patient with physical disease or injury to refuse an amputation, an operation, or medication, even when the choice may lead to a fatal outcome. The same reasoning applies to those with mental illness. There are two exceptions—emergencies and cases in which the person has been adjudicated incompetent. The former, narrowly defined, is a situation where the failure to treat would result in a substantial likelihood of physical harm to the patient or others.

The controversial issues here are (1) the extent to which the state may act paternalistically in protecting citizens who can't decide matters rationally and are dependent upon others for their survival (grievous mental illness) and (2) the paradox that if the state acts to involuntarily admit such individuals, it thereby deprives them of their right to treatment. The paradox is clear, for by exercising the right to refuse treatment, the person forfeits the right to an early restoration of the freedom from hospitalization and illness (Applebaum and Gutheil, 1981).

Types of Patients Who Refuse Treatment

Why patients refuse treatment. The most common reason for refusal is: the patient was not told the treatment was ordered or why. Unpleasant side effects in a previous experience, the desire to remain in control of oneself, and lack of trust in staff are common reasons for refusal according to a study made by Applebaum and Roth on seven wards in four medical hospitals who noted 105 instances of refusal (Applebaum and Gutheil 1981).

Less common are the more dramatic reactions found in a variety of more serious mental disorders. A patient may scream until exhausted, or take flight in panic, be delirious, be unresponsive because of profound depression or withdrawal, believe attempts to medicate or to restrain are intended to poison or kill, or may violently attack those present. Three groups of refusers were identified by Applebaum and Gutheil in a three month study period on a forty bed inpatient ward of a mental facility. There were 72 episodes of refusal in 23 patients. Although the sample was too small to permit generalizations, it suggested that in one heterogenous group, with a variety of mental illnesses (13 patients) no episode of refusal lasted more than one day. A second group (5 patients, 39 episodes) refused restraints for a period of from 1 to 3 days. Many of the episodes ended without the therapist learning of the patients' refusal. The patients appeared to be those with more serious mental illnesses, often paranoid, with refusal a means of communicating the distress suffered. A third group (5 patients, including 4 with schizophrenia) suffered from deep-seated delusions but phrased their refusal in the language of civil rights and resolutely held to their position for a period of from 7 to 65 days. Applebaum and Gutheil concluded that refusal is not a homogeneous concept but a set of behaviors whose meaning and consequences vary with the clinical state. The first two groups pose no serious barrier to treatment, for all the episodes were short. The role of the nurse was pivotal to secondary compliance. However, refusal in the third group was directly related to the illness, with serious consequences if not treated.

Judicial Actions to Establish the Right to Refuse Treatment

In Rennie v. Klein a qualified right to refuse treatment in non-emergency situations was established in New Jersey. In his 1978 decision in that case Judge Brotman ruled that except in emergencies, psychotropic drugs can be given only when there is a signed informed consent. Both voluntary and involuntary patients may be given medication when there is a sudden change in behavior which creates a danger to self and others. In nonemergency situations, an involuntary patient can be given medications only after review of the case by a court-appointed independent psychiatrist and after a hearing with patient or legal counsel present (Curran, 1980; *NCP,* 1980). In Rennie, the qualified right to refuse considered the physical danger to self or others, the patient's capacity for decision making, alternative treatment methods available, and the risk of untoward side effects (*Mental Disability Law Review,* 1980).

A broader declaration of the right to refuse treatment is that in Rogers v. Okin, the Boston State Hospital Case of 1979. There, Federal Judge Tauro, in a ruling that applied to both voluntary and involuntary patients, said, "henceforth, patients have a constitutional right to refuse medication" except where there is a substantial likelihood of extreme violence, personal injury, or attempted suicide (Ford, 1980). The patient in this case had rolled a coat hanger around his fist and threatened to punch those at hand. He was forcibly medicated and put in seclusion. Over thirty days, his time out of confinement was lengthened until control over his behavior was evident. The judge held that one can't "be given another forcing emergency treatment despite the known clinical finding that seclusion and medication work well together to control an acute episode of psychiatric excitement, agitation, or self-destructiveness" (Gutheil, 1980).

When Rogers v. Okin reached the Supreme Court as Rogers v. Mills (1982) no definitive ruling emerged. Rather, that body returned the case to the First Circuit Court of Appeals on grounds it was more in touch with Massachusetts law, with the comment that "Massachusetts recognizes liberty interests of persons adjudicated incompetent that are broader than those protected directly by the constitution" (*Clinical Psychiatry News*, 1982). It can therefore be inferred that the ruling of Judge Tauro applies only in that state.

In that ruling, the constitutional right of hospitalized mental patients to refuse treatment was affirmed, except in narrowly defined emergencies. The decision was based upon the First Amendment and cited the right to produce a thought and possible interference with the right of privacy by powerful mind-altering drugs.

The notion that medication is mind control and that drugs interfere with the production of thought seems strange to those who work in the mental health field. We use psychotropic drugs to counter the control of the mind by delusions, hallucinations, and mental disorder, and through drug action restore control over decisions to the patient. The Rogers v. Okin case illustrates the very considerable gap that exists between abstract legal concepts and the practical realities encountered in relieving human suffering and seeking remission of symptoms which deprive patients of rational control over themselves.

Problems Created When Patients Refuse Treatment

- Loss of credibility of physicians and mental health workers before the courts and lack of confidence in their therapeutic interventions
- The hazard of treating patients by alternative methods that are not medically indicated
- The prolongation of hospitalization from days to weeks and months
- An increase in disability and chronicity
- Disruption of the patient-therapist dyad, with loss of confidence and the inclusion of an advocate or independent negotiator
- Increased cost of care (longer hospitalization, court costs, legal fees, guardianship, and delay of the patient's return to earning a living)

Steps to Treatment When the Patient Refuses

The concept of mental illness implies the presence of a disorder of cognition, thought, or affect or of disturbed behavior that impairs ability to understand, to reason, or to make rational choices.

The legal view holds all individuals competent (except children under the legal age) unless adjudicated incompetent. Mental health professionals acknowledge the validity of this view in principle but encounter operational problems putting it into practice. When a person is involuntarily admitted for a mental illness but refuses to be treated, it subverts the purpose of the admission. Some states—Vermont is one—preserve all civil rights but specify treatment may be given to those involuntarily admitted. A few states determine competence at the same time a decision to admit is made. Where there is no statute covering such matters, treatment may be given only in an emergency situation where the patient may harm himself or others.

Fortunately, most patients who refuse treatment do so only for a short time. The therapist or nurse must have the patience to explain, to listen, and to negotiate an agreement. It usually works. It may take a day or two, but it is worth taking the time to gain patient cooperation.

When the patient refuses treatment and is believed incompetent to make the required decision, the process of securing a legal guardian may be initiated. Although this takes time to accomplish, a guardian may give consent to medical or other professional care, counsel, treatment, or services (Gutheil, Shapiro, and St. Clair (1980). If a relative will serve the patient's interests, this may provide a solution to the general scarcity of individuals willing to assume the burden of guardianship. Involuntary admission may well be a speedier process than that of appointing a substitute decision maker.

Alternate remedies suggested by Gutheil et al. (1980) include determination of competency at time of admission; external review by an independent psychiatrist or review board to study any previous response to treatment, to evaluate the patient's ability to make a rational choice, and to advise a course of action; and impartial review by an institutional medical standards committee.

It would therefore be wise for the administrator to develop a written policy governing the voluntary and involuntary use of medication, seclusion, and restraint. Rules governing steps to be taken should be outlined in detail for the protection of both patient and staff.

Fortunately, most patients realize their need for help and can be persuaded to give consent. When a stalemate results, it is essential to enter into the patient's clinical chart a written statement signed by the patient, if possible, and by responsible relatives indicating refusal of treatment. Failing this, an account of the actions taken should be entered, signed by the therapist, and witnessed. This may be useful in the event of any subsequent liability claims. It may also be wise to secure the advice of legal counsel as to what further steps may be taken.

The intensely suicidal patients, the mute, posturing patient with schizophrenia, and the violent and destructive patient respond to treatment and make care by hospital staff possible. A patient may starve to death if force feedings are not given over objections. With knowledge that mental illness may inhibit rational decisions and induce bizarre behavior, the psychiatrist is unwilling to accept the view that all persons possess the judgment to refuse treatment. But some do. The law asks us to be aware of this fine line and to follow due process whenever an individual's rights and liberty are involved.

LEGAL RIGHTS

A diagnostic label of mental disorder or mental retardation is not in itself sufficient cause to restrict an individual's freedom. Each must have *the right to live in the least restrictive environment* appropriate to treatment needs. Correlated as a fundamental principle is *freedom of choice* within the individual's capacity to make decisions. The principle implies competence to make a reasoned decision and to give informed consent. Admission to an institution, under commitment, does not by itself constitute a determination of the individual's competency or incompetency. A patient may need hospital care and be fully competent; another may not need hospitalization but be quite incapable of managing himself and his affairs, and may require a guardian (AAMD, 1973).

Living in one's own home and attending an outpatient clinic for treatment is the least restrictive of all treatment alternatives. Care in a mental hospital's open ward, with access to a variety of programs essential to treatment and rehabilitation, may be the appropriate environment and be less restrictive of freedom than the alternative of minimal or no psychiatric treatment in a nursing home. Emphasis is upon placement in an environment appropriate to treatment needs that least restricts the patient's freedom.

A recommendation of the President's Commission on Mental Health urges states to review guardianship laws and to revise them if necessary. As guardianship may lead to a deprivation of legal rights, procedural protection is necessary as well as limitation of the guardian's authority to "those activities in which a person has demonstrated an incapacity to act competently."

The U.S. Supreme Court was expected to rule on the patient's right to treatment, in O'Connor v. Donaldson, 1975. In a decision of June 1975 it failed to do so. The court unanimously held that "a state cannot constitutionally confine *without more* a non-dangerous individual who is capable of surviving safely in freedom by himself or with the help of willing and responsible family members or friends." The curious phrase in the above decision—"without more"—probably means "without more than custodial care." The implication is that those who are involuntarily committed, who receive only custodial care, who are not dangerous to themselves or to others, and who can survive outside the hospital alone or with available help must be given their freedom. The right to prompt release when the cause for involuntary detention no longer exists is thus stated.

The U.S. Supreme Court (Youngberg v. Romeo, June 18, 1982) noted the difficult problem in the right to treatment: the Constitution guarantees no substantive services to anyone. The court did establish the principle that the involuntarily committed receive the "training" to function safely in the hospital without hurting themselves or others, thus avoiding restraints on freedom.

Freedom of speech without fear of reprisal and the *right to communicate* with others should be guaranteed. The patient must have access to his or her physician, ward nurse, family, and lawyer. Some hospitals provide a patient advocate to handle special problems. The fundamental freedom of speech must not be denied by reason of mental illness. The hospitalized mental patient may wish family and friends to know of his admission to the hospital, may wish to have help with unfinished business matters at home, may wish to protest admission and secure release, and may wish to protect himself from neglect and abuse. There must be no arbitrary suppression of the patient's efforts to communicate with those whose help he seeks.

The court in Wyatt v. Stickney gave a much broader mandate: "Patients shall have an unrestricted right to send sealed mail and an unrestricted right to receive sealed mail from their attorneys, physicians, other mental health professionals, from courts and from government officials."

There are patients who write obscene letters to people whose names they have learned by chance; some write of torrid fantasied love in letters to a married person with whom they have the most superficial acquaintance; some patients order things by mail they can't pay for. Others threaten to kill the President. To require that all patients' mail be sent sealed when it is known it will cause harm is obviously wrong; the court's intent should apply to sealed letters sent to attorneys, physicians, etc. Where there is no evidence of abuse, all mail may be sent sealed. Violation of any social code is discussed with the patient. When a proven offense has occurred and consequent distress has been reported, stern reprimands and the unswerving expectation that there will be no further violations usually controls most such objectionable letter writing.

A lawyer retained by the patient or in his behalf by friends or relatives may see the patient at any reasonable time. If the patient demands a lawyer, he is given permission to write or phone one of his own choosing.

Other rights that apply to institutionalized patients are listed below. The *right to worship* in the religion of his or her choice is a recognized right. The *right to physical exercise* and to get out of doors should be provided for. The right to move about is encouraged on open wards and by freedom from physical restraint and excessive medication. The opportunity for interaction between men and women and with peers is afforded. The same rights of visitation afforded patients in general hospitals should apply in mental hospitals, unless it has been shown that the illness is made worse by visiting.

There should be an *opportunity to work* and to seek gainful employment, as soon as the individual's condition makes this possible. Some additional rules on patient labor were formulated in Wyatt v. Stickney:

• No patient shall be *required* to perform labor which involves the operation and maintenance of the hospital or for which the hospital is under contract with an outside organization.

• Privileges or release from the hospital shall not be conditional upon performance of such work.

• Patients may *volunteer* to engage in such labor if the work is compensated in accordance with the minimum wage laws under the Fair Labor Standards Act (29 USC P206) as amended in 1966.

• Patients may be required to care for their own living space.

• The right of release from hospital, at the earliest possible time his or her mental condition will allow, is recognized.

• Patients may be required to perform therapeutic tasks which do not involve operation and maintenance of the hospital provided these tasks are:

• an integral part of the treatment plan,

• approved by the responsible therapist,

• supervised by a staff member to ensure that it is:

  • a therapeutic activity,

  • paid for under the Fair Labor Standards Act if it is a therapeutic assignment meeting the requirements of approval,

  • part of treatment plan and supervised if it is work the hospital would otherwise pay an employee to do.

Other rights follow:

The very old right of the patient to challenge both the order for involuntary admission or continued institutionalization is expressed in a writ of habeas corpus which provides for a judicial review. Other review mechanisms have been established as well.

Basic constitutional guarantee of due process of law contained in the Fifth and Fourteenth Amendments gives the patient the right to a hearing before involuntary removal to a mental hospital on a long-term basis. One is entitled to present evidence to rebut the government's assertion that one is "insane"; one is entitled to be represented by counsel at any proceeding which ensues as the result of any criminal charges that have been placed against him or her.

Vermont may serve as a prototype of states with statutory appeal procedures to insure patients the right of release. The senior author serves as a member of the Vermont Mental Health Board, a seven-member body (the statute requires two physicians and one lawyer with staggered six-year terms) with investigative authority to review both individual patient complaints and alleged systems failures, as well as justification for hospitalization or discharge, the treatment prescribed, and the condition of the facility environment. Action may be taken by the Board on its own initiative or on request of a patient or someone acting on his behalf.

Vermont law also provides for judicial review on request of the person in residence in the state hospital or training school, or of an attorney or other interested party. A special unit of the district court conducts the review, hears interested parties, and may order the patient discharged.

In a democracy, one is perfectly free to be eccentric if one wishes, so long as one is not dangerous to oneself or others. While a person may be able to satisfy the court that he is not dangerous and hence no longer in need of involuntary commitment, he may well not convince the judge that recovery has occurred. Courts frequently order conditional release where continuing treatment and supervision seem necessary, but not to the extent of involuntary inpatient care. When the patient can show he either never was or is no longer dangerous, then he is entitled to release. One does not have to be normal or nice, merely not dangerous. As habeas corpus was created to prevent people from being held for insufficient reason in medieval dungeons, so today it is being used to allow people to leave hospitals when they can be cared for in less restrictive environments. It should be noted, however, that comparatively few decisions have been reported in which psychiatrists in good faith examined a patient and decided he was still dangerous, only to have a court overrule their professional judgment (*JAMA*, 1972).

CIVIL RIGHTS

There exists a right to equal treatment under the law without regard to race, ethnic group, religious preference, sex, or age.

"Section 504 of the Rehabilitation Act of 1973 prohibits discrimination on the basis of mental or physical handicap in federally assisted programs" (President's Commission, 1978). The Federal programs potentially available to mentally handicapped persons include, among others, Supplemental Security Income, Medicare, Medicaid, Social Services, Old Age and Survivors Disability Insurance, food stamps, CHAMPUS, VA, Vocational Rehabilitation, family planning, maternal and child health services, and institutional programs for the elderly.

The right to vote is acknowledged, as is the right to make contracts including marriage, if the person has not been judged incompetent.

The Arizona Mental Health Law, Section 36–513 (civil rights not impaired; discrimination prohibited), states:

A. Every person undergoing evaluation shall not be denied any civil right including but not limited to, the right to dispose of property, sue and be sued, enter into contractual relationships and vote. Court-ordered treatment or evaluation is not a determination of legal competency. . . .
B. A person who has been evaluated or treated in an agency for mental disorder shall not be discriminated against in any manner, including but not limited to:
1. seeking employment;
2. resuming or continuing professional practice or previous occupation;
3. obtaining or retaining housing;
4. obtaining or retaining licenses or permits including but not limited to: motor vehicle license, motor vehicle operator's and chauffeur's license, professional and occupational license.

C. Discrmination for purposes of this section means any denial of civil rights on the grounds of hospitalization or outpatient care and treatment unrelated to a person's present capacity to meet the standards applicable to all persons.

In practice, the civil rights of a hospitalized mental patient are often suspended by the act of involuntary admission, although in only four states—Colorado, Indiana, Virginia, and Washington—are they officially suspended. So great is the state-by-state variation in dealing with the many aspects of civil rights that only with difficulty may common principles be adduced. It may safely be said, however, that the nationwide trend is definitely toward retention of full civil rights.

HUMAN RIGHTS

The authors believe that the right to be treated with dignity, courtesy, and respect, to retain one's self-identity, and to wear one's own clothes and keep personal possessions and a reasonable sum of money for incidental purchases, is desirable. Restricted only are articles the therapist feels might be dangerous or inappropriate to therapeutic goals. A place to keep personal possessions is an essential.

Privacy is a human right; it should be provided in sleeping areas (in multipatient rooms, with dividers, screens, or draw curtains) and in toilet and shower areas with separate stalls with doors.

Confidentiality is an ethical responsibility of all staff members on the treatment team.

The right to be protected from exploitation, demeaning treatment, and abuse is acknowledged. The professional and public outcry over the use of experimental methods of treatment, particularly upon the institutionalized mentally ill and retarded, has led to the formulation of standards to protect individuals from exploitation in human experiments. Protocol review by an outside agency or body, informed consent, access to consultation, and monitoring are but a few of the safeguards in this area.

When patients are dangerous to themselves or to others, there is a requirement that an attempt be made to prevent the active expression of destructive impulses. It must be safe to go to sleep in a hospital ward in full knowledge that one will be protected by nurses and aides from the aggressive impulses of others. If an act of violence does occur, it must be fully investigated and the patient and family must be informed of the findings.

Freedom from excessive medication or restraint which interferes with function is a desirable goal to be attained as promptly as possible.

Staff attitudes and values have a direct bearing on the practice of assuring human rights. Staff addressing patients by their last names (Mr. Jones, Mrs. Smith, etc.) and caring for them as one would wish oneself to be cared for exemplifies thoughtful regard.

A safe, wholesome environment that meets the minimum standards of the Joint Commission on Accreditation of Hospitals is essential. This includes requirements of space, heating, ventilation, lighting, plumbing, and fire safety. Repair of buildings is essential, as is an attractive, bright, and clean environment.

ACHIEVING PATIENT RIGHTS

The achievement of patient rights begins with a written policy statement and rules and regulations assuring that practice at any psychiatric facility is in conformance with policy. In the public system this is the responsibility of the state mental health authority. In the private sector, this duty is that of the chief executive. In both systems, it is the administrator who directs operations and makes certain that practice in the patient rights area is in conformance with written policy.

The administrator's task is a threefold one of education, standard development and internal review to assure compliance.

As regards education, it is not enough to hand out to each patient a statement of rights and to post a copy. The actual relationship of attitudes and values to daily practice is of overriding importance. The reasons for patient rights, the problems that emerge in their observance, and the solutions to case management require discussion of the issues with the patient and often the family, and by both treatment and support personnel of an institution.

Standards must be developed that include rigorous criteria for determining compliance. Assistance toward this end, including examples, can be found in NIMH's *Implementing Standards to Assure the Rights of Mental Patients* (DHHS Publication No. [ADM] 8–860, 1980).

Lastly, a mechanism should be established for internal review by a patient's self-reporting check list, a patient advocate or case manager, or an institution's Human Rights Committee.

RESPONSIBILITIES OF PATIENTS AND CLIENTS

While there is no legal basis for pairing rights with responsibilities, we believe it proper to include such considerations along with the statement of rights. The following statement of responsibility may be given to each patient.

1. *Every individual is responsible for the maintenance of his own health* and should actively seek resolution of the problems that brought him into treatment. To this end full and frank information is required on all facts pertaining to the illness, including related data on family and personal life, medication received, previous treatment for this condition and other disorders, and previous hospitalizations.

2. The patient is expected to *cooperate fully with the treatment plan* proposed. The reasons for any part of the program will be discussed and questions answered by the therapy team.

3. It is essential to *keep appointments* for treatment. Prompt notice is required if the scheduled appointment cannot be kept so that a new appointment may be made.

4. The right of freedom from control presumes *mature and trustworthy behavior*.

5. *Consideration of others* and concern for their welfare and property are expected, as are good manners.

6. As a reponsible member of the facility, the patient is expected to *observe all rules*.

7. The patient is expected to *communicate and reach out* to the staff, and to request assistance and aid from the doctor, therapist, nurse, and social worker.

8. *The community and state in which the patient lives have the responsibility to supply the resources essential to carry out the mission of the psychiatric facility.* All citizens have an obligation to press their representatives in government, both local and state, to make certain the resources essential for evaulation and treatment are made available.

SUMMARY

We have presented patient rights to health, to access to treatment, and to refuse treatment. The legal rights to freedom, to see an attorney, to a writ of habeas corpus, and to judicial review were also discussed. A method for handling individual complaints and alleged systems failure was discussed using Vermont's Mental Health Board method as an example.

The patient's civil rights include equal treatment without discrimination and the rights to vote and to make contracts, including the right to marry.

Human rights refer both to one's person and to one's environment. Personal human rights include respect, privacy, confidentiality, protection, retention of dignity and identity, and freedom from excessive medication or restraint. Environmental issues include a safe, wholesome setting, compliance with standards for fire safety, space, heat, ventilation, lighting, utilities, etc. The provision of attractive, bright, and clean buildings is desirable.

To achieve patient rights it is suggested that there be staff education, development of standards against which performance can be checked, and an internal review mechanism to assess compliance.

QUESTIONS

1. What factors have influenced the development of the concept of right to treatment?
2. What are some of the issues in right to treatment?
3. Describe Wyatt v. Stickney, Morales v. Turman, and Rogers v. Okin. Why were these cases important?
4. Describe the concept of right to freedom and its relevance to involuntary admission to a hospital.
5. What are the issues in the right to refuse treatment? Suggest remedies.
6. What legal and civil rights do patients retain when admitted involuntarily to a mental hospital?
7. Who is responsible for patient rights policy? What action is expected?

8. Who is responsible for assuring compliance with patient rights?
9. Describe steps an administrator might take to assure patient rights.
10. Should a statement on patient responsibilities be developed?

REFERENCES

* AAMD (1973), Rights of mentally retarded persons: Official statement of American Association of Mental Deficiency. *Mental Retardation,* Oct.
* *American Journal of Psychiatry* (1980), Special Section: The Right to Refuse Treatment. *Amer. J. Psychiat.,* 137 (3), March.
Applebaum, P. S., & Gutheil, T. G. (1980), The Boston State Hospital case: "Involuntary mind control," the Constitution, and the "right to rot." *Amer. J. Psychiat.,* 137:720–728.
Barton, W. E. (1962), *Administration in Psychiatry.* Springfield, Ill.: Charles C Thomas.
Barton, W. E., Farrell, M. J., Lenehan, F. T., & McLaughlin, W. F. (1961), *Impressions of European Psychiatry.* Wahington, D.C.: American Psychiatric Association.
Barton, W. E., & Sanborn, C. J., eds. (1978), *Law and the Mental Health Professions.* New York: International Universities Press.
Burrier, D. S. (1969), *The Right to Treatment.* New York: Springer.
Byrne, G. (1981), Wyatt v. Stickney: Retrospect and prospect. *Hosp. Community Psychiat.,* 32:123–126.
Casey, J. F., & Rackow, L. L. (1960), *Observations on the Treatment of the Mentally Ill in Europe.* Washington, D.C.: Veterans Administration.
Clinical Psychiatry News (1982), Supreme Court decision on treatment issues in mentally ill. *Clinical Psychiatry News,* 10:1–13, Aug.
* Curran, W. J. (1971), Law-medicine notes: The right to health in national and international law. *N. Engl. J. Med.,* 284:1258–1259.
Curran, W. J. (1980), The management of psychiatric patients: Courts, patient representatives and the refusal of treatment. *N. Engl. J. Med.,* 302:1297–1299.
* Doudera, A. E., & Swazey, J. P., eds. (1982), *Refusing Treatment in Mental Health Institutions: Values in Conflict.* Ann Arbor, Mich.: Health Administration Press.
Ford, M. D. (1980), The psychiatric double bind: The right to refuse medication. *Amer. J. Psychiat.,* 137:332–339.
Furman, S. S. (1965), *Community Mental Health Services in Northern Europe.* Bethesda, Md.: National Institute of Mental Health.
Gutheil, T. G. (1980), Restraint versus treatment: Seclusion as discussed in the Boston State Hospital case. *Amer. J. Psychiat.,* 137:718–719.
Gutheil, T. G., Shapiro, R., & St. Clair, L. (1980), Legal guardianship in drug refusal: An illusory solution. *Amer. J. Psychiat.,* 137:347–352.
HCP (1980), New Jersey district court says patients have a qualified right to refuse psychotropic drugs. *Hosp. Community Psychiat.,* 31:65–69.
JAMA (1972), Right to release from mental hospital. *J. Amer. Med. Assn.,* 220:1405–1406.
Joint Commission (1981), *Consolidated Standards Manual for Child, Adolescent*

and Adult Psychiatric, Alcoholism and Drug Abuse Facilities. Chicago: Joint Commission on Accreditation of Hospitals.

Kopolow, L. E. (1976), A review of major implications of the O'Connor v. Donaldson decision. *Amer. J. Psychiat.*, 133:379–383.

* Law and Psychiatry (1982), *Psychiatry 1982,* Part IV. Washington, D.C.: American Psychiatric Press.

Leaf, P. (1977), Wyatt v. Stickney: Assessing the impact in Alabama. *Hosp. Community Psychiat.*, 28:351–356.

McDonald, M. D. (1979), Ruling balances treatment rights with patient needs. *Psychiatric News,* 14:1–12, Dec. 21.

Mental Disability Law Reporter (1980), Summary and analysis. *Mental Disability Law Reporter* 4:3–4, Jan.–Feb.

President's Commission (1978), *Report of the President's Commission on Mental Health,* Vol. I. U.S. Government Printing Office, Washington, D.C.

Psychiatric News (1979), Judge puts Alabama hospitals in receivership. *Psychiatric News,* 14:1–6, December 4.

Ray, I. (1869), *American Law Review,* 3:193.

Slovenko, R. (1973, *Psychiatry and Law.* Boston: Little, Brown.

Smith, C. M., & McKerracher, D. C. (1964), The comprehensive psychiatric unit in the general hospital. *Amer. J. Psychiat.*, 121:52–57.

* Stone, A. A. (1975), Overview: The right to treatment—comment on the law and its impact, *Amer. J. Psychiat.*, 132:1125–1134.

Tancredi, L., & Clark, D. (1972), Psychiatry and the legal rights of patients. *Amer. J. Psychiat.*, 129:328–330.

Veatch, R. M. (1980), Voluntary risks to health: The ethical issues. *J. Amer. Med. Assn.*, 243:50–58.

Chapter 11

Judicial Actions Affecting Treatment

> The standards of the law are standards of general application. The law takes no account of the infinite variations of temperament, intellect and education which make the internal character of a given act so different in different men.
> —*Oliver Wendell Holmes, Jr. (1841–1935)*

Case example. The parents of Jane Doe, aged 14, a severely retarded girl with an IQ of 26, have cared for her at home since birth. Jane is inattentive, distractable, sometimes impulsive, and requires an enormous amount of supervision.

The girl's personal hygiene, a task performed by the mother, is difficult since Jane is not toilet trained. When the girl began to menstruate the mother expended heroic efforts to help the girl understand the use of sanitary napkins and tampons. Even so, the girl refused to leave any hygienic device in place. When menstruating she left a trail of blood through the house. After a year of this, the parents found the situation intolerable and brought the girl to a gynecologist, requesting a hysterectomy be performed so the present situation would be resolved.

Should the surgeon secure consultation and with agreement carry out the requested operation? Does Jane have the right to retain her

231

normal uterus? What rights do the parents have after a lifetime of dedicated care of a retarded child? If the parents find the problem more than they can tolerate, would the girl be better off cared for outside of the home? (Stone, 1975).

"The loss of liberty is the most grievous penalty in a democratic society," Stone (1975) commented, as he traced a judicial trend during the last few decades that sought to develop procedural safeguards for criminal defendants and then to examine the loss of liberty in other contexts.

Morton Birnbaum, a physician and lawyer, proposed in 1960 that

> the courts, under the traditional powers to protect the constitutional rights of our citizens, begin to consider the problem of whether or not a person who has been institutionalized solely because he is sufficiently mentally ill to require institutionalization for care and treatment actually does receive adequate medical treatment so that he may regain his health, and therefore his liberty, as soon as possible. [*Frontiers*, 1974]

The recent upsurge of interest in the constitutional rights of the mentally ill is unprecedented. The courts have become a force in the establishment of policy and have defined standards and ignited controversy.

From concept to actions in the courts, this process has given rise to principles profoundly affecting treatment in psychiatric facilities. Intertwined are the strands arising from legislation and those emerging directly from court decisions. Both impinge on practice. We have chosen to discuss in detail in this chapter several of the recent legislative acts and some of the significant judicial actions which affect treatment.

In 1973 an amendment to the Social Security Act created the Professional Standards Review Organization, PSRO. The law intended to make certain that health care paid for by Federal funds was medically necessary, met professional standards of quality, and was appropriately administered, either in a hospital or, more economically, in an outpatient service.

Some physicians, seeing themselves as a learned profession with the obligation to regulate themselves, saw in PSRO a threat to setting their own standards and a formidable intrusion into the confidential patient-doctor relationship. Action to force physician compliance was tied, after a process of notices and appeals, to denial of payment if cause existed and failure to substantially comply to standards was proven. Others saw accountability and regulation an inevitable consequence of the need to watch over Federal funds used to purchase health care. Stone (1975) calls the development of required standards for mental health practice "a stroke that cuts the Gordian knot. It fills a void which now exists in every instance of involuntary confinement to a hospital or hospital-type facility; it offers the court a tangible standard by which it can evaluate the treatment component of confinement." Boon or bomb, PSRO significantly determines which patients will be admitted and what treatment they will receive. Criteria for hospitalization and length of stay have been established for each diagnosis, and the appropriateness of various treatments has been judged.

Restrictions on Accepted Treatment

Psychosurgery, some have held, should be prohibited because it severs brain connections and removes or destroys brain tissue with the intent of modifying behavior or of altering thought content and mood. The frequency of convulsive seizures following psychosurgery has also been used as an argument to ban its use. Others argue for it because of its demonstrated success in ameliorating symptoms when all else has failed, and for its use in alleviating otherwise intractable pain. Well-documented studies of its results seem to have been forgotten with the decline in use of the procedure. Alleged misuse of psychosurgery and a rise in its frequency led to statutory controls which required approval from an impartial group of experts. These experts must verify that there are indications for such surgical intervention and that the surgery planned is appropriate.

An interesting approach to ensure the appropriate use of psychosurgery without statutory controls was developed by a task force in Massachusetts. The procedure required the facility to submit evidence that it had instituted a two-tiered review system and could qualify for designation as a psychosurgery center. The review required was clearance by a Human Experimentation Committee and a review panel with a neurosurgeon, a psychiatrist, a neurologist, a neuroscientist, a psychologist and a social worker as members. A protocol on each proposed patient was required for examination, with a two-year follow-up of results, risks, and evaluation of the success of the system after the trial period.

Electroconvulsive treatment (ECT) is an accepted effective treatment for severe and agitated depressions, catatonic states, and (though to a lesser degree) some cases of acute schizophrenia. Its use, slowed by the introduction of drug therapies, has been accelerating in the 1980s. Typically, an average of seven treatments are given over a two-week period, with effects comparable to those of other therapies. Symptom improvement is prompt and the risk is minimal in these short courses. Critics express alarm at the application of electricity to the brain but accept it to the heart in cardiac resuscitation (Connell, 1982). Some critics believe it coercive and call it torture, while others hold it poses an unacceptable risk to the elderly, and upon occasion causes memory impairment (Brady and Brodie, 1978). While these claims are doubtless exaggerated, it must nonetheless be admitted that ECT has been over-prescribed: too long a course of treatment, too many treatments in a day, too many patients treated without proper indication.

To control these abuses, several states, California, Alabama, and Michigan among them, have instituted statutory or regulatory controls. Today, in states with controls, the treatment is allowed only when an impartial group of experts agree that it is reasonable and necessary or that all other appropriate treatments have failed to relieve the disorder. It is true that in the past some practitioners employed ECT for many conditions in which other therapies would have been more appropriate. It is equally true that for many years the medical profession did not act effectively to remedy the situation.

Appropriate use and prevention of abuse are legitimate and essential goals. The development of peer review, PSROs, and quality assurance reviews are appropriate tools for the correction of such abuses. The legal procedural approach imposes a barrier to prompt application determined by sound clinical judgment; it also is a poor agent for behavioral change in therapists. Education of practitioners in the peer review process is a better tool in the long run than a cumbersome legal procedure substituted for clinical judgment.

In Minnesota the courts consider prolixin, a long-acting drug, to be an intrusive treatment similar to ECT, and require that it be shown in each case to be a reasonable and necessary treatment.

OBLIGATION TO TREAT

In June 1975 the U.S. Supreme Court held in the Donaldson case that Donaldson had posed no danger to others during his long confinement and had never been suicidal. His frequent requests for release from a Florida state mental hospital were supported by responsible persons willing to provide him care. The evidence showed that his confinement was enforced custodial care and not a program designed to cure his illness. The court stated that the purpose of involuntary hospitalization must be treatment and not mere custodial care or punishment if a patient is not a danger to himself or others. The case led to the finding that mental illness alone cannot justify locking a person up against his will and keeping him indefinitely in custodial confinement. Involuntary commitment to a mental hospital is a deprivation of liberty. Confinement must be justified and must cease when the reasons for confinement no longer exist.

But the Donaldson case left unanswered the questions of constitutional right to treatment and the involuntary detention of nondangerous mentally ill individuals for the purpose of treatment. Chief Justice Burger's concurring opinion did, however, touch on the latter issue:

The idea that a state may not confine the mentally ill except for the purpose of providing them with treatment is of very recent origin and there is no historical basis for imposing such a limitation on state power. A state may confine individuals solely to protect society from the dangers of significant antisocial acts or communicable disease. Despite many recent advances in medical knowledge, it remains a stubborn fact that there are many forms of mental illness which are not understood, some of which are untreatable in the sense that no effective therapy has yet been discovered for them and the rates of *cure* are generally low. Given the present state of knowledge regarding abnormal human behavior and its treatment, few things would be more fraught with peril than to irrevocably condition a state's power to protect the mentally ill upon providing of *such treatment as will give them a realistic opportunity to be cured* nor can I accept the theory that a state may lawfully confine an individual thought to need treatment and justify that deprivation of liberty solely by providing some treatment. Our concepts of due process would not tolerate such a trade-off.

The right to liberty has been affirmed. The medical practitioner also has the obligation to treat if an effective therapy exists. We believe committed patients have a right to a level of treatment reasonably calculated to improve their mental condition. We also acknowledge that even if such a right exists, there will be times when the resources essential to the required therapy will not be available. Just who is responsible for providing these resources has not been finally determined, although in Wyatt v. Stickney the court has made a valiant attempt to compel the state to provide them.

Litigation and Mental Health Services (Kopolow, Brands, Burton, and Ochberg, 1975) presents summaries of recent court actions and classifies them under three headings: *Institutional psychiatry,* covering right to treatment, commitment procedures, rights of mentally disordered juveniles, and voluntary consent for persons under eighteen; *civil rights,* covering wages, education, freedom from discrimination, and confidentiality; and the *criminal justice system.*

Welsch v. Likins held that due process in civil commitment of the mentally retarded must ''be accompanied by minimally adequate treatment designed to give each committed person a realistic opportunity to be cured or to improve his or her mental condition'' (Connell, 1982). Also included in the decision is the order that provision be made for protection from assault, reasonable access to exercise and outdoor activity, and basic hygienic needs. The court held also that the practice of secluding residents in barren isolation rooms without strict supervision or monitoring, the use of various forms of restraint to control behavior without first attempting less restrictive measures, and the use of tranquilizers as a means of controlling behavior may have infringed on the patients' rights under the Eighth and Fourteenth Amendments to the U.S. Constitution.

Institutional psychiatrists and mental health professionals who wish to avoid the charge of cruel and unusual punishment must find some other means to stop the rare violent and destructive patient who frightens those who must remain in attendance. We have personally known some patients that illustrate the problem of implementing the wise and sound principle of the right to be free from cruel and unusual punishment. One patient would repeatedly run full speed, head down, to crash into the wall, battering and injuring himself. Another, a mere child, would creep up behind other patients, some of whom were adults, and garotte them with rope or strips of torn cloth. Another patient jammed his hand up the rectum of another and eviscerated him. For these few very dangerous mentally ill patients some form of control, some limit to their harmful behavior, is necessary.

Transfer of an incarcerated prisoner to a mental hospital for treatment was the subject of a U.S. Supreme Court decision (Vitck v. Jones). Nebraska's statute had permitted transfer when a psychologist or psychiatrist found proper treatment could not be given in prison. When Jones challenged the law as a violation of Fourteenth Amendment rights, the U.S. District Court held that section of Nebraska law unconstitutional. The Supreme Court declared a prisoner is entitled to an adversary hearing before an independent decision maker, with advance notice, before he can be involuntarily transferred to a mental facility to receive treatment the prison cannot provide. The independent decision maker conducting the adversary hearing need not come from outside the prison or hospital administration (McDonald, 1980).

We have already referred to the U.S. Supreme Court decision in Youngberg v. Romeo (1982), which again failed to establish a right to treatment but did declare the obligation to provide "training" to enable safe functioning without restraints.

Working Patients To Be Paid

Once social philosophy held that wards of the state had an obligation to contribute to their support if able to do so. The patients in mental hospitals worked on farms, cared for dairy herds and poultry, stoked the boilers, disposed of solid wastes, cleaned buildings, prepared foods, and washed clothing and linens. Their productive labor reduced institutional costs.

There were other justifications for industrial therapy. Work was part of the Puritan ethic; productive work led to a sense of personal achievement; relationships with others prevented deterioration induced by idleness and withdrawal; work was reality testing; it provided an outlet for hostile and aggressive feelings; work prepared one for a return to the community. Many still hold the view that the able-bodied on welfare should contribute labor.

Stone (1975) quotes a study made in 1972 to the effect that in three-fourths of all U.S. institutions for the mentally retarded, 20 percent of the residents perform nontherapeutic labor. The distinction between work as therapy and nontherapeutic labor may be clear at the extremes but certainly becomes blurred in such instances as the sharing of tasks in a rehabilitation ward or halfway house.

Several schizophrenic patients come to mind who illustrate that some can be brought out of total withdrawal into satisfying participation in work. One patient who had a mechanical aptitude and manual dexterity became apprenticed to the institution's plumber and learned the trade so well he became highly skilled and was in demand for the difficult jobs. All efforts to persuade him to leave the institution and get a job outside were rejected, for he enjoyed his work and the dependence of others upon him. Pressure to leave the hospital inevitably produced severe and acute schizophrenic symptoms. Another delusional patient learned patient care, cleaned soiled patients, did the dirty work of nursing care, and was an indispensable bedmaker. He accepted the suggestion that he find employment as a nursing technician in another hospital, where he became self-supporting. Both patients found work therapeutic, and both were performing tasks normally carried out by paid employees.

Nontherapeutic illustrations also come to mind: linen folders in the hospital laundry, floor moppers on wards, and trashmen emptying waste cans. The performance of repetitive tasks, days on end, may be associated with no change in schizophrenic symptoms.

Souder v. Brennan and Dale v. State of New York were class actions brought under the Fair Labor Standards Act passed in 1938 and amended in 1966. In the former case the court ruled that the act applied to patients and fair payment should therefore be made for their work. Included in the decision was the idea that there was such a thing as therapeutic work; along with this there was recognition that the handicapped may be paid less than the minimum wage when an ordinary rate of work is not maintained. In the Dale case, the New York Court of Claims was asked to distinguish between slavery and therapy. The plaintiff claimed that her work in various hospital jobs violated the Thirteenth Amendment, which forbids slavery. The court ruled against her in May 1974 and appeal affirmed the lower court ruling (Kopolow et al., 1975).

The social policy reflected in these applications of the Fair Labor

Standards Act holds that patients should be compensated for work that normally would be done by an employee and that only tasks validly a part of therapy or of a vocational program may be paid for at less than the minimum wage. The principle is a sound one, but again problems arise in its application.

The Souder v. Brennan case in 1973 (U.S. District Court, D.C.) stimulated the Department of Labor to enforce the provisions of the Fair Labor Standards Act. The consequences are far-reaching and affect every institution's industrial therapy program and all patient-workers. Souder, the subject of the court action, had been a worker in the kitchen of an Ohio institution for the retarded. He was paid a token sum for eleven hours of work a day. He recovered $10,000 in back pay (no more because of the statute of limitations) and $10,000 in damages.

Many similar suits were entered into the courts following Souder. In Montana, when back pay was claimed, the state countered with a claim for payment of room and board. Under the Eleventh Amendment it is held that a citizen of a state may not sue that state in a Federal court, and some courts have refused to hear such cases on those grounds. Another suit for over five million dollars was dismissed in a ruling that the state had not violated the Thirteenth Amendment because a choice of jobs had been offered and the right to refuse existed. In Tennessee the right to sue the state was upheld. It may be hard to prove violation of the Thirteenth Amendment when it can be shown that the patient participated willingly. In Pennsylvania the court ordered an end to forced labor by patients, and specified a maximum of fifteen hours per week of work justified as treatment or rehabilitation with documentation. Many institutions responded by abandoning all patient work.

By September 1975, there were 30,300 patients working under certifications issued by the Labor Department. Certificates are issued for work activities centers, for evaluation and training centers, and for centers for the multihandicapped unable to engage in competitive employment.

Safier (1976) gives an example of the cumbersome calculations necessary for each patient at work. He cites two types of wage situations:

1. Wage floor of not less than 50 percent of the Federal minimum

wage and commensurate with that paid nonhandicapped workers in industry for work of essentially the same quality and quantity. (Paid hospital employees' salaries provide these bases of comparison.) A patient-worker moves up from 50 percent according to productivity. Safier cites a patient who is 75 percent as productive as a regular employee receiving $3.50 an hour. With the Federal minimum rate at $3.10 an hour, the patient must be paid $2.32 an hour.

2. With no floor, wages are related to productivity. If the patient-worker is producing at the level of 33 percent of a regular employee's $3.50 an hour, the wage to be paid is $1.17 an hour.

The Department of Labor, in September 1975, had completed 72 investigations in as many institutions. In this survey it found that 21 employed no patients, 17 had no violations, 11 had record-keeping deficiencies, 21 had minimum-wage violations, and 2 had record-keeping violations. Three separate sets of regulations have been issued to cover sheltered workshops, subcontract shops in hospitals, and patient-workers engaged in institutional operations. Tokens or script are not acceptable, and board and room charges may not be deducted but must be a separate transaction.

The advantages of the system are the restoration of dignity to patient-workers through recognition of the worth of their labor, elimination of coercion to work at menial or repetitive tasks and scutwork that regular employees find boring or demeaning, and the opportunity to build regular work habits and learn to manage money. The disadvantages are the creation of another costly bureaucracy of Federal and state surveyors; the need for a facility payroll unit, records, income tax and social security deductions and reports; and the added expense. For example, before the Fair Labor Standards Act, St. Elizabeths Hospital operated its patient work-for-pay programs for $60,000 annually. In 1975 it filed a budget request for $800,000 and instituted a training program to enable work supervisors to evaluate patient performance and to estimate quality and quantity of their work.

A U.S. Supreme Court (League of Cities v. Usery, June 1976) decision prevented the Department of Labor from regulating the payment of patient-workers in non-Federal public hospitals. This decision limited action begun under Souder v. Brennan which held that patient-workers were to have the same protection under the Fair Labor Standards Act as regular hospital employees. It is unclear at this time whether state-operated group homes, halfway houses, or private but government-funded facilities are also exempt from minimum wage requirements. For the present, the requirements do apply to sheltered workshops under an order by the Department of Labor. The interference with state sovereignty was the basis for the Supreme Court action. It is likely the Department of Labor may gain legal authority to regulate wage and hour standards in public facilities that receive any Federal funds. It is known that work on revising regulations is proceeding. It is proposed that requirements presently necessary for certificates (both evaluation-and-training and individual) be eliminated. The minimum wage certificate would still be required for groups where productivity is at least 50 percent that of employees, and an activity center certificate would then be expanded to cover all those with less than 50 percent productivity. After one year at a group minimum, payment of the 50 percent rate would be mandated unless proof to justify a continued lower rate was accepted by the Department of Labor.

In the present economic crunch, the value of work programs must be reassessed. Does work by patients speed release, increase their chances of getting a job in the community, or contribute to maintaining jobs once secured? In controlled studies where groups of wageworkers are compared against nonworkers, what are the differences, if any, in remission and ability to get and hold a job? There is ample evidence already that long-term patients, those most likely to be patient-workers, do poorly in holding jobs in the community and have a high incidence of return. The basic questions to be answered are: Is the cost of patient work programs worth the expenditure? And what is the cost of having no work program?

Until these questions are answered by research, we can only observe that most patients prefer work to idleness and that it restores their identity and self-esteem. We believe the patient should have the option to choose to work or not, and to select the task from among a number of options. The essential operation of the facility should be the responsibility of paid employees. Payment for work done during a patient's convalescence is a valuable aid to recovery.

IMPACT UPON THE DELIVERY SYSTEM

PL93–282, the Comprehensive Alcohol Abuse and Alcoholism Prevention Treatment and Rehabilitation Act Amendments of 1974, prohibits a general hospital which is receiving funds from any Federal source from discriminating in admission or treatment procedures solely on the basis of alcohol abuse. Since most hospitals receive funds from Federal sources, the law has general applicability. It also has provisions which preserve confidentiality, allowing release of information without patient consent only to medical personnel in a bona fide emergency and to qualified personnel for research or evaluation, with no disclosure of patient identity.

Actions that make the mental health delivery system responsible for treatment *under the least restrictive condition* came in December 1975 when the U.S. District Court of D.C. ruled in Dixon v. Weinberger, or St. Elizabeths Hospital (D.C.) patients v. HEW and the District Govt. The court said that 43 percent of patients confined in St. Elizabeths must be released to less restrictive and more appropriate community facilities. St. Elizabeths, like most public mental hospitals, had already reduced its population by 50 percent at the time of the court order. It was in fact data developed for the hospital's internal use which suggested that 43 percent of the remaining patients could be placed in the community if appropriate facilities existed. That decision by the court was another test of the judicial system's ability to set priorities for the legislative system in the allocation of resources. The court order gave St. Elizabeths and HEW forty-five days to develop a plan for disposition of the 43 percent and four months to finalize it. It specified the number of patients to be sent to alternate facilities within six, twelve, and eighteen months. Any problems that presented barriers to execution of the plan—standards of care, procedures, personnel requirements, as well as needed funding—were to be presented to the court (*Psychiatric News,* 1976).

The problem cited above is not peculiar to the District of Columbia or to St. Elizabeths. There are many patients in public institutions who could be placed in less restrictive environments. The catch is everywhere the same: "When alternatives to hospitalization don't exist, can they be ordered to appear?" Is the mental health system to be responsible for the creation, construction, and maintenance of facilities, many of which might otherwise have been a part of the welfare system?

Expansion of the community mental health center to include halfway houses, cooperative apartments, and transitional facilities was a part of the 1975 amendments added to existing community mental health centers legislation by Congress. This expansion has been going slowly and has received only lukewarm support. New funding mechanisms are needed, and employees and their unions in the existing state facilities are resistive to such deployment of patients, as it would result in a drop in the number of state jobs.

We would not wish to convey the impression that we do not favor the principle of the least restrictive environment. Its application is indeed a highly desirable goal. Professional leadership has pressed for program development and has conducted extensive demonstrations that prove its feasibility. Home visiting teams to upgrade programs in nursing homes and community facilities have also been used. A place to live, a job, and social relationships in an accepting and integrated community are goals the mental health professional would have patients attain. We do have doubts, however, that these desirable goals are solely the responsibility of the mental health system. We also question whether courts that properly articulate a principle in this area should also attempt to take on the responsibilities of the legislative and executive branches of government in the implementation phase. They have neither the background, the access to resources, nor the skills that are required.

DIMINISHED SEXUAL CONTROL

Thirty-one states have laws for the detention of sexual psychopaths or sex offenders (Stone, 1975). These statutes confine those who lack control over their sexual impulses or who have been convicted of a crime manifesting a sexual abnormality. The term of confinement is usually indeterminate.

In the 1930s the tendency was to provide an alternative to imprisonment for two major classes of persons seen as having diminished sexual control: those whose sexual acts are threatening or aggressively violent and those whose acts involve minors. The intent was to substitute treatment in special programs and facilities. Statutes described individuals who were not able to conform their conduct to requirements of the law, who lacked control of sexual impulses, and who suffered from sexual psychopathy or from sexual deviations arising from mental illness or defect. Laws were directed both to those who had committed a sex crime (rape, incest, sodomy, indecent liberties, sex acts with minors) and to those perceived as having a high potential for dangerous behavior.

Some persons caught in the legal net had actually committed no crime but could be defined as "sexual psychopaths" under the statute because of deviant sex practices such as homosexuality with consenting adults, transvestism, exhibitionism, or voyeurism (GAP, 1976).

The vagueness of statutes, the abrogation of liberty because of sexual status, the preventive detention of nonviolent and nondangerous persons, and the lack of convincing proof that detention solved the problem led to the view that "sexual psychopath" laws had failed as a social experiment.

Dissatisfaction with the present statutes is evident, as is a trend toward the repeal of present state sex-offender laws. The evidence on successful treatment is contradictory. Some studies point to a significant reduction in recidivism when offenders are treated, while others deplore a recidivism rate of 25 to over 40 percent for some types of offenses. Many problems remain unsolved. There are reforms underway in handling the victims of rape. The recognition of rape as an act of violence rather than of diminished sexual control is a recent rediscovery. Other means of dealing with deviant sex exist: it is more apparent in the 1980s than it was in the 1930s that prison is not the place to detain the sex offender. Rape, sexual torture, and abuse, long covert practices of confined criminals, have evoked horror recently among the informed public, and efforts are being made to decrease their frequency. Placing sex offenders in prisons where deviant sex is rampant is certainly no solution to the problems they pose for society.

Still, the alternative to confinement for sex offenders, now that the mental hospital, the prison, and the special facility for sexual offenders are believed unsuitable, is yet to be determined. More is needed than repeal of the statutes: sharper definition, clearer criteria, and due process to eliminate certain categories of troublesome but nonviolent persons who offend society. The citizen must join with the legal, medical, and health professions in creating a new system that will segregate the dangerously violent and change the behavior of others who violate the limits of tolerance of the community. Freedom to infringe on the rights of others was never the intent of the framers of the Constitution.

PREDICTION OF DANGEROUSNESS

In the Tarasoff case referred to in chapter 8, the California Supreme Court ruled that psychotherapists have a legal duty to warn the intended victims of a patient they conclude is dangerous, and that such warnings are not a breach of patient-therapist confidentiality (Curran, 1975; *Psychiatric News*, 1975).

The reader may recall that in that case a request was made to campus police that the male graduate student involved be sent for observation to a mental hospital. However, the police simply questioned him and extracted a promise from him to stay away from the girl. For several months he lived with the victim's brother, who did not detect any potential for homicide. When Miss Tarasoff returned to school, the student killed her. Her parents sued the university, the police, the therapist, and the psychiatrist who was the director of psychiatric services at the university. Police and university were dismissed from the suit on the basis of statutory immunity. The ruling of duty to warn was made, for the due process required under California statutes had been followed.

The problems with the court decision are several. The prediction of degree of dangerousness cannot be made with accuracy. As we have said, many patients verbalize hostility during treatment, including threats to kill someone. Needless anxiety would be created if all threats were interpreted as dangerous. Admittedly, some of these threats are carried out, but just which ones should be taken seriously cannot be decided on anything more than a hunch. The breach in confidentiality required to inform a potential victim destroys the very purpose of treatment and could create an even greater hazard: a dangerous person prematurely terminating the therapeutic relationship.

Threats can be a therapeutic ventilation of felt hostility; they may also be a preview of tomorrow's behavior. We are among those who believe that mental patients are less likely to commit dangerous or criminal acts than is the population at large. Some recent studies challenge this view, suggesting that an observed increase in criminal acts by patients may be the consequence of limiting admission to those who demonstrate clear and convincing evidence of danger to self and others. The problem of false positives arises when prediction of rare events is attempted. "Even if an index of violence-proneness could be developed so as to identify fifty percent of the individuals who will commit violent acts, the continued employment of such an index would identify as many false positives as true positives'' (APA, 1974). An attempt to predict the rare dangerous event would create enormous anguish. Let us let the statement stand: We are unable to predict dangerousness. The Tarasoff ruling of requirement to warn is unworkable and creates an even greater hazard in the breach in confidentiality which would drive from treatment those most likely to require it.

The spate of judicial actions has led to the suggestion that a legal advocate represent the patient in admission proceedings, in therapy to ensure informed consent, and in release to the least restrictive environment. The legal approach, it seems to us, sets the patient against the facility and uses suits and complaints to protect patient freedom and ensure due process. There must be a better way to secure desired goals than to destroy the trust of patients that is so esential in psychiatric treatment.

To turn to a lawyer for the solution of every social problem and to the courts for determination of social policy is wrong. The balance in our system of government calls for social policy to be determined by the legislative branch, by representatives of the people who are held accountable for their actions by the electoral process.

On a small scale, an alternative to judicial action is developing in the form of a patient advocacy program. An ombudsperson ensures that patient interests are paramount and assists patients in the exercise of their civil rights. From our perspective, physicians and mental health professionals have always seen themselves as the clients' or patients' advocates. A reaffirmation of traditional roles, with patient rights in ascendancy and the institutional role secondary, might be a better course to follow in the long run.

SUMMARY

In the 1970s an unprecedented interest in the rights of the mentally ill and mentally retarded led to a series of legislative acts and judicial decisions that affected practice.

In 1973 the Social Security Act was amended to establish PSROs to monitor the necessity for treatment, its appropriateness, and its quality, in an effort to control costs under Federal health care programs. In 1974, PL93–282, the Comprehensive Alcohol Abuse and Alcoholism Prevention, Treatment and Rehabilitation Act, prohibited general hospitals from receiving any Federal funds if they discriminate against the admission of those who abuse alcohol. There was also a general disaffection with sex-offender statutes and a movement toward repeal of legislation. Two states, Michigan and California, passed laws to limit the use of psychosurgery and electroconvulsive therapy.

In 1972 Wyatt v. Stickney detailed patient rights, while 1973 saw payment for patient labor established in Souder v. Brennan, where it was ruled that the Fair Labor Standards Act applied to hopsitals and to mentally ill and mentally retarded patients.

Welsch v. Likins (1974) produced the ruling that committed mentally retarded persons must receive minimally adequate treatment to give each individual a realistic opportunity to be cured or improved. It was also ruled that there must be reasonable protection from assault.

The U.S. Supreme Court found in the Donaldson case (1975) that when the reasons for confinement no longer exist, the patient must be released, for involuntary commitment is a deprivation of liberty. In Dixon v. Weinberger (1975), St. Elizabeths Hospital in Washington, D.C. was directed to release patients to the least restrictive environment and to more appropriate community facilities. The court ordered that a plan be developed with a time schedule for fulfillment of the orders. Since the facilities did not exist, the hospital became responsible for developing the resources.

In California, the Tarasoff case produced the catchy phrase, "the right of privacy ends where public peril begins." The court ruled (only in the state of California) that the intended victim must be warned by the therapist. Since it is not possible to predict dangerous behavior without including many false positives and because psychotherapy cannot proceed where there is no trust, a dilemma of some magnitude was created: the therapist has a duty to warn. This alarms the designated victim, who would not really be safeguarded by the mere warning. It may violate the patient's right of privacy and in consequence the therapist may later be found guilty of a breach of confidentiality.

Who are the individuals most likely to be dangerous? They are the drunk driver, the adult who as a child was cruel to animals or who was abused and battered by violent parents, the poor minority group member who is enraged at the injustice of society, and the angry person who is threatened. Noise, heat, crowding, and invasion of one's territory may release aggression. Alcohol may release inhibitions and result in violence (McGarry, Schwitzgebel, Lipsitt, and Lelos, 1978). The best predictor of dangerousness is a history of violent acts (Farnsworth, 1977). Unknown victims (often threats are directed at no one in particular) cannot be warned, and those who are not certifiably ill cannot be preventively detained. The problem the Tarasoff case brings into focus is the difficulty of knowing when threats are likely to eventuate in violent acts. There are no reliable guidelines. It is easier to make a prediction of dangerousness over a period of a few days than it is to foretell what may happen in a critical situation a year later. The therapist will judge that in some cases the threat is real and will discuss the need for hospitalization; in California, he will breach confidence and give warning (Roth and Meisel, 1977). Such action will, however, carry with it the hazard of terminating a therapeutic relationship.

QUESTIONS

1. What legislative acts in the 1970s had significant impàct upon practice?
2. What was the impact of Souder v. Brennan?
3. Why was the ruling of the U.S. Supreme Court in the Donaldson case of such general significance? What problems did it produce? What significant issue did it not address?
4. What was the finding in Dixon v. Weinberger?
5. How would you minimize abuses in the use of ECT?

REFERENCES

APA (1974), *Task Force Report 8: Clinical Aspects of the Violent Individual.* Washington, D.C.: American Psychiatric Association.
* Brady, J. P., & Brodie, H. K. H., eds. (1978), *Controversy in Psychiatry.* Philadelphia: Saunders.
Connell, R. A. (1982), A review of the use of electro-convulsive therapy. *Hosp. Community Psychiat.,* 33:469–473.

Curran, W. J. (1975), Law-Medicine Notes: Confidentiality and the Prediction of Dangerousness in Psychiatry, *N. Engl. J. Med.*, 293:285–286.

Farnsworth, D. L. (1977), Dangerousness. *Psychiatric Annals*, 7:55–70.

Frontiers (1974), Whose right to what treatment and who foots the bill? *Frontiers of Psychiatry*, 5:1–2, Oct.

GAP (1976), Psychiatry and the sex psychopath: Premises, promises and performance. New York: Group for the Advancement of Psychiatry.

* Kopolow, L. E., Brands, A. B., Burton, J. L., & Ochberg, F. M. (1975), *Litigation and Mental Health Services*. Rockville, Md.: National Institute of Mental Health.

McDonald, M. C. (1980), Court orders hearings in hospital transfers. *Psychiatric News*, 15:1–12 June 20.

McGarry, A. L., Schwitzgebel, R. K., Lipsitt, P. D., & Lelos, D. (1978), *Civil Commitment and Social Policy*. Rockville, Md.: National Institute of Mental Health.

Psychiatric News (1975), Court sets rehearing in Tarasoff warning case. *Psychiatric News*, 10:1, April 2.

Psychiatric News (1976), St. Elizabeths ordered to give less restrictive care. *Psychiatric News*, 11:1, Jan. 21.

Roth, A., & Meisel, A. (1977), Dangerousness, confidentiality and the duty to warn. *Amer. J. Psychiat.*, 134:508–511.

Safier, D. (1976), Patient work under fair labor standards: The issue in perspective. *Hosp. Community Psychiat.*, 17:89–92.

Stone, A. A. (1975), *Mental Health and Law: A System in Transition*. NIMH DHEW Publication (ADM) 75–176, Washington, D.C.: U.S. Government Printing Office.

Chapter 12

Competency

An insane person cannot contract any business
whatever, because he does not understand what
he is doing.
—*Ancient Roman Law*

Case example. A 42-year-old man was admitted to the hospital with
a major depressive episode. For the previous month he had lost interest
in his family, his job, and in his usual pleasures of golf and bridge.
He was sad, ate poorly, lost weight, was unable to sleep, and talked
about his worthless life and wished he were dead. On two previous
admissions, accompanied by similar symptoms, he had had prompt
remissions following a course of ECT.

In the interview there were long pauses before he responded either
positively or negatively with a nod or a shake of his head. There was
no audible speech, all movement was slow, and he appeared profoundly
depressed.

He appeared to recognize the psychiatrist who had treated him on
his last admission. He nodded affirmatively in response to the question,
"Do you know where you are?" The doctor explained he wished to
give him ECT, which had helped him last time. The procedure was
explained, as were the risks and benefits and other treatment options.
The patient made no audible response but nodded his head when asked

250

if he understood, as also in response to the question, "Will you permit us to give you a course of ECT?" It took him a long time to sign his name to the treatment permit. It was not possible to determine if he read it. Was this man competent to give an informed consent?

Competence is a legal concept concerned with the mental capacity of an individual to perform a transaction. Mental health professions may define competence as the level of judgment required to make decisions. In either definition there is implied an ability to understand and appreciate both the context and the act. The law differentiates the capacity required for specific legal situations. One always asks, competent to do what? The level required varies in contracting into a marriage, handling one's affairs, making a will, or standing trial for a criminal act.

Two basic assumptions concerning competence are expressed in two legal principles (1) Every adult is assumed to be competent. Proof is required to establish the contrary. (2) Under ordinary circumstances, society should not interfere "to protect fools against their own folly" (Guttmacher and Weihofen, 1952).

In certain extraordinary circumstances, society does take action to protect its citizens. Minors, the mentally retarded, and the mentally ill constitute special groups that may require that legal guardians or conservators be appointed. According to Davidson (1965), to prove a person incompetent by reason of mental illness, it is necessary to show that:

1. A serious mental illness is present.
2. As a result of mental illness, there is a defect in judgment.
3. The defect in judgment has caused (or is likely to cause) an impairment of ability to act evidenced by such things as (a) a tendency to squander money; (b) falling prey to designing persons; (c) hoarding money to the detriment of one's own and one's family's support.

We would add another point, (d): evidence that one lacks understanding of a transaction and its consequences and capacity to execute it. Competence has many applications, as we shall see.

The neurotic patient is nearly always competent. The psychotic patient is usually competent to carry out most transactions. The patient on Social Security knows her check when she sees it, can endorse it, and instruct the nurse to deposit it in her account or to buy her a pair of needed new shoes. We once had a patient who "squandered" several hundred dollars getting a record cut of a song he had composed. It turned out he was a better judge of his talent than we were. We could easily have erred in ruling him incompetent to manage his money.

Each case must be decided on its merits in relationship to a specific transaction. One must ask, "Is he or she competent for this particular action?" A mental patient may be able to manage five dollars but not ten thousand; may be competent to change the beneficiary on a life insurance policy but be incompetent to sell a house or stocks and bonds.

WILLS

Testamentary capacity requires that the individual have a "sound and disposing mind and memory." Unlike contracts, testaments require judicial approval and are admitted to probate after the testator is dead. Testamentary capacity exists if the *nature of the act* is understood and the person is aware of the *nature and extent of property* and the *natural objects of one's bounty* (kinfolk, lifelong friends, loyal associates, and persons most helpful). The failure to mention a child, for instance, could be the basis of a challenge to a will.

The presence of a mental illness or of a major psychosis does not invalidate a will unless one of three conditions is present: (1) confusion, disorientation, delirium, or a semiconscious state; (2) inability to recognize those about one; (3) lack of knowledge that one is making a will. Many of the situations that cause the validity of a will to be challenged are classifiable as disorders of old age (Usdin, 1957). It is also necessary to know the nature and extent of property: what one owns—a house, a car, stocks, bonds, savings, other property—in reasonable detail. If the patient has grandiose notions of wealth which he does not possess, he does not know the nature and extent of his property.

A sister, Letha, may be given one dollar and brother Lothar a portrait of the grandparents, with the bulk of the estate going to nephew

Charles, in whose home the testator lived for years. One can be whimsical and eccentric without destroying the validity of a will. If, however, the principal beneficiary is a deceased person who died when the testator was a child, or if the estate is left to someone other than the surviving spouse by reason of a delusion that that person was unfaithful, the capacity to make a will may be later judged invalid.

In a few states, "commitment" to a mental hospital or adjudication of incompetency may be presumptive evidence of incapacity to make a will. Curran (1957) cites examples that reveal the complexities involved. The psychiatrist's task is to define the boundaries of the mental disease. Symptoms and objective signs serve as evidence to support an opinion. If the will is a product of the mental illness, and if comprehension and judgment are warped by disease, it is the psychiatrist's duty to make this explicit to the court. The majority of states, according to Curran (1957), agree that the psychiatrist should not be asked whether his patient had the capacity to make a will but should be asked about the patient's "soundness of mind" and the patient's capacity to understand the nature and extent of his property and who might logically expect to receive it.

CONTRACTS

An agreement or contract between parties is binding when consent is "fully and freely given" (Slovenko, 1973). To be valid, the parties to the contract must know what they are doing. If by reason of mental illness or defect, the individual did not understand the nature and consequences of the transaction, the contract is void. The test of competence has two parts: does a mental illness or defect exist, and if it does, does the illness or defect affect the understanding of the transaction. The law attempts to reconcile two conflicting intentions: (1) to uphold the integrity of contracts and the reasonable expectations of the two parties making an agreement; and (2) to protect the mentally ill and the defective from the consequences of their own acts taken without reason or understanding and from the acts of others who may seek to take advantage of them. A purchase agreement made by an incompetent is voidable provided the goods are returned without damage. Certain contracts for necessities may be allowed under an "implied contract."

The "implied contract" for necessities includes the physician's reasonable fee, medical service, food, and essential electrical or plumbing repairs. An automobile purchased by a mentally ill person who doesn't have the money to pay for it may be returned to the seller, and that would be deemed sufficient restitution.

In general, a contract or deed will be held void if it can be shown the person was mentally ill and incompetent at the time it was executed. However, if the patient, although mentally ill, was alert, in contact with reality, had a good memory, and comprehended the nature of the transaction, the contract or deed may be held valid in spite of the existence of a psychiatric disorder.

> In determining whether or not a person is competent to make a contract the usual test is whether the party's mind has been so affected as to render him incapable of understanding the nature and consequence of his acts. In other words, does he understand what he did? The general capacity to convey or mortgage real estate . . . has the added provision that the person must appreciate the fact that he will no longer own the land if he deeds it. [Davidson, 1965]

MARRIAGE

The degree of competence required for the contract of marriage is minimal. About all that is required is mutual consent and an understanding of the significance of the ceremony.

A marriage is void (considered as though it never existed), says Slovenko (1973), if either party at the time of marriage was mentally ill to such an extent as to be incapable of understanding the nature of the ceremony or to have acted under the influence of delusions. Many states have laws which forbid former patients of mental hospitals to marry without a certification by hospital authorities. We believe these laws are ineffective and improper and should be repealed. There is, however, need for annulment procedures.

To make a contract of marriage the law holds that individuals must be reasonably free of mental disorder which would render them incapable of giving free consent or would deprive them of the ability to understand the implications of marriage. Did the person understand the nature of the marriage relationship entered into and the obligations assumed under it? If the patient did not (was drunk or psychotic), many states would make it possible to annul the marriage contract. In practice, a mentally incompetent person can initiate the action to annul, but the other party can do so only if it can be proven that he or she was ignorant of the fact that the person was drunk or mentally ill at the time of the marriage. Concealment of a prior mental illness has been ruled not fraudulent, although there is a case on record (Schaeffer v. Schaeffer, NY, September 1959) in which the court ruled concealment constituted a fraud. By contrast, concealing epilepsy or a hereditary nervous ailment, even though the person is sane, *is* fraudulent.

Incapacity to perform sexual intercourse and impotence may result from emotional causes. Nonconsummation of the marriage may be grounds for annulment. There are states where desertion is a cause for divorce and where the inability to perform sexual intercourse may be defined as desertion.

DIVORCE

The presence of "incurable insanity" may be the basis for a divorce action in about half of the states. When this provision is made, a spouse may file for divorce after two to five years of involuntary confinement with failure to respond to treatment. The psychiatrist may be asked to establish that a serious mental illness exists, that recovery is unlikely, and that the patient has been continuously confined in the hospital for several years.

When a spouse is mentally ill, desertion, adultery, and mental cruelty may not be used to justify a divorce.

Divorce has become so common that new family law (in California, Colorado, Connecticut, Iowa, Michigan, North Dakota, and Texas) allows irreconcilable differences between partners to be the principal basis for divorce. Irreconcilable differences that have caused irremediable breakdown of the marriage or incurable insanity may be the basis for a "no fault" action. The right to divorce is not the problem but the practical reality of "the division of money and property" and custody and visitation of children (Slovenko, 1973).

LICENSES

The Wyatt v. Stickney case produced the following court ruling on the rights of mental patients: "Patients have a right to manage their own affairs (including retaining driver's license, right to marry, right to vote, right to engage in contracts) even while in the hospital unless it is specifically indicated that they are incapable of exercising such judgment." This changes the legal emphasis from automatic disqualification of the right to hold a license to proof of mental disability so pervasive that the public safety will be endangered. State statutes and regulations lag behind this landmark approach.

In rural and suburban areas a car may be the only means of getting to a job. Loss of license may mean loss of job if riding in a pool is not possible. The wisdom of preserving the right to drive is obvious. The right should be suspended only, as was said, when the mental disability is so pervasive that it is likely to endanger public safety. When treatment employs a drug with soporific side effects, a hazzard to safety may exist. The patient may be warned not to drive until it is possible to lower the dosage.

In states that require a license to drive an automobile and examination of the operator, the right to drive may be automatically suspended by the act of legal "commitment." It may be restored only upon complete discharge. While on trial visit or convalescent leave, the person is not eligible to reapply. In states with this restrictive view, when the patient is discharged, the psychiatrist may certify that there are no physical or mental contraindications to the patient's driving a car, if this is true.

In most states, some special licenses, such as those required of airplane pilots, physicians, and nurses, are also suspended or revoked by the act of legal "commitment." States may require notification of the appropriate licensing authority when the individual is involuntarily hospitalized for a mental illness. Restoration of privilege usually requires an application by the discharged patient and a supporting statement from the psychiatrist.

VOTING AND HOLDING OFFICE

In some states the act of legal "commitment" may make a mental patient ineligible to vote or to qualify for elective office. In others the right to vote is upheld. In our experience, however, open ward patients often vote and several have stood for election. Competent patients should be encouraged to vote where statutes permit it.

ADOPTION

Courts faced with the rising tide of divorce actions, and increasing numbers of warring parents fighting for custody of their children, have tried to make judgments in the best interest of the children. The need for standards by which to judge what is the "best interest" led Michigan to define it, in its Child Study Act of 1970, as the sum total of the following factors as determined by the court:

1. The love, affection and other emotional ties existing between the competing parents and the child.
2. The capacity and disposition of competing parties to give love, affection, and guidance and to continue to educate and raise the child in his or her religion or creed, if any.
3. The capacity and disposition of competing parties to provide the child with food, clothing, medical or other remedial care . . . and other remedial needs.
4. The length of time the child has lived in a stable satisfactory environment and the desirability of maintaining continuity.
5. The permanence as a family unit, of the existing or proposed custodial home.
6. The moral fitness of the competing parties.
7. The mental and physical health of the competing parties.
8. The home, school and community record of the child.
9. The reasonable preference of the child, if the court deems him or her to be of sufficient age to express preference.
10. Any other factor considered by the court to be relevant to a particular child custody dispute. [Benedek, 1972]

Usually in practice the child is sent to the mother unless she is reluctant to accept responsibility or is deemed unfit. The presence of alcoholism, drug addiction, promiscuity, or incest may be determinants of unfitness. The emotional harm a parent may do to a child is seldom a factor unless the parent in question is incompetent and involuntarily hospitalized for incurable mental illness.

CHILD ABUSE AND NEGLECT

Many states have laws that define child abuse as injury or disability from physical abuse or neglect or evidence of malnutrition inflicted on a child (under 16 years of age) by other than accidental means. When there is reasonable cause, not necessarily certainty, to believe that a child has been abused this must be reported to a designated agency, usually the Department for Children and Family Services. The nature of the abuse may be beatings; cutting; burning; sexual abuse; malnutrition; lack of clothing, shelter, medical care or supervision; or serious emotional injury. If court action is instituted to remove the child from the parents the psychiatrist may be required to testify in court (Slovenko, 1973).

Studies of the syndrome of child battery have found a defect in mothering or fathering in the abusing parent. The defect is one of attitude not ability or willingness to care for the child. The defective attitude views the child as existing for the parent's pleasure and satisfaction and repeats what the parents themselves experienced when they were children. Few cases of psychosis, sociopathy, or mental retardation were found in the population studied. Social and economic factors were not significant. Some studies emphasized the demand by parents that children supply them with love and gratification. Another study found parents projecting on to the child a hated part of their own personalities. Abusing parents are often angry, dependent people lacking warmth. Flynn's cases (1970) demonstrated an extraordinary reliance on the defense mechanisms of repression, denial, and projection and an incapacity to learn from experience and to appreciate the consequences of their actions. However, most child abuse is a manifestation of narcissistic rage and doesn't necessarily result from any lack of warmth. More important in our view, child abuse is likely to occur where there is insufficient support of adult levels of narcissism.

COMPETENCE TO STAND TRIAL

Interest in the issue "not guilty by reason of insanity" and preoccupation with rules for determining criminal responsibility have overshadowed the far more fundamental issue of competence to stand trial. The relative importance of the two issues is illustrated by a survey of mentally ill offenders reported by the APA's Joint Information Service (Scheidemandel and Kanno, 1966). Fifty-two percent of all mentally ill offenders admitted are incompetent to stand trial, and 4 percent are not guilty by reason of insanity. While the survey was made using a selected population and in consequence is not generalizable, there is recognition that competence to stand trial is a very different issue from responsibility for crime.

The test for competence to stand trial is the capacity to comprehend the nature and the objectives of the proceedings, to conduct a rational defense, and to cooperate with one's attorney. It is essential to make this determination prior to the trial. The defense counsel, the prosecutor, or the judge may request a hearing on competency. The failure to conduct such a hearing may, on review, be held to be a denial of due process of law (Smith, 1969).

A deaf-mute also said to be mentally retarded was apprehended in a robbery, and was unable to cooperate in his defense, yet no competency hearing was held before he was sent to a state institution. The U.S. Supreme Court found that he had been deprived of his constitutional rights (Curran, 1972). Persons under the influence of drugs or alcohol may be unable to participate in their defense. To participate in defense one must be able to remember events and relate the story to one's lawyer, "to help counsel obtain, examine and cross-examine witnesses" (Task Force, 1963). The defendant should be capable of coping with attacks under cross-examination as the adversary system of justice seeks to get at the truth. Often the mentally retarded and the mentally ill will be unable to meet these requirements.

"Typically, psychiatric evaluations of competency have focused on the need for hospitalization or upon mental health issues and not on legal issues" (Bukatman, Foy, and Degrazia, 1971). The question to be answered is, can the accused understand the nature of the proceedings against him and render effective assistance in his defense?

The legal criteria of competence to stand trial formulated by the Georgetown University Law Center (Bukatman et al., 1971) require that the following six points be determined with certainty by careful questioning. The defendant must be able to:

1. Understand the Current Legal Situation.

2. Understand the charges.
3. Understand the legal issues and procedures.
4. Understand the possible dispositions, pleas, and penalties.
5. Understand the relevant facts in the case.
6. Identify and locate witnesses.

Seven other issues may fluctuate and require prediction of future behavior. To help in this determination Bukatman et al. have included in their article a suggested list of questions designed to arrive at the defendant's ability to communicate with counsel and to:

7. Comprehend instructions and advice.
8. Make decisions after advice.
9. Follow testimony for contradictions or errors.
10. Maintain a collaborative relationship with the attorney.
11. Testify if necessary and be cross-examined.
12. Tolerate stress of trial or while awaiting trial.
13. Refrain from irrational behavior during trial.

A sentence-completion instrument called the Competency Screening Test proved reasonably reliable in a study of its use by Lipsitt, Lelos, and McGarry (1971). It is another device to objectify and standardize the determination of competence to stand trial.

The mental health professional or psychiatrist with the task of testifying as to the competence of an individual to stand trial will make a thorough mental examination and then ask how the impairments noted affect the capacity to understand the legal issues, the charges, and the other factors noted above. The Group for the Advancement of Psychiatry's *Misuse of Psychiatry in the Criminal Courts: Competency to Stand Trial* (GAP, 1974), will be a most helpful guide to the clinician's preparation.

Competency examinations are frequently used for purposes other than determining the defendant's mental competence to stand trial. A study of differential rates of referral for examination in a series of one thousand arrests showed the referral rates for those charged with homicide, arson, sex crimes, and armed robbery to be higher than for those charged with such lesser crimes as assault, burglary, and larceny. This led Cooke, Johnston, and Pogany (1973) to conclude that competency hearings are often employed as a strategy "to remove public pressure for severe punishment, to avoid a jury trial on the responsibility issue or to lay the ground work for a not guilty by reason of insanity plea where the crime would result in a long sentence. Referral is frequently based on some strategy rather than on a legitimate concern over the mental status.''

A referral for determination of competency might be used to delay trial or to secure a mental examination for certain troublesome offenders for whom no criminal disposition appears appropriate, in the hope that confinement in a mental hospital might more easily be accomplished. Another interesting finding of the study was that in big cities judges and attorneys are more knowledgeable about competency examinations and employ them more frequently than is the case in rural areas.

The constitutional rights of a defendant include the right to confront accusers and to consult with counsel. We have already noted the defendant, under most statutes, must have the capacity to understand the nature of the proceedings and the peril of his position. The clinician asked to determine competence to stand trial is faced with an often difficult judgment as to the ability to assist counsel, especially when amnesia is claimed regarding the events surrounding the alleged crime.

To assist the court in making an appropriate determination, advise Koson and Robey (1973), ''the clinician should examine several aspects of the memory defect. Is the inability to remember real or feigned? If it is real what is the cause? Is it temporary or permanent? If it is temporary, is it treatable? Is it crucial to the case [on psychiatric grounds] that the defendant be able to remember?''

Competence to stand trial includes memory, but obviously justice would not be done if all who claim loss of memory were declared incompetent. The courts grappling with the problem have declared persons competent to stand trial when the defendant is not totally incapacitated to assist counsel. Those with temporary amnesia may have the trial postponed to enable treatment to be instituted, but those with permanent amnesia may be ruled incompetent. Some decompensate while waiting for trial and manifest an acute psychosis, regressive symptoms, or suicidal depression that requires treatment for relief.

Temporary amnesia (or recall) may occur after intoxication, trauma, acute reversible brain damage, in the repression in hysteria, or in psychosis; perceptual and attention defects may follow drug ingestion, sleep disturbance, alcoholism, or psychosis. Brain damage, epilepsy, and, more rarely, electroconvulsive therapy may cause long-term memory impairment. Irreversible brain damage with permanent amnesia may follow a vascular accident, be present in presenile and senile chronic brain damage, and in Korsakoff's syndrome or brain tumor. The need for a psychiatrist to carefully evaluate the defendant with amnesia is evident. Malingering is a real possibility and calls for great care in arriving at a diagnosis (Koson and Robey, 1973).

The ultimate decision regarding fitness to stand trial will be determined by the court. It is the clinician's job to supply the evidence that the patient is or is not competent based upon an examination. The Massachusetts Division of Legal Medicine noted in one year that 1,888 defendants were sent for observation for determination of competency and only 76 were found incompetent (Bendt, Bolcanoff, and Tragellis, 1973). This is a far smaller percentage than was found by the New York City Forensic Psychiatry Clinic. Goldstein (1973) has reported the work of this clinic, which serves the New York City Criminal Court. The clinic does competency examinations with the objective of expeditious return for trial of all who can fulfill the basic criteria of competence even if seriously disturbed or dangerous. It is better to speedily determine guilt or innocence of a crime than to resort to indefinite involuntary confinement in a mental hospital awaiting return to competence. The New York City clinic found 71 percent fit to stand trial; 21 percent unfit and sent to a state hospital; and 8 percent sent to the prison service of a metropolitan hospital for a longer period of evaluation. (Formerly, 42 percent were sent for hospital observation; the numbers returned to stand trial remained constant.) It appears, then, that most mentally disturbed offenders are fit to stand trial. A most useful checklist that embodies the criteria for competence has been developed by Robey (1969).

COMPETENCE TO GIVE INFORMED CONSENT

A patient with a mental illness who is able to understand his need for an operation or procedure and who can appreciate the risks involved, may give permission for the action. When the patient is involuntarily admitted and gives consent, the clinician should also append a statement that the patient is competent for this act. As an added safeguard, a relative or a friend who has demonstrated a genuine interest in the patient's welfare may join in executing the consent.

In an emergency when a surgical operation must be done to save a life, it may be performed on the theory of implied consent (Curran, 1972). To do so it must be shown that a true emergency exists, that the patient was not able to give consent or lacked the competence to do so, and that relatives or a guardian could not be reached to give permission or that time did not permit such a delay. The effort to reach relatives or guardian must be made as soon as possible afterwards, in order to inform them of the action.

Summary

The legal concept of competence involves the mental capacity of an individual to enter a transaction. The level of judgment required to make decisions varies with the situation—making a will, entering a marriage contract, disposing of property, or standing trial. Capacity to carry out a specific legal act is the focus in each determination. The law assumes every individual competent unless proof is established to the contrary, and allows society wide latitude in not interfering "to protect fools against their own folly."

A finding of incompetence requires evidence that a serious mental illness exists and that consequently there is a defect of judgment which interferes with the capacity to execute a specific transaction or the ability to understand its consequences.

Making a will requires that an individual understand the nature of the act and have knowledge of what he possesses and the natural objects of his bounty (kinfolk, friends, loyal associates, and most helpful persons). To make a contract, the same basic rules apply. To be valid the parties to the contract must know what they are agreeing to do. Contracts for necessities are usually allowed to stand. Restitution through return of purchased item may void a contract made by one who is incompetent. Free consent and understanding of the implications is about all that is required for a marriage contract. Divorce and adoption pose special problems, as does child abuse.

Competence to stand trial requires a capacity to comprehend the nature of the proceedings and the ability to participate in one's own defense and to cooperate with one's attorney.

QUESTIONS

1. What are two basic assumptions made in legal practice with regard to competence?
2. What evidence is reqired to prove an individual incompetent?
3. What three capacities are required of an individual making a will?
4. What degree of competence is required of parties in a marriage?
5. Can a spouse secure a divorce on grounds that the partner is mentally ill?
6. Does a mentally ill and involuntarily confined patient have the right to retain a driver's license? a medical license? an airline pilot's license?
7. How does one determine the competence to stand trial of a person suspected of having a mental disorder?
8. Under what circumstances can one conduct a procedure or a surgical operation on an incompetent patient?

REFERENCES

Benedek, E. P. (1972), Child custody laws: Their psychiatric implications. *Amer. J. Psychiat.*, 129:326–328.
Bendt, R. H., Bolcanoff, E. J., & Tragellis, G. S. (1973), Incompetency to stand trial. *Amer. J. Psychiat.*, 130:1288–1289.
* Bukatman, B. A., Foy, J. L., & Degrazia, J. D. (1971), What is competency to stand trial? *Amer. J. Psychiat.*, 127:1225–1229.
Cooke, G., Johnston, N., & Pogany, E. (1973), Factors affecting referral to determine competency to stand trial. *Amer. J. Psychiat.*, 130:870–875.
Curran, W. B. (1957), Medicine and the law, *J. Amer. Med. Assn.*, 165:65–70, Sept. 7.
* Curran, W. B. (1972), Competency of the mentally retarded to stand trial. *N. Engl. J. Med.*, 287:1184.
Davidson, H. (1965), *Forensic Psychiatry.* 2nd ed. New York: Ronald Press.
Flynn, W. R. (1970), Frontier justice: A contribution to the theory of child battery. *Amer. J. Psychiat.*, 127:375–379.
GAP (1974), *Misuse of Psychiatry in the Criminal Courts: Competency to Stand Trial.* New York: Group for the Advancement of Psychiatry.
Goldstein, R. L. (1973), The fitness factory: Part I, the psychiatrist's role in determining competency. *Amer. J. Psychiat.*, 130:1144–1147.

Guttmacher, M. S., & Weihofen, H. (1952), *Psychiatry and the Law*. 3rd ed. New York: Norton.

Koson, D., & Robey, A. (1973), Amnesia and competency to stand trial. *Amer. J. Psychiat.*, 130:588–592.

* Lipsitt, P. B., Lelos, D., & McGarry, A. L. (1971), Competency for trial: A screening instrument. *Amer. J. Psychiat.*, 128:105–109.

Robey, A. (1965), Criteria for competency to stand trial. *Amer. J. Psychiat.*, 122:616–623.

Scheidemandel, P. L., & Kanno, C. K. (1966), *The Mentally Ill Offender: A Survey of Treatment Programs*. Washington, D.C.: Joint Information Service, American Psychiatric Association.

* Slovenko, R. (1973), *Psychiatry and Law*. Boston: Little, Brown.

Smith, W. B. (1969), Mental competence to stand trial. *J. Amer. Med. Assn.*, 207:1581–1582, Feb. 24.

Task Force (1963), *Report of the Task Force on Law, The President's Panel on Mental Retardation*. Washington, D.C.: U.S. Government Printing Office.

Usdin, G. L. (1957), Making a will. *Psychiatry*, 114:249, Sept.

Chapter 13

Criminal Responsibility

A madman is not responsible for a criminal act.
—*Dominus Ulpiamus (170–228* A.D.)

Case example. Thomas Vanda was arrested in November 1971 and charged with the knifing murder of a minor. In June 1975, Vanda was found not guilty by reason of insanity and was committed to the Illinois Department of Mental Health. He was diagnosed as schizoid and described in the records as a borderline psychotic with a lengthy history of violence. In April 1976 he was released on certification by the attending psychiatrist to the court that he was no longer dangerous to himself or others. He was continued on medication and attended an aftercare clinic upon release. Slightly more than a year later, on a day he attended the clinic, he stabbed to death Marguerite Bowers, a girl whom he had met in a Bible class. The attending psychiatrist and the Commissioner of Mental Health were sued for negligent release and failure to supervise (Bowers v. DeVito). The U.S. District Court in Illinois exonerated the defendants, basing its decision on the U.S. Supreme Court findings in Martinez v. State of California, in which the releasing officers were found to have no reason to be aware of any special danger to others and the event was deemed too remote a consequence of the action to release to be actionable.

A crime is an act that violates a law and does injury to others. The

266

law states that for a crime to exist there must be both an overt act and the intent to commit it. Responsibility is the answerability for one's acts. Society usually demands some form of reparation for acts that harm. A finer focus on the intent to carry out an act that violates a law reveals that children, the mentally retarded, and the mentally ill may have diminished responsibility.

In recent years the insanity defense has been used more and more often. For example in the period 1965–1970 it was used successfully in New York 53 times and in the next period, 1971–1977, 225 times (Tancredi, 1979). Critics say it is employed to delay justice or to avoid guilt and punishment. Societal acceptance of the defense was made possible by the protracted removal of the offender from society (Carnahan, 1978). Placement in the state mental hospital years ago often meant months to years of confinement. But as state mental hospitals changed into places of treatment with open wards and short stays, they were no longer appropriate for all criminals using the insanity defense. In addition, challenges to the indefinite confinement of individuals in state hospitals and demands for substantive and procedural protection unsettled an already unstable system of incarceration and care.

The Adversary Position

Mental health professionals and psychiatrists use a *process approach* to problem solving; they identify all the components and seek causal connections. An action may be understood when biological, psychological, and social factors can be shown as relevant to motivation and to the accused's behavior. There is a saying, "To understand all, is to forgive all". The "understandable" crime might result in a more lenient punishment and the unequal application of sanctions for the same crime.

The law has derived, a simpler, less costly *attributive approach* to problem solving. The quality of a problem is attributed to an individual of free will who has a choice of action. The relevant questions to be answered are: Was a wrongful act done by the accused? Was it intended? To get at the truth the courts have evolved a system which allows both sides in a controversy equal presentation of their views (Payson 1982).

David L. Bazelon, Chief Judge, U.S. Court of Appeals for the District of Columbia Circuit, indicated he approached the issues "as one charged with monitoring and supervising the decisional process." Judge Bazelon explained:

> The court's proper role is not to determine whether the decision is correct or wise but whether there has been a full exploration of all relevant facts and possible alternatives, and whether the results of the exploration relate rationally to the ultimate decision. And, finally, whether constitutional, statutory and procedural safeguards have been faithfully observed. As Felix Frankfurter said, "The history of liberty has largely been the history of the observance of procedural safeguards."
>
> This is also the role of courts in questions relevant to psychiatry. Who can be held morally responsible for a crime? Who can be ordered into a hospital for compulsory treatment? What kinds of treatment can be imposed involuntarily and for how long? What standards should govern the imposition of solitary confinement and other restrictive measures? Such questions pose issues that require a delicate balancing of power between the state and the individual, where the stakes are the highest for human and personal rights.
>
> Let me emphasize at the outset that the adversary process does not create *adversity*. (I use the term adversity to mean opposition and conflict.) The adversary process in the courtroom is merely the decisional mechanism for attempting to reconcile the adver*sity*—the adversity, for example, which exists in the practice of psychiatrists who work for institutions.
>
> We use the adversary process in the law to deal with both factual and value conflicts. In dealing with *factual conflicts,* we rely on an exhaustive inquiry; adversary roles are assigned to bring into the open the reality of the underlying dispute. Parties and counsel must make the best possible case for themselves; and must check and correct their adversary's material.
>
> Specific rules have been developed to make the system both skeptical and objective. These rules presuppose that people are biased; that their testimony and opinions are inevitably shaped by their backgrounds, personalities, interests and values. Cross-examination challenges witnesses for their veracity, accuracy and bias. Steps are taken to select fact-finders—the jury members—who are hopefully impartial. The legal profesion is expected to be sensitive to its own conflicts of interest and to make sure that counsel do not serve more than one master.
>
> In addition to the discovery of facts, the law also deals with competing interests and values which seem irreconcilable. In this task, the common law does not seek final solutions. It maturely recognizes the continuing nature of deep-rooted conflicts. A judge reviews and fashions criteria for resolving each case as it comes. The criteria are made known to the public

in written opinions; the competing values are ventilated. Consequently, the judgments are never fixed or frozen; they can be altered in response to new information, new understanding, or new public demands. [Bazelon, 1974]*

CRIMINAL INTENT AND PUNISHMENT

If the fact of act and intent to violate a law is established, the criminal is punished. This may be by imposing a fine, by granting probation, or by segregating the individual in prison for a specified time. The correctional system seeks to deter the repetition of crime through making offending behavior public, warning offenders that society will not tolerate or overlook its repetition, or removing criminals from society and depriving them of freedom. On occasion society decrees that a criminal shall be put to death in the belief that the extreme penalty will serve as a deterrent to others who might contemplate a similar crime. In the 1970s there was pressure to restore capital punishment, but convincing evidence is lacking that it serves as a deterrent to others. Much has been written for and against capital punishment. The arguments advanced by McClellan (1961) and Weihofen (1956) are still cogent in that regard.

In recent times some effort has been made to understand the motivations and behavior of criminals. The tendency has been to separate out hard-core recidivists as responsible for most crimes committed and to lengthen their sentences. There is some evidence that extensive investigation can bring to light past offenses previously unascribed to recidivists; once blame is laid, it is argued, future crime rates can be cut in these individuals. As a counterbalance, an enlightened approach realizes that cruel and inhuman management increases the likelihood of repetition of criminal behavior so a humane punishment system needs to operate well. Additionally, efforts are made to change the criminals' attitudes and behavior and to rehabilitate those who on examination seem to offer some hope that the increased efforts may pay off.

Those who would abolish the insanity defense were given a cause around which to rally when, in June 1982, a jury found Charles W.

---

* Permission to reprint granted by the Honorable David L. Bazelon, Chief Judge, U.S. Court of Appeals, Washington, D.C., and by the *American Journal of Psychiatry* (131:1317–1322, 1974). Copyright © 1974, The American Psychiatric Association.

Hinkley, Jr. would-be-presidential assassin not guilty by reason of insanity. Hinkley, a son of a well to do family, was a loner, drifter and underachiever who was enamored of an actress he saw in a film. His fantasied love for her was acted out in love letters, phone calls, and visits to her hometown without response from the actress. He determined he would gain her attention by securing media coverage and began stalking the president. He shot and wounded President Ronald Reagan, two Secret Service officers and permanently injured Press Secretary James S. Brady. At the trial the fact that he shot and wounded four persons was admitted but his responsibility for the act was the subject of dispute with the usual battle of the experts. The defense claimed he was insane and the prosecution that he demonstrated the ability to formulate an intent and while a troubled person was sane and responsible.

The public outrage following the jury's decision gave voice to a demand to change the system. In the wake of the verdict two states (Idaho and Montana) abolished the insanity defense and eight states (Alaska, Connecticut, Georgia, Illinois, Indiana, Kentucky, Michigan and New Mexico) have enacted versions of the "guilty but mentally ill" verdict, according to the Division of Government Relations of the American Psychiatric Asociation (State Update, Oct. 1982). The Idaho statute introduces evidence of insanity only after the jury decides whether the defendant has in fact committed the crime of which he stands accused. This evidence is available to the judge in determining where the sentence will be served. Other features of the Idaho law include court-appointed examiners to determine the defendant's competence; a limit of nine months' confinement of those found incompetent without an involuntary civil commitment hearing; and the loss, upon conviction, of the right to refuse treatment (Bower, 1982).

Colorado is one of a very few states which have instituted a bifurcated trial. The issue "sane or insane" is determined first. If the person is found sane, then relevant evidence on his mental state may be introduced at the second stage, at which guilt or innocence is determined. The bifurcated trial gives the defendant "two bites at the apple," because exactly the same evidence may be presented and heard at both proceedings (Watson, 1979). Michigan follows a slightly different approach: guilt and mental illness are determined in the first phase, with a second phase undertaken in order to determine an appropriate disposition when both guilt and mental illness are judged present.

California, which in an earlier period had a bifurcated trial, abolished the legal defense of "diminished capacity" over the objection of the psychiatric profession in that state. The new legislation permits judges to limit the scope of testimony of court-appointed psychiatrists in criminal cases, and allows judges to prohibit testimony as to the ultimate issue of a defendant's sanity at the time of the crime (Jancin, 1981).

RULES FOR RESPONSIBILITY

Until at least 1800 the insanity defense nurtured and grew in purely legal soil, with no influence or contribution from medical men. For centuries society has recognized that all individuals are not equally accountable for their acts. The principle was stated in 1765 by Blackstone in his commentaries: an insane person cannot be tried or convicted of a crime. The assumption undergirding this principle is that the mentally ill lack the ability to formulate a criminal intent and that the illness is a proper defense and a bar to conviction for a criminal act. A fairly recent expression of this concept is the Freeman Rule:

The Freeman Rule

A person is not responsible for criminal conduct if at the time of such conduct, as a result of mental disease or defect, he lacks substantial capacity either to appreciate the wrongfulness of his conduct or to conform his conduct to the requirements of the law.

The M'Naughten Rule

The standard used by courts changed in 1843, with the formulation of what has come to be known as the "M'Naughten Rule."

M'Naughten had well-systematized paranoid delusions when he killed the private secretary to the Prime Minister. Unanimous medical testimony that M'Naughten was mentally ill led to acquittal. The public outcry was so vociferous that the House of Lords requested fifteen judges to clarify the responsibility of the insane. The concept of insanity in medical use at the time included the demented, the psychotic, and the compulsive, as well as the idiot and the imbecile. What came to be known as the M'Naughten Rule was a part of the opinion handed down by this panel of judges. It was stated that to acquit an individual of a crime *"it must be clearly proved that, at the time of committing the act, the party accused was laboring under such defect of reason, from disease of the mind, as not to know the nature and quality of the act he was doing; or if he did know it, that he did not know that he was doing wrong."*

The psychiatrist or mental health professional asked to determine the mental condition of a person accused of a crime in a jurisdiction that still employs the M'Naughten rule will seek the answers to the following questions: At the time of the act, was there a mental disease which impaired thinking and feeling? Was mental deficiency present to such an extent that it impaired the capacity to reason? Was knowledge of the nature of the act present? (Required here is knowledge that the instrument with which a blow is struck may knock the victim unconscious, that the knife will cut and blood will flow, that the gun when fired will discharge a bullet that will strike a person.) Was the accused aware that what he did would harm the other? ("The quality of the act" refers to the capacity to appreciate that the individual would be harmed.) Was the accused aware that what he did was wrong? (This implies an understanding, at the time, that the action taken was wrong—not that he must have believed it justified, but only that he was aware that society punishes those who do harm in that way.)

All states except Idaho, Illinois, Indiana, Kentucky, Massachusetts, Missouri, New York, Vermont, and Wisconsin follow the M'Naughten Rule. The nine states noted follow the American Law Institute (ALI) test of criminal responsibility (to be described later), as do ten Federal jurisdictions. The first Federal circuit (Maine, Massachusetts, and New Hampshire) does not employ the ALI rules (Slovenko, 1973).

Irresistible Impulse

There is added to the M'Naughten Rule, in military law, in many Federal jurisdictions, and in about sixteen states, the recognition of an *"irresistible impulse"* that impairs the accused's capacity to control his or her behavior. In most states an irresistible impulse is not an acceptable defense which diminishes responsibility. Where it is acknowledged and when the accused knew the nature and quality of the act and that it was wrong but was nonetheless compelled to act by an impulse he was unable to control because of a mental condition so pervasive as to dethrone reasoning and to paralyze the will to resist, the individual may be not guilty by reason of insanity.

Davidson's (1965) practical question, relevant to establishment of an irresistible impulse, is, "Would the person have yielded to the impulse if there was a policeman at his side?" Such an impulsive act was viewed by a TV audience when Lee Harvey Oswald, the suspected assassin of President Kennedy, was gunned down by Jack Ruby in a heavily guarded police station corridor.

The Durham Rule

Judge Bazelon, in 1954, formulated a rule stressing the link between an existing mental illness and the performance of a criminal act. According to the Durham Rule, *"an accused is not criminally responsible if his unlawful act was the product of mental disease or defect."* Psychiatrists hailed the rule as a philosophical and conceptual advance that allowed medical opinion to be expressed based on knowledge of the accused's mental state. The jury may accept the testimony of experts as to mental disease or defect and determine the question of guilt on the basis of the evidence presented. Descriptions of the Durham Rule can be found in Weihofen (1956) and in Reid (1960), who also reviewed the New Hampshire rule.

New Hampshire Doctrine

A copy of Isaac Ray's *A Treatise on the Medical Jurisprudence of Insanity* (1838) was purchased in 1854 by Charles Doe, who later became Chief Justice of the New Hampshire Supreme Court (Quen, 1978). Doe was unhappy with many of the legal tests in criminal and civil law. He sought one doctrine that would apply in all situations. He wrote a scholarly dissent in Boardman v. Woodman (1868) on the development of the concept of responsibility of the insane. In it he held there should be a consistent legal approach based on legal principles rather than on the shifting state of medical knowledge. He held that *if an act was the offspring of insanity, the individual could not be held responsible for it.*

In 1870, Doe instructed the jury in State of New Hampshire v. Pike that "all symptoms and all tests of disease are purely matters of fact to be determined by the jury." What had been an eloquent dissent in Boardman now became the New Hampshire Doctrine put forth by that state's Supreme Court.

Reid (1960) maintains that the doctrine is misunderstood by psychiatrists, who persist in testifying in the language of M'Naughton, and often by judges, who confuse it with Durham or M'Naughton. Quen (1978) has said, "the beauty of the ruling lay in its simplicity, its reliance on first principles and its insistence on preserving the functional distinction between matters of law and matters of fact. It would not require the law to conform to changing medical theories." The doctrine worked well until the 1970s, by which time it was frequently manipulated and no longer considered fair. In fact, it seemed rather capricious in allowing those who behave most outrageously to escape responsibility for their actions (Souter, 1978). In New Hampshire in the 1980s, the opinion of the clinician-expert is the crucial determinant, not the jury. When the insanity defense is raised, the plea of insanity is accepted by the prosecution and the court, thereby subverting Judge Doe's concept of the jury as finder of fact. As a result, precisely the situation Doe inveighed against prevails once again. One wonders whether the New Hampshire Doctrine might not be truly timeless, if only it were understood and applied as intended.

In Carter v. United States, the court elaborated upon the meaning of "product of" a disease and formulated a rule on the admissibility of expert testimony:

> The problems of the law in these cases are whether a person who has committed a specific criminal act—murder, assault, arson, or what not—was suffering from a mental disease, that is, from a medically recognized illness of the mind; whether there was a relationship between that specific disease and the specific alleged criminal act; and whether that relationship was such as to justify a reasonable inference that the accused

would not have committed the act if he had not had the disease. The law wants from the medical experts medical diagnostic testimony as to a mental illness, if any, and expert medical opinion as to the relationship, if any, between the disease and the act of which the prisoner is accused. The conclusions, the inferences, from the facts are for the trier of the facts.

In McDonald v. United States, the same court defined "mental disease or defect" to include "any abnormal condition of the mind which substantially affects mental or emotional processes and subsequently impairs behavior controls" (Portnow, Magee, and Foster, 1974).

Judge Bazelon (1974) commented on the failure of the Durham Rule to live up to its promise as follows:

> The experiment undertaken by my court in its 1954 decision in *Durham v. United States* is a real lesson in this regard. That case involved formulation of a new test of criminal responsibility: it held that an accused is not criminally responsible if his unlawful act was the product of a mental disease or defect. Durham's purpose was to grant the psychiatrist his one-hundred-year-old request to be allowed to tell what he knows and (just as importantly) what he does *not know* about the phenomenon of human behavior—rather than face demands for conclusions resting on ethical, moral, and legal considerations that were beyond his expertise.
>
> The purpose of *Durham* was not fulfilled. Clinician-expert witnesses adamantly clung to conclusory labels without explaining the origin, development or manifestations of a disease in terms meaningful to the jury. The jury was confronted with a welter of confusing terms such as "personality defect," "sociopathy," or "personality disorder." What became more and more apparent was that these terms did not rest on disciplined investigation with facts and reasoning, as was required for the fulfillment of *Durham*. We regret to say they were largely used to cover up the lack of relevance, knowledge and certainties in the practice of institutional psychiatry.

The Currens Formula

The Currens formula was a transitional rule advanced by Judge Biggs of the U.S. Court of Appeals, Third Circuit (1961). Having knowledge of a model code under development by the American Law Institute (ALI) since 1952 and unhappy with both the M'Naughten and the Durham rules, Judge Biggs formulated a rule for the incapacity for self-control in United States v. Currens. The rule stated that "criminal responsibility will not be imposed upon one who is suffering from a disease of the mind who does not possess substantial capacity to conform his conduct to the requirements of the law at the time for the criminal act'' (Slovenko, 1973).

American Law Institute (ALI) Rule

In 1962 the American Law Institute published its model code, the results of a decade of study, that included, in Section 4.01, the ALI Rule. It read: *"A person is not responsible for criminal conduct if at the time of such conduct, as a result of mental disease or defect, he lacks the substantial capacity either to appreciate the criminality of his conduct or to conform his conduct to the requirements of law."*

In 1966 the Court of Appeals reviewed the M'Naughten and Durham Rules and added comments to the ALI Rule in United States v. Freeman, noting:

> For reasons which will be more fully set forth, we believe this test to be the soundest yet formulated and we accordingly adopt it as the standard of criminal responsibility in the Courts of this Circuit.
>
> The gravamen of the objections to the M'Naughten Rules is that they are not in harmony with modern medical science which, as we have said, is opposed to any concept which divides the mind into separate compartments—the intellect, the emotions and the will. The Model Penal Code formulation views the mind as a unified entity and recognizes that mental disease or defect may impair its functioning in numerous ways.
>
> The rule, moreover, reflects awareness that from the perspective of psychiatry, absolutes are ephemeral and graduations are inevitable. By employing the telling word "substantial" to modify "incapacity," the rule emphasizes that "any" incapacity is not sufficient to justify avoidance of criminal responsibility but that "total" incapacity is also unnecessary. The choice of the word "appreciate" rather than "know" in the first branch of the test also is significant; mere intellectual awareness that conduct is wrongful, when divorced from appreciation or understanding of the moral or legal import of behavior, can have little significance (Portnow, 1974).

The *M'Naughten Rule* was not in harmony with modern medical science. The application of the *Durham-McDonald Rule* did sweep away the disadvantages of the M'Naughten Rule. *Durham* failed because of the clinician-expert's failure to explain origin, manifestations and relationship of mental disorder to the act. It allowed acquittals of persons manifesting personality disorders under the "product of mental disease." *McDonald* endeavored to remedy this deficiency by defining mental disease or defect. This definition, however, did not solve the problems of the jury. As a result, the American Law Institute adopted Section 4.01 quoted above.

The ALI rule substitutes the concept of "appreciation" for that of cognitive understanding and thus introduces an affective and more personalized approach for evaluating the nature of a defendant's knowledge or understanding. A total lack of appreciation of the nature of one's conduct is not required only that the accused "lacks substantial capacity"; and it *adds* an ability to control one's actions. The American Psychiatric Association (1982)* favored a new standard proposed by Richard L. Bonnie:

A person charged with a criminal offense should be found not guilty by reason of insanity if it is shown that as a result of mental disease or mental retardation he was unable to appreciate the wrongfulness of his conduct at the time of the offense. As used in this standard, the terms mental disease or mental retardation include only those severely abnormal conditions that grossly and demonstrably impair a person's perception or understanding of reality and are not attributable to the voluntary ingestion of alcohol or other psychoactive substance [Bonnie, 1982].

The proposed standard above limits criminal responsibility to those with severely abnormal mental conditions and does provide a clearer definition.

At the interface between the two systems of psychiatry and the law the search for standards, guidelines, and criteria goes on. Psychiatrists and mental health professionals present findings and opinions; in the process of examination and cross-examination the reasoning behind their opinions is exposed, in the trial, as true, false, or conjecture. Often the psychiatrists or mental health professionals feel that in the

---

* A four member work group, chaired by Loren Roth, M.D. (Director of the Law and Psychiatry Program at the University of Pittsburgh) produced a document circulated to 75 nationally known experts on the insanity defense and incorporated their suggestions into the final statement approved by the Assembly and issued by the Board of Trustees December 1982. The document, a comprehensive statement is titled "American Psychiatric Association Statement on the Insanity Defense".

process of questioning for ''relevant'' information the whole truth is concealed. Be that as it may, their evidence and opinions are essential to the establishment of the client's competence to stand trial and determination of responsibility for the criminal act.

The judicial system is adverse to enlarging the scope of the insanity defense. Lay persons as well are unwilling to believe that a person who knows his act was wrong can be driven to perform a forbidden act as a result of conflicting drives of whose nature he or she is unaware. The psychiatrists and mental health professionals are often asked to predict future behavior, something they cannot do. What is the least restraint under which an individual can live without endangering others? If released, will the illness operate similarly and the offense be repeated? Arens (1974) believes verbal formulations to test criminal responsibility have to be substantially increased, that the abandonment of the rational and compassionate Durham Rule was a disaster, that judicial activism has only limited the effectiveness of the courts and professionals. Arens is horrified at the thought of throwing in the sponge and abandoning the insanity defense because of problems existing with its usage and definition.

We cannot urge too strongly that mental health professionals, psychiatrists, administrators and legislators contemplating revision of statutes familiarize themselves with the ''Statement on the Insanity Defense'' prepared by the American Psychiatric Association (APA, 1983). Summarized below are the findings after debate on the issues of abolition of the insanity defense, modification of existing rules, limitation of psychiatric testimony, and disposition after trial including release.

Should the insanity defense be abolished?

- No, for it rests upon one of the fundamental premises of criminal law: punishment for wrongful deeds should be predicated upon moral culpability.
- Retention of the insanity defense is essential to the moral integrity of the criminal law.

Should ''guilty but mentally ill'' verdict be adopted?

- APA ''extremely skeptical of this approach (9 states experimenting with it (1982). Michigan the first to adopt it found it discharged 55% of the ''not guilty'' group in 60 days after confinement.
- It could be an easy way out for juries to avoid grappling with the tough moral issues in guilt or innocence.

- Prisons lack resources for essential treatment.

Should the legal standard be modified?

- Limit to severe mental disorder and mental retardation.

Should the burden of proof rest with the prosecution?

- Further study needed. (Presently in one-half of states and all Federal courts the prosecution has the burden of proving the defendant sane when the insanity defense is introduced by the defendant. An equal number of states and the District of Columbia assign the burden of proof to the defendant who must prove insanity by a preponderance (or a higher standard) of evidence.
- Psychiatric evidence is not sufficiently clear-cut to prove or disprove many legal facts beyond a reasonable doubt.

Should psychiatric testimony be limited?

- Psychiatrists must be permitted to testify fully about psychiatric diagnosis, mental state and motivation at time of alleged act so as to permit judge or jury to decide on the "ultimate issue"; whether sane or insane, responsible or not—these are legal matters not medical.

What should the post trial disposition be following a finding of "not guilty by reason of insanity"?

- Significant reforms indicated.
- Design special legislation for persons charged with violent offenses acquitted under insanity defense. Mental hospitals have changed markedly with open doors, early release and aftercare. Long term confinement is uncommon. Courts have ruled those acquitted to be treated like other non-criminal patients. Society has hardened its attitude toward crime and opposes exploitation of the insanity defense as an easy way out.
- Confinement and release decisions to be made by a Board. (Favored is the Oregon Security Review Board composed of a psychiatrist, a psychologist, a lawyer, a probation officer and a citizen). The Board determines the degree of confinement security, the release, and the conditions of release and supervision (Rogers, Bloom & Manson, 1982).
- Release conditional upon a treatment plan with resources to implement it.
- Board has jurisdiction over released with clear authority to reconfine.

• If confinement is still necesary after maximum hospital benefit attained, Board has authority for transfer to an appropriate facility (APA, 1983).

Coercive Persuasion

Should responsibility for criminal behavior be diminished when the behavior is claimed to have resulted from exposure to a systematic course of coercive persuasion? This contention did not prevail in one of the longest courts-martial ever conducted.*

Robert Garwood, a Marine private and captive of the Vietcong for fourteen years, was charged with violation of Art. 104 of the Uniform Code of Military Justice for acts of collaboration with the enemy during his captivity. Garwood allegedly had acceded to the demands of his captors without resistance, taken a Vietnamese name and worn an NVA uniform, participated in the interrogation and guarding of other American prisoners, and urged Americans in the field to defect. These offenses are potentially punishable by death.

Garwood's story emerged during the testimony of the many mental health professionals who examined him. He was portrayed as an unsophisticated and immature young man who, ten days before he was to leave Vietnam, was captured while out on patrol. During the struggle, he killed two Vietnamese and was himself wounded. Thereafter, he endured a forced march, naked, through the jungle; physical abuse; starvation; confinement in a camp where he was the sole American, in a cage six feet square. Intensive daily political reeducation sessions were coupled with promises of food, clothing, and release from the cage. Garwood eventually signed a "confession" and was freed from the cage. Despite his debilitation from malaria, dysentery, and tropical parasites, he made escape attempts, which ended in recapture, beatings, and punishment by being kept for prolonged periods in a pit into which his captors urinated.

Although in time Garwood was joined by other American POWs, he became close only to one: a Green Beret officer who, he claimed, taught him to regard survival as the ultimate form of resistance. By

---

* The remainder of this section is an abstract of Merton and Kinscherff (1981) prepared by V. Merton, who has authorized its use here.

the time Garwood had been captive for a year, he had learned to speak Vietnamese and to live in the jungle by imitating and cooperating with his captors. He began to develop the mannerisms and affect of a Vietnamese. Soon he was not only parroting the Vietcong political cant, but taking an active part in the "reeducation" of his fellow POWs. Their understandable contempt isolated him further. Finally he crossed the line: the man who now answered to the name Nguyen Chen Dao picked up a gun. At his court-martial fifteen years later, the five officers, all Vietnam veterans, who heard his case were not persuaded to absolve him from responsibility for his behavior.

The expert witnesses who testified at the court-martial disagreed on virtually every forensic issue raised: whether the phenomenon which journalists call "brainwashing" and psychiatrists call "coercive persuasion" exists; whether, if it does, some are more susceptible to its pressures than others; whether Garwood, whose life before his enlistment in the Marines at seventeen had been far from happy, was such a person; whether coercive persuasion can precipitate the conditions identified by the United States psychiatric community in the 1980 edition of the Diagnostic and Statistical Manual as "post-traumatic stress disorder" and "atypical dissociative reaction"; and whether those conditions had substantially impaired Garwood's ability to evaluate and control his behavior, and therefore constituted "mental disease" satisfying the legal standards for an insanity defense.

Some observers see the Garwood court-martial as a landmark case, raising questions that first surfaced after the Korean War with accounts of Chinese "thought reform," and which are likely to appear again in connection with proceedings involving not only those taken hostage by extremist or terrorist groups (e.g., Patty Hearst), but those who freely join such unorthodox organizations as the Moonies or the People's Temple. Can an environment of total dependency, great stress, physical suffering, and adroit psychological manipulation and indoctrination induce not only adaptively compliant behavior but genuine identification with those in power? If we decide that involuntary ideological conversion is possible, then we will have to confront the troubling question of whether to hold such converts morally accountable and legally responsible for their actions.

While the outcome of the Garwood trial clearly does not resolve these issues, it is instructive. The same five officers who convicted Garwood also meted out his sentence. They did not choose to send him to prison for the rest of his life. Instead, they ordered him dishonorably discharged and deprived of some accumulated back pay. Clearly they were affected by the account they heard of his experience; perhaps they shared the opinion of many commentators that the appropriate role of coercive persuasion in our legal system is to mitigate punishment, rather than to excuse the offense.

Degree of Illness

More than a hundred years after Isaac Ray's and Judge Doe's attempts at clarification, we are still troubled by the question, How much pathology or mental illness is necessary to escape responsibility for one's acts? What degree of handicap may we classify as "substantial"? The late Bardwell Flower, M.D., who served the courts in Vermont for many years, wrote us as follows*:

> We psychiatrists are responsible for much of the difficulty. We have carelessly used the words *psychosis, mental disease, personality disorder, sociopath,* and others pretty much as synonyms. The lawyers have taken us at our words. So just what is mental disease or defect as used in the ALI code?
>
> In exasperation the jurists have tried to clarify the confusion. An example appears in the charge to the jury given in a recent Vermont case (Pray). "A mental disease or defect is any abnormal condition of the mind, regardless of its medical label, that distorts or impairs the mind and prevents the person from maintaining adequate control over his will." It was further stated in that charge that "a defect is a permanent impairment of these controls." Is it any wonder that the jury found him "not guilty by reason of insanity"?
>
> We are still quibbling over terms and their precise meaning. Just what is "mental disease"? Out of uncertainty arise varying interpretations and shades of meaning, all honest differences of opinion which from the witness stand convey conflict and confusion to the jury. The general public in the reading of newspaper accounts is prone to conclude from this "battle of the experts" that if a defendant only has money enough he can get any opinion that he wants. Or, to put it more kindly, it may seem that "those fellows don't know what they're talking about."

* Permission to use this quote granted by Dr. Flower.

Perhaps the APA recommended "Bonnie Rule" cited above will diminish the confusion by limiting those to be found "not guilty by reason of insanity" to severe mental conditions. How "severe" will still be a debatable issue. It appears when psychiatric testimony is restricted to medical and scientific issues it is about 80% reliable. An area of uncertainty remains. Sensible suggestions for improving the post trial confinement of those acquitted by reason of insanity should reassure the public that experts in the psychiatric field do not wish to release on the streets the criminal offender without appropriate safeguards for the public.

As difficult as the determination of the influence of mental illness or defect on criminal behavior may be for the psychiatrist or mental health professional, the determination of the influence alcohol, drug addiction, and sexual deviation may have on criminal behavior is even more complex.

ALCOHOLISM

Public drunkenness is a crime in almost all states. In Kansas drunkenness that disturbs the family or others even in one's own home is a crime. The Diagnostic and Statistical Manual (DSM III) of the American Psychiatric Association lists alcohol intoxication, withdrawal delirium, and hallucinosis as mental illnesses. However, the defense of drunkenness, unlike mental illness, is no escape from responsibility because in the eyes of the law drinking alcohol to the point of intoxication is a willful act. Yet, an organic brain syndrome induced by alcohol may make the individual unfit to stand trial and may diminish responsibility.

In the well-publicized Easter v. District of Columbia decision, the U.S. Court of Appeals held that "when expert medical and psychiatric evidence establishes that a defendant is a chronic alcoholic who has lost control over his use of alcoholic beverages, chronic alcoholism is a defense to the charge of 'public drunkenness' " (Slovenko, 1973). Easter had been arrested seventy times. He could be given treatment but not be punished for his addiction.

The law has moved to differentiate persons who commit crimes while intoxicated from those whose chronic alcoholism has produced a psychosis. The former are held responsible for their crimes, while the latter are not. Society is only beginning to develop a treatment system for alcoholism with detoxification units, treatment clinics, and rehabilitation centers. In the meantime, drunk drivers continue their slaughter on the highways, and the police sweep the streets clear of drunks, charging them with disorderly conduct if a charge of public drunkenness won't hold up. Social policy and a viable treatment system awaits administrative leadership. The beginnings of such programs are in place, the technology exists, but only with the significant help of Federal funds has it been implemented, and then only in a few places.

DRUG ADDICTION

In spite of a seventy-year battle to eradicate drug addiction by the promulgation of strict laws and vigorous enforcement procedures, there are more addicts and more abuses of illegal drugs today than at any other time in American history. It seems probable that the focus of the law on addiction as a crime has contributed to this legacy. There is evidence that criminal sanctions had failed when drug abuse reached epidemic proportions in the 1960s. A massive Federal program was launched as part of an effort to educate youth on the perils of drug use. This backfired, however, by apparently stimulating curiosity so much that many teens and preteens began experimenting. The youth rebellion of the 1960s gave way to the more serious struggle for survival of the 1970s. With that shift, drug abuse declined somewhat. While addiction continues at a high level, it is difficult to measure the impact of the Federal program on the decline.

Most arrests involving addicts are for simple possession and use. But because a drug habit is costly, many addicts steal to support it. Psychiatrists and mental health professionals often view such stealing as a product of the addiction. The law, meanwhile, holds the addict responsible for such criminal behavior.

The Federal government plays a role in trying to control the traffic in drugs. Hospital pharmacies are subject to governmental control. Physicians in the conduct of their practice, if they prescribe narcotic drugs and other "controlled substances," are also subject to state and Federal laws. Nearly all states have statutes modeled on the Uniform Narcotic Drug Act. That act defined narcotic drugs, regulated importation and limited possession, authorized physicians with a registration number to prescribe, administer, and dispense drugs, and required records to be kept of each use. Since the passage in 1970 of the Comprehensive Drug Abuse Prevention and Control Act, states have repealed earlier laws and modeled new ones on the Federal statute. The Control Act deals not only with narcotics but also with a wide variety of depressant, stimulant, and hallucinogenic drugs that are now controlled. Administrators of psychiatric facilities and physicians prescribing drugs should familiarize themselves with state and Federal legislation governing requisition of drugs, required records, and control procedures necessary to prevent abuse, theft, or diversion.

Personal abuse of controlled drugs by those with access to them is not common but does occur. Physicians, pharmacists, nurses, and ward clerks all have ready access. A few with access to drugs may prescribe them for a fee to known addicts, sell drugs on the street, or abuse them themselves. Penalties are severe: loss of hospital privileges, loss of license to practice, loss of job, exclusion from specialty societies, imprisonment, fines, etc. Physicians who abuse drugs or alcohol to the point where it clouds their judgment and endangers patients can be brought into treatment and their practice interrupted under "sick physician" statutes where these exist.

The law does not hold addiction in itself to be a crime, though possession of controlled substances is; when a California statute made addiction illegal, the U.S. Supreme Court (Robinson v. California, 1962) declared the law unconstitutional. Marijuana has been so widely used (it is said that over twenty-five million people have used it at least once) that most states (more than half) have reduced its possession to a misdemeanor.

PORNOGRAPHY AND OBSCENITY

Pornography—the lewd portrayal of sexual acts, genitals, or excretory functions—and obscenity—revolting, vulgar, or filthy material or behavior that is offensive—are mentioned here only because psychiatrists and mental health professionals have a propensity for getting involved in this legal wilderness. Nearly all states have laws that prohibit the distribution of obscene materials. Federal laws prohibit their mailing, importation, and transport. Because most of society is uneasy about vulgar, erotic displays, and a sizeable segment of the population is outraged and firmly believes exposure corrupts and leads to asocial behavior, efforts are made to enforce obscenity laws which are on the books. Courts have struggled with the lack of definition. Cases reaching the U.S. Supreme Court have produced rulings that did not settle the matter; in fact, they made local efforts at enforcement even more difficult.

Neighborhood adult bookshops have brought pornography into public view. The motion picture industry has found that sagging box office receipts could be swelled by the portrayal of deviant and explicit sex. Even staid Boston has designated several blocks downtown the "combat zone"—open territory for the obscene and the pornographic. In a society struggling to preserve its sense of decency and values while it accommodates to a looser moral code, the courts have been trying to formulate acceptable legal standards. To that end they have suggested that the test of obscenity be whether the material has as its dominant theme appeal to prurient interest, whether it affronts community standards, and whether it is utterly lacking in redeeming social value.

Psychiatrists and mental health professionals have been asked to determine whether the materials or display "would appeal to the prurient interest of the average or normal person." They may also be asked what the impact of a single exposure and of multiple exposures might be on behavior. Professionals who deem themselves expert in these matters are often frowned upon by those within their profession and the local community. Meanwhile, studies in countries such as Denmark, where "anything goes," show no increase in criminal behavior and, if anything, a reduction in certain forms of deviant behavior. Evidently, a society quickly becomes bored with such flagrant displays, since only a few get their satisfactions exclusively from voyeurism.

We are also aware that repetition over time is an advertising technique that influences consumer behavior. It is also a learning technique. The association of violence and sex in multiple exposures may lead some to put into practice what they have learned. We are not so sanguine as to accept the unproven statement that pornography does no harm.

Most will agree that a step in the right direction was taken in the 1967 Supreme Court decision (Redrup v. New York) that "obscenity convictions should be limited to material sold to juveniles or thrust upon unwilling adults or pandered" (Slovenko, 1973). (Let the TV stations beware: "pander" means to cater to the desire of others.)

SEX OFFENDERS

Society focuses intense anger on certain sexual behaviors. This angry reaction has led over half the states to enact laws to segregate the sex offender. Examples of behavior stimulating this societal outrage: the kneeling girl praying in church is stabbed to death by a knife-wielding youth; an apprehended rapist in psychiatric treatment on release returns to the same school to murder another adolescent; a couple of homosexuals capture, tie up, torture, kill, and bury a number of youths; a man kidnaps, sexually molests, and murders a 7-year-old child; a number of 14-year-old girls all living in the same neighborhood disappear one after the other and when their bodies are discovered, are found to have been raped and murdered. The panic that follows the news broadcasts and newspaper headlines forces action by legislatures. The sex statutes described in chapter 11 need not be repeated here in any detail. These laws were passed largely to control the type of acts described above. When legislators were importuned, often a commission was formed with psychiatrists and other mental health professionals. Often very involved diagnostic approaches and treatment plans emerged from such undertakings. In most of the "sexual psychopath laws" the sex offender is "*defined as one lacking the power to control his sexual impulses or having criminal propensities toward the commission of sex offenses*" (Rubin, 1965). In states which have civil statutes, the state's attorney initiates the procedures for the determination of the accused's ability to control sexual urges that allegedly have resulted in a crime. The examining psychiatrist or other mental health professional, after a hearing, certifies lack of control and dangerousness, the offender is civilly committed for an indeterminate period to a designated facility or mental hospital for treatment and released if recovered. Some states require no proof of crime, but the trend is toward laws that authorize determination of sexual psychopathy only after conviction.

Some of the dissatisfactions with current laws involve (1) apprehension and detention of homosexuals who use a public toilet wall to advertise availability and are caught when a willing adult partner responds, fetishists who snip a lock of hair or pilfer women's undergarments, touchers and feelers, exhibitionists who unzip their pants when a female is looking, those who perform unnatural sex acts with animals, and those who engage in fellatio or cunnilingus; (2) the indeterminate period of confinement; (3) the expectation of recovery after confinement and treatment and the guarantee there will be no repetition of the crime; (4) disparities in length of sentence between jurisdictions and between judges; (5) common sexual practices between consenting adults being held to constitute criminal acts; (6) failure to deal effectively with the rapist, the rape-murderer, and the child molester; (7) the lack of proven efficiency of psychiatric treatment for sex offenders; and (8) the absence of psychiatric treatment in some of the facilities incarcerating sex offenders.

The time for reappraisal of sex offender laws has arrived. We suggest that the first step be decriminalization of sex acts performed in private between consenting adults; next, that the law focus its attention on sex acts that do violence to others and to sexual acts by adults which involve children. The indeterminate sentence and the inequality in sentencing for similar offenses requires revamping the legal system.

SUMMARY

In the eyes of the law a crime must involve both an overt act and the intent to commit it. Society usually demands reparation for acts that harm. It has recognized that with the focus on "intent," responsibility for one's acts is diminished in children, the mentally ill, and the mentally retarded.

To explore all relevant facts and alternative conclusions, the courts employ the adversary system to assist in decision making. Mental health professionals are not asked to determine criminal responsibility, but are asked only to state the information, observations, and reasoning that lead to the conclusion that a mental illness or defect existed at the time the crime was committed, and in such degree that it affected the ability to appreciate that an act was wrong or that it impaired the defendant's ability to control his behavior. A diagnosis or label is not helpful. The exposition of the basis for an opinion is. The judge and the jury decide if the evidence presented is sufficient to diminish responsibility.

In 1843 the M'Naughten Rule was formulated. It still stands in all but nine states and in three others in the first Federal circuit. Isaac Ray's influence on Judge Doe produced the New Hampshire Doctrine. The Durham Rule of 1954 was intended to provide professional freedom to describe the disease or defect and whether the criminal act was its product. In Carter v. United States, the court elaborated the meaning of "product" in Durham, and in McDonald v. United States mental disease or defect was defined. The Freeman Rule and the Currens formula were transitional versions of the 1962 American Law Institute (ALI) Rule that serves as the current standard for criminal responsibility.

The ALI Rule states that a person is not responsible for criminal conduct if at the time of such conduct, as a result of mental disease or defect, he lacks the substantial capacity either to appreciate the criminality of his conduct or to conform his conduct to the requirements of the law.

Alcoholism is no escape from responsibility, for drinking alcohol is viewed by the law as a willful act. The same applies to the ingestion of drugs. However, both alcohol and drug abuse may lead to a mental disorder such as organic brain syndrome which may damage the capacity to appreciate the wrongness of an act and may undermine the ability to control behavior.

Recently society has been outraged at legal maneuverings that interfere with local efforts to control the pornographic and the obscene. Society has also been disaffected with statutes to control sex offenders.

In 1982 public outrage at the verdict of not guilty by reason of insanity in the case of a would-be presidential assassin revived a move to abolish the insanity defense. The arguments for abolition included the need for a change to a more rational system which first establishes guilt and only then, in the disposition, takes the mental condition or the facts of childhood into account. Such changes would spare loss of respect for courts, avoid discrediting psychiatrists and psychologists, and protect society from premature release of dangerous defendants.

Arguments against abolition of the insanity defense include the legal and moral necessity of recognizing the diminished responsibility of children, those of limited intelligence, and the mentally ill; and the fact that the defense is seldom used—chiefly in homicides and in only 2 percent of those.

QUESTIONS

1. What is criminal responsibility?
2. Define the following rules or tests: M'Naughten; New Hampshire; Durham; Freeman; Currens; American Law Institute.
3. What are the principal problems with the M'Naughten and Durham Rules and how does the ALI Rule seek to correct them?
4. Is an irresistible impulse recognized as a cause for diminished responsibility?
5. Is an individual who was intoxicated and punched another who subsequently died from the injuries sustained responsible for his act?
6. What is a sexual offender? What objectives have been raised against present statutes?
7. What are the reasons advanced for the retention of the insanity defense?
8. What would be some of the consequences of eliminating the insanity defense?

REFERENCES

* Arens, R. (1974), *Insanity Defense*. New York: Philosophical Library.
* Barton, W. E., & Sanborn, C. J., eds. (1978), *Law and the Mental Health Professions*. New York: International Universities Press.
Bazelon, D. L. (1974), The Perils of Wizardry, *Amer. J. Psychiat.*, 131:1317–1322.
Bower, B. (1982), Insanity defense dropped. *Psychiatric News*, 17:1–2, June 4.
Carnahan, W. A., ed. (1978), *The Insanity Defense in New York: A Report to Gov. Hugh L. Carey*. Albany, N.Y.: Department of Mental Hygiene.
Davidson, H. A. (1965), *Forensic Psychiatry*. 2nd ed. New York: Ronald Press.
Jancin, B. (1981), California abolishes the legal defense of "Diminished Capacity." *Clinical Psychiatry News*, 11:3–21.
McClellan, G. L. (1961), *Capital Punishment*. New York: H. W. Wilson.
Merton, V., & Kinscherff, R. (1981), Coercive persuasion and the culpable mind: The court-martial of Bobby Garwood. *Hastings Center Report*, 11:5–8.

NYSOMH (1980), Recommend retention of insanity defense. *This Month in Mental Health* (N.Y. State Office of Mental Health), 3:1–8, June.

Payson, H. (1982), *Workshop on Forensic Evaluation*. Presented by West Central New Hampshire Community Mental Health Service. West Lebanon, NH, Dec. 17.

Portnow, S. L., Magee, W. E., & Foster, H. (1974), Testimony on S1 and S1400 before the Subcommittee on Criminal Laws and Procedures, U.S. Senate, May 15, 1974 on behalf of the American Psychiatric Association.

Quen, J. (1977), A history of the Anglo-American legal psychiatry of violence and responsibility. *Bull. Amer. Acad. Psychiat. Law.*

Quen, J. M. (1978), Issac Ray and Charles Doe: Responsibility and justice. In: *Law and the Mental Health Professions*, ed. W. E. Barton and C. J. Sanborn. New York: International Universities Press.

Ray, I. A. (1838), *A Treatise on the Medical Jurisprudence of Insanity*. Boston: Little, Brown.

Reid, J. (1960), Evaluation of the New Hampshire Rule, *Yale Law J.*, 69:367.

Rogers, J. L., Bloom, J. D., Manson, S. (1982), Oregon's innovative system for supervising offenders found not guilty by reason of insanity. *Hospital & Commun. Psychiat.* 33:1022–1023.

Rubin, S. (1965), *Psychiatry and Criminal Law: Illusions, Fictions, and Myths*. Dobbs Ferry, N.Y.: Oceana Publications.

* Slovenko, R. (1973), *Psychiatry and Law*, Boston: Little, Brown.

Souter, D. H. (1978), Attorney General, State of New Hampshire. Personal communication, March.

Tancredi, L. R. (1979), Associate Professor of Law and Psychiatry, New York University. Personal communication, Nov. 29.

* Watson, A. S. (1977), *Psychiatry for Lawyers*. New York: International Universities Press.

Watson, A. S. (1979), Professor of Psychiatry in the Medical School and of Law in the Law School, University of Michigan. Personal communication, Nov.

Weihofen, H. (1956), *The Urge to Punish*. New York: Farrar, Straus and Cudahy.

Chapter 14

Malpractice

There is always one more thing that could be done.
—*A. Wildovsky's Medical Uncertainty Principle*

Case example. A white male of 48 was under treatment for recurrent depression. The psychiatrist had successfully treated him about one year previously with daily doses of 100 mg of Amitriptyline HC1. When seen in the office, the patient appeared depressed and agitated, and complained of sleeplessness and loss of appetite. He talked of joining his deceased wife and of ways he might kill himself. The physician called the local general hospital and arranged admission to the psychiatric section with the doctor on call. A daughter transported the patient to the hospital admitting room at about 6:00 P.M. No orders were written on the chart and nurses' notes described the patient as depressed, cooperative, and wakeful.

The patient got up the next morning when requested, but while breakfast was being served he ran the length of the dayroom and dove headlong through a thick plateglass window, plunging to his death. The psychiatrist on service saw the patient for the first time in the morgue. A suit entered by the daughter against the hospital for negligence was successful and the jury awarded damages.

The malpractice crises of the 1970s began to subside at the end of the decade, when premiums for physician liability insurance declined. Unfortunately, the beginning of the 1980s was marked by a renewed upward trend in both the cost of settling claims and in their number. The return of shockingly high premiums for malpractice insurance was the consequence.

The administrator's concern should be the safety of the patients, the ability of staff to provide them quality care, and the protection of the organization and its staff from liability actions insofar as that it possible. Let us look first at why the crisis developed, its dimensions, and the legal concepts on which malpractice claims are based, and then at the steps that can be taken to prevent them. Let us also remember that mental health professionals, physicians excepted, were not drawn into the vortex of the malpractice crisis. While liability claims have been lodged against a few mental health professionals, most are directed toward physicians held responsible for patient care. As more and more mental health professionals practice independently, however, they may expect an increase in claims. The discussion that follows will therefore be equally relevant to their practice.

Through the nineteenth century and in the twentieth until 1930, there was no malpractice "problem." Massachusetts Law in 1876 stated that charitable hospitals were immune from liability to patients for any negligent acts of its servants. In 1930, however, California witnessed a spurt in the number of malpractice claims and the tempo elsewhere was to increase after World War II. Hospitals operated by the U.S. Government were removed from malpractice immunity by the Federal Torts Claim Act in 1945. Since then the erosion has continued to the point that the immunity principle appears to be no longer socially desirable (Southwick, 1962). It is staggering to learn that "90% of all malpractice suits ever filed in the U.S. have come since 1964" (*U.S. News,* 1975).

We all probably conjure up the image portrayed in the painting of the doctor seated at the bedside of the sick child, with distraught parents illuminated by lamplight in the background. Compassion and expectant waiting for a natural crisis in the disease process characterized the doctor's behavior. How different the painting would depict contemporary practice. Today it would need to convey a physician too busy to visit the home, with too many patients to spend much time with any one, relying on laboratory tests and x-rays to assist him in arriving at the correct diagnosis, and then prescribing a powerful medication that interrupts the course of the disease so that the patient experiences speedy recovery.

Technical advances at times allow the physician to restore life to a patient's arrested heart; to perform a kidney transplant to avert an untimely death; and to prescribe a course of penicillin to prevent the psychosis and dementia of untreated syphilis. In spite of the physician's greater capacity to treat and cure disorders, today he is more vulnerable to malpractice suits than ever before. Each of the new procedures carries with it the possibility of injury or side effects. Powerful drugs, effective immunization procedures, and life-preserving blood transfusions have a built-in risk for harm. If the doctor does nothing, he might be judged negligent for not applying an appropriate treatment; if something is done and the patient suffers some injury, even though good judgment was used and there was no negligence, the doctor may still be dragged through a costly malpractice action that may damage his professional reputation.

In the late 1960s, rumblings of trouble ahead led a Senate subcommittee to produce a massive, well-documented report. In it, Senator Abraham Ribicoff made a prophetic statement: "The number of malpractice suits and claims is rising sharply and so are the size of judgments and settlements. The publicity given to the higher malpractice judgments and settlements is likely to increase litigation. The situation threatens to become a national crisis" (U.S. Senate, 1969). The Senator was not the first prophet to be ignored.

Very little remedial action was taken until the situation exploded in 1975, precipitated by the announced withdrawal of several principal carriers from this form of insurance. Because of escalating claims and litigation that dragged on for years, the companies were unable to project rates for coverage. When they were also hit by investment losses due to the economic depression, they found this line of business too unprofitable to continue.

The announced loss of insurance protection in the face of more claims and greater settlement charges precipitated a panic. Doctors switched to salaried posts in nonclinical jobs or quit their practices rather than risk a suit without protection. Others organized slowdowns, refused all but emergencies, or participated in strikes to call attention to their plight. The uproar produced a torrent of action unique in the history of medical law in this country (Curran, 1975). The malpractice crisis was primarily an insurance crisis. It developed at a time when medical care was better than it had ever been and at a time when the clinical competence of practitioners was at an all-time high. The four dimensions of the crisis were (1) multiplying malpractice claims, (2) diminishing availability of insurance, (3) skyrocketing premiums, and (4) the escalating cost of medical care:

Multiplying malpractice claims. In the period 1970–1975, claims increased 225 percent. In 1974, there were about 40,000 claims with the projection of 82,000 by 1980 (AMA, 1975). One insurance company's experience showed 2,434 claims filed in 1970 or one claim against every 21 physicians covered. In nine months of 1974 the claims filed had jumped to 5,015, involving one out of every ten physicians (*Malpractice Digest,* 1974).

In some states patients were quicker to sue than in others. Cardiac surgeons were the most vulnerable specialty group, followed by orthopedic surgeons, neurosurgeons, and anesthesiologists. The least likely to be sued were internists, pediatricians, psychiatrists, and pathologists. Board-certified specialists were 1.5 times more likely to have a claim against them than noncertified physicians. Foreign medical graduates were infrequently sued.

While psychiatrists were not as vulnerable to claims for malpractice as were other specialists, there was little comfort in statistics. Under the American Psychiatric Association's Professional Liability Program, statistics covering experience are subject to analysis: with over 8,000 psychiatrists covered, 50 to 60 claims were received in each of the years 1979 and 1980. In 1980 the program recommended that 31 be defended and 20 be settled; a few remaining cases were held for more data. The most frequent allegations (see Slawson, 1981) were failure to restrain and resulting suicide (15), improper medication (11), improper diagnosis (10), improper treatment (9), and wrongful detainment (7).

Slawson's survey (1979) of 3100 psychiatrists who practiced in California in a five-year period revealed 166 malpractice claims or notification of potential claims. This amounts to a claim rate for this period of 3 per 100. A follow-up study of the claims showed that over 25 percent involved suicide; 19 percent claimed a diagnostic error or improper treatment; and 16 percent related to drug reactions. As far as settlements are concerned, 54 percent remained as threats and no legal action was taken; 21 percent were characterized by legal action; 19 percent were settled by payment, the average being $22,000; and 6 percent were tried in court (all but one of which involved inpatients). Slawson's findings indicate that there is about one chance in two hundred that a psychiatrist will subject an insurance carrier to a significant loss. In general, then, psychiatric practice presents a low risk to insurers.

Diminishing availability of insurance. Insurance carriers wanted to quit malpractice coverage for very good reasons. Although about 50 percent of claims were settled within eighteen months, the rest dragged on, with 10 percent still open after six years. This protracted litigation, the escalating number of suits, and the increasing size of settlements made it difficult for companies to set rates with any degree of accuracy. When companies began to lose money as a result, many stopped writing this type of insurance. By 1978 malpractice insurance was available only in Arkansas and Nevada, though even there with some problems (*AMA News,* 1978a).

Skyrocketing premiums. Premium rates paid by hospitals and by physicians soared as a consequence of greater amounts paid to settle malpractice claims. In 1970 more than half of the settled claims were closed for less than $3,000. In 1974 the average settlement was in the range of $8,000 to $12,000. The range of malpractice awards has pushed upward in recent years according to the *Wall Street Journal* (Bronson, 1980). By 1978 there were 24 awards of more than $1 million and the largest was $4.5 million compared with $2.5 million in 1976. A 1978 study by the U.S. Justice Department concluded that malpractice insurance costs hospitals about $1.2 billion a year and adds about $5.00 a day to every patient's bill (Bronson, 1980).

Michigan, not a high-risk state, demonstrated another dimension of cost increase. The Henry Ford Hospital in Detroit paid a liability premium of $72,000 in the year 1968. In 1976 the same coverage earned a premium of $3.5 million! Premiums for individuals in the lowest risk group, such as psychiatrists, paid $1,185 a year, and neurosurgeons paid $12,000 (*U.S. News*, 1975). In 1976 premium rates in twenty states increased anywhere from 100 to 600 percent. Premium cost to some specialists was as much as $35,000 a year.

The fear of large awards in court led to a greater willingness on the part of physicians and insurance companies to accept out-of-court settlements at a high average cost when there was a better than even chance the complainant would win in court.

The escalating cost of medical care. The cost of increased individual premiums to physicians and to hospitals was borne by patients through higher rates for services. The patient paid the runaway costs as well as the cost for the practice of defensive medicine; it was the patient who suffered the penalty of less risk-taking on his behalf because of the likelihood of a malpractice claim being filed.

A few other characteristics of claims may be of interest. Fifty-eight percent of the claimants were women. Two-thirds of all the alleged injuries were temporary; however, 19 percent of claimants sustained permanent damage and 18 percent died. Sixty percent of claims were filed by persons who alleged they had no income. Fifty-seven percent of claims were against physicians and 38 percent against hospitals, with 5 percent directed to others (*AMA News*, 1975).

An analysis of the claims showed that most were stimulated not by actual negligence but by an adverse event in the course of treatment or by an injury, real or imagined. Today's less personalized care and more advanced technology have given rise to a greater distance between patient and physician. This has created an atmosphere of greater willingness to blame the physician if the patient's expectations for cure are not realized.

There were other factors behind the escalating claims and costs:

• Reimbursement when adverse results or unavoidable injury occurred reinforced claim-seeking behavior.

• Expectations for cure no matter the odds appeared to have the support of courts in their decisions for the claimants.

• Publicity in the news media of million-dollar awards promoted more claims.

• Lawyers were attracted to a profitable enterprise by contingency fees. There are 5,000 lawyers who specialize in malpractice cases. The Inner Circle of Advocates, it is alleged, recognizes those who win million dollar awards.

Despite technological advances and despite physicians' best efforts, more claims were filed. It was a myth that only the incompetent were being attacked, for far more often it was the more able who were being sued. The more claims and settlements and the higher the awards, the fewer were the carriers willing to write liability insurance even at astronomical premiums.

Mental health professionals have seldom been sued for malpractice. In mental health facilities, even when a nonmedical therapist has had full responsibility for patient care, it is customary to sue the assigned psychiatrist for clinical mishaps. As more mental health professionals assume administrative responsibility for organizations with patient care obligations, and as more go into independent practice, they may expect to be as vulnerable to suits as psychiatrists presently are. While most of what follows has evolved from the experience of physicians, it applies with equal force to all professionals involved in the delivery of health services to the mentally ill and mentally retarded.

LEGAL DOCTRINES

Malpractice

In its simplest definition malpractice is an unwarranted departure from accepted clinical practice resulting in an injury to a patient (MMS, 1975). A more formal definition follows: *Malpractice is negligent or substandard practice by a professional person or a failure to perform his or her duty that results in an injury to patient or client.* Other definitions specify professional misconduct, ignorance, carelessness, or criminal intent that results in harm to the patient or another.

Legal Duty of a Clinician

In accepting a patient or client, the clinician assumes certain obligations that are recognized as essential in clinical practice.

Possession of a valid license to practice. A license to practice in a state requires evidence of education and training and an examination to ensure clinical competence for the protection of the public. The personal character and professional conduct of the clinician are also considered relevant to obtaining a license.

Possession of skill and knowledge equivalent to that of other clinicians. Actual practice is expected to be limited to conform to the clinician's ability and qualifications. Once the standard was measured solely by comparisons within the physician's locality; however, as graduates of professional schools often live in and practice in many states after they leave school, courts are increasingly moving toward a single national standard.

Extraordinary skill is required of the medical specialist. The psychiatrist must meet a national standard of skill and knowledge. Membership in the state psychiatric society and in the American Psychiatric Association is one way to gain recognition in the field. Becoming a Diplomate of the American Board of Psychiatry and Neurology is used in legal settings as evidence of specialty status.

Exercise of skill, knowledge, and judgment in the best interest of the patient. The physician is expected to use methods of diagnosis, treatment, and aftercare that are generally accepted; to keep abreast of advancing knowledge; to perfect skills; and to apply them wisely.

The doctor must uphold these obligations to the patient whenever service is rendered, even gratuitously or as an employed member of a hospital staff. The contractual relationship between doctor and patient is assumed on the basis of implied acceptance by the doctor of the patient for treatment. The physician is not obligated to accept a case against his wishes. In an emergency a physician is required only to give first aid. In such cases, the physician is obligated to stand by until the patient has been picked up by an ambulance for transport to a hospital or until the patient is actually turned over to another doctor. Obligation by the physician ends when a patient discharges the doctor. Alternatively, the physician may give notice to the patient of a wish to be relieved of responsibility. The obligation to serve in this instance is ended when another physician accepts responsibility for the patient.

Malpractice occurs when a clinician fails in his duty to the patient and as a result harm is done. It must be proven that a failure in duty did occur, that it was more than an error in judgment, and that the patient's injury was a result of the failure.

The clinician whose practice is limited to psychotherapy conducted in an office setting, and who makes no promise of cure, is unlikely to face a claim for malpractice. If electroconvulsive therapy or drugs are used, the risk goes up. The psychiatrist with an institutional practice is at greater risk of being charged with failure to treat or with errors in treatment that harm or injure the patient.

Negligence. Negligence is the omission of something a reasonable person would do or the doing of something a responsible and prudent person would not do. It is conduct that falls below the standards of care. To recover damages it must be shown that a duty was owed, that failure to do that duty occurred, and that as a consequence an injury took place to which the plaintiff did not contribute. Eighty-five percent of all malpractice claims allege negligence. An honest mistake in judgment is not malpractice unless the action taken was contrary to accepted medical practice. Judge Learned Hand said, "Negligence occurs whenever it would cost less to prevent a mishap than to pay the damages predicted to result from it" (quoted in Slovenko, 1973).

Contributory negligence doctrine precludes recovery of damages by a person whose injury was in part caused by his or her own negligence. Courts are reluctant to follow this doctrine for the individual's negligence may have been substantially less than that of the person sued. Preferred as a doctrine in such cases is that of comparative negligence. Recovery of damages is not necessarily precluded when a person's own negligence has contributed to his own injury. Damage is reduced to the extent that the injury was proximately caused by a patient's own negligence. (If equally responsible no damage, but if hospital or facility 51% and 49% by patient then damages are assigned at but 51%.) An example of the above: an aged patient smoked a pipe and carelessly set his gown on fire with severe burn injury. The hospital was negligent in its supervision and the patient careless (negligent) in the use of his pipe (Miller, 1982).

Abandonment. Abandonment of the patient may be charged if the doctor agreed to make a visit or provide care and failed to do so. For instance, the clinician may leave for a weekend holiday or vacation without arranging for another doctor to care for his or her patients; the resident physician may leave a post of duty in the hospital uncovered, may refuse to respond to an emergency call, or may leave a patient unattended on the examining table to answer the phone. If it can be shown that the patient suffered an injury as a direct result of abandonment, there may be a basis for a malpractice claim.

Errors in diagnosis. All clinicians make mistakes in diagnosis. Symptoms are not disorder specific. The clinical state may be characterized by conflicting clues that point to any one of a number of disorders, and the examining psychiatrist must use judgment in sorting out clues to arrive at an appropriate diagnosis. Honest mistakes in judgment are not of concern here. What is of concern is the failure to make the necessary observations and tests that any competent psychiatrist would be expected to perform in arriving at a diagnosis. Typical of errors in diagnosis is the failure to recognize the presence of an organic disorder and consequent use of exclusively psychological treatment, e.g., treating a patient for anxiety when the patient actually has thyrotoxicosis or carcinoma of the head of the pancreas. It is slight protection to ignore symptoms of organic illness because the patient was referred by another physician who had "cleared" the patient of organic problems. Once the psychiatrist has accepted the patient for treatment, the responsibility for the patient is total. Various specialty consultations should of course be secured when these are indicated and, if appropriate, referrals made. If the consultant recommends further diagnostic tests, these must be promptly done to prove or disprove the presence of the suspected disorder.

Unnecessary "commitment." There are no cases on record of a claim against a psychiatrist for *failure* to "commit" a patient to a mental hospital (Slovenko, 1973). One of the three risks most frequently encountered by psychiatrists is *improper* "commitment"—the others are treatment problems and suicide, (Bellamy, 1968). The most obvious negligence is the certification as to examination of a patient for involuntary admission to hospital when, in fact, the psychiatrist has not examined the patient. In some instances an involuntary admission certificate may be filled out by a doctor on the basis of a story given by relatives, without any actual examination of the patient. Unverified tales have been circulated of the practice in some busy general hospitals of leaving signed certifications, otherwise blank, in the ward office for the use of residents at night. If such stories are true, they point to instances in which involuntarily admitted patients may never have been seen by the certifying physician. Legislative hearings in Massachusetts did produce testimony from many patients that no doctor had examined them before their admission to hospital.

As a result, a change in the law was made. In a typical case, a patient was properly certified by a psychiatrist who found her dangerous to others and in need of treatment. Though she had been discharged by the mental hospital on the grounds she was not psychotic, she was unable to present evidence, as is required, that the psychiatrist had acted in bad faith and without probable cause. The court decided in favor of the psychiatrist (AMA, 1970).

Failure to treat. (the right to treatment). Several recent court actions have established the right to treatment of a patient involuntarily committed to a mental hospital. A 15-year-old boy (Gault) was arrested for making obscene phone calls. He was sent to the juvenile correction system and incarcerated. The Supreme Court castigated the system for nontreatment and established rules to make it more difficult to admit juveniles (Stone, 1974). The Gault decision of 1967 outlined the essentials of due process which must be observed in involuntary commitment: (1) a notice of the charges, (2) representation by counsel, (3) protection against self-incrimination, (4) opportunity to confront and cross-examine witnesses.

In 1960 a patient by the name of Rouse was arrested carrying an arsenal in his suitcase and pleaded not guilty by reason of insanity. He was confined in a security section for criminal offenders at St. Elizabeths Hospital in Washington, D.C. There he received milieu therapy and once-a-week group therapy. Rouse introduced the challenge to his confinement on the basis that he had been detained longer in the mental hospital than he would have been had he gone to prison for the offense. Judge Bazelon ordered his discharge from St. Elizabeths because of the staff's failure to treat him. Bazelon raised "due process" questions, cited "violation of equal protection under the law," and stated that failure to treat might be so inhumane as to constitute "cruel and unusual punishment" (Slovenko, 1973).

Judge Frank Johnson articulated in Wyatt v. Stickney "a clear and constitutional basis to the right to treatment" (Stone, 1974): "To deprive any citizen of his or her liberty upon the altruistic theory that the confinement is for humane and therapeutic reasons, and then fail to provide adequate treatment, violates the very fundamentals of due process."

A legal decision that frightened psychiatrists was that rendered in the Donaldson case. The concern among the profession was that it opened the door for similar actions. The decision held Florida state hospital psychiatrists responsible for failure to adequately treat a committed patient. Donaldson had been confined for fourteen years with a diagnosis of schizophrenia, paranoid type. A Christian Scientist who refused medication for religious reasons, he sued his psychiatrist and won an award of $3,500 in damages. Judge John Wisdon wrote: ''We hold that the 14th Amendment guarantees involuntarily civilly committed mental patients a right to treatment'' (Stone, 1974). However, the U.S. Supreme Court, upon hearing this case in June 1975, issued a ruling which did not reach this conclusion. It instead dealt with a narrower issue: mental illness alone cannot justify incarceration of a person against his will and keeping him indefinitely in a custodial setting.

In 1974, the American Psychiatric Association asked the U.S. Supreme Court to rule on the right to treatment of the mentally ill and on the legal responsibility of psychiatrists. On the first point the APA brief asked, ''Does the involuntarily committed patient at a state mental institution have a constitutional right to a level of treatment reasonably calculated to improve his or her condition?'' And on the second point: ''Assuming such a right, who should be responsible for providing the remedy when an institution has inadequate resources to provide that level of treatment?'' The brief argued that lower courts committed a grievous error in holding psychiatrists responsible for inadequate resources, a fact over which they have no control. A further argument was that the lower courts' decisions conflicted with other case rulings in which state officials who work in good faith were not held liable for inadequate resources beyond their control. It was also noted that fourteen years ago, when Donaldson was first admitted, no constitutional right to treatment had been established; it would have been impossible to plan in advance for a new policy in law not made until years later (APA, 1975). The Supreme Court, however, did not address the questions directly; as mentioned above, its decision advanced only the principle that mental illness is insufficient to justify indefinite and involuntary incarceration in a custodial setting.

The case raises an important issue, since state mental hospitals have difficulty enough in recruiting staff, and are often marginally financed.

The specter of suits against hospital psychiatrists can only further increase the difficulty in recruiting competent staff. (In the Florida case, a hospital superintendent who had retired and a ward psychiatrist responsible for six hundred patients were both sued; payment of $10,000 by each defendant was made in the final consent agreement in 1977.) In the end, patient treatment must suffer even more. It is evident that involuntarily admitted patients must be placed in intensive treatment programs tailored to individual requirements or released if not dangerous to self or others and capable of survival on their own.

A 30-year-old male, in and out of prisons and mental hospitals since he was a teenager, was diagnosed schizophrenic, paranoid type, with heroin addiction. There was a history of violent behavior. It was known he had on several occasions threatened to kill his mother. When his behavior stabilized after a stay in Michigan's Northfield Psychiatric Hospital, he was released. Two months later he went to the home of his mother in Alabama and killed her. In the trial for first degree murder, he was acquitted by reason of insanity. After a year in an Alabama institution, the man was returned to Detroit. A Wayne County jury found the psychiatrist who released the patient liable for wrongful discharge (*AMA News,* 1981).

The dilemma arises when judgment indicates overt symptoms no longer require inpatient care, but the history of violence and of threats makes recurrence of dangerous behavior a possibility. "Liability is imposed if a patient who causes harm was negligently released," cautions Slovenko (1973). Prediction of future behavior is difficult if not impossible. One uses one's best judgment, carefully assesses the patient's condition, and records the findings and opinion in discharge notes. This is the therapist's best protection but is by no means an absolute safeguard.

Another example of improper discharge is the failure to admit a patient brought to the emergency room who, when turned away, injures himself or another. The potential exists here for litigation for negligence. We have earlier noted the emergency room as a site that generates a high proportion of claims. Here also the best protection is an adequate record of examination and of treatment, including refusal of treatment.

Suicides. When a person has attempted suicide or has threatened it, the "reasonable apprehension" standard applied by courts assumes the likelihood of another attempt, or of a realization of the threat. If the patient is known to be depressed and suicidal, there is a duty to protect the patient from suicidal impulses, depending on the history, clinical course, and treatment response. To demonstrate negligence, the clinician may be shown to have been insufficiently diligent in securing an adequate history, one that would have brought to light previous self-destructive actions or suicidal thoughts. Appropriate treatment may not have been prescribed, or hospital staff may have failed to carry out orders or to carefully supervise the patient. It makes no difference whether the patient is on voluntary or involuntary status, or is paying or not paying for care.

When it is not known that the patient is likely to kill himself, and it can be shown that careful examination failed to uncover any clue whatsoever of suicidal tendency, claims made for negligence because of a sudden impulsive act that results in death rarely result in clinician or hospital being found liable. Negligence may be established if reasonable precautions to protect the potentially suicidal patient are not taken. When a patient thwarts precautions and commits suicide, even though the therapist and the hospital are aware of the danger and do their best to provide adequate treatment and supervision, negligence is rarely proven (*JAMA*, 1971).

Hospitals should be constructed so that they provide protection and safety to the patients. Care should be taken to ensure that there are no open invitations to suicide in multistory buildings, e.g., open access to the roof or to stairwell windows. Drug and poison control systems should safeguard unauthorized access to medications or chemicals. The notation "suicide precautions" on the clinical chart should alert staff to more than routine surveillance of a patient.

The contention that "if only the patient had been watched suicide could have been avoided" is invalid. So also are such statements as "If only the door had been locked," or "If the plateglass window had been a steel-mullioned window the tragedy could have been averted." Suicides are no more frequent today in an entirely open hospital than they were during the era of patient control on closed wards. Formerly, there was a reliance on locked doors, iron-barred windows, control of all sharp objects, and constant surveillance. Depressed and suicidal patients were subjected to the degrading practice of being tied down with sheet restraints "spread eagle" fashion on a bed: the ultimate in control. The active treatment found in today's hospitals can actually be said to reduce the risk of suicide. Even so, our experience includes a patient committing suicide despite there being a nurse in constant attendance. The patient concealed a glass fragment which she used to sever an artery under a blanket where the nurse could not see it. The patient bled to death under the blanket, undetected by the nurse at her bedside until it was too late.

Adverse reactions from drugs. Every psychiatrist who uses drug therapy assumes additional responsibilities for care in prescribing, administering, and monitoring. The psychiatrist doing investigational drug research assumes extraordinary risks (Slovenko, 1973). Negligence may be proven if a suicide results from a lethal overdose of a drug given in quantity to a patient for self-medication when that individual was known to have had suicidal impulses. Negligence may also be claimed when the patient was harmed as a result of an improper dosage prescribed by the psychiatrist (e.g., 1 gram written where it should have read 0.1 gram). The potential harm from side effects of drugs must be fully explained and understood by the patient. The thalidomide disaster that resulted in deformities of offspring set off an alarm that was heard around the world. Many drugs in daily use have side effects that can be harmful. Package inserts now carry warnings that alert the user to toxic reactions. If toxic reactions are not explained to the patient, or if the physician or nurse does not monitor the patient to detect them, negligence may be claimed.

Some drugs exhibit an adverse effect when they become addictive. Drugs controlled under the Omnibus Drug Act require detailed records and strict accountability. Laxity in control or careless prescribing that produces addiction or harm can result in a claim of negligence. The use of methadone therapy for heroin addiction requires clear evidence of addiction to opiates and care to ensure that the substitute drug is taken by the patient and monitored during treatment. The busy private practitioner who fails to maintain the standard of care given in a methadone clinic runs the risk of a negligence claim.

The physician shares the responsibility to make certain that the nurse administers the prescribed drug accurately, completely, and on time, and keeps proper records (*JAMA*, 197). It is also important to keep track of how prescriptions are being filled—can the nurse call in a refill prescription? If the nurse does, is it noted on the chart for the information of the rest of the treatment team?

Some antianxiety drugs can be addictive if prescribed for years on end. Careful monitoring of the length of time a prescription has been used, as well as its effectiveness and any signs of tolerance or chronic withdrawal symptoms, should be routine.

Errors in prescribing drugs do occur, but not as often as a Senate subcommittee has charged. The media, of course, gave this charge wide coverage. In response, an editorial in a medical journal (*JAMA*, 1976) cited two studies showing faulty prescribing to be infrequent. One of these showed that in 827 autopsied cases of adverse drug reactions only 25 (3 percent) were due to therapeutic errors. The second study, of 7,423 hospitalized patients, showed the incidence of error to be only 0.22 percent.

Judge Squire of the Court of Claims ruled the State of New York negligent and liable when it failed to use reasonable care and to act in conformity with the standard by not providing a patient with medication after her supply ran out. The facts of the case showed she had been released from Marcy State Hospital without her prescription. After repeated attempts on her part to obtain more medication, and without the stabilizing effect it had on her, she attempted suicide. The court assessed $228,000 in damages.

Another case, which received wide coverage in the press, and resulted in a successful claim for damages, involved the administration of a drug, mistakenly given, which harmed the patient. Damages were also awarded a patient who sustained an injury as the result of an auto accident: the patient had not been warned of the soporific action of a tranquilizer.

The problem of avoidance of liability due to adverse reaction to drugs is in essence the answer to the question: What is reasonable professional behavior in communicating to patients the risks of medications? It is evident that it is impractical, if not impossible, to recite every known risk, nor has the law required it. Remote and improbable side effects need not be communicated. The patient's mental condition may be such that concentration is impaired and attention wanders.

When in acute discomfort, there may be an impatience with delay in beginning a drug that brings relief. Some might reject a drug that could dispel their symptoms because of being frightened by potential hazards.

We recommend participatory management: therapists should discuss with their patients the possible alternative approaches to treatment and accept the patient's right to reject at least some of the alternatives. The more frequent side effects should be communicated. A handout sheet of frequently encountered side effects and what to do should they occur is much appreciated by patients. There is a more extensive discussion of this subject in chapters 7 and 10.

Complications/concerns of electroconvulsive therapy (ECT). The most common cause of claims following ECT is a fracture or dislocation. As the use of ECT declined, suits for injuries also decreased. Because injury can occur in treatment even when proper care is taken, many claims are based on failure to disclose to the patient the possibility of such injuries. In one instance, the courts found a psychiatrist negligent when he failed to conform to the APA standard and gave further treatments after the patient complained of back pain. A complaint of pain calls for examination and x-rays. Had the psychiatrist taken an x-ray, he would have discovered a compression fracture and not aggravated the injury (Slovenko, 1973). Fractures may also occur if patients recovering from ECT are unattended and allowed to fall off a wheeled litter or out of bed. Failure to provide protective restraints or to instruct an attendant to observe the patient closely may be ruled negligence. Another aspect of the treatment is cessation of voluntary breathing. This requires resuscitation and advance preparation for a possible respiratory emergency. Some hospitals have an anesthesiologist in attendance during ECT to provide adequate respiratory support and emergency treatment should complications arise.

Memory impairment and confusion are often transient complications of ECT that require advance explanation to patients and their families. Even more important than the above, perhaps, is explaining to the mental patient the possible side effects before obtaining consent. The use of a signed consent form and an oral explanation of complications is recommended. In states such as Michigan, the written form is required.

The procedure of ECT has become much simpler and less risky with the use of intravenous short-acting barbiturates and succinylcholine, a muscle relaxant. Fractures are now almost entirely eliminated in the use of ECT. Use of consent to treatment forms and thorough review with the patient of the potential complications of ECT will further reduce the risk of a malpractice claim.

On October 31, 1974, a bill was signed into law in California which threatened to virtually eliminate ECT as a treatment modality in standard clinical practice. Intended as a measure to strengthen informed consent and requiring that every aspect of risk involved be explained to the patient and to a relative, it went on to allow ECT to be used "only after all other appropriate treatment modalities have been exhausted." This would have eliminated its use as primary therapy in extremely suicidal, agitated depressed patients who obviously cannot wait the three weeks it takes for antidepressant medications to work their effect. The law required a review by a committee of three physicians, one from the institution and two appointed by the local mental health director. Applicable to voluntary and involuntary patients alike, the law carried penalties including fines of up to $10,000 plus revocation of license to practice, as well as encouraging damage suits against any psychiatrist administering the treatment (*Psychiatric News,* 1975). Action to repeal the legislation was initiated and enforcement was prevented by injunction. In April 1976 the statute, which also limited the use of psychosurgery, was declared unconstitutional by the California State Court of Appeals (4th District, San Diego).* Some of the court's findings will prove relevant as efforts continue to use the courts to control overuse or abuse of these therapies. The opinion set forth the following principles:

• The regulation of intrusive or possibly hazardous forms of medical treatment is a proper exercise of the state's police power. The objective of the law was to ensure certain medical procedures are not performed on unwilling patients.

• The requirement that a procedure be "critically needed for the patient's welfare" offers no guide to the degree of need and is impermissibly vague.

• The state's interest is the protection of the right to refuse treatment

---

* A revised version became law Jan. 1, 1977. It requires unanimous approval of a three-man board for psychosurgery, and agreement by two physicians that ECT is "definitely indicated."

and the prevention of unnecessary administration of a hazardous and intrusive treatment. But the procedure is in violation of the patient's rights of privacy and the right to confidentiality established by law. When voluntary consent is confirmed, the state has little excuse to invoke a substitute decision making process. The patient and the physician are the best judges of health, safety, and welfare.

The case illustrates how abuses often stimulate the quest for a solution. Later in this chapter we use a similar situation in Massachusetts that effectively controlled abuses. Also illustrated is the very real importance of monitoring prospective health legislation, both while it is being formulated and after bills are introduced in hearings.

Failure to request consultation. "Not every treatment of a patient which turns out to be less than a complete success is malpractice because the attending physician has failed to consult a specialist" (AMA, 1970). It must be shown that the clinician knew or should have known that the patient had a disorder that was beyond his competence to treat and that a consultant should have been called. Also it must be shown that such referral would have benefited the patient. The failure to refer will not constitute negligence unles the average clinician would have done so.

Other negligent acts. There are cases on record where negligence was alleged when mental hospitals failed to properly identify a patient. A notice of death sent to relatives led to their discovery that the deceased was not in fact their kinsman. We know of a case where two patients had identical names. Through error the wrong set of relatives was summoned to the bedside of a critically ill patient. For several days they faithfully maintained their vigil and claimed the body for burial. It was only a rare visit by a relative of the other patient with the same name which led to discovery of the mix-up. It took extra compassion to avoid a claim on the part of all concerned.

Rarely, it may be shown that substandard care was responsible for an aggressive assault by a patient that injured another.

Res Ipsa Loquitur (The Thing Speaks for Itself)

Where a situation is demonstrated to be under the control of the accused, the injured party has not contributed to the injury in any way, and it is obvious that harm could not have occurred without negligent conduct, no further proof of the physician's liability is necessary. Instead, when the legal principle *res ipsa loquitur* is invoked, the physician must prove he is *not* responsible for the harm done. The surgeon who leaves a forceps or sponge in the patient's belly illustrates this principle. There are few situations in psychiatric practice where this doctrine might apply. Infusing boric acid intravenously instead of saline; breaking a needle while doing a spinal tap and making no attempt to remove the broken fragment; or tossing a lighted cigarette into a wastebasket and setting a fire which burns a patient are possible examples.

Battery

Touching a person without permission is battery in legal terminology. Unauthorized bodily contact may be an assault, as in slapping a person for allegedly therapeutic purposes without his permission. Battery can also be charged when manipulations, procedures, or injections are performed without consent. In a suit for battery, the patient does not need to prove injury.

The Discovery Rule and the Statute of Limitations

The law requires that a person injured by another seek legal redress as soon as possible. All states have established time limits for filing claims. These are known as statutes of limitations. Laws vary, but in seventeen states it is required that a suit for personal injury be initiated within one to three years of the time the incident occurred. The remaining states rely on similar statutes governing other civil action damages (Chayet, 1966).

In recent years there has been a trend toward adopting a "discovery rule" whereby these statutory periods do not begin to elapse until such time as the patient discovers that a wrongful and injurious act has occurred (AMA, 1970). In most cases the patient's awareness of harm and the incident that caused it will occur in close temporal succession, but in some instances they may not. Protracted nondiscovery is more commonly encountered in surgery or radiology than in psychiatry.

In another use of the term "discovery" by lawyers, it is used to refer to the "digging" they do before trial to learn what evidence the other side has. Discovery prevents surprise and may lead to an out-of-court settlement. The strategy for this type of discovery is comprehensively covered in an outline prepared by Crawford Morris (1970). Scanning it will give the administrator some idea of the breadth of inquiry and search usual in a well-prepared malpractice claim or defense against one. Some of the points covered are:

• Review of the law, for it determines what facts are needed;
• Review of the petition of the plaintiff and formulation and definition of the legal issues;
• Reading opinions and briefs in similar cases;
• Reading the patient's medical chart;
• Determining the proof needed and securing evidence in records behind the medical record, as in worksheets, log entries, maintenance and service records on equipment, financial records, x-rays, pathology slides, etc.;
• Studying medical literature, hospital review committee findings, applicable standards, and hospital regulations;
• Identifying all personnel involved and refreshing their recollection of the event;
• Examining the scene of the accident;
• Checking on plaintiff's total hospital experience in previous admissions as well as present;
• Ascertaining plaintiff's experts and their theory of the case.

LIABILITY FOR THE ACTS OF OTHERS

A physician or an administrator may incur liability for the acts of others (Southwick, 1962; AMA, 1970; *U.S. News,* 1975; Andrade and Andrade, 1979). Under the legal principle of *respondeat superior* (let the one higher up answer for it), administrator and physicians have been held responsible for the acts of those under their supervision. This rule has been applied even when due care has been exercised in selection of staff. Recent rulings have held hospital, nursing home, and other facility employees jointly responsible in providing health care, thus making them responsible for their own misdeeds. However, a physician who employs another physician or mental health professional may still be held responsible for any injuries to patients caused by the employed person's negligence. A physician who knowingly employs a physician or clinical psychologist not licensed in the state may be guilty of aiding the unlawful practice of medicine or psychology and could lose protection under malpractice insurance.

A psychiatrist giving ECT might be liable for the negligent act of an anesthesiologist, even though the latter is a specialist and is usually regarded as an independent professional.

If an office assistant who has been properly trained gives an injection at the physician's direction and an injury occurs through negligence or giving the wrong drug, the physician might be held liable. The same risk extends to paramedical personnel assigned tasks under a physician's direction.

Incidentally, interns and residents who "moonlight" answering calls for physicians may involve the employing physician or administrator in liability. Interns and residents also run risks in emergency room service and other practice. They should be protected under their own liability policy or that of the employing institution.

TOWARD CORRECTIVE LEGISLATION

A crisis was precipitated when one of the largest malpractice insurance carriers announced that as of June 30, 1975, it would stop writing the traditional coverage and offer only a claims-made policy. The traditional policy provides coverage for any claims made in the future for services provided while the policy is in effect. The claims-made policy would cover the physician only for claims reported during the year the policy is in effect. The change was made because the number and size of potential claims could not be predicted, and companies were increasingly finding themselves behind in rates. To be protected under a claims-made policy for a claim filed in 1982 for an incident that occurred in 1979, the policy must have been in effect in 1979 and be still active in 1982. The claim would not be covered if in 1982 the policy had been dropped or changed to another carrier.

The American Medical Association's House of Delegates took steps in June 1975 to ease the crisis (slowdowns, strikes, doctors leaving practice in droves) by the establishment of an AMA reinsurance company to cover excess losses for state medical societies that had established their own liability insurance companies (*AMA News,* 1975c). To enroll, states were required to have a minimum of three thousand physicians in participation. Smaller states banded together to meet the requirement (AMA News, 1975a). At the close of 1979, the AMA's wholly owned insurance company (The American Medical Assurance Company—AMACO) was providing a portion of the reinsurance for ten physician-owned companies. There were, in 1979, twenty-three physician- or medical society-owned companies, which covered about 92,000 physicians constituting about 40 percent of the market.

Welch (1975) suggested joint underwriting mechanisms as the favored short-range solution to the malpractice crisis. For the long run he favored shortening the statute of limitations, limiting lawyer's contingency fees, elimination of *res ipsa loquitur* and *ad damnum* clauses (the latter a specification of the amount asked as damages from a defendant), and "powerful malpractice arbitration boards whose conclusions and evidence would be submitted on further appeal."

It was suggested that no-fault insurance be tried in a circumscribed locality for its speedy settlement of claims according to a predetermined benefit schedule. It would not eliminate disputes, however, and it could well escalate the number of claims. Schwartz and Komesar (1978) believed that no-fault schemes might abolish the deterrent effect of litigation. It was their position that damages awarded in malpractice suits not only compensate victims but also deter health care providers from negligent behavior. Their studies of patient records revealed a large number of mishaps due to negligence, with only one in fifteen leading to a claim. Some 40 percent of file entries held by insurance companies reported mishaps that were not pursued by patients. Of 24,000 instances of malpractice in California hospitals in 1974 only 4,000 of the injured parties filed claims. The extent of the problem, Schwartz and Komesar held, required a mechanism for deterrence which the present system supplied. However, they favored a rating of physicians by individual performance, for 1 percent of physicians account for 10 percent of all claims and a full 30 percent of payments.

By 1978 every state had passed some type of remedial legislation. As a consequence of the general discussion of the malpractice problem and with the impact of new laws, the number of claims dropped in 1977 (*AMA News*, 1978a). Perhaps screening and review mechanisms were partly responsible for reducing spurious claims. Canel noted a reduction in the number of suits pending in Cook County (Illinois) Circuit Court from 400–500 per month in 1975 to 40 per month in 1977 (*AMA News*, 1978a). Of 1,100 claims filed, 97 were sent to trial judges, where 80 were resolved in favor of the defendant and the remaining 17 dropped. Some decrease in the filing of irresponsible claims may have resulted from 100 countersuits filed against attorneys and their clients.

Premium rates for hospitals were reduced in 1978 by action of the Massachusetts Insurance Commission when companies asked for a 32 percent increase. The action followed a two-year experience with screening claims, with more than half the cases files being rejected (*AMA News*, 1978a). In Kansas, hospital malpractice rates were reduced by 40 percent below what they were in July of 1972 (AMA News, 1978b). Favorable loss experience was the reason given, but it may be that the original increases were unjustified and an evidence of overreaction by insurance companies.

Legislation enacted by the states to remedy malpractice difficulties fell into three major categories (*Psychiatric News*, 1976):

1. Insurance coverage change:
    a. Joint underwriting (twenty-four states) with pooled risk. Wisconsin's law is the model most are using.
    b. Maximum liability set at $500,000 (thirteen states).
    c. Some states allowed or required claims-made policies (coverage only for claims reported during the year the policy was in effect) or occurrence methods (coverage for any claim made in the future for service provided while the policy was in effect).
2. Legal reforms:
    a. Screening panels to eliminate spurious claims (twelve states) and to encourage early settlement.
    b. Fundamental reforms, including agreements by parties to submit their dispute to an impartial arbitrator or a panel of arbitrators for settlement (twenty states).
    c. Shortened statute of limitations (seventeen states).

   d. Restrictions on lawyers' contingency fees (twelve states).
   e. Defined informed consent (nine states).
   f. Restrictions on plaintiff's right to state a specific monetary damage—the *ad damnum* clause (nine states).
   g. Redefined scope of standards of care.
   h. Limited amount of awards (nine states).
3. Strengthening medical disciplinary boards (twelve states):
   a. Require disclosure of negligent acts to Board (nine states).

   Some of the impact of the actions taken in the various states can now be assessed. Indiana enacted a law in 1975 establishing a medical review panel to screen all claims. Findings were admissible as evidence in court; the limit of liability to physicians was set at $100,000. A patient's compensation fund was limited to $500,000, with the stipulation that a dollar amount could not be included in a claim, and a statute of limitations was set at two years from the date of the act. As a result, 90 percent fewer claims were filed. An average of thirty-two claims per year were received, and all resolved cases were settled out of court. The steep rise in malpractice insurance premiums was halted (Munro, 1982).

   Massachusetts changed its statutes, enacting a law which established a new Board of Registration in Medicine to provide stricter controls, reduced the statute of limitations for minors; eliminated specification of the amount of money sought in damages; created a joint underwriting mechanism which included all casualty insurance companies doing business in the state; and provided for a tribunal (a supreme court judge, an attorney, and a physician from the same field as the defendant physician) to screen out frivolous or nonmeritorious cases. In the first three years of operation 45 percent of cases fell into that category and subsequently this percentage rose to 50 percent. The tribunal model has demonstrated its value and is being copied by other states (Kruger, 1977).

   Premium rates for malpractice protection for psychiatrists, according to McDonald (1980), were reduced 22.5 percent in 1980. California, with the highest rate among the states, showed a 44 percent decrease from an annual rate of $2700 to $1500, while North Carolina psychiatrists, paying but $189 per year (the lowest rate), got no cuts. Also noted was a drop in the surcharge for ECT from 50 percent to 25 percent.

LIABILITY OF NURSES AND OTHER MENTAL HEALTH PROFESSIONALS

The nurse or other mental health professional may be responsible for an injury to a patient or client through negligence, battery, or failure to meet a standard of care. While there have been few malpractice claims made, they can occur, and few of these individuals carry liability insurance. The expanded role and increased responsibility of the professions carry with them a greater risk of mishaps, and these can occasion malpractice claims. Nurses, when administering drugs, may make a mistake in dosage. If they are in doubt, it is essential they verify the dose by checking with the physician. The nurse is obligated to observe the patient and report anything unusual to the physician (Andrade and Andrade, 1979).

Some of the areas of concern in the area of liability claims against mental health professionals are the following: informed consent, confidentiality, protection of the patient from harm by patients known to be assaultive, suicide, failure to note change in behavior or symptoms of illness, protection of patients from falls, limiting practice to areas of competence, and failure to seek consultation.

PROTECTION WHEN RENDERING EMERGENCY CARE

"Good Samaritan" statutes have been enacted in nearly all states to exempt physicians from liability for negligence when they provide emergency care to victims of accidents. These statutes vary widely, however. Some cover all physicians, others only those licensed in the particular state; some cover any emergency, others only an accident or only a roadside accident; some cover any person who gives first aid, others cover only services rendered without payment.

As far as we can ascertain, there is not a single case on record of any suit involving a person rendering emergency aid which has reached an appellate court in the U.S. Psychiatrists and mental health professionals can take comfort in the fact that standards of practice in an office or hospital do not apply to the emergency situation. To stop and give first aid to the best of one's ability and to stand by until the patient is placed in an ambulance for transport to the hospital is all that is required. It is unlikely that liability will be found against the "Good Samaritan."

THE BEST DEFENSE IS PREVENTION

The best defense against malpractice claims is prevention. Observation of the following guidelines should render physicians and other health care professionals less liable to malpractice claims:

1. *Establish a good rapport with each patient.* The therapist's compassion, understanding, and concern contribute to the development of the patient's confidence, trust, and willingness to work in cooperation. Courteous, helpful attention to involved relatives is also part of building rapport. If possible, engage them in a harmonious relationship. The therapist who has established good rapport is seldom sued when things go wrong.

2. *Give each patient care that meets the standards of good clinical practice everywhere.* Examine each patient completely. Order laboratory tests, x-rays, EEG and psychological tests when they may lend support to the diagnosis. If there is an untoward complication, side effects, or injury, take time to explain it fully. Beware of an arrogant, defensive reaction to questioning by the patient or family of what you have done. Make no overly optimistic prognosis and avoid even a casual remark that could be construed as a guarantee of cure.

3. *Maintain current clinical records.* Document symptoms and signs; develop a formulation that justifies the diagnosis. Record the treatment directed to patient problems and note its effect. When a procedure or therapy is chosen over other alternatives, it is helpful to indicate the reasoning that led to the action. Courts assume that the clinican will use judgment, and while not demanding infallibility, they do ask that opinion be justified. When an error is made in a record, it is important not to deface the chart. One draws a line through the incorrect portion, writes "error," and initials it before entering the correct statement. This simple procedure is extremely important. Records should also be legible and easily decipherable.

4. *Practice within the limits of your competence. Use consultants*

whenever indicated. The obscure disorder, the refractory case, and the unusual or alarming symptom provide the basis for referral to the consultant. Seeking help when in doubt and refusing to undertake a procedure beyond one's competence is evidence of good judgment. If the situation is not compatible with your methods of practice, arrange to sever the relationship and take appropriate steps to transfer responsibility to another physician or therapist.

5. *Be responsible in setting a value on your services. Discuss fees with the patient and avoid overcharging.* Make certain the patient understands the fee before starting treatment. Review carefully any case that has had an unsatisfactory outcome before applying pressure for the collection of an unpaid bill for services. It may be advantageous to write off the charges when the patient is disgruntled with the service. Taking care to avoid any acknowledgment of liability, one can shift the guilt to the patient for receiving free care. He or she may later pay the bill in installments (Vaccarino, 1976).

6. *Always secure an informed consent* for a procedure such as ECT, drug therapy, or surgery, as well as autopsy. Use a consent form and oral explanation. (See also Slovenko, 1973, pp. 431–433; MMS, 1975, pp. 21–41.) If a new or experimental drug is employed it may be best not to request a fee for its use or to accept any consideration from the manufacturer. (It is difficult to avoid the allegation that the patient was used as a ''guinea pig'' if payment of some kind was made.) An experimental procedure requires clearance through a human subject research group and extra care in insuring that the patient understands the risks involved and the alternative courses of action.

7. When a complaint or threat of action is received, *communicate* the knowledge to the administrator, legal counsel, or patient advocate. Shared knowledge permits determination of an appropriate course of action that may avoid suit.

8. *Educate patient,* families, and the public that all diseases can't be cured or all risks avoided. The variable response of each patient cannot be predicted. Public expectation that medical science can overcome every obstacle if only enough effort is expended is unrealistic, the product of TV and other media fiction. Related to the need for education is an effort which should be made by the clinician to offset the shock the patients receive when the bill for a serious illness is

received following a period of hospital care. The assumption is often made that the cost will be about $100 per day and that insurance will pay most of it. It takes advance preparation to create an awareness that the bill may be many thousands of dollars and that the amount not covered by insurance may be a great deal more than the amount originally held in mind as the total cost. The educational effort may also alert the public that it is paying the enormous cost of expensive malpractice actions. They need to understand that the injured party receives only a small fraction of any settlement and that the rest goes for costs. They need to learn that users of service pay for unbelievably high malpractice premiums.

    9. An experimental approach to the prevention of malpractice actions is reported to work at Halifax Hospital and Medical Center in Daytona Beach, Florida. The basic element in the plan is to *catch mistakes before the patient discovers them*. When an error occurs the patient and his family discuss with the doctor and the hospital what can be done. In ten years the 500-bed hospital recorded about 20,000 instances in which something went wrong. It took steps to correct them. Payments were made in only 150 cases (Auerbach, 1975).

SUMMARY

Ninety percent of all malpractice suits ever filed in the United States have come since 1964. The crisis of the 1970s was largely an insurance crisis, for medical practice was never better nor practitioners more competent than they are now. The multiplying number of claims, the diminishing availability of insurance, the astronomical premium costs, and the escalating cost of medical care were aspects of the problem.

    Malpractice is negligent or substandard practice by a professional (or a failure to perform a duty) that results in an injury to patient or client. Negligence is the omission of something a reasonable person would do, or the doing of something a responsible and prudent person would not do. Some forms of medical negligence involve abandonment, errors in diagnosis, unnecessary commitment, failure to treat, improper discharge, suicide, adverse reaction to drugs, injury following ECT, and failure to request consultation.

    In addition to negligence, other legal doctrines were defined: *res ipsa loquitur,* battery, discovery, statutes of limitations, and informed consent.

Legislative remedies for the crisis in medical liability have been enacted in almost all states. They fall into three categories: changes in insurance coverage, legal reforms, and the strengthening of medical disciplinary boards.

The best defense against a malpractice action is prevention. To prevent claims one can establish rapport with patients, give each one care that meets the standards of good medical practice, maintain current clinical records, practice within the limits of one's competence, secure informed consent, communicate with others when an error is made or a complaint received, let people know that all diseases cannot be cured or all risks avoided, and catch errors before the patient does and remedy them if possible.

In 1977 the number of malpractice claims fell dramatically, and the first reduction in premium rates followed in 1978. Screening out frivolous claims was partly responsible for the lower rates, and perhaps countersuits played a small part, but most important was the open discussion of the problem and the awareness that the patient paid the higher costs.

While liability insurance is available again in the 1980s and the number of claims seems to be decreasing, the cost of settlements is soaring and awards are often astronomical. In New York State two major carriers have filed for substantial premium increases in consequence of increasing claim costs. For every 100 physicians there were 8.8 claims. It has been estimated that by the time all 1981 claims are settled the cost for every physician will amount to $16,968. If the requested increases are allowed, some specialists will have to pay an annual premium of $60,000. The pressure for tort reforms has increased, as well as for a state-established catastrophe fund to pay 90 percent of claims over $250,000 (Golin, 1982).

In Florida, increasing costs of professional liability coverage in Dade County for 1982 cause high-risk specialists to pay an annual premium of $19,816 and add $701 to the annual cost of every hospital bed in the county (Tokarz, 1982).

Administrators, psychiatrists and mental health professionals, with a one in thirty chance each year of being sued, have a cause to support in legal reforms that will reduce the cost of medical care to patients.

QUESTIONS

1. What are four factors that contributed to the present malpractice crisis?
2. How is malpractice defined? negligence?
3. List six common situations that may constitute negligence.
4. What are three legal doctrines other than negligence that may be invoked in a malpractice action? How are they defined?
5. What are some of the legislative remedies enacted?
6. What steps are recommended to prevent malpractice claims?

REFERENCES

AMA (1970), Liability of the committing physician. In: *The Best of Law and Medicine 1968–1970*, reprinted in book form from *J. Amer. Med. Assn.* articles, pp. 9–10. Chicago: American Medical Association.

AMA (1975), Malpractice in focus: An AMA source document prepared by the editors of *Prism*. Chicago: American Medical Association.

AMA News (1975a), AMA liability reinsurance. *AMA News,* June 23. p. 1.

AMA News (1975b), Liability woes spread. *AMA News* Feb. 24, p. 1.

AMA News (1975c), Malpractice problems widen. *AMA News,* Feb. 3. p. 1.

AMA News (1978a), Malpractice update. *AMA News* (Impact, pp. 1–14), April 28.

AMA News (1978b), Premium cuts stir new malpractice questions. *AMA News,* June 23, p. 4.

AMA News (1981), MD liable for releasing patient. *AMA News,* 24:7, July 24.

Andrade, P. D., & Andrade, J. S. (1979), Professional liability of the psychiatric nurse. *J. Psychiat., & Law,* 7:141–186.

APA (1975), Amicus curiae brief in the Donaldson case. *Amer. J. Psychiat.,* 132:109–115.

Auerbach, S. (1975), Malpractice: The doctor's dilemma. *Washington Post,* May 18, p. C3.

Bellamy, W. A. (1962), Malpractice risks confronting the psychiatrist. *Amer. J. Psychiat.,* 188:769–779.

Bronson, G. (1980), A malpractice lawyer, Charles Kramer, wins respect and big awards. *Wall Street Journal,* Feb. 19, p. 1.

Chayet, N. L. (1966), Malpractice: The statute of limitations. *N. Engl. J. Med.,* 275:42–45.

Curran, W. J. (1975), Malpractice crises: The flood of legislation. *N. Engl. J. Med.,* 293:1182–1183.

Golin, C. B. (1982), Potential deficits trouble New York's liability carriers. *AMA News,* 25:1–7, June 11.

*Halleck, S. L. (1980), *Law and the Practice of Psychiatry: A Handbook for Clinicians.* New York: Plenum.

JAMA (1971), Law and medicine: Liability for patient's suicide. *J. Amer. Med. Assn.,* 215:1879–1888.

JAMA (1976), Adverse drug reactions and associated deaths. *J. Amer. Med. Assn.*, 236:592.

Kruger, I. D. (977), Important developments in malpractice. The Bulletin (ACP) 18:30-31, September, 1977.

McDonald M. (1980), APA malpractice carrier reduces premium rates. *Psychiatric News*, 15:1–7, Feb. 15.

Malpractice Digest (1974), Nov./Dec. issue. St. Paul, Minn.: St. Paul Fire and Marine Insurance Co.

MMS (1975), Professional liability guide. Boston: Massachusetts Medical Society.

Miller, L. J. (1982), Comparative negligence. *J. Amer. Med. Assn.* 248:1443–1444.

Morris, C. (1970), Strategy of discovery for the defendant physician and hospital in medical malpractice actions. *Scalpel and Quill: The Bulletin of the Pittsburgh Institute of Legal Medicine,* 4:4, Dec.

Munro, P. (1982), Malpractice insurance tribunal. *Physicians East,* 4:22.

Psychiatric News (1975), California enacts rigid shock therapy controls. *Psychiatric News,* 10:3, Feb.

Psychiatric News (1976), Medical liability: Update, The Bulletin American College of Physicians. *Psychiatric News,* 17:22–23, March.

* Schwartz, W. B., & Komesar, N. K. (1978). Doctors' damages and deterrence: An economic view of medical malpractice. *N. Engl. J. Med.,* 298:1282–1289.

Slawson, P. F. (1979), Psychiatric malpractice: The California experience. *Amer. J. Psychiat.,* 136:650–654.

Slawson, P. F. (1981), Report of loss control committee to the Board of Trustees. American Psychiatric Association, Washington D.C., March 1.

* Slovenko, R. (1973), *Psychiatry and Law.* Boston: Little, Brown.

Southwick, A. F. (1962), Current legal trends in hospital liability. *Hospital,* 36:43–47.

* Springer, E. W., ed. (1970), *Nursing and the Law.* Pittsburgh: Health Law Center, Aspen Systems Corp.

Stone, A. A. (1974), The right to treatment and the psychiatric establishment. *Psychiatric Annals,* 4:21–42.

Tokarz, W. (1982), Liability woes hit Florida, *AMA News,* 25:3, June 18.

U.S. News (1975), Malpractice crisis: How it's hurting medical care. *U.S. News and World Report,* 78:32–34, May 26.

U.S. Senate (1969), Medical malpractice: The patient versus the physician: A study by the Subcommittee on Executive Reorganization, Committee on Government Operations, U.S. Senate. Washington, D.C.: U.S. Government Printing Office.

Vaccarino, J. (1976), Malpractice insurance. Lecture at Dartmouth Medical School, Nov. 1.

Welch, C. E. (1975), Medical Malpractice, *N. Engl. J. Med.,* 292:1372–1376.

Chapter 15

Presentation of Evidence

Avoid any material misrepresentation of data
upon which an expert opinion or conclusion is
based.
—*Code of Ethics, American Academy of*
Forensic Sciences

Case example. A 26-year-old cook has had several discrete episodes
of loss of control which resulted in an attack on the chef with a knife,
on an assistant cook with a pan of dough, and extensive destruction
of the hotel kitchen. Behavior in the above instances was grossly out
of proportion to the minor criticism of his work that preceded the
outbursts. Between the episodes of rage he was a good cook, attended
to his duties, was friendly, and related well to fellow workers. Associated findings were frequent barroom brawls and a history of hy-
peractivity as a child. The EEG was normal. It is your opinion the
man has an intermittent explosive disorder. (You have ruled out brain
lesion, epilepsy, schizophrenia, and antisocial personality disorder,
this last because of the absence of aggressiveness and impulsiveness
between episodes.) The man feels a sense of tension before he loses
control, fails to resist the harmful act, and experiences a pleasurable
sense of relief afterwards but no self-reproach or guilt.

Is he competent to stand trial? Is he responsible for his criminal
behavior of assault and destruction of property?

Psychiatrists and psychologists are more frequently involved in court actions than they once were. The law is extending its interest in the mental health field. As the number of actions increases, so does the demand for experts in human behavior. Most try to avoid requests for help in a legal action.

In their own world, psychiatrists are invested with medical authority centuries old, an inheritance from their predecessors, the priests. In their practice, doctors seek to understand the patient as a whole person with values, emotions, intellect, attitudes, and as a biological, psychological, and social totality (Bromberg, 1969).

The courtroom is a very different setting from the clinician's office. Its rituals and practices are designed to portray the majesty of the law. Somehow it has retained some of the flavor of another ancient method of determining guilt, trial by ordeal. Under the guise of the intent to reveal bias and error, the lawyer in the courtroom resorts to such strategems as trickery, bullying, and intimidation to unsettle the witness or to arouse anger that may make testimony less credible. The lawyer takes a part of the story, a single symptom, an exception to the textbook picture, and worries it and treats it as the whole and then seeks to destroy the whole by ridiculing the inconsistency. Clinicians unfamiliar with the feudal metapsychology of the legal profession condemn the cross-examination as a device to confuse or to impute dishonesty to the witness (*Medical World News*, 1967).

Many believe affidavits setting forth the findings and opinion would be of greater value and eliminate the need for the clinician in court. Lawyers oppose affidavits because they are aware that experts disagree and believe their adversary system separates fact from opinion and identifies errors in both in the cross-examination. The same objection often is used to approve the admission of evidence on tapes or videotapes where the opportunity for cross-examination would be limited. The evolution of common law and rules of evidence has produced a system of discovery of truth that merits respect.

Earlier we quoted Judge Bazelon's explanation of the adversary process. We also found helpful another lawyer's comment on the different approach to discovery of truth used in courts. Weinstein (quoted in Slovenko, 1974, p. 672) remarks that the artificial world the law demarcates by establishing parameters is not a valid basis for objection. The same reasoning might be applied to the artistic quality of a painting that distorts a scene or might be used to criticize a distinguished writer of a biography that does not include everything that is known about the subject. The artist's world and the legal world are to be tested within a frame of reference. Neither presents the whole truth but only what is deemed relevant.

The legal trial presents facts that are regarded material and allows protagonists of a point of view to argue their case. More than what happened must be known in order to resolve a conflict. Courtroom goals are to search for truth, economize on resources by employing rules of procedure and evidence, inspire confidence, support social policies, establish rulings that are generalizable, pacify the disputants, and keep the peace.

DIFFERENCES IN APPROACH OF THE JUDICIAL AND MENTAL HEALTH SYSTEMS

Even when aware of these differences in approach, the clinician often goes to court with feelings of distaste, uneasiness, embarrassed anxiousness, even panic, and emerges from the experience with frustration and anger (Bromberg, 1969). To cope, more is needed than an understanding of the differences in approach and an awareness of the court's goals. Lawyers approach problems with deductive reasoning, while physicians and mental health professionals employ inductive reasoning. Lawyers build their case piece by piece on bits of evidence. Psychologists and psychiatrists deal with whole persons. Lawyers use the information relevant and material to their adversary position. They believe the adversary system puts champions of a cause in opposition and allows them to do battle, each trying to demolish the other, and that the observance of this ordeal makes the judgment less difficult than it would be if facts and opinion were gathered, studied, and evaluated in a calm, unemotional setting.

Science sets up an hypothesis and an experimental procedure to test its validity. After time and replication by others, an established fact may emerge. It may take years to discover what is true. A trial is not an investigation. Its function is to settle a dispute. Only the evidence available and relevant at the time of the trial is considered. The lawyers, as advocates for their clients, present only that evidence that will advance their position. "Loyalty to the client comes before loyalty to the truth," says Slovenko (1973).

Evidence can be suppressed which might establish guilt if it was obtained by evasion of the law. Elaborate rules of evidence govern what information may be admitted and how it is presented. The lawyers must be alert to the testimony being given, for the judge will consider only those objections the attorneys urge.

The judicial system holds that many psychological and behavioral problems are a part of common knowledge and do not require evaluation by an expert. Someone who knew the person well, a lawyer who understands the legal rules that apply to the situation, or the trial judge may report their observation as a finding on an individual's conduct (Curran, McGarry, and Petty, 1980).

Strange and eccentric behavior may be observed and reported by a witness. The accused may have been heard to say he planned to kill the milkman because he was having an affair with his wife. The question "Was the defendant suffering from delusions which were present at the time of the murder of the milkman, and which caused the act?" requires the opinion of an expert in human behavior.

Mental health professionals should be aware of antipsychiatric attitudes. Antagonism is frequently expressed against treatment (ECT, psychoactive drugs, and behavior modification), as well as against such concepts as "adjustment" or "control of behavior." Civil libertarians and young lawyers, often drilled in the controversial issues in the field, may be particularly alert to weaknesses in the testimony of mental health experts, and may in fact be opposed to all mental hospitals.

Some lawyers may believe, wrongly, that not only are physicians, psychiatrists, and mental health professionals experts in the evaluation of human behavior, but that they are also knowledgeable in all areas of forensic psychiatry. In reality, only a very few are expert in both fields (Curran, et al., 1980).

WHO MAY TESTIFY

Courts in general are lacking in standards for the qualification of clinicians to determine competence to stand trial or make wills and contracts, or to give an expert opinion on an individual's responsibility for criminal conduct. In consequence, almost any physician, even those with little or no training in psychiatry, may be asked to report findings and to give an opinion to the court. Psychiatrists who have completed an approved residency training and are Diplomates of the American Board of Neurology and Psychiatry are qualified to give expert opinion. Only a few of the latter have by experience and training the knowledge of the interrelated clinical and legal standards applicable in the situation.

Because psychiatrists have a broad medical training, they are assumed to possess the knowledge to give a complete opinion or diagnosis. Some courts limit psychologists to reporting findings and a partial opinion.

Most courts now recognize clinical psychologists with Ph.D. degrees as qualified to give both findings and an opinion, even with no special qualification to provide forensic testimony (Curran et al., 1980).

Some of the weak credibility of expert witnesses, both psychiatrists and psychologists, is the consequence of their lack of understanding of the legal issues to which their clinical findings relate. Inadequate, incomplete reports, personal bias, and irrelevant information are vulnerable to cross-examination.

SITUATIONS IN WHICH TESTIMONY OF EXPERTS IN HUMAN BEHAVIOR IS REQUIRED

Since 1965, litigation of all types has greatly increased and with it the need for the testimony of experts in human behavior. The cases fall into two categories, civil and criminal. Below we have listed the more common situations in which experts participate. Before the mental health administrator agrees to give testimony in court, it is imperative that one know precisely what is desired and for what purpose. If an examination is to be made, and an opinion presented in court, will the expert be granted access to background information? Access is desired to the charge, the statements of witnesses, and reports of mental health facilities, hospitals, and other relevant informants. Will a report be required? What fee will be paid?

The categories of litigation which require human behavior experts are:

Claims for Injury or Disability
- Personal injury alleging pain and suffering or mental disorder
- Third-party insurers where mental and emotional disorders and the ensuing disability are in dispute
- Malpractice allegations
- Workmen's Compensation

Divorce and Child Custody
- Mental illness, and psychosexual and personality disorders
- Ability of a parent to provide proper care for a child

Competence
- Mental capacity to make a will
- Need for guardian or conservator to manage affairs or finances
- Ability to negotiate a contract to participate with attorney and to stand trial

Commitment
- Need for involuntary admission to hospital
- Readiness for release from hospital

Criminal Litigation
- Determination, under statute in the jurisdiction, of criminal responsibility
- Capacity to formulate intent to commit a crime
- Evidence of mental illness or defect that affects actions, control, and judgment
- Assessment of ability to adhere to requirements of probation or parole

PROBLEMS AND ISSUES

The legal standards of "clear and convincing evidence" required for involuntary admission to hospital, and "beyond a reasonable doubt" required in criminal cases may be very clear standards from the point of view of the law. However, the absence of objective measures of mental and emotional disorders handicaps the clinician.

A step toward more precise definition of psychiatric disorders was taken with the adoption of the Diagnostic and Statistical Manual, DSM III, The degree to which anxiety disorders, somatoform disorders, psychosexual disorders, and personality disorders impair control over an individual's action is still largely a matter of subjective judgment.

Even with agreement on essential findings, experts may disagree as to theory, diagnosis, and prognosis. Differences of opinion lead to the "battle of the experts" which continues to undermine faith in the reliability of psychiatrists and psyhologists. It is often difficult to determine the exact onset of a mental or emotional disorder. In consequence it may be uncertain whether the condition discovered on examination of the client was present when an act was committed. The uncertainties and variability in human behavior often make it impossible to give the truth, as one interprets it, in response to "yes or no" questions.

PREPARATION OF THE REPORT

The court, or the attorney for a client, may request that an examination of the accused be made when mental disorder or defect is suspected or the defendant introduces a mental or emotional condition. While the accused cannot be compelled to answer questions and thus be exposed to self-incrimination if a plea of mental illness or pain and suffering is entered, an examination is required.

The client is informed of the nature of the examination—that it is not a therapeutic relationship and that the findings will be reported to the court and be available to the attorneys of both parties. The purpose is to determine the mental and emotional state at present and at the time of the incident, and not to determine guilt or innocence. The examiner must be alert to the possibility of malingering, and assume the individual is of sound mind unless proven otherwise. The examiner should allow enough time and effort to accomplish the purpose. This might include examination of documents, records, and any other pertinent data available, a physical and mental examination, appropriate psychometric tests, and laboratory tests. The examiner should be certain to understand the reason for examining the defendant.

The report to the court should contain, in addition to the usual identification data on the defendant, the court status (awaiting trial, competent to stand trial, probation, etc.) the date of the incident and its description, and the precise purpose of the examination. The report will include the number of interviews; where, when, and time spent in each; other sources of information; a statement that the client's informed consent to the examination was obtained; and the degree of cooperation with the examiner. The content of the report should include pertinent background of the circumstances surrounding the incident and, if possible, an evaluation of motivation and mental state at the time. Significant past history will be included. Objective findings of the examination will be documented.

The specific legal issues should be addressed and an opinion given as to how the mental and emotional state of the individual is relevant to it. Finally, a diagnosis and a dynamic formulation of the salient facts that support it are made, together with a statement as to how it bears on the legal issues. The report is dated and signed, including degrees and board certification.

PRETRIAL PREPARATION

When one is to testify in court, the prepared report will be available to both parties. The review of the report with the lawyer who invited the clinician to make the examinations offers time for education of the psychologist and psychiatrist in the legal issues, and of the attorney in clinical theory and significance of the data. Controversial points will be discussed, as well as probable line of questioning. The actual questions to be asked and the expected answers may be discussed. This is not to put answers in the expert's mouth to distort the collected data, but simply to let the lawyer know what the responses will be. One does not seek surprises on direct examination.

It is well to refresh one's memory of the latest literature and one's own published work, if any. One reviews the report carefully and formulates responses to possible challenges during cross-examination.

Not all reports require the expert to be present in court. Sometimes a hypothetical case will be presented which embodies the essential facts of the case on trial. If that is the course to be taken, questions and responses may be reviewed in advance.

On The Witness Stand

To play their part in the courtroom drama, clinicians must come emotionally prepared, and must project in dress, manner, and response warm, concerned, compassionate, highly competent, clinical specialists. Lines must be delivered with clarity, in layman's language. They must forgo the professional style of communication with colleagues and attempt to explain concepts as if addressing high school students hearing about psychiatry for the first time. This must be done without ostentation, behaving as a fact-finding agent of the court.

Clinicians should make certain each question is understood before answering. It is proper to request clarification or to request that the question be repeated. Pausing and taking time to reflect before answering, is also quite acceptable. Speaking clearly, distinctly, and loudly enough for those present to hear is best. If a yes or no answer is not possible, a turn to the judge with a request: "Your Honor, may I explain my answer?" is useful.

One's thoroughly prepared written report should produce a comprehensive overview in which each symptom or finding builds toward a totality such that the conclusion is obvious to the court, and is both logical and supported by objective facts and tests.

The cross-examination may challenge the expert's authority and knowledge and attack the conclusions in order to diminish the force of the testimony. One should calmly formulate a direct, clear, short response, answering one question at a time. One does not volunteer information that would extend the scope of the question asked.

The most effective professional witness is often the one who admits the areas of uncertainty and possible bias, reluctantly offering conclusions while pointing out that they are the court's prerogative. If the presented observations succeed in building a logical totality, and if deference is paid to the court's wisdom, the psychistrist or psychologist will enhance the public image of the profession and be in demand as an expert witness.

Usdin (1977) has offered some practical guides for the mental health professional testifying as an expert witness:

• make a thorough examination of the client;
• ensure access to records, testing, and consultants;

- conduct the examination in a proper setting;
- hold a pretrial conference with judge and opposing attorneys to clarify expectations;
- avoid partisanship, jargon, and unsupported statements;
- admit uncertainties; have the courage to say, "I don't know";
- acknowledge limitations of examinations made;
- discuss the established fee without hesitation.

Videotapes may be presented in evidence if available and relevant. Graphics often clarify when words can't. Be thorough, study background and related material, be prepared to explain alternatives and contingencies, give clinical opinions only if they are supportable, not those desired by one or the other of the litigants. Someday, when those in the legal profession are as much concerned about their problems and image as mental health professionals are about theirs, maybe we will see videotape used to show the patient before and after the event, as well as the interaction of clinician and patient during an interview. The stored file will then be fresh and ready for use when the time of trial arrives some three years or more later. The procedure can then move swiftly without the staggering loss of time and inconvenience to witnesses. It could also help in avoiding the badgering of witnesses, for most of us can't remember exactly what we did on the night of ———.

Another proposal for reform in expert medical testimony was made by Aring (1976): physicians should refuse to testify in legal proceedings unless called as a witness by the court rather than by one of the parties. Both the AMA and the American Bar Association, as long ago as 1961, endorsed in principle the concept of impartial medical testimony (Bergen, 1976). Most physicians would welcome the restructuring of their role to that of an unbiased friend of the court to report on findings, with testimony to be used by one or both sides as they see fit.

However, as we have commented earlier, lawyers favor the adversary system because the outcome of a trial may be influenced by expert opinion. They hold medicine to be an inexact science, and argue that opinions may differ, that experts are not infallable, and that miscarriages of justice might well follow a one-sided presentation that did not openly acknowledge uncertainties and disagreements.

Testimony on the issue of dangerousness was crucial in Smith v. Estelle (U.S. Court of Appeals, 5th Circuit, September 13, 1979). In an armed robbery in which a store clerk was killed, Smith accompanied another whose weapon fired the fatal shot. A psychiatrist was asked to determine whether the defendant was competent to stand trial. The physician answered in the affirmative when asked, "Is there a probability that the defendant would commit criminal acts of violence that would constitute a continuing threat to society?" It was also stated that the defendant was a "sociopath" who would continue his previous behavior. Smith's attorneys were never told their client had been examined, and Smith was not told the psychiatrist was examining him for anything other than competence to stand trial. The Appeals Court ruled that "a criminal defendant may not be compelled to speak, or to discuss his alleged crime, to a psychiatrist who can use his statements against him at the sentencing phase."

The APA-filed amicus curiae brief held that predictions of dangerousness are judgments of relative risk of a group and have low reliability.

The expert witness should derive the following guides to behavior from the Smith case:

• Always inform the patient as to the purpose of the examination.

• Make certain it is understood that a report will be sent to the court, that the interview is not for therapy, and that there is no confidential relationship.

• If evidence is to be presented, the defendant, with knowledge of the relationship, and of the purpose and intended use of his comments, must voluntarily consent to the examination.

• The court and the attorneys on both sides should know that the examination was held and for what purpose.

• Psychiatrists and psychologists have no expertise that allows a prediction of dangerousness in an individual on the basis of a mental examination.

SUMMARY

Psychiatrists and psychologists are more frequently involved in court actions than they once were. Because the courtroom is a very different setting from the therapist's office, we have attempted to clarify some of the reasons for this difference. The deportment of the expert witness and the need for preparation must be stressed. Communication with laymen, the construction of evidence to justify diagnosis and interventions, and the admission of biases and of knowledge limited by the state of the art are esential aspects of testimony. Videotape and graphics may clarify the presentation.

While most lawyers continued to favor the adversary system, some call for reforms whereby the expert witness, as friend of the court, would present testimony that could be used by both sides however they see fit.

QUESTIONS

1. What is the legal system's procedure to discover truth?
2. What are the standards for qualification of experts in human behavior?
3. In what situations are experts usually called?
4. What are some of the problems that experts in human behavior encounter when serving the judicial system?
5. What preparation is essential for the expert witness?
6. What are some of the suggested guides to presentation of testimony?
7. Should expert testimony be given only as a friend of the court and not as witness for a litigant?

REFERENCES

Aring, C. D. (1976), Expert medical testimony. *J. Amer. Med. Assn.*, 236:569.

Bergen, R. P. (1976), Medical witness and the adversary system. *J. Amer. Med. Assn.*, 236:592.

Bromberg, W. (1969), Psychiatrists in court: The psychiatrist's view. *Amer. J. Psychiat.*, 125:1343–1347.

* Curran, W. J., McGarry, A. L., & Petty, C. S. eds. (1980), *Modern Legal Medicine* (Chapter 43, pp. 963–987). Philadelphia: F. A. Davis.

Medical World News (1967), Witness stand need not be a personal trial for M.D. *Medical World News*, 8:28–42, April 7.

* Slovenko, R. (1973), *Psychiatry and Law*. Boston: Little, Brown.

Slovenko, R. (1974), Psychotherapist-patient testimonial privilege: A picture of misguided hope. *Catholic U. Law Rev.*, 23:649–673.

* Usdin, G. L. (1977), Psychiatric participation in court. *Psychiatric Annals*, 7:42–51.

Appendix A

Rights of Patients

The required minimum standards for adequate treatment of the mentally ill as defined in Wyatt v. Stickney are presented below as ordered on April 13, 1972 and amended April 1972 by Judge Frank Johnson, U.S. District Court, Alabama:

1. Patients have a right to privacy and dignity.
2. Patients have a right to the least restrictive conditions necessary to achieve the purposes of commitment.
3. No person shall be deemed incompetent to manage his affairs, to contract, to hold professional or occupational or vehicle operator's licenses, to marry and obtain a divorce, to register and vote, or to make a will *solely* by reason of his admission or commitment to the hospital.
4. Patients shall have the same rights to visitation and telephone communications as patients at other public hospitals, except to the extent that the Qualified Mental Health Professional responsible for formulation of a particular patient's treatment plan writes an order imposing special restrictions. The written order must be renewed after each periodic review of the treatment plan if any restrictions are to be continued. Patients shall have an unrestricted

right to visitation with attorneys and with private physicians and other health professionals.

5. Patients shall have an unrestricted right to send sealed mail. Patients shall have an unrestricted right to receive sealed mail from their attorneys, private physicians, and other mental health professionals, from courts, and government officials. Patients shall have a right to receive sealed mail from others, except to the extent that the Qualified Mental Health Professional responsible for formulation of a particular patient's treatment plan writes an order imposing special restrictions on receipt of sealed mail. The written order must be renewed after each periodic review of the treatment plan if any restrictions are to be continued.

6. Patients have a right to be free from unnecessary or excessive medication. No medication shall be administered unless at the written order of a physician. The superintendent of the hospital and the attending physician shall be responsible for all medication given or administered to a patient. The use of medication shall not exceed standards of use that are advocated by the United States Food and Drug Administration. Notation of each individual's medication shall be kept in his medical records. At least weekly the attending physician shall review the drug regimen of each patient under his care. All prescriptions shall be written with a termination date, which shall not exceed thirty days. Medication shall not be used as punishment, for the convenience of staff, as a substitute for program, or in quantities that interfere with the patient's treatment program.

7. Patients have a right to be free from physical restraint and isolation. Except for emergency situations, in which it is likely that patients could harm themselves or others and in which less restrictive means of restraint are not feasible, patients may be physically restrained or placed in isolation only on a Qualified Mental Health Professional's written order which explains the rationale for such action. The written order may be entered only after the Qualified Mental Health Professional has personally seen the patient concerned and evaluated whatever episode or situation is said to call for restraint or isolation. Emergency use of restraints or isolation shall be for no more than one hour, by which time a Qualified

Mental Health Professional shall have been consulted and shall have entered an appropriate order in writing. Such written order shall be effective for no more than 24 hours and must be renewed if restraint and isolation are to be continued. While in restraint or isolation the patient must be seen by qualified ward personnel who will chart the patient's physical condition (if it is compromised) and psychiatric condition every hour. The patient must have bathroom privileges every hour and must be bathed every 12 hours.

8. Patients shall have a right not to be subjected to experimental research without the express and informed consent of the patient, if the patient is able to give such consent, and of his guardian or next of kin, after opportunities for consultation with independent specialists and with legal counsel. Such proposed research shall first have been reviewed and approved by the institution's Human Rights Committee before such consent shall be sought. Prior to such approval the Committee shall determine that such research complies with the principles for research involving human subjects published by the American Psychiatric and Psychological Associations and with those required by the United States Department of Health, Education and Welfare for projects supported by that agency.

9. Patients have a right not to be subjected to treatment procedures such as lobotomy, electroconvulsive treatment, adversive reinforcement conditioning or other unusual or hazardous treatment procedures without their express and informed consent after consultation with counsel or interested party of the patient's choice.

10. Patients have a right to receive prompt and adequate medical treatment for any physical ailments.

11. Patients have a right to wear their own clothes and to keep and use their own personal possessions except insofar as such clothes or personal possessions may be determined by a Qualified Mental Health Professional to be dangerous or otherwise inappropriate to the treatment regimen.

12. The hospital has an obligation to supply an adequate allowance of clothing to any patients who do not have suitable clothing of their own. Patients shall have the opportunity to select from various types of neat, clean, and seasonable clothing. Such clothing shall be considered the patient's throughout his stay in the hospital.

13. The hospital shall make provision for the laundering of patient clothing.
14. Patients have a right to regular physical exercise several times a week. Moreover, it shall be the duty of the hospital to provide facilities and equipment for such exercise.
15. Patients have a right to be outdoors at regular and frequent intervals, in the absence of medical considerations.
16. The right to religious worship shall be accorded to each patient who desires such opportunities. Provisions for such worship shall be made available to all patients on a nondiscriminatory basis. No individual shall be coerced into engaging in any religious activities.
17. The institution shall provide, with adequate supervision, suitable opportunities for the patient's interaction with members of the opposite sex.
18. The following rules shall govern patient labor:
   A. Hospital Maintenance. No patient shall be required to perform labor which involves the operation and maintenance of the hospital or for which the hospital is under contract with an outside organization. Privileges or release from the hospital shall not be conditioned upon the performance of labor covered by this provision. Patients may voluntarily engage in such labor if the labor is compensated in accordance with the minimum wage laws of the Fair Labor Standards Act, 29 U.S.C. S206 as amended, 1966.
   B. Therapeutic Tasks and Therapeutic Labor
      (1) Patients may be required to perform therapeutic tasks which do not involve the operation and maintenance of the hospital, provided the specific task or any change in assignment is:
         a. An integrated part of the patient's treatment plan and approved as a therapeutic activity by a Qualified Mental Health Professional responsible for supervising the patient's treatment, and
         b. Supervised by a staff member to oversee the therapeutic aspects of the activity.
      (2) Patients may voluntarily engage in therapeutic labor for

which the hospital would otherwise have to pay an employee, provided the specific labor or any change in labor assignment is:

  a. An integrated part of the patient's treatment plan and approved as a therapeutic activity by a Qualified Mental Health Professional responsible for supervising the patient's treatment, and

  b. Supervised by a staff member to oversee the therapeutic aspects of the activity; and

  c. Compensated in accordance with the minimum wage laws of the Fair Labor Standards Act, 29 U.S.C. §206 et. seq. as amended, 1966.

C. Personal Housekeeping. Patients may be required to perform tasks of a personal housekeeping nature such as the making of one's own bed.

D. Payment to patients pursuant to these paragraphs shall not be applied to the costs of hospitalization.

19. *Physical Facilities*

A patient has a right to a humane psychological and physical environment within the hospital facilities. These facilities shall be designed to afford patients with comfort and safety, promote dignity, and ensure privacy. The facilities shall be designed to make a positive contribution to the efficient attainment of the treatment goals of the hospital.

A. Resident Unit. The number of patients in a multi-patient room shall not exceed six persons. There shall be allocated a minimum of 80 square feet of floor space per patient in a multi-patient room. Screens or curtains shall be provided to ensure privacy within the resident unit. Single rooms shall have a minimum of 100 square feet of floor space. Each patient will be furnished with a comfortable bed with adequate changes of linen, a closet or locker for his personal belongings, a chair, and a bedside table.

B. Toilets and Lavatories. There will be one toilet provided for each eight patients and one lavatory for each six patients. A lavatory will be provided with each toilet facility. The toilets will be installed in separate stalls to ensure privacy, will be clean and free of odor, and will be equipped with appropriate safety devices for the physically handicapped.

C. Showers. There will be one tub or shower for each 15 patients. If a central bathing area is provided, each shower area will be divided by curtains to ensure privacy. Showers and tubs will be equipped with adequate safety accessories.

D. Day Room. The minimum day room area shall be 40 square feet per patient. Day rooms will be attractive and adequately furnished with reading lamps, tables, chairs, television and other recreational facilities. They will be conveniently located to patients' bedrooms and shall have outside windows. There shall be at least one day room area on each bedroom floor in a multi-story hospital. Areas used for corridor traffic cannot be counted as day room space; nor can a chapel with fixed pews be counted as a day room area.

E. Dining Facilities. The minimum dining room area shall be ten square feet per patient. The dining room shall be separate from the kitchen and will be furnished with comfortable chairs and tables with hard, washable surfaces.

F. Linen Servicing and Handling. The hospital shall provide adequate facilities and equipment for handling clean and soiled bedding and other linen. There must be frequent changes of bedding and other linen, no less than every seven days to assure patient comfort.

G. Housekeeping. Regular housekeeping and maintenance procedures which will ensure that the hospital is maintained in a safe, clean, and attractive condition will be developed and implemented.

H. Geriatric and Other Nonambulatory Mental Patients. There must be special facilities for geriatric and other nonambulatory patients to assure their safety and comfort, including special fittings on toilets and wheelchairs. Appropriate provision shall be made to permit nonambulatory patients to communicate their needs to staff.

I. Physical Plant
   (1) Pursuant to an established routine maintenance and repair program, the physical plant shall be kept in a continuous

state of good repair and operation in accordance with the needs of the health, comfort, safety and well-being of the patients.

(2) Adequate heating, air conditioning and ventilation systems and equipment shall be afforded to maintain temperatures and air changes which are required for the comfort of patients at all times and the removal of undesired heat, steam and offensive odors. Such facilities shall ensure that the temperature in the hospital shall not exceed 83°F nor fall below 68°F.

(3) Thermostatically controlled hot water shall be provided in adequate quantities and maintained at the required temperature for patient or resident use (110°F at the fixture) and for mechanical dishwashing and laundry use (180°F at the equipment).

(4) Adequate refuse facilities will be provided so that solid waste, rubbish and other refuse will be collected and disposed of in a manner which will prohibit transmission of disease and not create a nuisance or fire hazard or provide a breeding place for rodents and insects.

(5) The physical facilities must meet all fire and safety standards established by the state and locality. In addition, the hospital shall meet such provisions of the Life Safety Code of the National Fire Protection Association (21st Edition, 1967) as are applicable to hospitals.

19A. The hospital shall meet all standards established by the state for general hospitals, insofar as they are relevant to psychiatric facilities.

20. Patients, except for the non-mobile, shall eat or be fed in dining rooms. The diet for patients will provide at a minimum the Recommended Daily Dietary Allowances as developed by the National Academy of Sciences. Menus shall be satisfying and nutritionally adequate to provide the Recommended Daily Dietary Allowances. In developing such menus, the hospital will utilize the Moderate Cost Food Plan of the Department of Agriculture. The hospital will not spend less per patient for raw food, including the value of donated food, than the most recent per person costs of the

Moderate Cost Food Plan for the Southern Region of the United States, as compiled by the United States Department of Agriculture, for appropriate groupings of patients, discounted for any savings which might result from institutional procurement for such food. Provisions shall be made for special therapeutic diets and for substitutes at the request of the patient, or his guardian or next of kin, in accordance with the religious requirements of any patient's faith. Denial of a nutritionally adequate diet shall not be used as punishment.

QUALIFIED STAFF IN NUMBERS SUFFICIENT TO ADMINISTER ADEQUATE TREATMENT

21. Each Qualified Mental Health Professional shall meet all licensing and certification requirements promulgated by the State of Alabama for persons engaged in private practice of the same professions elsewhere in Alabama. Other staff members shall meet the same licensing and certification requirements as persons who engage in private practice of their specialty elsewhere in Alabama.
22.
   a. All Non-Professional Staff Members who have not had prior clinical experience in a mental institution shall have a substantial orientation training.
   b. Staff members on all levels shall have regularly scheduled in-service training.
23. Each Non-Professional Staff Member shall be under the direct supervision of a Qualified Mental Health Professional.
24. *Staffing Ratios.* The hospital shall have the following minimum numbers of treatment personnel per 250 patients. Qualified Mental Health Professionals trained in particular disciplines may in appropriate situations perform services or functions traditionally performed by members of other disciplines. Changes in staff deployment may be made with prior approval of this Court upon a clear and convincing demonstration that the proposed deviation from this staffing structure will enhance the treatment of the patients.

Classification	*Number of Employees*
Unit Director	1
Psychiatrist (3 years' resident training in psychiatry)	2
M.D. (Registered physician)	4
Nurse (RN)	12
Licensed Practical Nurse	6
Aide III	6
Aide II	16
Aide I	70
Hospital Orderly	10
Clerk Stenographer II	3
Clerk Typist II	3
Unit Administrator	1
Administrative Clerk	1
Psychologist (Ph.D.) (doctoral degree from accredited program)	1
Psychologist (M.A.)	1
Psychologist (B.S.)	2
Social Worker (MSW) (From accredited program)	2
Social Worker (B.A.)	5
Patient Activity Therapist (M.S.)	1
Patient Activity Aide	10
Mental Health Technician	10
Dental Hygienist	1
Chaplain	5
Vocational Rehabilitation Counselor	1
Volunteer Services Worker	1
Mental Health Field Representative	1
Dietitian	1
Food Service Supervisor	1
Cook II	2
Cook I	3
Food Service Worker	15
Vehicle Driver	1
Housekeeper	10
Messenger	1
Maintenance Repairman	2

Individual Treatment Plans

25. Each patient shall have a comprehensive physical and mental examination and review of behavioral status within 48 hours after admission to the hospital.

26. Each patient shall have an individualized treatment plan. This plan shall be developed by appropriate Qualified Mental Health Professionals, including a psychiatrist, and implemented as soon as possible—in any event no later than five days after the patient's admission. Each individualized treatment plan shall contain:

   a. a statement of the nature of the specific problems and specific needs of the patient;

   b. a statement of the least restrictive treatment conditions necessary to achieve the purposes of commitment;

   c. a description of intermediate and long-range treatment goals, with a projected timetable for their attainment;

   d. a statement and rationale for the plan of treatment for achieving these intermediate and long-range goals;

   e. a summary of each physical examination which describes the results of the examination;

   f. criteria for release to less restrictive treatment conditions, and criteria for discharge;

   g. a notation of any therapeutic tasks and labor to be performed by the patient in accordance with Standard 18.

27. As part of his treatment plan, each patient shall have an individualized post-hospitalization plan. This plan shall be developed by a Qualified Mental Health Professional as soon as practicable after the patient's admission to the hospital.

28. In the interests of continuity of care, whenever possible, one Qualified Mental Health Professional (who need not have been involved with the development of the treatment plan) shall be responsible for supervising the implementation of the treatment plan, integrating the various aspects of the treatment program and recording the patient's progress. This Qualified Mental Health Professional shall also be responsible for ensuring that the patient

is released, where appropriate, into a less restrictive form of treatment.

29. The treatment plan shall be continuously reviewed by the Qualified Mental Health Professional responsible for supervising the implementation of the plan and shall be modified if necessary. Moreover, at least every ninety days, each patient shall receive a mental examination from, and his treatment plan shall be reviewed by, a Qualified Mental Health Professional other than the professional responsible for supervising the implementation of the plan.

30. In addition to treatment for mental disorder, patients confined at mental health institutions also are entitled to and shall receive appropriate treatment for physical illnesses such as tuberculosis. In providing medical care, the State Board of Mental Health shall take advantage of whatever community-based facilities are appropriate and available and shall coordinate the patient's treatment for mental illness with his medical treatment.

31. Complete patient records shall be kept on the ward in which the patient is placed and shall be available to anyone properly authorized in writing by the patient. These records shall include:
    a. identification data, including the patient's legal status;
    b. a patient history, including but not limited to:
       (1) family data, educational background, and employment record;
       (2) prior medical history, both physical and mental, including prior hospitalization;
    c. the chief complaints of the patient and the chief complaints of others regarding the patient;
    d. an evaluation which notes the onset of illness, the circumstances leading to admission, attitudes, behavior, estimate of intellectual functioning, memory functioning, orientation, and an inventory of the patient's assets in descriptive, not interpretive, fashion;
    f. a copy of the individual treatment plan and any modifications thereto;
    g. a detailed summary of the findings made by the reviewing Qualified Mental Health Professional after each periodic review of the treatment plan which analyzes the successes and

failures of the treatment program and directs whatever modifications are necessary;

h. a copy of the individualized post-hospitalization plan and any modifications thereto, and a summary of the steps that have been taken to implement that plan;

i. a medication history and status which includes the signed orders of the prescribing physician. Nurses shall indicate by signature that orders have been carried out;

j. a detailed summary of each significant contact by a Qualified Mental Health Professional with the patient;

k. a detailed summary on at least a weekly basis by a Qualified Mental Health Professional involved in the patient's treatment of the patient's progress along the treatment plan;

l. a weekly summary of the extent and nature of the patient's work activities described in Standard 18, *supra,* and the effect of such activity upon the patient's progress along the treatment plan;

m. a signed order by a Qualified Mental Health Professional for any restrictions on visitations and communication, as provided in Standards 4 and 5, *supra*;

n. a signed order by a Qualified Mental Health Professional for any physical restraints and isolation, as provided in Standard 7, *supra*;

o. a detailed summary of any extraordinary incident in the hospital involving the patient to be entered by a staff member noting that he has personal knowledge of the incident or specifying his other source of information, and initialed within 24 hours by a Qualified Mental Health Professional;

p. a summary by the superintendent of the hospital or his appointed agent of his findings after the 15-day review provided for in Standard 33 *infra*.

32. In addition to complying with all the other standards herein, a hospital shall make special provisions for the treatment of patients who are children and young adults. These provisions shall include but are not limited to:

a. opportunities for publicly supported education suitable to the educational needs of the patient. This program of education must, in the opinion of the attending Qualified Mental Health Professional, be compatible with the patient's mental condition and his treatment program, and otherwise be in the patient's best interest;

b. a treatment plan which considers the chronological, maturational, and developmental level of the patient;

c. sufficient Qualified Mental Health Professionals, teachers, and staff members with specialized skills in the care and treatment of children and young adults;

d. recreation and play opportunities in the open air where possible and appropriate residential facilities;

e. arrangements for contact between the hospital and the family of the patient.

33. No later than fifteen days after a patient is committed to the hospital, the superintendent of the hospital or his appointed, professionally qualified agent shall examine the committed patient and shall determine whether the patient continues to require hospitalization and whether a treatment plan complying with Standard 26 has been implemented. If the patient no longer requires hospitalization in accordance with the standards for commitment, or if a treatment plan has not been implemented, he must be released immediately unless he agrees to continue with treatment on a voluntary basis.

34. The Mental Health Board and its agents have an affirmative duty to provide adequate transitional treatment and care for all patients released after a period of involuntary confinement. Transitional care and treatment possibilities include, but are not limited to, psychiatric day care, treatment in the home by a visiting therapist, nursing home or extended care, out-patient treatment, and treatment in the psychiatric ward of a general hospital.

MISCELLANEOUS

35. Each patient and his family, guardian, or next friend shall promptly upon the patient's admission receive written notice, in language he understands, of all the above standards for adequate treatment. In addition, a copy of all the above standards shall be posted in each ward.

Appendix B

Informed Consent and Release of Information from Patient Records

There follow a short, concise, readable Consent to Treatment form (page 351) and one to use when consent is refused (page 352). Both require full explanation, for the patient's signature attests that he or she has been informed in the manner stated.

Also presented is a Federal form 522 (page 353). It is used in obtaining consent for the administration of anesthesia, and for surgical and other procedures. While slightly more difficult to read, it is suitable for all purposes if properly filled out, striking out paragraphs which do not apply.

The three forms are not suitable as a consent for participation in a research study using an experimental drug or procedure; in such cases, the purpose of the study, the name of the drug (or a description of the procedure), the possibility one will be a control subject, the side effects that may occur, and prohibitions (such as driving a motor vehicle) should be spelled out. It is well to include mention of the right to withdraw and the names of research investigators available to answer questions. It is usually inappropriate to include a statement releasing the investigator from responsibility for adverse effects. Some do include a release in legal terminology such as the following:

349

The said members of the medical staff hereby agree the exercise of their best judgment in prescribing, carrying out, or causing to be carried out such medical treatment shall relieve and release them and each of them, including the director of said hospital, as well as the Board of Administrators of said hospital severally or collectively of any liability whatsoever, kind or nature to me, my successors or assigns as well as the undersigned for any consequences which may result from anything done or directed to be done, in the performance of said treatment as aforesaid.

Such a statement will please lawyers, confuse patients, and comfort physicians without at all diminishing the potential for legal action when malpractice is alleged.

Lastly, a release authorization (page 354) in use in Michigan is presented. It serves the purpose of establishing need-to-know in regard to information in a patient or client's record. It indicates the specific nature of the disclosure and to whom it is to be made.

CONSENT TO TREATMENT

Patient _____ Age _____

Date _____ Time _____ A.M. Place _____
                                        P.M.

I hereby authorize Doctor _____, and such assistants as he
may designate, to perform upon _____ treatment
                                    (Name, Myself)
appropriate for the following condition: _____
The nature and purpose of this treatment, possible alternative methods
of treatment, the risks involved, and the possibility of complications
have been fully explained to me. I acknowledge that no guarantee or
assurance has been made as to the results which may be obtained from
this course of treatment.

I certify that I have read and fully understand the above consent to
treatment, that the explanations therein referred to were made, and that
all blanks or statements requiring insertion or completion were filled
in before I signed my name below.

                         Signed _____
                         (patient, or both parents or guardian of minor)

Witness: _____

(NOTE: If parents or guardian sign they should specify relationship to the
patient.)

REFUSAL TO CONSENT TO TREATMENT

Patient _____ Age _____

Date _____ Time _____ A.M. Place _____
　　　　　　　　　　　　　　P.M.

I have been advised by Doctor _____ that it is necessary for me to undergo the following treatment: _____

_____

(describe operation or treatment)

The effect and nature of this treatment have been explained to me.

Although my failure to follow the advice I have received may seriously imperil my life or health, I nevertheless refuse to consent to the recommended treatment. I assume the risks and consequences involved and release the above-named physician, the hospital and its staff from any liability.

Signed _____

Witness: _____

(NOTE: If the patient refuses to sign such a statement, he cannot be forced to do so. If this occurs, the form should be filled out, witnessed, and the statement on the form "signature refused.")

MEDICAL RECORD	REQUEST FOR ADMINISTRATION OF ANESTHESIA AND FOR PERFORMANCE OF OPERATIONS AND OTHER PROCEDURES

A. IDENTIFICATION

1. OPERATION OR PROCEDURE

B. STATEMENT OF REQUEST

1. The nature and purpose of the operation or procedure, possible alternative methods of treatment, the risks involved, and the possibility of complications have been fully explained to me. I acknowledge that no guarantees have been made to me concerning the results of the operation or procedure. I understand the nature of the operation or procedure to be _____ (Description of operation or procedure in layman's language)

which is to be performed by or under the direction of Dr. _____

2. I request the performance of the above-named operation or procedure and of such additional operations or procedures as are found to be necessary or desirable, in the judgment of the professional staff of the below-named medical facility, during the course of the above-named operation or procedure.

3. I request the administration of such anesthesia as may be considered necessary or advisable in the judgment of the professional staff of the below-named medical facility.

4. Exceptions to surgery or anesthesia, if any, are: _____ (If none, so state)

5. I request the disposal by authorities of the below-named medical facility of any tissues or parts which it may be necessary to remove.

6. I understand that photographs and movies may be taken of this operation, and that they may be viewed by various personnel undergoing training or indoctrination at this or other facilities. I consent to the taking of such pictures and observation of the operation by authorized personnel, subject to the following conditions:

    a. The name of the patient and his/her family is not used to identify said pictures.

    b. Said pictures be used only for purposes of medical/dental study or research.

(Cross out any parts above which are not appropriate)

C. SIGNATURES (Appropriate items in Parts A and B must be completed before signing)

1. COUNSELING PHYSICIAN/DENTIST: I have counseled this patient as to the nature of the proposed procedure(s), attendant risks involved, and expected results, as described above.

(Signature of Counseling Physician/Dentist)

2. PATIENT: I understand the nature of the proposed procedure(s), attendant risks involved, and expected results, as described above, and hereby request such procedure(s) be performed.

(Signature of Witness, excluding members of operating team) (Signature of Patient) (Date and Time)

3. SPONSOR OR GUARDIAN: (When patient is a minor or unable to give consent) I, _____ sponsor/guardian of _____ understand the nature of the proposed procedure(s), attendant risks involved, and expected results, as described above, and hereby request such procedure(s) be performed.

(Signature of Witness, excluding members of operating team) (Signature of Sponsor/Legal Guardian) (Date and Time)

PATIENT'S IDENTIFICATION (For typed or written entries give Name - last, first, middle, grade, date, hospital or medical facility)

REGISTER NO.	WARD NO.

STANDARD FORM 522 (Rev. 10-76)
General Services Administration &
Interagency Comm. on Medical Records
FPMR 101-11.806-8
522-109

☆U.S. GOVERNMENT PRINTING OFFICE 1981 341-489/4634

MICHIGAN DEPARTMENT OF PUBLIC HEALTH

Client Information Release Authorization

1._____ , hereby authorize_____
    (clients name)   (program name)
its director or designee,_____, to release information contained
              (program director or designee)
in my client records to the individuals or organizations and only under
the conditions listed below:

1. Name of person(s) or organization(s) to whom disclosure is to be
   made: _____
   _____

2. Specific type of information to be disclosed:_____
   _____

3. The purpose and need for such disclosure: _____
   _____

4. This consent is subject to revocation at anytime except in those
   circumstances in which the program has taken certain actions on
   the understanding that the consent will continue unrevoked until the
   purpose for which the consent was given shall have been accomplished. However, any consent shall have a duration no longer than
   that reasonably necessary to effectuate the purpose for which it is
   given.

5. Without expressed revocation this consent expires for the following
   specified reasons:
   A. Date: _____
   B. Event: _____
   C. Condition: _____

_____   _____
Witnessed By   Client's Signature

_____   _____
Date Witnessed   Date Signed

APPENDIX C

Legal cases cited in the text

Addington V. Texas 1979, U.S. Supreme Court

Bartley v. Kremens 1979, U.S. Supreme Court (2MDLR 548) (402 F Suppl. 1039 E.D.Pa. 1975)

Bell v. Wayne County General Hospital 1974, Fed. Dist. Ct. M1 (384 F Supp. 1085)

Binder v. Ruvell 1952, Circuit Ct. of Cook County Ill. Civil docket 52C2535

Boardman v. Woodman 1868, (47 N.H. 120)

Bowers v. DeVito 1980, U.S. District Ct. N. Ill. (77C2850)

Caesar v. Mountanos 1974, U.S. District Ct. of Appeals 9th Cir. CAL. 74-2271

Canterbury v. Spence 1972, D.D. Circuit Ct. (464 F 2nd 772)

Carroll Towing Co. v. United States 1947 (159 Fed. Reporter 2d 169)

Carter v. General Motors 1961 (361 Mich. 577) (106 N.W. 2d 105)

Cobb v. Grant 1972 (8 CAL. 3rd 229, 502 P 2d 1)

Currens v. United States

Dale v. State of New York 1974, N.Y. Ct. of Claims

Dinnerstein, intre, 1978, Mass. Ct. of Appeals (Sh 763)

Dixon v. Weinberger 1975 U.S. Dist. Ct. D.C. (CA 74 285) (405 F Supp 974)

Doe v. Gallinot U.S. Dist. Ct. Central Div. CA.

Donaldson v. O'Connor 1975 U.S. Supreme Ct. (95 S. Ct. 2486) (422 U.S. 563)

Durham v. United States 1954 U.S. Dist. Ct. D.C. (214 F 2d 862)

Easter v. District of Columbia 1966 (361 F 2d 50)

Eichner v. Dillon 1981, N.Y. Ct. of Appeals (658 Mar. 31, 1981)

Fox, Brother (see Eichner)

Freeman v. United States 1966 (357 F 2d 606)

Gault, in Re 1967, U.S. Supreme Court (387 U.S. 1)

Glotkin v. Miller 1974, U.S. Ct. of Appeals 2nd Cir. (74-2138)

Hawaii Psychiatric Society v. Arisyoshi 1979, Fed. District Ct. Hawaii (CV 79-0113)

Karmowitz v. Michigan Dept. of Mental Health 1973 Mich. Circuit Ct. (Civ. 73-19434AW)

League of Cities v. Usery 1976, U.S. Supreme Court

Lessard v. Schmidt 1972, Fed. Dist. Ct. Wis (349 F Supp. 1078 E.D. Wisc.)

Lifschutz, in re 1970, CAL. Sup. Ct. (2 CAL. 3d 415; 476 P 2d 557) 85 CAL Reporter 829

Lipari v. Sears Roebuck 1980, (497 F 185 D.C. Neb. July 17)

McDonald v. United States

Martinez v. State of California 1980 CA. Sup. CT (100 S. CT 553)

Morales v. Turman 1974-1977 Ct. of Appeals and U.S. Supreme Ct. (383 F Supp 53 ED Texas 1974) (535 F 2nd 864 5th Cir. 1974) (430 U.S. 322 1977) (562 F 2nd 993 5th Cir. 1977)

Parham v. J. Land Jr. 1979, U.S. Supreme Ct. (2 MDL9 188) (70 N.J. 10, 355 A 2d 647, 1977)

Quinlan, in Re, 1976, 1977, (70 N.J. 10 355 A 2d 647, 1976)

Redrup v. New York 1967, U.S. Supreme Ct. (386 U.S. 767)

Rennie v. Klein, 1978, (462 F Supp 1131 D.N.N.) (79-2576) (79-2577)

Robinson v. California 1962 (370 U.S. 660)

Roe v. Wade, 1973, U.S. Supreme Ct. (935.4 705)

Rogers v. Okin 1979 U.S. Dist. Ct. Mass. (75-161 OT) (478 F Supp 1342 890) Rogers v. Mills 1982.

Rone v. Fineman 1979 U.S. Dist. Ct. Ohio

Rouse v. Cameron 1966 Dist. D.C. (373F 2d 451)

St. Elizabeths v. HEW and D.C. govt. 1975 U.S. Dist. Ct. D.C.

Saikewicz v. Supt. of Belchertown Mass. 1977 (370 NE 2d 417)

Schaeffer v. Schaeffer 1959, N.Y.

Small v. Gifford Memorial Hospital 1975 Vt. Supreme Ct.

Smith v. Estelle 1979 U.S. Ct. of Appeals 5th Cir.

Souder v. Brennan 1973 U.S. Dist. Ct. D.C. (42 U.S.L.W. 2271)
(367 F Supp 808)

State v. Pike 1870 (49 N.H. 399)

Tarasoff v. Regents Univ. of California 1974, Cal. Superior Ct. 405694
(Dec. 1974) (118 Cal. Reporter 129)

Vitck v. Jones 1980 U.S. Supreme Ct. (78 1155)

Welsch v. Likin 1974 Dist. Ct. Minn.

Wyatt v. Stickney 1971-3 U.S. Dist. Ct. ALA (325 F Supp 781 MD
Ala. 1971) (334 F Supp. 1341) (344 F Supp 373) (344 F Supp
387) (72-2634 5th cir. 1973)

Youngberg v. Romeo 1982 U.S. Supreme Ct.

Zurcher v. Stanford Daily 1978, U.S. Supreme Court

AUTHOR INDEX

359

SUBJECT INDEX